1850 1920
THE WONDERFUL WORLD OF
Ladies' Fashion

Edited by Joseph J. Schroeder, Jr.

Associate Editor, Barbara C. Cohen

FOLLETT PUBLISHING COMPANY
CHICAGO

ISBN: 0-695-80221-6   Library of Congress Catalogue Card Number: 70-148723

Foreword

The Wonderful World of Ladies' Fashion was originally conceived to be a comprehensive collection of fashion illustrations from a variety of old fashion periodicals and catalogues. Once we began to review the source materials, however, we realized we had a far more exciting prospect to explore — one that presented a much broader picture of how a woman's world was really *fashioned* 50, 100 or more years ago.

This is not to say that we have abandoned fashions as the central theme of the book. Instead, we have supplemented an array of dresses, cloaks, hats, handbags, shoes and other items of woman's garb with contemporary humor, recipes, etiquette, poetry, husband-hunting and home-making — indeed, with a broad spectrum of "The Wonderful World of Ladies' Fashion."

Introduction

This book is first and foremost an illustrated history of the evolution of women's fashions. It covers a period beginning with the mid-19th century and continuing through the end of the first World War, starting when the hoop skirt was high fashion and extending through the age of the bustle on into the adoption of the tubular or sheath styles that are still current today. The changes in fashions that occurred during this extended period are illustrated by means of contemporary woodcuts, steel engravings and half-tones selected from dozens of rare old books, periodicals and catalogues. The original descriptive material accompanies most of the illustrations, and in many cases entire pages of fashions and related advertising are reproduced exactly as they originally appeared many decades ago.

However, the pages of this book contain not only a record of women's *fashions* but also of women's *fashion* — the many factors in addition to apparel that served to fashion a woman's life in those earlier and seemingly simpler times. The material we have selected includes humor, advice, commentary and poetry. It covers practically every aspect of a woman's life from education and etiquette through courtship, raising children and the high price of household help. It presents a surprisingly complete story of the American woman and how she lived her life while the nation was moving from an agrarian to an industrial society.

We trust you will find your travels through *The Wonderful World of Ladies' Fashion* as entertaining and educational as we have.

Joseph J. Schroeder, Jr.
Glenview, Illinois
May, 1971

Joseph J. Schroeder, Jr. is the editor of the 1894 Montgomery Ward & Company, 1896 Marshall Field & Company, and 1900 and 1908 Sears, Roebuck & Company replica catalogues. He has authored a number of articles for electronics technical journals and firearms periodicals, and is co-author of the book, System Mauser, *a history of the Mauser 1896 pistol.*

Acknowledgements

Finding suitable source materials for this book proved to be almost as much of a challenge as the task of assembling them into the book itself. It is only through the wealth of materials and generous assistance supplied by the following individuals and organizations that we are able to present *The Wonderful World of Ladies' Fashion* as it was for our mothers, grandmothers, great-grandmothers . . .

Eugene M. Adler
Mr. and Mrs. William Anderson
Frederick Asher
Cookbook Collector's Library
Robert Cromie
Mrs. Joseph J. Schroeder, Sr.
Mr. and Mrs. Roy R. Stewart
The Chicago Historical Society
Harper and Row, Publishers, Inc.

Contents

Part I

The Cycles of Fashion

The Cycles of Fashion

Historically, an analysis of skirt contours provides a valid system for classifying women's fashions. In the past two centuries there have been only three different basic skirt forms; the hoop, the bustle and the sheath. During this period, these basic styles have appeared and reappeared in a recurring pattern, each enduring (with some modification) for extended period of time, but then being replaced—rather quickly—by its successor.

At first blush this might seem to be too simple a basis on which to classify a subject as complex as women's fashions, but upon reflection one realizes that it is the skirt that literally forms the foundation of a woman's costume. This is not to say a given skirt style does not in itself show change, or that the many other parts of a woman's garb are not changing, for of course they are, almost constantly. But for the most part these are detail changes which are more subtle, and indeed form the very essence which distinguishes this year's style from last and there-fore establishes what is currently "fashionable."

The three basic styles and how they appear on the female figure are shown in the drawings below. With the hoop or bell-shaped skirt the wearer stands squarely in the middle of the skirt,

while with the bustle the front is fitted snugly and the back is built out with padding. The sheath is almost a cylinder, not much larger at the bottom than at the top.

Illustrations from history books show that the bustle was in favor at the time of the American Revolution. By 1800, however, fashion evolution was following its predictable course and more form-fitting styles, often showing distinct Grecian or Roman influence, were the vogue. This sheath skirt period lasted until the mid 1820s, when increasingly wider hems finally reached the point where skirts were more bell-like than tubular, and the third phase in the cycle of women's fashion began. It must be noted that this phase is called the "hoop" skirt era more for convenience than accuracy. In practice, the use of an actual mechanical hoop to form the skirt contour occurred only in the later years of "hoop skirt" dominance. Earlier versions achieved their proportions by the use of voluminous petticoats, padding and later crinoline—a semi-rigid skirt made from a coarse horsehair and cotton fabric.

That the hoop skirt, particularly in its later, more extreme forms, did not meet with universal approval is evidenced by the number of cartoons and jokes directed toward it in the late 1850s. A representative sampling of these appears in Part II, along with discussions of the current fashions and their unrestrained endorsement of the style. As in the case with present day fashions, practicality and male approval were of little or no concern to the style setters. As long as they considered a style to be in fashion it *was,* and that was that.

Shortly after the end of the Civil War the hoop skirt began to lose its symmetry. The full-

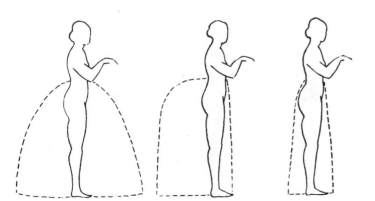

ness at the front was replaced by an exaggerated build up at the rear, and by 1870 the bustle was back in style. Following the same course as its predecessor the style became more and more exaggerated with time, resulting in some bizarre effects in and on its wearers during the final years of its popularity.

The emancipated woman of the 1900s was not only ready for voting rights and equality—she was ready for a new style. Thus it was that the sheath again came to the fore, and by 1907 or 1908 the bustle was definitely passe. The relative simplicity of the sheath style has suited twentieth century women well — only hem length has changed since its last introduction. Initially falling to the ankle, the hem line has been moving almost inexorably upward ever since. Even in the relatively few remaining years of our coverage this trend is clearly established. Although during the past several decades both hoop and bustle-like costumes have re-experienced brief periods of popularity, primarily for formal wear, it is the sheath that still remains dominant.

The recurring pattern in the evolution of fashions is graphically illustrated by the accom-

panying silhouettes, reproduced by courtesy of Harper and Row. Though details and even forms change, each silhouette is unmistakable in its classification.

As established in the Foreword and Introduction, this book contains far more than a history of fashions. Fashions are, after all, only one manifestation of a woman's life and as such cannot truly be divorced from her other activites, duties and pleasures. So it is that "The Wonderful World of Ladies' Fashion" encompasses many subjects, some closely related to fashions and some not. The sources are as diverse as the subjects. It is fascinating to see how much of what concerns modern day woman was also important to her forebearers.

Part II of this book begins its coverage with the early 1850s. This was not an arbitrary choice, for a contemporary (November 1854) source has provided an excellent discussion of the evolution of fashions up to that time. This discussion, reproduced exactly as it appeared in *Harper's New Monthly Magazine* well over 100 years ago, is as relevant and readable today as it was then.

 1780  1790   1805  1815    1830  1850

 1860  1870  1875  1880 1890 1895 1910 1920

THE "MERVEILLEUSE," 1793.

THE GENERATIONS OF FASHIONS.

IF there be one earthly object more deserving of pity than another, what do you think it is, curious reader? As a Yankee, with all your inherited traditionary 'cuteness, you will never guess! I leave that to a Frenchman; and, not to keep you longer in suspense—the worst possible policy for an author—I will tell you. It is an "*old fashion!*" How many delicately-chiseled noses are turned up at that irrevocable sentence of condemnation, while disgust at the sight, and amazement at the audacity of the shopkeeper, play about the lines of the fairest mouths, as their lovely possessors turn their backs peremptorily upon an article which but a month before was the coveted object of all eyes—" a perfect beauty" —a " sweet love"—with an exclamatory " Pooh ! it is old-fashioned." To use an expressive, though vulgar phrase, that is " a clincher." The fate of an old pot is not more hopeless. When once that Mede and Persian fiat has gone forth from feminine lips.

every body is at liberty to give it another crack. A shopkeeper might as profitably employ his time in searching for the philosopher's stone, as his eloquence in endeavoring to sell any thing once put under the ban of fashion. The interdict of beauty is upon it. Accursed of good taste has it become, and excommunicated from the depths of every well-filled purse. No matter how becoming it has been considered a few short weeks before, whatever may be its intrinsic merits of elegance, art, or costliness ; however much human brains and hands have labored to make it a combination of utility and beauty, it is now a sunken, degraded thing, despised of women and scorned of men, barely tolerated by the necessities of poverty, or reduced to seek a home in the haunts of vice.

This caprice, which looks only to change for its aliment, is as old as human invention. I make no doubt that Eve never wore twice the same pattern of fig-leaves, while Adam searched diligently the forests through to diversify the colors of his vegetable breeches. The Polynesian turns to nature for his book of fashions, and seeks to rival the hues of the bird of Paradise in the ample folds of his brilliant-colored " tappas." Every savage finds his greatest wants in the bright gewgaws of civilization. If there be a nation on earth that clings to its old clothes and furniture because they are good and useful, that deprecates change as innovation upon good habits and customs, that does not dive into the bowels of the earth, fish the seas, and penetrate the heavens, racking nature to find material wherewith to distort and crucify nature in form, stuff, and pattern, out of sheer disgust of the old and capricious love for the new, I have yet to discover it.

A passion so universal must be productive of more good than evil, or else it would die of neglect. At first glance, nothing appears more unreasonable, and more destructive of excellence, than this devotion to variety. The " love" of one season is the " fright" of the next. No sooner have we reconciled our eyes and shoulders to one fit, and begun to think it tolerable, than we abandon it for some fresh abomination of the tailor or modiste, and recommence our penance of new-formed inexpressibles and new-cut whalebone. Every change of coat or boot is another martyrdom. The rack has indeed left the halls of justice, but it has taken up its residence on the counters of St. Crispin and kindred saints. Human flesh has become a mere machine—a sort of clay model—for the masters and mistresses of the shears and needles to fit their garments upon. Bone and muscle are secondary in their system ; the primary object is to display their " fashions," which, as they are mainly of late of the " grotesque" order, we may class, according to the views of Ruskin's architecture, rather as the *labor* of little minds than the *repose* of great.

So in other things. We no sooner combine utility and beauty, forming an article which is truly excellent in itself, than we abandon it, and content ourselves with some crude novelty, to be discarded in its turn, as soon as it has advanced

1760.   THE CHANGES OF FASHION.   1793.

through its several degrees of fashion to any thing like comfortable excellence. An individual who ventures to like what suits and fits him well, in opposition to the novel and fashionable, becomes a pariah at once. He is abandoned of society; lucky if known as nothing worse than an "odd, old-fashioned fellow," and of no more account in creation than a dead leaf. In usual they are doomed to equal consideration with an old hat, substituting a stale joke for the decided kick, either of which is an effectual barrier to the firmament of fashion.

If this love of variety had no other recommendation than to prevent repletion in the purses of the rich, it would still be a social blessing. It feeds, clothes, and houses half the world. It feels the way to artistic perfection, opens the doors to ingenuity, favors invention, and prevents mental stagnation: Costly and annoying to the individual it may be, but to the nation it is beneficial. The very whims of beauty are so much bounty to industry and art. Mere dandyism is the rust of civilization. Like corroded steel, it shows the most where the polish is most brilliant.

Paris is the central star of fashion. Whatever is seen elsewhere is a ray from her light, diminishing in lustre as it recedes from that city. The French under Napoleon, by force of arms, sought to win a universal empire. Failing in this, they have since employed the more subtle weapons of taste and fashion to attain the same end. Their conquests extend with a rapidity that far surpasses the warlike exploits of the "grand Empereur." There is not a race on the globe that does not seem destined to lose its national identities of costumes and habits before the invincible power of French fashions. They have penetrated the huts of the South Sea savages. They march with the rapidity of commerce along the steppes of Central Asia, and have climbed the Chinese wall. The turban of the descendants of the Prophet rolls in the dust before the hat of the infidel. This infiltration of Parisian fashions is seen every where; sometimes with an elegance that rivals Paris itself, but more often with an awkward imitation destructive of every grace of the original. It threatens to subjugate every European costume, however venerable from antiquity or picturesque in effect. The traveler must hasten if he would see what remains of the beautiful or odd in the dresses of the Italian, the national costumes of the Swiss, the furred robes of the Pole, and the medley mediæval civilization of the Asiatic and European tribes that now are ruled by

1820.   THE CHANGES OF FASHION.   1850.

the Autocrat of all the Russias. The conquests of the *modistes* are wider than those of the marshals.

A French army of "artistes" have insinuated themselves, as worms into old books and furniture, into every cranny of past civilization. They are rapidly undermining every habit, both of the body and for the body, of the past. At present the adulterine mixture is becoming to neither condition; but before the army of French cooks, dancing-masters, tailors, modistes, coiffeurs, valets, femmes-de-chambres, and mechanics of knick-knackery, every other knick-knackery and fashion not absolutely Parisian in its origin and education is rapidly giving way. Whether this is an incipient stage of the millennium or not, when mankind are to be all brethren, alike in speech, habits, and rule, remains to be seen. This much we know, that French millinery is the dominant power of civilization. England's Queen and Russia's Czar alike acknowledge its supremacy. Parisian fashion, which, like all others, once had a local character of its own, has now become a cosmopolite, making itself equally at home in Timbuctoo as in the Champs Elysées.

Whether the world will gain in picturesque effect by the obliteration of national costumes may well be doubted; but whether French taste has not a wide gulf yet to pass, before it can make any thing graceful and comfortable of the stove-pipe hat, dismal colors, and swaddling clothes to which it dooms its male devotees, is no matter of doubt at all. It is in the infancy of its empire, and has yet much to learn before mankind will acknowledge its sway an easy one. The most that can now be said in its favor is, that in its restlessness it may by chance hit upon some combination which shall reconcile comfort and beauty. But we very much fear, if it succeeded in this, that it would not allow it to live a month.

One secret of Parisian success in the empire of fashion is this: In the past, it cunningly borrowed of all nations every peculiarity that could be turned to account in its own rage for novelty. The Romans admitted the deities of conquered nations into their mythology without scrutiny. Their great scheme of government comprehended every worship, provided it was not purer than their own. Parisians borrowed every hue and cut from rival costumes, and transformed them to their own tastes and purposes. Receiving every

"CLASSICAL COSTUME," 1796.

thing in the beginning, they have ended by giving every thing, and the whole world now looks to Paris as the arbitress of fashion, as the Jew does to Jerusalem, and the Romanist to Rome, for the seat of their religions.

With all this, however, the French once had fashions peculiarly their own. Indeed their empire is of very recent date, and it is well worth our trouble to go back a little, and see by what strange metamorphoses French taste has assumed its present shape. To do this, I shall be compelled to illustrate freely, for two reasons. I detest the technicalities of dress, and if I employed the terms in description, I could neither understand the costumes myself or make them intelligible to my readers; therefore I shall adopt the better plan of letting them see for themselves.

After gunpowder had put an end to metallic armor, the French nobles, by the usual force of contradiction, ran into the opposite extreme, and from iron by the pound on their necks, began to wear

HEAD DRESSES, 1813.

COURT DRESS, 1775.

"L'AGIOTEOR," 1795.

costly lace and ribbons by the yard. This in time subsided into the most elegant of court-dresses, though too effeminate in its character for any but aristocratic idlers. Such was the costume of the perfumed gallants who crowded the ante-chambers of Pompadour and Dubarray. Intrigue was the business of their lives; they looked, acted, studied, and above all dressed with the paramount view of captivating the fairer sex. Dressing therefore was a laborious and protracted operation, which demanded all the powers of the mind. It was well if the gallant who commenced it as soon as he rose from his couch at noon, finished his labor of love by three o'clock. The hands, withdrawn from the night-gloves, must be soaked for a long time in lotions and washes, to remove any discoloration or roughness; the cheeks were to be tinted with carminatives to give a bloom to the complexion, palid from last night's debauch; every envious pimple must be hidden by a patch; the clothes must be perfumed, the linen powdered to overcome the smell of soap. The proper tying of the cravat was the great labor of the day; this performed, the wig and hat properly adjusted, the most captivating attitudes and graces carefully studied before the mirror, and the French noble of the few years before the Revolution was prepared for the conquests of the day. But before this elaborate costume was finally swept away by the Revolution, there was a brief episode of simplicity. Franklin made his appearance at court in a suit of sober brown. All heads were turned. Lace and embroidery and powdered curls were discarded. Straight brown coats and straight cut hair became the mode of the moment.

The habit succeeding this was based upon the old English frock-coat, with its ample and awkward folds, which by some unaccountable freak became all at once the rage at Paris. The Duke de Lauroquais used to say that the English frock-coat gave a mortal wound to the costume of the French noblesse, which speedily degenerated, with its brocade and gay colors, into a disguise for the carnival or a dress for a masquerade ball; while the new costume, which was half adopted by the ladies, became in 1787 as we see it in the cut which we present of the fashions of that year.

Black, which heretofore had been the obscure color confined to lawyers, authors, and all those who then formed the connecting link between the vulgar and the fashionable world, now suddenly took a start, and became the "ne plus ultra" of gentility. The pre-eminence then attained by it for gentlemen has been retained to this day, while colors are banished to the street or masquerades. At this time, too, that abomination of abominations for the covering of the head, known as the modern hat, began to assume its present hideous shape, for which the transformer deserves the pains of decapitation. Expensive lace became the passion of the dandies, who piqued themselves upon having a different variety for each season.

It was the fashion also for gentlemen to wear much costly jewelry, as another mode of distinguishing themselves from the plebeian crowd. In 1780 was introduced the singularity of wearing two watches at once, burdened with immense chains. This was also adopted by the ladies. The custom now appears ridiculous, but in reality it is no more so than the present one of loading a vest with a huge bundle of non-descript jewelry — coral and

THE FASHIONS FOR 1787.

CARICATURE, 1778.

bone arms, legs, and death's-heads—under the name of charms. The Marshal Richelieu was one of the first to carry two watches. One day a caller, by some mischance, threw them both on the floor. He began to overwhelm the Marshal with excuses. "Make yourself easy," replied the veteran of politeness, "I never saw them go so well together before."

The ladies, not to be outdone in extravagance by their lords, turned their attention to their hair, and invented the strangest coiffures. The Roman ladies, in their rage for red perukes, frequently sacrificed their own raven locks altogether, and accumulated several hundred of different shades in a short time. The passion of the French was for white. A caricature of 1778 gives an idea of the height to which they carried their new fashion, which, after all, was not much above the truth.

The chronicles of the day are filled with scandalous stories of the relations

HEAD-DRESS, 1785.

between the grand dames and the artists thus admitted to the solitude and privacy of their bedchambers. The art of the coiffeurs became a great one in the eyes of fashion. A work on the subject was published at eight dollars the volume. The professors became rich and distinguished. The handsome Leonard, who was the coiffeur of the Queen, Maria Antoinette, succeeded in using upward of fourteen yards of gauze upon a single head, which acquired for him a European renown.

The turbans and bonnets of this epoch were equally extravagant. The coiffures of the ladies became so high that the face seemed to be in the middle of their bodies; and the director of the Opera was compelled to make a rule that no lady with a head-dress above a certain height should be admitted into the amphitheatre, because the spectators were unable on account of them to see the stage. If the ladies are induced to class these specimens as "frights," let them consider that in *their* day they were considered equally as becoming as the present styles.

It was in vain that the caricaturists leveled their weapons at these towering head-dresses. "Top-knots" would not "come down." They waxed higher and higher, threatening to rival the tower of Babel; until the Queen was attacked by a violent illness which occasioned the loss of the flaxen locks that had called forth the genius of the coiffeurs. At once down went the towering piles, like castles in the clouds. Every lady at court appeared

HEAD-DRESSES, 1802.

with a flat head. The next great change in ladies head gear was wrought by a philosopher and poet. St. Pierre put forth his *Paul et Virginie*, and all Paris went mad for simplicity and nature. He attired his heroine in simple white muslin with a hat of plain straw. The volatile *Parisiennes* were captivated. Silks and satins, powder and pomatum vanished as if by magic, and from queen to waiting-maid nobody appeared except in white muslins and straw hats.

Geography was ransacked to find names for these remarkable superstructures for the head. Thus there were bonnets *à la Turke*, *à la Autriche*, and, even as early as 1785, America was honored in having one style, called *à la Philadelphie*; finally, the wits or the geographical knowledge of the milliners being exhausted, in despair they christened their last invention the "anonymous bonnet."

Paris, in 1851, no sooner set eyes on the would-be American fashion of Bloomerism, with its short skirts and trowsered legs, than it completely extinguished it by one blast of its all-powerful ridicule. Yet, as long ago as 1772, it had adopted a mode, compounded from the Polonaise, equally as open to objection, so far as scantiness of petticoats was concerned, with the additions of heels several inches

BONNET, 1786.

BONNET, 1786.

in height, and walking-sticks which might easily be mistaken for boarding-pikes.

The extravagance and luxury of the fashionables of both sexes immediately preceding the Revolution, which was destined to engulf them and their fortunes, were such as almost to palliate the excesses of the people who had so long and patiently borne with the heartlessness and vices of the aristocracy. There was a rivalry among the great lords and bankers as to who should ruin themselves soonest for the favorite actresses of the day. Then courtesans rode in their carriages made with panels of porcelain, silver spokes, drawn by six horses, and attended by mounted servants in livery. Even royalty was scandalized and outdone by the magnificence of their equipages, hotels, and houses of pleasure. The nobles, as if with a presentiment of their coming fate, hastened to pour into the laps of their mistresses their entire fortunes, seeking to drown in refined debauchery the thunder of the storm that already began to roll over their heads.

Among the follies which the fashions of this date presented was the confusion which arose between male and female attire. Men borrowed the laces, ruffles, belts, jewelry, and finery of the women. They, in revenge, took the coats, vests, open shirts, cravats, powdered queues, canes, and even cloth frock-coats of the men. The fashion

THE FASHIONS, 1787, '88.

of the male for one month was frequently adopted for the mode of the female for the next. Sexual proprieties in dress were utterly confounded, and this medley of apparel extended in some degree to habits and pursuits. The ladies seized upon the studies and occupations of men. Many of their conquests they have retained to this day, as any one conversant with Paris can perceive.

In the midst of this extravagance came the Revolution. The etiquette and magnificence of the old society disappeared in the vortex of the social whirlpool. Diamonds and lace, flowers and plumes, embroidered coats and satin robes, all the luxurious and costly creations of past fashion, sunk more rapidly than they arose. Fortunes were annihilated in a day. Royalty even put on plebeian shoes, mounted the coarse cap of the worker, and shouted the hollow cry of "*Egalitè!*" Universal brotherhood was on the lips of men, and universal hate in their hearts. Religion and decency fled in affright. It was the advent of *sans-culottism.* For a while, coarseness and vulgarity, under the garbs of equality and fraternity, reigned triumphant. For a time they took the form of *Anglo-mania.* This was before the advent of the "classical" era. The clubbists carried enormous cudgels, wore thick

shoes and coarse coats, and in all ways endeavored to transform themselves into blackguards, with the most complete success. The stones of the Bastile were made up into patriotic breastpins for the bosoms of beauty. Copper buckles replaced the gold and silver of former years. Wealth and fashion, once so inordinately displayed, were now the sure tokens of destruction. Safety was only in abject humility and conspicuous poverty. But French nature, though it could endure the tyranny of political Jacobinism, was restless under the extinction of fashion and obliteration of clean breeches. It soon rebelled, discarding all past inventions, struck out new and tenfold more ridiculous costumes than before. The fashion-plates of that time reveal this rebellion against *sans-culottism* in a thousand comical ways. A view of the rendezvous of the fashionable world, the garden of the famous "Palais Royal," as it existed in 1792, would better illustrate the "cut" of the day than pages of description. The different political parties displayed their mutual hatred, not so much in words which they dared not utter, as in the silent but mocking eloquence of dress. The popular tri-colors and cut and unpowdered hair remained, however, in the ascendency. But neither the horrors of the scaf-

"INCROYABLE," 1796.

for a time a strange turn. A year before men went in red night-caps, and magistrates wore wooden shoes. Now the citizens emulated the times of the Regency in the extravagance if not in the elegance of their costumes. The most popular entertainments were the *bals à victime*. To be admitted to these one must have lost a relative by the guillotine. The dancers wore crape about the arm, and gayly danced in honor of the deceased. It became the fashion to show the profoundest abhorrence of the Reign of Terror. Instead of Robespierre's *tappedurs*, "hard-crackers," young *muscadines*, or dandies, in swallow-tailed coats, with their hair plaited at the temples, and flowing behind in military fashion, made it a duty to knock down any shag-coated Jacobin they chanced to encounter. The ladies, too, expressed their horror of the bloody time in a fashion of their own. The Jacobins had made a virtue of destroying life; the production of life must be

fold nor the brutalities of Jacobinism could long suppress the pretensions of the young elegants to dress as they pleased. Indeed, it became a species of heroism, by extravagant finery and outrageous taste, joined to a mincing, effeminate voice, to throw contempt upon the coarseness of their political opponents. The "*jeunesse dorée*" of this period were clerks, young lawyers, and others of equally humble origin, who, having aided in destroying the old aristocracy, now sought to excel them in vice and folly.

Each succeeding year gave origin to fashions if possible more absurd than the preceding. The moral chaos that prevailed in France affected all material things. Dress was not only more or less typical of politics, but illustrative of the classical theories of the times. The military scholar of the school of Mars in 1793, wore a mongrel uniform, invented by the painter David, and intended to be partly Roman, partly Grecian, but which any old legendary or phalanx veteran of Cæsar or Alexander would have indignantly rejected as wholly French.

Upon the overthrow of Robespierre, fashion took

PROMENADE COSTUME, 1801.

BONNET, 1801.

"MERVEILLEUX," 1793.

the grand virtue under the new state of things. Hence in 1794 it was noticed that every fashionable *citoyenne* was either really or apparently far advanced in maternity.

The "*Merveilleuse*" of the same year, by the capacity of her bonnet and the slimness of her skirts, will recall a fashion which undoubtedly some of my readers thought "extremely elegant" in its day, but which would now be likely to consign its wearer to a mad-hospital.

The male specimen of this species was scarcely less remarkable in his choice of attire ; while the "*Agioteur*"—a political bully, a blackguard, on a par in principles and practice with some of his kindred who disgrace our republic—wore a costume which, like the stripes of a hyena, distinguished him at once from the more respectable citizen.

The attempt, under the auspices of David, to revive the classical toga, and to model the fashions for the ladies after the costumes of Aspasia and Agrippina, met with but transient success, owing to the severity of the climate—which was particularly unfavorable to bare throats and legs,

and transparent muslin. Besides, none but those whom nature had bountifully clothed with charms could with complacency thus dispense with dress. Coughs, rheumatisms, and ridicule, soon extinguished all classical ardor among these few, though many of the fashionable women of the day were willing to sacrifice both modesty and health in their desire to carry back the civilization of the world two thousand years, when silk was worth its weight in gold and cotton an unknown thing. While the fashion lasted its want of adaptation to the climate gave rise to some ludicrous scenes. Thus at the famous "Feast of Pikes," when all Paris was gathered in the open air, a sudden storm of rain came down. The thin muslins with which the females had attired themselves "like the women of the free peoples of antiquity," were soaked through in a moment, and clung closely around their wearers, so that, as the dry chronicler remarks, "the shape was clearly discernible." "Titus" and "Alcibiades" would have been more than human to have refrained from laughing at the spectacle presented by the bedraggled "Clorinda" and "Aspasia."

THE MODE, 1800.

The *coup de grace* was given to the classical fashion by the appearance of a favorite actress in the character of a Chinese girl. Her costume would hardly have been recognized in Pekin; but such as it was it struck the fancy of the town; and the Parisiennes loaded themselves with frills and ruffs, fancying that they were habited *à la Chinoise.*

The classical party were divided into Romans and Athenians, whose simplicity of attire gave rise to another sect in the world of fashion called "*Incroyables.*" They protested against the invasion of antiquity by an opposite extreme in dress; so that, what between superfluity of coat collar, cravat, and hat, it was difficult to see that they had any head at all.

At this epoch the confusion, or, more properly speaking, medley of fashions—in which every extreme and incongruity was represented—was at its height. Each taste and political sentiment wantoned in its own masquerade. The liberty of dressing as one pleased for once reigned triumphant. The Jacobins reveled in dirt and dishabille; the classical scholars in nude simplicity; the fops in perukes, powdered heads, three-cornered hats, and hair cut *à la Titus;* the ladies as simple country girls with bonnets *à la butterfly;* robes *à la Cybèle;* chemises *à la Carthaginoise;* in short, *à la* any thing their caprices or ingenuity could devise. Each one strove after originality; and a more extraordinary crowd than that of the streets and salons of Paris under the Consulate the world will never again see. It was fashion run crazy. The world of "ton" were more like the inmates of a mad-house than the rulers of society. Madame Tallien—the beauty of the day—wore *transparent* costumes, in imitation of the Olympian gods. Her stockings were flesh-colored and divided at the toes, on which she carried rings and jewels. Her friend

THE MODE, 1812.

Josephine—afterward Empress—was her rival in fashion. Feminine whims did not stop even at this degree of immodesty, but went to such lengths as I shall not undertake to describe. Suffice it to say that dresses "*à la sauvage*" became in vogue; while the pictures and ornaments openly displayed would have scandalized even the Roman world, and been thought not quite "the thing" in Sodom.

I shall run hastily over the intervening space between that era and our own, depending mainly upon illustrations to show by what changes of cut, and gradations in taste, our present costumes have been formed; and how Paris—having for a while rioted in every species of extravagance that a depraved and licentious taste could conceive—has at last quietly and indisputably assumed the supreme rank in the world of fashion. From being the butt of mankind for her grossness of garments, she has become the arbiter of civilization as to what it shall wear, and how it shall live. Not a rival disputes her sway.

As the Revolution receded so luxury augmented. At the commencement of the present century dress had simplified wonderfully, and the worst features of previous absurdities had disappeared, although it would not be quite safe for man or woman to walk the streets in our day in the attire of that. The grand passion, after the Egyptian expedition, was for India shawls, pearls, diamonds, and lace of the highest price. Men rivaled women in their desires for these luxuries. The debts of Josephine for her toilet in a short time amounted to one million two hundred thousand francs. She had ordered thirty-eight new bonnets in one month; the feathers alone cost eighteen hundred francs. With such an example, the Court followed so rapidly in the path of extravagance that even Napoleon was scandalized, although he had said to his wife, "Jose-

25

CRAVAT "A OREILLES DE LIEVRE," 1812.

LEG-OF-MUTTON SLEEVE, 1828.

phine, I wish that you shall astonish by the beauty and richness of your dress;" following up the precept with action one day, when she was not clad with sufficient elegance to satisfy him, by throwing the contents of his inkstand upon her costly robe. Josephine owned one hundred and fifty cashmere shawls of remarkable beauty and great price. She offered Madame Murat for one that pleased her fourteen thousand francs.

Judging from the past, nothing admits of greater variety of form than the modern bonnet; while its rival—the male hat—is restricted to the slightest possible variation of its pipe shape. *Now*, the fashionable ladies wear their bonnets merely suspended from the back of their heads, like the outer leaf of an opening rose-bud. *Then*—in 1801—they overhung the forehead much after the manner of a candle extinguisher.

In 1812, the modern hat had assumed the general shape which it has unfortunately ever since retained, and with which it seems likely to make the tour of the globe. The ladies have at times made various assaults upon it, and even attempt-

ed to take it into their own possession—a conquest which, luckily for the influence of their charms, they never wholly accomplished. He would be a benefactor to the human race who could invent a suitable covering for the head, which should utterly annihilate the present source of torture and ugliness which surmounts the front of him made in the image of God.

In 1812, the leg-of-mutton sleeve, which descended in its full amplitude to the present generation, was in full vogue; also *low* necks and backs, which have ever maintained their popularity, by a strange sort of anomaly, as *full* dress; while short petticoats—which are so convenient—have been lengthened into untidy skirts that save the street-cleaners half their trouble.

I have brought together, in one tableau, the four principal types of dress that have swayed the fashionable world for the past century. The striking changes therein depicted are indicative of what we may look for in the future. With so plastic a many-colored material as dress, there can be no limits to the varieties of costume.

Part II

Hoop Skirts and Crinoline

1850–1870

Its diameter growing steadily in the years following its introduction in the late 1820s, the hoop skirt reached maximum circumference about 1854. The mechanical engineering problems this growth presented were resolved when layers of petticoats and padding were replaced with a hoop-shaped whalebone framework. This substructure gave the hoop skirt its name.

At the time the hoop was the dominant fashion, Europe, in particular Paris, Vienna and Berlin, was the world center of style. In America, the women most concerned about fashions lived in the major cities of the eastern seaboard, though in the raw frontier town of Chicago a few brash upstarts like Potter Palmer and Marshall Field were finding success by bringing the benefits of culture to the wilderness.

News of fashions in American journals was largely replaced by war news during the Civil War years. Excellent current fashion coverage was available in many European publications, however, and thus *Der Bazar*, one of the leading women's magazines of the continent, was selected for use in presenting the fashions of this period. A comparison of some 1870 and subsequent issues of *Der Bazar* with contemporary issues of *Harper's Bazar* reveals many of the same illustrations in both.

Despite the apparent universal acceptance of the hoop, it was not regarded with unqualified enthusiasm in all quarters. Criticism of the hoop was manifested in the vast number of cartoons, jokes and poems deriding it that appeared at the time. The following offering from an 1857 issue of *Harper's Weekly* is quite representative.

A WHOOP ABOUT HOOPS

For when a smitten wretch has seen
Among the lost in crinoline,
　　The one his heart holds dearer,
Oh! what a chill to ardent passion,
To feel that through this hollow fashion
　　He never can be nearer!

That instead of timidity drawing near,
And pouring into her thrilling ear
　　The flood of his soul's devotion,
He must stand and bellow in thunder tones,
Across half an acre of skirts and bones,
　　As if hailing a ship on the ocean.

Fashions for June.

Furnished by Mr. G. Brodie, 51 *Canal-street, New York, and drawn by* Voigt *from actual articles of Costume.*

FIGURES 1 AND 2 VISITING AND WALKING COSTUMES.

THE Illustrations which we present require but brief comment. Figure 1 is a VISITING DRESS. It is *à disposition*, although for this may be substituted a trimming of embroidery, braid, or *bouillonée*. Figure 2 is a WALKING DRESS for a young lady. It is high in the neck at the back, with a *basque* somewhat deeper in front and behind than at the sides. The sleeves are cut at the outside in points, which are united by fancy buttons, forming lozenge-shaped openings, through which the under-sleeves appear. The under-sleeves are plain with embroidered wristbands. The body is ornamented with a shirred ribbon, which terminates in small bows at the sleeves. When the hair is copious the mode of dressing given above is very becoming.

BONNETS are made of almost every material and combination of materials. Though smaller than have previously been worn, they are extremely pretty; and recede further than ever from the face. The ornaments are chiefly displayed upon the edges and front, the crown being comparatively plain. Redundancy of ornament is the distinguishing characteristic of the foreign modes. Flowers, laces, marabouts, and ribbons are used with the utmost profusion. The cap-crown is a special favorite. Transparent tissues are in great request. The same profusion of trimming is worn upon dresses. Flounces and *basques* are the prevailing modes.

In MANTELETTES the modistes have put forth all their resources, and never has their success been so decided. Every variety of this beautiful costume has tasked their inventive powers—the stately Pelisse, the bewitching Mantilla, the graceful Scarf, the elegant Talma, and combinations of all these—every thing, in short, that the exigencies of any style of figure or complexion could require, is at the disposal of the fair.

FIGURE 3.—THE TALMA MANTLE.

Composed of taffeta wrought upon tulle, forming a *guipure*. This is outlined with needle-work, and finished by a massive fringe.

FIGURE 4.—L'EMPERATRICE.

A double scarf formed of two shades of *poult de soie;* the outlines, embroidery, and fringes alternating in color upon the ground of the scarf.

FIGURE 5.—THE ZULEIKA BERTHE.

This graceful mantelette is composed of a vandyked *berthé*, trimmed with a crimped fringe, and terminated by a rich *velour guipure*, fringed.

ETIQUETTE FOR LADIES AND GENTLEMEN.

A few plain directions, fashioned not after an imaginary model, but upon the world as it is.

The Person.

Cleanliness, absolute purity of person, is the first requisite in the appearance of a gentleman or lady. Not only should the face and hands be kept clean, but the whole skin should be subjected to frequent ablutions. Better wear course clothes with a clean skin, than silk stockings drawn over dirty feet. Let the whole skin be kept pure and sweet, the teeth and nails and hair, clean; and the last two of medium length, and naturally cut. Nothing deforms a man more than bad hair-cutting, and unnatural deformity in wearing it. Abstain from all eccentricities. *Take a medium between nature and fashion,* which is perhaps the best rule in regard to dress and appearance that can be given.

Dress.

The importance of dress can scarcely be overrated, but by comparison. It is with the world the outward sign of both character and condition.

A well bred man may be ever so reduced in his wardrobe—his clothes may be coarse and thread-bare, but he seldom wears a coarse, and never a dirty shirt.

The boots should always be clean, and invariably well blacked and polished.

Make a point of buying a good hat. One proper fur-hat worth four or five dollars, when a year old, looks more respectable, than a silk one bought yesterday.

Be as particular as you like about the cut of your pantaloons. Buy strong cloth that will not be tearing at every turn, and if you consult economy and taste at the same time, let them be either black or very dark grey, when they will answer upon all occasions.

The vest allows of some fancy, but beware of being too fanciful. A black satin is proper for any person or any occasion. Nothing is more elegant than pure white. Some colors may be worn for variety, but beware of every thing glaring, in materials or trimmings.

If you have but one coat, it will be a black dress-coat, as there are occasions where no other will answer. Frock-coats are worn in the morning, riding or walking, but never at evening visits, at weddings, or parties. Overcoats are worn for comfort; they need not be fine, and should not be fanciful. Most gentlemen wear a simple, plain, black silk cravat, neatly tied in a bow-knot before. Parties require white or light kid-gloves. Black, or very dark ones, of kid, silk, or linen, are worn upon all other occasions, except in driving, when buff leather-gloves are preferable.

The best dressed men wear the least jewelry. Of all things avoid showy chains, large rings, and gewgaw pins and broaches, All these things should be left to negroes, Indians, and South Sea islanders.

The most proper pocket-handkerchiefs are of white linen. If figured, or embroidered, they should be very delicately done.

Gloves are worn in the street, at church, and places of amusement. It is not enough to carry them—they are to be worn.

Ladies are allowed to consult fancy, variety, and ornament, more than men, yet nearly the same rules apply. It is the mark of a lady to be always well shod. If your feet are small, don't spoil them by pinching—if large, squeezing them makes them worse.

As you regard health, comfort, and beauty, do not lace too tightly. A waist too small for the natural proportion of the figure, is the worst possible deformity, and produces many others. No woman who laces tight can have good shoulders, a straight spine, good lungs, sweet breath, or is fit to be a wife and mother.

The most elegant dresses are black or white. Common modesty will prevent indecent exposure of the shoulders and bosom. A vulgar girl wears bright and glaring colors, fantastically made; a large, flaring, red, yellow, or sky-blue hat, covered with a rainbow of ribbons, and all the rings and trinkets she can load upon her. Of course, a modest well-bred young lady chooses the reverse of all this. In any assemblage, the most plainly dressed woman is sure to be the most lady-like and attractive. Neatness is better than richness, and plainness better than display. Single ladies dress less in fashionable society than married ones, and all more plainly and substantially for walking or travelling, than on other occasions.

In my opinion, nothing beyond a simple, natural flower, ever adds to the beauty of a lady's head-dress.

It is a general rule, applicable to both sexes, that persons are the best dressed, when you cannot remember how they were dressed. Avoid every thing out of the way uncommon or grotesque.

Behavior in the Street.

When you meet a gentleman with whom you are acquainted, you bow, raising your hat slightly, with your left hand, which leaves your hand at liberty to shake hands if you stop. If the gentleman is ungloved, you must take off yours, not otherwise.

Meeting a lady, the *rule* is that she should make the first salute, or at least, indicate by her manner, that she recognises you. Your bow must be lower, and your hat carried further from your head; but you never offer to shake hands; that is *her* privilege.

The right, being the post of honor, is given to superiors and ladies, except in the street, when they take the wall, as farthest from danger from passing carriages, in walking with or meeting them.

In walking with a lady you are not bound to recognise gentlemen with whom she is not acquainted, nor have they in such a case, any right to salute, much less to speak to you.

Should her shoe become unlaced, or her dress in any manner disordered, fail not to apprise her of it respectfully, and offer your assistance. A gentleman may hook a dress, or lace a shoe, with perfect propriety, and should be able to do so gracefully.

Whether with a lady or gentleman, a street talk should be a short one; and in either case, when you have passed the customary compliments, if you wish to continue the conversation you must say, "Permit me to accompany you."

Don't sing, hum, whistle, or talk to yourself in walking. Endeavor, besides being well-dressed, to have a calm, good natural countenance. A scowl always begets wrinkles. It is best not to smoke at all in public, but none but a ruffian will inflict upon society the odor of a bad cigar, or that of any kind, on ladies.

Ladies are not allowed upon ordinary occasions to take the arm of any one but a relative, or an accepted lover, in the street, and in the day time; in the evening—in the fields, or in a crowd, wherever she may need protection, she should not refuse it. She should pass her hand over the gentleman's arm, merely, but should not walk at arm's length apart, as country girls sometimes do. In walking with a gentleman, the step of the lady must be lengthened, and his shortened, to prevent the hobbling appearance of not keeping step. Of course, the conversation of a stranger, beyond asking a necessary question, must be considered as a gross insult, and repelled with proper spirit.

Visiting.

Of course, you ring or knock, and await the opening of the door. When this is done, you ask for the mistress of the house, not the master.

Should she not be at home or engaged, you leave your card, where cards are used, or your compliments. Where there are several ladies in the family, you may ask for *the ladies.* Where people dine early, calls are not made until some time after dinner—in cities they are made from eleven till three.

You leave over-coat, cane, umbrella, &c., and if the call is of any length, your hat in the entry. A graceful bow, a pleasant smile, an easy way of paying the customary compliments, and suiting them to each person, no lesson can teach. In the presence of ladies, you are only silent when listening to them. You never yawn, nor lounge on your seat, nor interrupt nor contradict, but by insinuation—you never tell unpleasant news, nor make ill-timed observations. Study to please, by a respectful demeanor, and an easy gaiety. It is well to know how to enter a room, but it is much better to know when and how to leave it. If you have made a good impression, a long story may wear it off—if a bad one, being tedious only makes it worse. Don't stand hammering and fumbling, and saying, "Well, I guess I must be going." When you are ready, go at once. It is very easy to say, "Miss Susan, your company is so agreeable, that I am staying longer than I intended, but I hope to have the pleasure of seeing you again soon; I wish you a good morning;" and, bowing, smiling, shaking hands, if the hand be proffered, you leave the room, if possible without turning your back; you bow again at the front door, and if any eyes are following you, you still turn and raise your hat in the street.

Behavior at Dinner.

There is no situation in which one's breeding is more observed, than at the dinner-table; our work would therefore be incomplete without the proper directions as to its etiquette.

The best general rule for a person unacquainted with the usages of society, is to be cautious, pay attention, and do as he sees others do, who ought to know what is proper. Most of our blunders are the result of haste and want of observation.

If there are ladies, gentlemen offer their arms, and conduct them to the dining-room, according to their age or the degree of respect to be shown them.

The lady of the house sits at the head of the table, and the gentleman opposite at the foot. The place of honor for gentlemen is on each side of the mistress of the house—for ladies on each side of the master. The company should be so arranged that each lady will have some gentleman at her side to assist her. Of course, it is every gentleman's duty, first of all to see that ladies near him are attended to.

When napkins are provided, they are at once carefully unfolded, and laid on the knees. Observe if grace is to be said, and keep a proper decorum. If soup is served, take a peace of bread in the left hand, and the spoon in the right, and sip *noiselessly* from the side of the spoon. Do not take two plates of the same kind of soup, and *never* tip up the plate.

When regular courses are served, the next dish is fish. If silver or wide-pronged forks are used, eat with the fork in the right hand —the knife is unnecessary.

Next come the roast and boiled meats. If possible the knife should never be put in the mouth at all, and if at all, let the edge be turned outward. Any thing taken into the mouth not fit to be swallowed, should be quietly removed with the fingers of the left hand, to that side of the plate. The teeth should be picked as little as possible, and never with fork or fingers. Carefully abstain from every act or observation that may cause disgust, such as spitting, blowing the nose, gulping, rinsing the mouth, &c.

When the ladies leave the table, which they do together, at the signal of the mistress of the house, the gentlemen rise and conduct them to the door of the apartment, and then return to the table. This is in formal parties.

If at dinner you are requested to help any one to sauce, do not pour it over the meat or vegetables, but on one side. If you should have to carve and help a joint, do not load a person's plate —it is vulgar: also in serving soup, one ladleful to each plate is sufficient.

Eat PEAS with a dessert spoon; and curry also. Tarts and puddings are to be eaten with a *spoon*.

As a general rule, in helping any one at table, never use a knife where you can use a spoon.

Making a noise in chewing, or breathing hard in eating, are both unseemly habits, and ought to be avoided.

Never pare an apple or a pear for a lady, unless she desire you, and then be careful to use your fork to hold it; you may sometimes offer to *divide a very large pear* with or for a person.

At some tables, large colored glasses, partly filled with water, with a bit of lemon, are brought when the cloth is removed. You dip a corner of your napkin in the water, and wipe your mouth, then rinse your fingers and wipe them on your napkin.

Introductions.

The rule is, never to introduce one person to another without knowing that it is agreeable to both. Ladies are always to be consulted beforehand. Gentlemen are introduced *to* ladies, not ladies to gentlemen.

A common form is, "Mr. Jones, Mr. Smith—Mr. Smith, Mr. Jones." Messrs. Jones and Smith bow, shake hands, express their happiness at being made acquainted with each other.

When more ceremony is required, the introducer says, "Miss Smith, permit me to introduce Mr. Jones to your acquaintance," or, "allow me to present."

Coffee-house, steamboat, and stage-coach acquaintances last only for the time being. You are not obliged to know them afterwards, however familiar for the time.

Conversation.

The object of conversation is to entertain and amuse. To be agreeable, you must learn to be a good listener. A man who monopolises a conversation is a *bore*, no matter how great his knowledge.

Never get into a dispute. State your opinions, but do not argue them. Do not contradict, and, above all, never offend by correcting mistakes or inaccuracies of fact or expression.

Never lose temper—never notice a slight—never seem concious of an affront, unless it is of a gross character.

You are not required to defend your friends in company, unless the conversation is addressed to you; but you may correct a statement of fact, if you know it to be wrong.

Never talk at people, by hints, slurs, inuendoes, and such mean devices. If you have any thing to say, out with it. Nothing charms more than candor, when united with good breeding.

Do not call people by their names, in speaking to them. In speaking of your own children, never "Master" and "Miss" them —in speaking to other people of theirs, never neglect to do so.

It is very vulgar to talk in a loud tone, and indulge in hoarse laughs. Be very careful in speaking of subjects upon which you are not acquainted. Much is to be learned by confessing your ignorance—nothing can be by pretending to knowledge which you do not possess.

Never tell long stories. Avoid all common slang phrases, and pet words.

Of all things, don't attempt to be too fine. Use good honest English—and common words for common things.

General Rules of Behavior.

Having dressed yourself, pay no further attention to your clothes. Few things look worse than a continual fussing with your attire.

Never scratch your head, pick your teeth, clean your nails, or worse than all, pick your nose in company; all these things are disgusting. Spit as little as possible, and never upon the floor.

Do not lounge on sofas, nor tip back your chair, nor elevate your feet.

If you are going into the company of ladies, beware of onions spirits, and tobacco.

If you can sing or play, do so at once when requested, without requiring to be pressed. On the other hand, let your performance be brief, or, if never so good, it will be tiresome. When a lady sits down to the piano forte, some gentleman should attend her, arrange the music stool, and turn over the leaves.

Meeting friends in a public promenade, you salute them the first time in passing, and not every time you meet.

Never tattle—nor repeat in one society any scandal or personal matter you hear in another. Give your own opinion of people if you please, but never repeat that of others.

Meeting an acquaintance among strangers—in the street, or a coffee-house, never address him by name. It is vulgar and annoying.

Preliminaries for Marriage.

According to the uages of society, it is the custom of the man to propose marriage, and for the female to refuse or accept the offer as she may think fit. There ought to be a perfect freedom of the will in both parties.

When a young man admires a lady, and thinks her society necessary to his happiness, it is proper, before committing himself, or inducing the object of his admiration to do so, to apply to her parents or guardians for permission to address her.

Young men frequently amuse themselves by playing with the feelings of young ladies. They visit them often, walk with them, pay them divers attentions, and after giving them an idea that they are attached to them, either leave them, or what is worse, never come to an explanation of their sentiments. This is to act a truly dastardly and infamous character.

How to commence your Addresses.

A gentleman having met a lady at social parties, accompanied her to and from church, may desire to become more intimately acquainted. In short, you wish to commence formal addresses. This is a case for palpitations, but forget not that "faint heart never won fair lady." What will you do? Why, taking some good opportunity, you will say,

"Miss Wilson, since I became acquainted with you, I have been every day more pleased with your society, and I hope you will allow me to enjoy more of it—if you are not otherwise engaged, will you permit me to visit you to-morrow evening?"

The lady will blush, no doubt—she may tremble a little, but if your proposition is acceptable to her, she may say:

"I am grateful for your good opinion, and shall be happy to see you."

Or if her friends have not been consulted, as they usually are before matters proceed so far, she may say:

"I am sensible of your kindness, sir; but I cannot consent to a private interview, without consulting my family."

Or she may refuse altogether, and in such a case, should do so with every regard to the feelings of the gentleman, and if engaged, should say frankly:

"I shall be happy to see you at all times as a friend, but I am not at liberty to grant a private interview."

As, in all these affairs, the lady is the respondent, there is little necessity for any directions in regard to her conduct, as a "Yes," ever so softly whispered, is a sufficient affirmative, and as her kindness of heart will induce her to soften as much as possible her "No."

To tell a lady who has granted the preliminary favors, that you love her better than life, and to ask her to name the happy day, are matters of nerve, rather than form, and require no teaching.

Love Letters.

For a love letter, good paper is indispensable. When it can be procured, that of a costly quality, gold-edged, perfumed, or ornamented in the French style, may be properly used. The letter should be carefully enveloped, and nicely sealed with a fancy wafer—not a common one of course, where any other can be had; or what is better, plain or fancy sealing wax. As all persons are more or less governed by first impressions and externals, the whole affair should be as neat and elegant as possible.

Popping the Question.

There is one maxim of universal application—never lose an opportunity. What can a woman think of a lover who neglects one? Ladies cannot make direct advances, but they use infinite tact in giving men occasions to make them. In every case, it is fair to presume that when a woman gives a man an opportunity, she expects him to improve it.

In the country, the lover is taking a romantic walk by moonlight, with the lady of his love—talks of the beauties of the scenery, the harmony of nature, and exclaims,

"Ah! Julia, how happy would existence prove, if I always had such a companion!"

She sighs, and leans more fondly on the arm that tremblingly supports her.

"My dearest Julia, be mine forever!"

This is a settler, and the answer, ever so inaudable, "makes or undoes him quite."

"Take pity on a forlorn bachelor," says another, in a manner which may be either jest or earnest, "marry me at once and put me out of my misery."

"With all my heart, whenever you are ready," replies the laughing fair. A joke carried thus far is easily made earnest.

A point is often carried by taking a thing for granted. A gentleman who has been paying attentions to a lady, says,

"Well, Mary, when is the happy day?"

"What day, pray?" she asks, with a conscious blush.

"Why, every body knows that we are going to get married, and it might as well be one time as another; so, when shall it be?"

Cornered in this fashion, there is no retreat.

"Jane, I love you! Will you marry me?" would be somewhat abrupt, and a simple, frankly given "Yes!" would be short and sweet for an answer.

"Ellen, one word from you would make me the happiest man in the universe?"

"I should be cruel not to speak it then, unless it is a very hard one."

"It is a word of three letters, and answers the question, Will you have me?"

The lady, of course, says Yes, unless she happens to prefer a word of only two letters, and answers No.

And so this interesting and terrible process in practice, simple as it is in theory, is varied in a hundred ways, according to circumstances and the various dispositions.

One timid gentleman asks, "Have you any objection to change your name?" and follows this up with another which clenches its significance, "How would mine suit you?"

Another asks, "Will you tell me what I most wish to know?"

"Yes, if I can."

"The happy day when we shall be married?"

Another says, "My Eliza, we must do what all the world evidently expects we shall."

"All the world is very impertinent."

"I know it—but it can't be helped. When shall I tell the parson to be ready?"

LADIES' TOILETTE TABLE.

To prevent Loosening of the Hair.

Immerse the head in cold water, morning and night, dry the hair thoroughly, and then brush the scalp, until a warm glow is produced. In ladies with long hair this plan is objectionable; and a better one is to brush the scalp until redness and a warm glow are produced, then apply to the roots of the hair one or two of the following lotions.

Lotion for Promoting the Growth of the Hair, and Preventing it from Turning Grey.

No. 1.

Vinegar of cantharides, half-an-ounce
Eau de Cologne, one ounce
Rose-water, one ounce.

No. 2.

Eau de Cologne, two ounces.
Tincture of cantharides, half-an-ounce.
Oil of nutmegs, half-a-drachm.
Oil of lavender, ten drops.
Mix.

To cure Ringworm.

The head should be washed with a profusion of soap, and the hair carefully combed, to remove all loosened hairs and every particle of crust. Then bathe the head with ringworm lotion.

Ringworm Lotion.

Sublimate of mercury, five grains.
Spirits of wine, two ounces.
Tincture of musk, one drachm.
Rose-water, six ounces.
Mix well.

Style of Bonnet.

A person of delicate pale complexion should wear a hat with pink lining. A person of dark complexion should have white lining, with rose trimming. A person with very red or yellow complexion should not wear high colors.

Dress.

Have reference to the complexion. Tight sleeves without trimming are becoming to full forms, of medium height, or below it. A tall person appears graceful with drapery. A short form should not wear much drapery, and not a full skirt.

Flounces.

Flounces appear well upon tall persons, but never upon diminutive ones.

High-neck Dresses.

High-neck dresses are generally becoming, but not upon a very high-shouldered person. If the shoulders are only moderately high, the neck may be covered, and a narrow piece of lace, instead of a collar, put around the throat.

Evening Dresses.

Evening dresses of transparent materials, look well when made high in the neck. Make the dress loose over the chest, and tight over the shoulder blades. Long sashes fastened in front are preferable to belts, unless there is much trimming upon the dress.—Narrow lace at the wrist is becoming, and gives a finish to the dress. An extremely small and waspish-looking waist can never be considered handsome. It is exceedingly hurtful to those who attain it by tight-lacing, and doubly ungraceful, since it prevents all graceful movements.

Fashions for July.

Furnished by Mr. G. Brodie, 51 *Canal-street, New York, and drawn by* Voigt *from actual articles of Costume.*

FIGURE 2.—The Hat, from which our sketch is taken, is of fine Leghorn. Other fabrics of straw, made in similar style, are worn. The rim is looped up at the sides—more closely upon that side where the feather is worn—by two wide bands of white watered satin ribbon. A twisted band of this ribbon, together with rosettes and strings, also ornaments the hat, which is completed by a gracefully floating plume.—The Habit is composed of Cashmere or Saxon cloth. Light green is a favorite color, though this is not imperative, since the color should always be such as to harmonize with the complexion of the wearer. It is enriched by elaborate needlework of trailing vines and flowers, with an arabesque border. The sleeves, which are embroidered in like manner, are slashed upon the under-sleeve and cross-laced by cords which terminate in tassels. The sleeves are made flowing, and do not have the *mousquetaire* cuff.—The *Gilet* is of white *poult de soie*, likewise embroidered upon the collar. It is cut away rounding at the bottom, where it is fashioned like the old Continental waistcoat. Above this the breast of the coat may be confined by loops, which do not, however, slip over the button directly opposite, but over the one next below. The cords from the opposite sides thus form a cross-lacing with lozenge-shaped openings.—The Chemisette is of lace, fulled at the top, with an edging of Valenciennes lace. The size of our page does not admit of the insertion of the skirt in the illustration. This is made quite full, and may be ornamented with needle-work to match that of the boddice.

Of MANTILLAS there are several elegant novelties. Among the most noteworthy of Mr. BRODIE's recent importations are some elegant scarfs and mantillas of Chantilly and Guipure lace. The delicate tracery of the one of these materials, and the transparency and picturesque effect of the other, peculiarly adapt them for the summer months. There are also novel styles of open-worked Canton crape scarfs and mantles, the beauty of whose designs and the elaborateness of whose manufacture fully equal any thing that has been produced in the Flowery Land.

In BONNETS we notice no very special novelties. They still continue to be made small, very small, with round crowns, and of the most transparent tissues. They are worn a trifle closer to the cheeks than heretofore. The trimming is chiefly bestowed upon the inside and around the front, the back being comparatively unornamented.

FIGURE 1.—EVENING COSTUME FOR A BRIDE.

FIGURE 1.—The hair is arranged in bandeaux, half-puffed at the sides only; and, as illustrated in our last Number, it is crossed in front by a plait taken from the back hair, with which is entwined a garland of flowers. A second group of larger flowers is also placed upon the lower portion of the back of the head. These terminate in drooping sprays, falling upon the neck.—The Dress is of *moire antique*, low upon the shoulders, and *demi-basquée* before and behind. It is covered almost entirely with white blonde, three rows of which ornament the corsage, and being continued, drape the sleeves. The skirt also is covered with three blonde flounces overlapping each other. The first two are looped up at the side by clusters of orange flowers with branching sprays. Smaller bouquets also ornament the corsage and the sleeves.

FIGURE 2.—RIDING DRESS.

CANARY BIRDS.

General Directions.

Keep the cage washed and clean if you wish the birds to be healthy. Fresh lettuce, cabbage and plantain may be given them in July and August, two or three times a day. The seeds of plantain and lettuce are good to be given as food. Keep clean water in pans in the cage for them to wash and bathe in. A piece of cuttle-fish bone or sand ought to be in the cage, to keep them in a healthy condition. A little sponge cake may be given occasionally. Crackers, sweet apples, and worms are good. Never give salt.

How to distinguish the Male from the Female.

The male may be distinguished from the female by a streak of bright yellow over the eyes and under the throat; his head is wider and longer, and has richer colors, and larger feet. He also begins to warble first, which is often at a month old.

LETTER WRITER.

1. A letter of introduction, note of invitation, or reply, should always be enclosed in an envelope.
2. A letter of introduction should always enclose the card and address of the person introduced.
3. Notes of invitation should always be sent in the name of the lady of the house.
4. Invitations should be answered within two days.
5. Notes of invitation should not be sealed.
6. Figured and colored paper is out of style; pure white paper, with gilt edges, is more strictly in good taste.

CELEBRATED CHEMICAL
MIXTURE FOR WASHING.
BY ELIZABETH WATERS:
RICHLY WORTH TWENTY DOLLARS,
AS
IT SAVES POUNDING & RUBBING.

☞ *The Recipe, in a separate form, is generally sold at Fifty Cents and One Dollar each.*

MIXTURE.—Dissolve half a pound of Soda in a gallon of Boiling Water, and pour upon it a quarter of a pound of Lime. After this has settled, cut up ten ounces of common bar Soap, and strain the solution upon it, and mix perfectly. Great care must be taken that no particles of Lime are poured upon the Soap. Prepare the Mixture the evening before washing.

DIRECTIONS.—To ten gallons of water add the above Preparation, when the water is boiling; and put the clothes in while boiling. Each lot of linen must boil half an hour, and the same liquid will answer for three batches of clothes. The white clothes must be put in soak over night, and, if the collars and wristbands are soaped and rubbed slightly, so much the better. Clean cold water may be used for rinsing. Some prefer boiling them for a few moments in clean blueing water and afterwards rinse in cold water.

☞ *The Clothes may not appear perfectly white while wet; but when dry, will be clean white.*

DIRECTIONS FOR COLORING GARMENTS—&C.

Discharging Colors.—Colored silks are put into a copper vessel, in which water, with half a pound of soap dissolved. Then boil until the copper gives evidence of color. Then take out the silk, and rinse it in warm water. Then add more soap, and boil as before, until the color is discharged.

Re-Dyeing Silks, or Changing the Color.—You can dye all colors, black—blues, green or black—green, brown—and brown, green.

To Dye Silk, Light-Blue.—Boil your silk in a solution of white soap and water until it is white; then rinse in warm water. Put the silk into a wash-basin, and cover it with cold water. From your chemic blue-bottle drop one or two drops: this is sufficient, unless you wish to have the color darker—in which case, more of your chemic blue must be used. Move your silk in the water until the blue is expended, which can be ascertained by holding up some water with your hand, and looking through it as it falls.

To Dye Silks, Green.—A quarter of a pound of ground ebony-wood placed in a dish, and boiling water poured over it, stirred, covered over with a cloth a few moments, and strained off—will color the silk, if put into the mixture for half an hour, grass-green, inclining to laurel. After the half hour, take the silk out, and rinse in the same dish. Pour cold spring water into another dish, and put in a table-spoonful and a quarter of chemic blue; then rinse in spring water, and dry.

To Dye Silk, Brown, inclining to Mulberry.—Boil, about two hours, two ounces of sumach or one ounce of galls, one ounce of logwood, two or three ounces of camwood or madder. Pour in cold water, and cool it down. If necessary to incline more to mulberry, add a little purple archil. Put in the silk, and simmer it for half an hour or more. Rinse in two waters, and hang up the silk to dry.

To Dye Silks, Red, Crimson, &c.—Dissolve two ounces of white soap in boiling water. Stir your silk shawl or dress in the liquid, rubbing with your hand any places looking soiled, until it is as clean as possible. Then rinse in warm water. Put the silk in one or two more of the same kind. Then rinse in warm water. Put the silk in a solution, in hot water, of half an ounce of Spanish annatto, and stir for half an hour. Take it out, and rinse in clean water. Then put the silk into a solution of alum, (size of a common bean,) in warm water. Take out, and rinse in clear water. Boil in copper, 20 minutes, a quarter of an ounce of cochineal. Dip out into a pan. Put silk in for thirty minutes. For scarlet, add to the above half a wine-glassful of the solution of tin. When cold, rinse in cold water.

To Dye Black, common materials.—Four pounds of logwood for four pounds of goods. Soak logwood twelve hours in soft water. Boil an hour, and strain. Dissolve one ounce of blue vitriol in warm water, and dip goods into it. Then turn the whole into logwood dye. If they are cotton goods, boil fifteen minutes, stirring, to prevent spotting. Drain, and do not wring goods. Hang them up to dry. Put them into water boiling hot, in which there is half a tea-cupful of salt for two gallons of water. This sets the color. Goods must remain until the water is cold, and then dried without wringing. To set color for black silk, put it into boiling hot suds.

To Clean Silk Goods.—If dingy, rub dry bran on them carefully with a woollen cloth. Hard soap is best for washing silks of all colors except yellow—and soft soap for that. Dissolve soap in hot water, then add cold, to make it lukewarm. Take them in silks, and rub until clean. Take them out without wringing, and rinse in two portions of warm water. Add sulphuric acid enough to give it an acid taste, for bright yellows, maroons, and crimsons. To restore pink colors, add a little vinegar to the second rinsing water. For blues, purples, &c., add pearlash. For scarlet, a solution of tin. For olive-green, a little verdigris dissolved in the water. Fawn and brown, in pure water. Fold up silks while damp; after drying awhile, iron them on the wrong side, with irons just hot enough to smooth them.

To Clean Carpets.—Take up and shake at least twice a year, if used much; and once, if not used, to keep out moths. Put straw under, to prevent dust grinding them out. If any moths are found, sprinkle tobacco or ground pepper on floor underneath. To remove grease, grate on clay or chalk very thick; cover it with brown paper, and put on a warm iron. Repeat it until removed. If it needs cleaning all over, spread it on a clean floor, and rub on, with a new broom, pared and grated raw potatoes. Dry perfectly.

To Clean White Kid Gloves.—Rub on India-rubber, moist bread, or magnesia. If you cannot clean in this way, close the top of the gloves, and rub them over with a sponge saturated with saffron water. The color will be yellow or brown.

To take out Ink from Floors.—Scour with sand wet with sulphuric acid and water. Then rinse with strong pearl-ash water.

PICKLING.—*Cucumbers.*—Pick the small, green cucumbers. Turn on boiling water; and in four or five hours take them out, and put them in cold vinegar, with a spoonful of alum and a tea-cupful of salt to every gallon of vinegar. Turn the vinegar from the cucumbers; scald and skim it; then turn it on the pickles, and scald them, without boiling, a few minutes. Then put them hot in the vessel for keeping. To make them brittle, scald several times. Put in a few peppers.

Oysters.—Turn off the liquor from the oysters; strain and boil it. Rinse off the bits of shells. Put the oysters in the liquor while boiling. and boil one minute. Take them out, and put in the liquor a few pepper-corns, cloves, and a blade or two of mace. Add a little salt, and as much vinegar as oyster sauce. Boil the whole fifteen minutes, and turn it on the oysters. Bottle and cork them, if you wish to keep them several weeks.

Fashions for September.

Furnished by Mr. G. BRODIE, 51 *Canal-street, New York, and drawn by* VOIGT *from actual articles of Costume.*

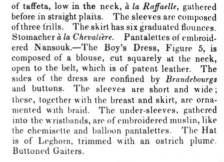

of taffeta, low in the neck, *à la Raffaelle*, gathered before in straight plaits. The sleeves are composed of three frills. The skirt has six graduated flounces. Stomacher *à la Chevalière.* Pantalettes of embroidered Nansouk.—The Boy's Dress, Figure 5, is composed of a blouse, cut squarely at the neck, open to the belt, which is of patent leather. The sides of the dress are confined by *Brandebourgs* and buttons. The sleeves are short and wide; these, together with the breast and skirt, are ornamented with braid. The under-sleeves, gathered into the wristbands, are of embroidered muslin, like the chemisette and balloon pantalettes. The Hat is of Leghorn, trimmed with an ostrich plume. Buttoned Gaiters.

FIGURE 2.—SLEEVE.

FIGURE 1.—MANTEAU.

THE transparent tissues of summer begin to give place to fabrics somewhat more substantial. The BYZANTINE, which we illustrate above, forms an appropriate link between summer and autumn styles. It is characterized by its dignified aspect, its elaborate embellishment, and its easy adaptation to the movements of the wearer. The material is Gros d'Ottoman, of a Napoleon blue color, ornamented with black velvet bands, adorned with Oriental figures. A richly tasseled fringe adds much to the unique effect of this garment. Its form is ample, being box-plaited in the back into a yoke, which is smoothly adapted to the figure.

SLEEVES.—We observe a sleeve which, besides being in itself beautiful, is admirably suited for elderly ladies, or those who prefer to have their wrists covered during the cool season. It is of very simple construction. The fullness of the sleeve is gathered in box plaits a scant inch wide (very little being folded under), and 3½ or 4 inches deep at the shoulder and wrist. The meeting edges of the plaits are seamed together; a cord may be inserted for ornament. The fullness of the drapery falls free from the termination of the plaits. Care must be taken that they be not too wide.

CHILDREN'S DRESSES.—Figure 3 is clad in a loose sack of black or dark colored taffeta, with a *revers* scalloped, as is also the outline of the garment, and enriched with a crochet ornament. The sleeves are open and laced upon the outside, back of the arms, and are also trimmed with bows. The skirt is very full. The Hat is of straw, with a feather, and band of white satin ribbon, No. 22, arranged full, with a rosette upon the side opposite the feather. Chemisette of lace, fulled into bands of insertion. Pantalettes of embroidered muslin. Gaiters of black patent leather, the quarters of the same color as the skirt.—Figure 4 has a bonnet of silk; dress

FIGURES 3, 4, 5.—CHILDREN'S DRESSES.

Fashions for October.

Furnished by Mr. G. Brodie, *51 Canal-street, New York, and drawn by* Voigt *from actual articles of Costume.*

FIGURES 1, 2, 3.—HOME DRESS AND CHILDREN'S COSTUMES.

FIGURE 4.—VELVET CLOAK.

FIGURE 5.—CLOTH CLOAK

THE Dress is of shot *Poult de Soie.* The corsage is closed to the neck, but exposes the chemisette through the graduated lozenge-shaped spaces, which are cut away. There are similar openings in the sleeves; these are divided into three large puffs. Ruches *à la vielle* trim the edges of these open spaces, which are further ornamented with a neat button at the points where the opposite sides are connected. The front of the skirt is similarly ornamented with *echelons* of ribbon. When the skirt is not lined these *bouillonérs* may be supported by a lining of stiff muslin. They are graduated from six inches at the top to four times that length at the bottom. The Head Dress is of Valenciennes.

The GIRL'S DRESS is composed of a striped *poult de soie* skirt. The *basquin,* of dark taffetta, is slashed at the sides and cross-laced. The sleeves are cut in a double rank of leaf-shaped lappets. Bows of satin ribbon trim the shoulders and the lower portion of the jacket. Lace under-sleeves and pantalettes. Gaiters, buttoned, matching in color the skirt, or of glazed leather.

The BOY'S DRESS is of velvet, of a dark color. The fly is of the same material as the blouse, and is lined with silk to match. The blouse is short, and confined by a belt. Breeches *a la Louis XIII. Mousquetaire* collar, which, as well as the wristbands, should be confined with gold buttons. Shoes of patent leather.

From the variety of CLOAKS presented for the present season, we select the two following as especially worthy of illustration.

FIGURE 4 is composed of velvet, of a dark color, ornamented with heavy needle-work and a massive fringe. In form it is very simple, being merely a plain skirt set with a trifling fullness upon a yoke, which is

hidden by a pelerine. It is lined throughout with plush, so that it may be worn with either side out; thus constituting in effect two garments, as the weather or fancy may dictate.

FIGURE 5 is composed of cloth. It forms a circle, taken in at the neck, the gores being covered by the collar. It is cut up, as far as to the level of the bend of the arm, leaving tabs in front. The slit is curved somewhat backward, which allows the cloth to be apparently turned over, forming what appears like a sleeve. The cloak is buttoned up in front. The trimming is of galoon. It is quilted, with a silk lining to match.

Fashions for November.

Furnished by **Mr.** G. Brodie, 51 *Canal-street, New York, and drawn by* Voigt *from actual articles of Costume.*

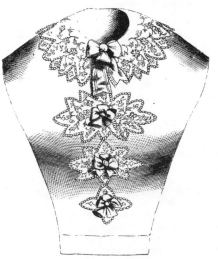

is passed a ribbon, which terminates in a three-looped knot. Similar nœuds ornament each of the other pieces of lace. The sleeve is in like manner

FIGURE 2.—CHEMISETTE.

FIGURE 3.—CAP.

enriched by a ribbon passing through the lace at the wrist. The laces illustrated are Valenciennes, but Maltese, or any other fabric, may be similarly fashioned.

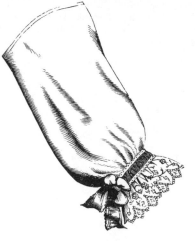

FIGURE 4.—SLEEVE.

FIGURE 1.—PROMENADE COSTUME.

THE distinguishing features which marked the prevailing styles for Cloaks during the past winter—yokes and box-plaited skirts—still remain favorites. They are, however, modified by being cut in such a manner that the lower portion of the skirt falls with great fullness. That which we illustrate this month is quite unique. It is composed of Napoleon blue satin. Its peculiarity consists in the cut and great depth of the cape, which occupies nearly one half of the length of the back. From the centre, which is left in a decided point, arches spring boldly to the sides, and from thence to the breast; the points thus formed being terminated with rich tassels. The skirt, box-plaited behind into a concealed yoke, is plain in front, the arm-holes being covered with flaps ornamented with drop buttons upon the rear sides. The whole garment is elaborately ornamented with needle-work.—In re-

gard to the materials for Cloaks, cloths are most extensively used. Satins dispute the favor which has been hitherto accorded to velvets, which they seem to be gradually displacing. In richness and elaboration of ornament, cloaks will exceed even those of last year. Every thing at present seems to indicate that furs, those especially of a costly character, will be a favorite trimming.—The Dress is of damask silk, of which the richest fabrics are displayed in profusion. The skirt is made in flounces alternately wide and narrow, of which the number is left to the discretion of the wearer.—The Bonnet is of light blue satin, having a soft crown, and is trimmed with marabout feathers.

The Chemisette, Cap, and Sleeve require but few words in explanation of the illustrations. It will be perceived that they are *en suite.* Through the fulling which borders the centre-piece of the cap

SOMETHING FOR THE LADIES ABOUT COLORS.

TO ladies who make cunning use of color—not by painting their faces, but by a deep and subtle study of costume ; to artists, house-furnishers, ornamental gardeners, and others, there have been officially delivered at Paris and Lyons, during the last quarter of a century, sundry lectures by M. Chevreul, upon the practical effect of certain laws connected with the contrast of colors ; and these lectures, which were formed by him into a book fifteen years ago, have been lately translated into English. Having read the translation, we write what follows :

Monsieur Chevreul, learned in the law of colors, was appointed long ago to superintend the dyeing department of the manufactory of the Gobelin tapestries. One of the first questions asked of him was, Why are the black tints bad that are employed as shadows in blue draperies? He answered that the black was of course spoiled by contrast. M. Chevreul followed up his hint by arranging together various masses of colored wool taken from the warehouse, observed how colors put side by side mutually affected one another ; and, from that point, carried on his researches in various ways to maturity. We state some of the results, chiefly having in mind the uses to which ladies may put them.

First must be set down two very plain rules. One concerns the setting side by side of two different shades of the same color. Put side by side squares tinted with Indian ink, each square having one uniform tint, but no two squares of the same intensity. Arrange them in a row, according to a regular scale, beginning with the lightest and ending with the darkest. Then every square will be seen to be modified by those on either side of it ; the border next a darker square will be lightened in effect—the border next a light square will be darkened in effect. The whole row of tinted squares, seen from a little distance, will be made in this way to appear not flat, but fluted. Such is the effect of tints upon each other.

The effect of hues, or contrasting colors, may be expressed in the second main rule—Contrasting or complementary colors are such as when blended together give rise to the perception of whiteness. The most perfect of these relations is that existing between blue, yellow, and red ; for, mix those three colors, and they produce white ; consequently a color complementary to each of these is made by blending the other two. Because blue with yellow creates green, green is the complement of red ; because red and yellow create orange, orange is the complement of blue ; because red and blue create violet, violet is the complement of yellow. The eye itself can perform these changes ; look upon a blue and a yellow, and in a little while both will appear to be green. Again, take a square colored red, and observe it. Take also a square colored blue, and observe it. Place them side by side. The red square where it is near the blue will have a yellower tinge than the rest ; and into the blue on the other border some little shade of green will enter. That is because every color tends to suggest its opposite (or complement) around its borders, and, as we have explained, the opposite of red is green—the opposite of blue, orange.

It is also to be remembered that the eye, fatigued with looking at one color, is disposed to receive the impression of its complement. Let us suppose, for example, that a lady in a draper's shop is looking at red stuffs ; and, after having seen five or six pieces, begins to complain of the bad color of those subsequently shown to her. The color is not bad ; but her eye, weary of red, no longer receives the impression of it vividly, or as a source of pleasure. Let the prudent tradesman not allow ten or eleven red stuffs to be looked at in succession ; but, after about the fifth, contrive to submit for inspection something green. A very good green it is sure to seem if it be only of a tolerable color ; and, after dwelling on it for a little time, the customer may go on looking at the reds, and will be sure to see them to the best advantage.

Accustomed to a little application of these principles, and knowing pretty well how colors stand related to each other, any person may avoid gross errors of taste in house-furnishing, in dressing, in the arrangement of a nosegay, and in all such matters. The main relations of color to be borne in mind are these : Green is the opposite, and complement, to red ; green, therefore, reddens adjacent hues, and red adds a green tinge to them ; but green and red set off each other to the best advantage when placed side by side— the green looking greener, the red redder—and this is, of course, most thoroughly the effect when the two colors are alike in depth of tone. What green is to red, yellow is to violet, and blue to orange. In the same way it may be said that the yellow tints of green suggest their complements and opposites, the violet-reds ; the yellow-oranges contrast with violet-blues, and the orange-reds with the blue-greens.

Thus the pink of the complexion is brought out by a green setting in dress or bonnet ; and any lady who has a fair complexion, that admits of having its rose tint a little heightened, may make effective use of the green color, but it should be a delicate green, since it is of importance to preserve harmony of tone. When there is in the face a tint of orange mixed with brown, a brick-red hue will result from the use of green ; if any green at all be used in such a case it should be dark.

But for the orange complexion of a brunette there is no color superior to yellow. This imparts violet to a fair skin, and injures its effect. A skin more yellow than orange has its yellow neutralized by the suggestion of the complement, and a dull white effect imparted. The orange skin, however, has the yellow neutralized and the red left ; so that the freshness of complexion is increased in black-haired beauties.

As the complement of violet is yellow, which no lady desires to see added to the color of her skin, it follows that violet is only suitable for dress when it is very deep in tone, and worn by those who wish to have the complexion whitened by contrast.

Blue imparts orange, which enriches white complexions and light flesh tints ; it also of course improves the yellow hair of blondes. Blue, therefore, is the standard color for a blonde, as yellow is for a brunette. But the brunette who has already too much orange in her face must avoid setting it in blue.

Orange suits nobody. It whitens a brunette, but that is scarcely a desirable effect, and it is ugly. Red, unless when it is of a dark hue, to increase the effect of whiteness by contrast of tone, is rarely suitable in any close neighborhood to a lady's skin. Rose-red destroys the freshness of a good complexion ; it suggests green. For this reason it ought not to be chosen for the lining and hangings of the boxes of a theatre, if ladies who frequent it are to look well in their evening toilets. Rose-red, wine-red, and light crimson boxes give a green tint to the ladies in them ; if they would rather have the best made of all natural rose in their faces, the hangings they should wish for ought to be light green. But they would suit best pale or fair complexions, just as the amber hangings at the opera-house in the Haymarket used to be best suited, and, in fact, only suited, for brunettes. The dark crimson of the draperies adopted at the rival house were more impartial, since they tended by contrast to the whitening of all faces to which they served as background.

Enough has been said now to display some principles that may be carried into application in a thousand ways. The painter upon canvas knows that if he places certain colors side by side, though they be as pure as tube can hold, yet they may look dirty because they spoil each other by the complements that they suggest. He knows that in painting from the model, wherever there is much contrast of color in small compass, he must not directly imitate each color that he copies with a stroke of the same color from his brush ; he is compelled to use false tints to get the true ones. Upon the same plan must a lady go to work in the compounding of a nosegay or the trimming of a bonnet, keeping apart those colors that can not come together without quarreling. Thus she would do well to trim a yellow bonnet with violet or blue, and a green bonnet with rose, red, or white flowers, and to follow the same general idea in grouping the colors of a dress.

Contrast of rich color is familiar to us in the dress of soldiers, and it has an economic use. The soldier in his bright mixture of green and yellow, blue and scarlet, or whatever else it be, will seem to be well clothed when all the seams of his coat, perhaps, are white, and he is really threadbare ; for if the colors be but well contrasted they will set each other off and remain to the last intensified. Just in the same way a civilian may wear in the summer a black coat that is not new, and over white trowsers it will be made to look by contrast excellent as to its color. But let him buy in the winter a new pair of black trowsers and put them on : the old coat causes them to seem fearfully black and glossy, and is made by them in return to look really much older and whiter than it is.

The same ideas M. Chevreul carries into the business of house-furnishing. Dark paper-hangings he proscribes, as absorbing too much light, red and violet as damaging the color of the skin, orange as tiresome by reason of intensity. He recommends only yellow and light tones of green and blue. Yellow combines well with mahogany furniture, but spoils the look of gilding. Light green suits well both with mahogany and gilding. Light blue suits with mahogany fairly, and with gilding admirably : it also combines better than blue with yellow and orange woods—is therefore good for drawing-rooms. A gray pattern on a white ground—pattern and ground being balanced pretty evenly—is, however, very strongly recommended. As a general rule, says M. Chevreul, the color of the covering of the chairs should be complementary to the prevailing color of the paper-hanging. The window curtains should be of the color of the chairs, having fringes of the color of the paper-hanging. The carpet should be chosen by the same rule, to give distinctness to the effect of the furniture ; green and black being better dominant colors under mahogany than red, scarlet, or orange. To mahogany chairs green covers are good when uniformity is not desired. In small rooms a harmony should be sought by carrying throughout an analogy of color—the contrast should be of tones and hues of the same color : it is only in large rooms that the contrast of color can be thoroughly well carried out.

It is not worth while to multiply examples of this theory. We have desired only to amuse ourselves and at least one section of our readers.

THE HAUNTS OF FASHION.

This is the Carnival of Fashion, when it puts on its gayest face, and prepares to deck itself in its most brilliant colors. Great preparations are made for the occasion. All Paris, Lyons, and London having been ransacked for the richest stuffs, the newest patterns, and the brightest colors, these are displayed on this opening of the Fall Season at all the haunts where our fashionables are in the habit of resorting. Dry-goods shops roll out their velvets, silks, and satins, and millinery establishments show their most attractive finery. It is during this week, when *the* world is supposed to have come back to the city, that shopmen and milliners send out their polite missives to the houses of all those who are supposed to have money and the disposition to spend it, informing the ladies that Messrs. Calico and Co., or Madame La Mode, have opened their new goods for the season, and inviting inspection. This is irresistible, and if desire only prompts some, curiosity impels all to accept the invitation. Accordingly there is hardly a lady who does not come out on the occasion, and make a round of visits to certain well-known stores and millineries.

Hats are the absorbing interest of the week, and uneasy will sleep that fashionable head that can not deck itself with the glories of the latest mode on the coming Sunday. We do not pretend that there is any necessary connection between Religion and Fashion; but we will venture to say that, if there should be any recreancy on the part of female church-goers on that day, it may be fairly put down to the account of unpunctual millinery. If the new hat don't come home on Saturday, we know of more than one devout worshiper of Fashion who will lose necessarily the opportunity of displaying her devotion at church the day after.

The new hat must be had, and there is no want of opportunities to secure the desired object. There is all Broadway hanging with its tempting baits, but it is not at these that the golden fish of fashion deign to rise. They are only to be caught in certain quiet and retired places, where the knowing ones throw out their irresistible lures. A fashionable woman in search of a new hat drives, of course, the round of all the stylish establishments, but finally alights at a respectable-looking and apparently private house in Waverley Place. She rings the bell, and being received by half a dozen coquettish-looking French mademoiselles, presiding over their various departments, is ushered at once into the inner sanctum of Fashion, where Madame herself does the honors of her establishment. Our

fashionable lady has passed contemptuously by the ranges of hats—pretty enough, but not sufficiently expensive—in the outer rooms, and keeps her admiration in reserve for the choice specimens which their weight in gold would hardly pay for, kept carefully concealed within from all vulgar eyes. Here, after repeated trials and nice adjustments before the mirror, and by the aid of a hand-glass, and the most emphatic assertion of Madame that our fashionable dame has got the hat that suits her exactly, and which, of course, is the only one of the kind in New York, the purchase is made. She has a costly hat, and one manufactured by the most fashionable milliner, and she is, of course, content. What it is we could not describe, and if we did, we probably would not be understood. It may be a straw, white, brown, or gray, with velvet, lace, and ribbons; or a rice-straw or leghorn, with feather, or a tulle bouillonné, or a crape, with silk—for all these are said by the oracles of fashion to be in vogue this autumn. You may rest assured, whatever it is, that it will cost thirty dollars, at least. When a milliner once gets a run of fashionable customers, her fortune is made; and trade can show no more remarkable cases of success than in this department. Several have already retired in succession with handsome independences, acquired in the same establishment.

The dry-goods stores, too, have their special days, although one would think, from the constant brilliancy of the shop-windows in Broadway, that there was a perpetuity of the opening season. There is always, however, at this time something "just arrived," supposed to be particularly new and attractive, to entice the butterflies of Fashion, and they may be seen just now fluttering in excited eagerness wherever a gay ribbon or flashing silken surface is spread to catch the eye. It is a glorious time for the dry-goods man, when each woman, what with the extended circumference of the hoop and the increased multiplication of flounces, wants as many yards for her dress as in old times would cover the nakedness of a whole family. We hear of no diminution in this respect, and notwithstanding the contraction in Wall Street, there is continued expansion in Broadway. The tarlatanes, the grenadines, the stamped velvets, or the moire antiques having been bought, they are of course to be made up according to the latest Parisian mode, and here it is:

"Skirts of dresses are ornamented either with flounces or quilles. Double skirts are still in great favor, and are generally seen in plain or very small checked pop-

lins. These dresses are completed by long, tight-fitting casaque, which forms a third skirt, each being bound with black velvet.

"Chinées dresses and robes à disposition, with fringe on the flounces woven in the material, are very pretty. The body is made pointed in front, and a Montespan basque behind, or rounded with a sash, the long, wide ends being trimmed with pinked ruches. When the skirt is ornamented with quilles, the body should be à basque, closed in front by Louis XIII. bows. Tarlatanes and silk grenadines are worn in full dress. The bodies of walking dresses are all made high. The sleeves of thin dresses are made in different forms. That called the Vénetienne is cut open, and hangs long at the back of the arm. Another is composed of a large puff, forming a short sleeve, from which hangs a deep frill caught up at the front of the elbow. The form of the burnous remains unaltered. We have seen some, intended to be worn in the country, made in plain material—brown or iron gray, trimmed round with a broad, crossway band of bright-colored plaid, some with a plaid border and plaid ground, and others of a light color, braided in two contrasting colors.

"The fichu is growing in favor daily. At one time we see the fichu Marie Antoinette, of black lace or richly embroidered muslin, trimmed with lace and ribbon to match the color or trimmings of the dress; or the fichu Paysanne, or guipure, or embroidered organdi, in large, flat plaits, drawn down on the shoulders and the middle of the back to form a low body. The fichu crosses in front, and is fastened with a large gold or silver pin; the ends fall on each side over the band. The fichu Lamballe, the prettiest among them, made of embroidered muslin, trimmed with narrow lace, crossed at the chest, finishing in long ends tied behind like a sash; or that novelty, full of grace and elegance, the little fichu Naomi; and for a more severe style, the fichu Maintenon, which discovers much less of the chest, hiding nearly the whole of the body, which it enriches by the profusion of its elegant trimming.

"Nor must we forget to mention the pélerine-berthe, with a seam on the shoulder to make it fit tightly to the figure. The body of the pélerine reaches half-way down the bust; it is cut square, and the same length behind and before, trimmed round with an insertion, which serves as a heading to a double frill which reaches to the waist. This pélerine buttons up to the throat, and is finished with a ruche. Lace is worn in profusion; it is used for trimmings of all kinds of lingerie. It is employed as flounces in bridal full dress; then in violettes, black or white (the latter are increasing in favor). With it the most charming mantles are made."

We must trust to the sharp eye and quick intelligence of Fashion to comprehend what we have quoted. All we pretend to know is that it comes from the best authorities, and when our fashionable readers are persuaded that it is so, we do not fear but that they will succeed in fathoming all its mysteries.

A HAUNT OF FASHION.

TO-DAY AND FIFTY YEARS AGO.

1857.   BALL TOILETTE.   1807.

"ARABELLA MARIA. "Only to think, Julia dear, that our Mothers wore such ridiculous fashions as these!"
BOTH. "Ha! ha! ha! ha!"

FASHIONS FOR FEBRUARY.

AT the present season, novelties in ball and evening costume are those which chiefly claim attention. For ball dresses, the most favorite materials are tulle illusion, lace, or tarletane, over slips of glacé silk. The flounces are elaborately ornamented with ribbon, fringe, feather trimming, &c. In addition to the ball dress shown in our illustration, we may mention one of a very simple and elegant description, composed of pink tulle illusion, with seven flounces, each edged by a narrow ruche of the same material, and below the ruche, by a row of narrow blond lace. Another beautiful ball dress, peculiarly appropriate to the season, is of white tulle illusion, with two skirts, each ornamented with a broad trimming of quilled satin ribbon, set on in zig-zag. Within each angle formed by this trimming there is fixed a bouquet, composed of the foliage and red berries of the holly. The corsage and sleeves are ornamented with corresponding bouquets.

THE ILLUSTRATIONS.

Evening Dresses. — The figure with the opera cloak wears a dress of pink silk, with a double skirt. Each skirt is trimmed with three rows of white feather fringe—one broad row being placed quite at the edge, and two narrower rows above it. The opera cloak is of white cashmere, trimmed with pink plush figured with white spots. The hood is ornamented with rich tassels of pink and white chenille and passementerie. The other figure represents a ball dress of white tulle illusion, figured with small sprigs worked in blue silk. The dress has three flounces, trimmed with festoons of blue terry velvet. The corsage has a berthe formed of rows of blonde and trimming of blue terry velvet. The sleeves are trimmed in corresponding style. Head-dress a double bandeau of gold and turquoise, with a plume of white and blue marabouts on one side. Bracelets of gold and turquoise, and a Chinese fan.

In-door Costume.—The lady whose face is seen in profile, wears a dress of very rich brown silk, crossed with chequers of black satin. The skirt has side trimmings formed of black velvet intermingled with pendent ornaments of black chenille. The corsage is trimmed with black velvet and fringe. The collar and under sleeves are of Maltese lace. The cap, also of Maltese lace, has lappets hanging at the back, and is trimmed with bows of peach-blossom ribbon and black velvet. Bracelets of malachite and coral. Gloves of pale yellow kid. The dress shown in the other figure is of violet color terry velvet. The skirt is trimmed with nine bands of black velvet, each graduating in breadth as they ascend to the waist, and each headed by a row of black guipure. The corsage and sleeves are nearly covered with narrow rows of black velvet, intermingled with black guipure, and one row of broad guipure is set on in the form of a berthe. Collar and under sleeves of Venetian lace. Lappets of the same, fixed very low at the back of the head, and flowing loosely over the shoulders. Bracelets and brooch of oxydised silver, set with amethysts.

THE HAIR, AND STYLES OF WEARING IT.

VARIOUS HEAD-DRESSES.

NATURE has given us no finer ornament than our hair; and the *torments* by fire and floods of oil to which in all ages it has been subjected, are enough to make "each particular hair stand on end" and protest against the cruel inflictions. But if they make no audible protest they are apt to stand on end, and avenge themselves by growing white, and falling untimely from the heads that have "plotted with devilish arts against their peace."

Fashion, we are happy to observe, is lately giving some indications of a gracious permission finally to uncoil the monstrous ropes, and flatten down the unnatural projections with which, for two or three years past, her votaries have been disfigured.

In its highest state of cultivation and preservation the hair requires only a simple arrangement, varied to suit the style of its possessor, to be the most glorious of all crowns. When we shall refine back to nature, and cease to paint the lily and perfume the rose, we shall have taken a great step toward elegant accomplishment.

We learn by the best authorities that the hair of women is coarser than that of men, disproving the common notion that continual use of the "abhorred shears" tends to coarseness and strength.

The ordinary length of women's hair is about twenty inches, and flaxen and chestnut hair are the finest, and white and black hair the coarsest. In confirmation of these observations, Whitoff tells us that 598 black, 648 chestnut, and 728 flaxen hairs are about the average number which a square inch of the skin of the head produces.

How the hair sympathizes with the diseases of the body we have all noticed, growing thin, and fading, and withering up under the influence of various maladies; and we have some very curious evidences of sympathy with emotion as well as disease. Byron makes his Prisoner of Chillon say,

"My hair is gray, but not with years,
  Nor grew it white
  In a single night
As men's have grown from sudden fears."

Several instances are recorded of the hair changing color under the influence of a few hours' suffering. The hair of Sir Thomas More is said to have turned white in a single night, and that of Mary, Queen of Scots, Marie Antoinette, and others, within a very short period of time. In the "Encyclopædia Metropolitana" a case is recorded of a banker whose hair became perfectly gray in the course of three days, in consequence of anxiety of mind.

No author has been able to account for this, nor, in fact, for the gradual growing white of the hair with age. Various theories have been proposed, but we are not warranted in adopting any of them. A celebrated German authority considers that the hair begins to turn gray about thirty, and another gives forty as the time of life at which this change begins to make itself seen; and it is the popular belief that dark hair turns gray much earlier in life than light, but probably the belief is not founded in fact. White streaks are readily recognized among dark hair; but as far as our observation goes, light hair is as liable to turn gray as dark, and scarcely do we know a man or woman beyond twenty-five who has not some white hairs, and we think of several of the age of thirty who are not only very gray but bald.

The coloring matter of the hair is supposed to be secreted in small glands in the scalp, and that its character is subject to alteration from disease and violent emotions, in consequence of which the hair changes its hue.

A variety of restoratives have been invented, each professing to recover the pristine character of this pigment, but a case of absolute restoration has never come under our observation.

Poets have exhausted all epithets of description in singing this crowning beauty of men and women—and sunshine, and snow, and raven darkness have been summoned again and again to do it reverence by their poor representations.

The different fashions of wearing the hair in different ages is a curious and interesting study. There is no torture, it would seem, to which the tresses of women have not been subjected — dyed and bleached, variegated and varnished, powdered and stiffened and frizzled. Among the ancient Greeks the custom of wearing false hair was at various periods excessively prevalent; indeed, it was only now and then that the classic head-dress we term Grecian was to be seen, so predominant were the pyramids of curls, plaits, and other elaborations. Pomatum was also in liberal use—a custom that is quite too prevalent at this day, for it neither advances the growth nor adds to the beauty of the hair, and cleanliness and refined taste are alike offended by it.

The ancient Roman ladies reduced their hairdressing to a positive science, and their slaves were taught by them how to rear their tresses into most magnificent edifices, together with curls, flowers, jewels, and coronals. They understood, too, a very ingenious method of twining the hair into multitudinous plaits, which it was the fashion to inclose in a caul or net woven of gold and silver thread and gems. Arrows of gold and silver, and dagger-shaped jewels of all precious metals, pinned the caul to the hair.

The Egyptians wore false hair, both mixed with their own and in wigs, and the fashion of using perfumes and pomatums was universally sanctioned by use. The ladies neither wore the caul nor adopted any other means of confining the tresses, except the wearing of a fillet, composed of precious stones, about the forehead to prevent their falling over the face. Having been perfumed and put into braids or plaits they were left to stream over the neck and shoulders, and as far down the back as they would reach: a profusion of flowers and gems adorned them.

In the British Museum there is a wig which is said to have been found among the ruins of the temple of Isis at ancient Thebes; and though it must have been manufactured thousands of years ago it is perfectly preserved, both in curl and color. But however successful their art of curling in those days, their ambition was not to emu-

late nature, as is shown by such specimens of their handiwork as have come down to us. It appears rather that they sought to destroy the identity of the hair altogether by painting, frosting, and gilding.

The earliest authentic records furnished by England on the styles of hair-dressing show them to have been very simple. The ladies wore their hair parted in the middle, put smoothly back from the face, and wound under a hood or coif—sometimes it was allowed to float in curls down the back. Many of the old court ladies are thus represented. Elizabeth, Queen of Henry VII., wore her hair with "a calle of pipes over it" on the day of her marriage. In one of the portraits of Anne Boleyn her hair is represented in the same way. In the pictures of Lady Jane Grey her hair is shown to be parted in the middle, braided across the forehead, and concealed behind under a vail or cap. It was not till the days of Queen Bess that "coming events cast their shadows before," and signs of the dreadful head-gear, which a century later rose to a ridiculous height, began to present themselves.

In some of the portraits of Elizabeth her hair appears to be folded over an enormous cushion; and, indeed, so fond was she of extravagant structures, that she had several entire wigs, which she caused to be reared into various ornamental pyramids of curls and frizzles, and set-off with gems and flowers.

Among the articles composing her wardrobe, the following is set down:

"Item. One cawle of haire set with pearles, in Number xlii. One ditto set with pearles of sundry sizes and bignchs. One cawle set with nine true-loves of pearle and seven buttons, in each a rubie."

Toward the close of the reign of the "goode Queen" perukes came in fashion, and the manufacture of them afforded employment to numberless decayed gentlewomen. So much false hair was worn, indeed, that a traffic in hair was established, and means not very honorable resorted to for supplying the requisite amount. Poor women were bribed to sell their hair, children induced by gifts to part with theirs, and the graves visited and the dead despoiled in frequent instances.

The custom of dyeing the hair prevailed largely at this period. A writer of the time says: "If any have hair of her owne naturall growing, which is not fine ynough, then will they dye it in divers colors."

The peruke, agreeably to the best authorities, was originated in France, and after the massacre in Paris introduced into England.

About 1630 Henrietta Maria, Queen of Charles the First, introduced the fashion of wearing the hair in a sort of cross, curled in short thick curls

along the forehead, and in falling ringlets along the neck. This style, under various modifications, prevailed for a good many years.

In the reign of Charles the Second perukes became the exclusive fashion. They were worn of all hues, and it was the custom of the ladies either to match or contrast the colors of their wigs and dresses.

The following is transcribed from Pepys's Diary:

"1664, *May* 13*th.*—This day my wife began to wear light-colored locks, quite white almost, which, though it made her look very pretty, yet, not being natural, vexes me that I will not have her wear them."

In 1690 a fashion of setting the hair out from the head upon wires prevailed, but whether the natural hair could be worn in this style does not appear.

In the beginning of the next century the most extravagant elaboration became the fashion in hair-dressing. Masses of ringlets were worn floating down the back, interspersed with flowers, ribbons, and jewels; also, immense fabrics of curls and *frise* were reared up on the top of the head, and surmounted with feathers and ornaments of jewels, flowers, and ribbons. About half a century later these fashions gave place to still more absurd and extravagant ones. Cushions of a monstrous size were placed on the head, and the hair drawn smoothly over them; sometimes, however, the extreme ugliness and stiffness of this coiffure was relieved by the wearing of curls along the neck. In the reign of George the Second, powder and pomatum were in excessive use, and false hair was worn to an inconvenient degree of profusion. At this time various stiff and unnatural styles of arranging the hair were in vogue; among them a kind of sausage-shaped curl, and the German, or roll-shaped curl, which was made stiff and round by being stuffed with frizzles. These elaborate fashions, of course, consumed a great part of every day, and required the skill of a hair-dresser. So much time and pains could not always be granted, indeed, and one hair-dressing, it is said, not unfrequently served for a week. To enable them to sleep in such gear must have taxed the ingenuity of the ladies heavily. But they are not likely to fail of doing "what fashion dictates to be done," nor of leaving undone what she warns them not to do. No doubt it is scandal upon the fair women of the times, but we find it stated that hair-dressers about this period were in the habit of advertising their competency to erect tires that would last for three months!

These ridiculous cushions were superseded by wigs closely resembling those worn by men; the only difference, in fact, consisting in the termination of the gentlemen's wig in a queue, and the ladies' in a fold of hair called a club. About 1800 powder began to be discontinued, but whether the powder-tax or common-sense discouraged the use of it is a point not easily answered at this day; probably, however, it was the tax that chiefly operated against it. False hair soon afterward began to disappear, and the ladies bestowed the time and pains on their own hair which was formerly given to their wigs. In some of the pictures of the times we find a profusion of ringlets, not only dropping down the neck and shoulders but also falling over the face like a vail.

About the beginning of the eighteenth century the French ladies began to rear their hair into turrets and pile it up to mountains, and for the purpose of supporting it great frames of whalebone and wire were invented, and cushions, and various other fabrics over which to train it, were brought into use.

In the reign of Louis XIV. a head-dress was introduced composed of rows of full curls raised one above another to the crown of the head. The curls were mixed with flowers, and strings of pearls were worn between each row; and curls, interwoven with various ornaments, floated down over the neck and shoulders. Altogether, it was not an unbecoming mode. In the centre of this head-dress it was the custom to place an ornament of highly elaborated jewel-work, so placed that its pendants should just touch the "white honor of the beauteous brow."

From the times of Louis XV. we take an illustration much less pleasing. The hair, it will be seen, is combed up from the forehead, and arranged in perpendicular rows of frizzed curls, over which a ruff is worn, fastening under the chin. Occasionally the fashion was varied by some royal caprice; but our illustration represents that which predominated.

Various modes followed each other in quick succession during the revolutionary period. Wigs obtained great favor, but pomatum and powder were unfashionable. Toward the close of the Reign of Terror Madame Talien introduced the fashion of cutting the hair short all round like that of a man, and this style was succeeded by a clustering crop of short curls, represented by our illustration.

About the opening of the nineteenth century a succession of monstrously grotesque head-dresses followed one another. One of them consisted of a pyramid of hair supported by a tall comb, and was called "the Giraffe," probably from its giving the neck a resemblance to that of the animal which gave name to the mode. Another style, called "the Casque," was made by combing all the hair together at the top of the head, like that of a Chinese woman, and there raising it in great bows and plaits over foundations of wire and whalebone. We give a specimen of another mode considered specially becoming in its time.

In the provinces of France the prevailing styles have been much more simple and beautiful. Some of the peasants, however, appear to have no pride in their tresses, and, when tempted by the hair-merchants, dispose of them for the veriest trifle. Those who retain their hair conceal it beneath a cap, and this fashion extends even to the little children.

The modern styles of most nations are, perhaps, familiar to our readers. Among the Portuguese and Italians it is the custom to plait the hair, and wear it beneath a loose silken net. The Turkish ladies plait their hair in a great many different tresses, and ornament them with gems, coins, and jewels. The Armenian women have a similar fashion of adding such quantities of false hair to their own that, when seated, they appear half-buried in disheveled locks.

DIFFERENT MODES OF WEARING THE HAIR.

WHY DOES CRIME INCREASE?

ALMOST without exception, the criminal returns in all parts of the country show a startling increase of crime—an increase wholly disproportionate to the increase of population. In this State, and especially in this city, where the development of the press enables us to keep a more accurate watch upon ourselves than most of our neighbors can, the increase in crimes of violence is perfectly appalling. Hardly a day passes that the papers do not contain some dreadful account of a murder—some peaceable citizen knocked down and robbed at his own door; or some gambler massacred for his gains; or some policeman shot for doing his duty; or, still oftener, some poor girl decoyed out of earshot, foully outraged, and thrown into the water. The horrid story is becoming so common that it has ceased to be exciting. Equally terrible is the increase of robbery. When the police took possession of Cancemi's rooms they found some five thousand dollars' worth of stolen property there, including an immense variety of female clothing; and as soon as the windfall became known, claimants for fifty thousand dollars' worth of stolen property made formal but unsuccessful applications to the police receiver.

It is true, of course, that allowance must be made for the peculiar condition into which the police system of this city has been thrown by the new police law, and the litigation to which it has led. But this excuse covers but a very brief period of time, whereas the increase of crime is of long standing.

The real cause, we apprehend, of this truly alarming feature of our society must be sought in the maladministration of the law. Our laws are complete enough for their purpose; but, on the one hand, a sad negligence on the part of those who are intrusted with their administration, on the other, a vicious tendency in the public mind toward undue compassion for criminals, combine almost wholly to neutralize and nullify them. Not one-fourth of the rogues, murderers, robbers, and rowdies—either here or in the other large cities of this country—are brought to justice, or even pursued with any thing like vigorous zeal; and the few who are caught, arraigned, and convicted are certain beforehand that the sentence passed upon them will prove a mere idle threat. The only important function of our Governors seems to be to let loose jail-birds upon society; our judges —seemingly from timidity—defeat the law by sentencing to a few years' penitentiary criminals whom the law clearly designed for the halter; between the two, vagabonds may well make light of the terrors of courts and prisons.

In the year 1856, on a full consideration of the criminal returns of England, the British Government came to the conclusion that no more sentences would be shortened, and the law carried out against convicts with the utmost rigor. That is a decision to which we must come. Tenderness to criminals is indeed proving cruelty to society; were our long sentences to the Penitentiary carried out, were our murderers hanged, our burglars taken out of harm's way, this would be a safer and more wholesome country to inhabit. It seems beyond a doubt that the abolition of capital punishment has simply had the effect of substituting innocent for guilty victims; our murderers live, while their victims die. It is time there were a reaction from the morbid sentimentality which has inspired our Judges, Governors, and the public of late years. Justice carries not only a pair of scales, but a sword also.

CHAT.

DIRT AND BEAUTY.

THE handsome, well-developed legs of the Parisian women, so boldly displayed to the admiration of the traveler, have been attributed to the dirty streets by Dr. Arnott, who is an excellent authority on female as well as male anatomy. He tells us that the effort of the pretty little French feet to pick their way through the mud, and the habitual poising of the weight of the whole-body upon the toes, cause a powerful muscular strain, and a consequent large development of the female calf. On this principle, there should be great hope for our American women of increased proportions, for we have already the mud in abundance, in New York at least. We shall look, with our ladies' permission, for the confirmation of Dr. Arnott's theory.

Why, by-the-by, do not our ladies learn to walk more gracefully? They might take a lesson from the Parisian beauty, who treads the dirty streets of Paris with the grace and dignity of a tragic queen. Mark how with one hand she gathers up her drapery, fairly lifting it from the ground, but still allowing it to hang with a graceful negligence, so as to show, with an artistic irregularity of revelation, her well-turned feet and ankles. You might suppose that she had borrowed a living grace from the famous Venus of Milo, in the Gallery of the Louvre. Now look at the New York belle, clutching her gown with her two hands, as if she were afraid of the sudden trundling away of her hoop, and crossing the dirty street like a blowzy countrywoman fording a creek. The newly-adopted female boot is not favorable, we fear, to either feminine grace or the picturesque in woman's steps. It justifies a great deal of duck-like wading; and as we look upon a pair of female boots plopping through the mud of New York, we are reminded of negro Pompey's legs in pursuit of woodcock in the swamp. The exercise is good and healthful, but it must be confessed to be rather trying to the taste for the beautiful.

NEW PATENT TRAVELING-CASE.

"How very absurd these dressmakers are! as though ladies bore any resemblance to such objects as these!"

LADY. "Don't you think the Dress *rather* low in the Neck?"
DRESSMAKER. Oh! no, ma'am: only *Dressy.*"

WHAT WE MAY NEXT EXPECT.

COOL REQUEST.

LADY CRINOLINE. "You won't mind Riding on the Box, Edward dear, will you?   I'm afraid, if we both go inside the Carriage, my New Dress will get so rumpled!"

THE DRESS CIRCLE AT A CONCERT—FRONT ROW.

FASHIONS FOR APRIL.

THE newest Parisian fashions manifest a decided approximation to the style of dress which prevailed during the reigns of Louis XV. and Louis XVI. The make and the trimmings of dresses, the style of arranging the hair, the designs for setting jewelry—all are accurately copied from pictures of the date above mentioned. In short, there is quite a rage for the style Louis XV. and the style Louis XVI.

Pearls were never worn in greater profusion than at the present time. Nets formed of strings of pearls, and just sufficiently large to inclose the torsade of hair at the back of the head, are favorite head-dresses. These nets are edged round by pearl fringe, and at each side and at the back are tassels of pearl. In front a cordon of pearls is passed between the bandeaux of hair. The same style of head-dress has a very elegant effect when composed of blue beads (imitation of turquoise), or of blue beads and pearls mixed together.

Châtelaines are regaining fashionable favor; but those recently introduced are somewhat different in style from the same kind of ornament worn a few years ago. The most elegant consist of two long chains of gold, confined together by a slide set with jewels or beautifully enameled. From one of these chains is suspended a watch, in the back of which is frequently set a valuable cameo. To the other chain may be affixed a jeweled cassolette, or any other trinket which taste may dictate.

OUR ILLUSTRATIONS.

Fig. 1. Ball dress of white tulle, over a slip of white glacé. The skirt is formed of three double jupes of tulle, gathered up in festoons by chains of pearl. The corsage is draped, and in the centre there is a bouquet of white camellias. The sleeves, which are exceedingly short, are formed of a single puff and frill; and on each shoulder there is an *agraffe* of pearls. Head-dress pearls, and blue and white marabouts. Necklace, bracelets, and eardrops of pearl.

Fig. 2. Dress of velvet, of a beautiful hue of brown, at present very fashionable in Paris, where it is designated *la nuance Teba*, in honor of the Empress, who, it will be remembered, bore prior to her marriage the title of Countess de Teba. The skirt of the dress is perfectly plain, without trimming of any kind; but it is made exceedingly full, and is sufficiently long behind to form a short train. The corsage is high, and has a round turn-over collar. The basque presents a novelty; being set on in large box plaits round the waist—a style which, be it observed, is suitable only to a very slender figure. The sleeves have a flat piece on the shoulder, and below it a puff and a broad frill. The under sleeves consist of large *bouillons* of plain muslin, with worked cuffs turned back, and the wrists are encircled by coral bracelets. A small round collar of worked muslin turns over the velvet collar of the dress. The bonnet, of emerald-green velvet, is shaped so as to form a small point in front of the forehead. In the inside of the brim a fall of black lace slightly veils the cap. The outside of the bonnet has also a trimming of black lace, which is carried round the curtain at the back. At each side there are three small black and green ostrich feathers. Strings of green velvet ribbon. Under trimming, bouquets of geranium.

Fig. 3 (Bridal Costume). Double skirt of white satin, richly trimmed with Brussels lace. The lace is disposed in a novel and highly effective style. It is set on in pyramidal groups, each formed of horizontal rows of lace gathers, in slight fullness. On the front of the lower skirt are two bows and ends of broad white satin ribbon, and a ceinture of the same ribbon is fastened in a bow, and long, flowing ends in front of the waist. The corsage, which is high to the throat, is trimmed with horizontal rows of lace and white silk fancy buttons. Spanish sleeves, loose at the ends, and entirely covered with rows of lace, one above another, with bows of white satin ribbon on the shoulders. Round the throat a small white lace collar. The veil is of white tulle, edged with a broad hem, within which is a running of white ribbon. The bridal wreath is composed of orange blossom and jasmine.

Fig. 4. The dress of this sitting figure, which is only partially shown in our Engraving, is of pink tulle, with three broad flounces edged with fancy ribbon of a flowered pattern. The head-dress consists of a wreath, or rather a narrow cordon, of pink flowers, passes across the upper part of the head; and on each side there is a tuft of pink and white marabouts, fixed by pearl-headed Italian pins.

SURPRISING INCIDENT.—*(From the Daily Papers.)*

"Captain Locust, of the Metropolitan Force, having chased two notorious Burglars to a house in Water Street, proceeded to search the premises; but, though it was known that many thieves must be concealed there, he obtained no trace of them till he entered a closet, which the lady of the establishment used as a Dressing-room. There, at infinite risk, he succeeded in dislodging fourteen Herculean Brigands from the inside of a Fashionable Hoop!"

THE GREAT TOBACCO CONTROVERSY.

CLARA (*emphatically*). "I don't care what you say, Frank—I shall always think it a *nasty, odious, dirty, filthy, disgusting*, and *most objectionable* Habit!"

FRANK. "Haw!—Now I'm really surprised, Clara, to hear such a Clever Girl as you are running down Smoking in such Strong Language—for it's admitted by all Sensible People, you know, that it's the *Abuse of Tobacco* that's Wrong!"

[*Which little bit of sophistry completely vanquished Clara.*

SONG ABOUT NOTHING.

I'm thinking just now of Nothing,
    For there's Nothing in all I see;
And I am well pleased with Nothing,
    And the world is Nothing to me.
So I sing the praise of Nothing,
    For Nothing is perfect and true;
And I'm madly in love with Nothing,
    Though that is Nothing to you.

I began my life with Nothing,
    And Nothing on Nothing lives;
For the world is good for Nothing,
    And Nothing for Nothing gives.
Moreover, I sprang from Nothing,
    And Nothing has sprung from me;
And my Muse is fond of Nothing,
    And Nothing her theme shall be.

At home they taught me Nothing,
    And Nothing I learned at school;
And I began to work at Nothing,
    And Nothing made me a fool.
So I have a taste for Nothing,
    For Nothing I ever would choose;
And all I am worth is Nothing,
    And Nothing I have to lose.

Hence I place my faith in Nothing,
    For Nothing will long endure;
And I've learned to count upon Nothing,
    For Nothing, you know, is sure.
And I keep on singing of Nothing,
    Because Nothing is on my mind;
And the world it tends to Nothing,
    And Nothing is in the wind.

Thus I've clung through life to Nothing,
    And in Nothing put my trust;
For the world amounts to Nothing,
    And Nothing is more than dust.
All I know is, I know Nothing,
    And Nothing ever shall be;
And that all things end in Nothing,
    Though that is Nothing to me.

NEW CONTRIVANCE FOR LADY'S MAIDS, Adapted to the Present Style of Fashions.

THE NEW YORK LABOR MARKET.

FEMALE HOUSE-SERVANTS.

Green "help," like all other raw materials, has experienced a rise in value during the past year, notwithstanding the heavy "consignments" from Ireland and Germany. The advance in market value of this description of labor is about 25 per cent., especially on the poorer qualities; as an article of maid-of-all-work, which could be had last year at $4 per month, now readily brings $5. This, too, while tea, sugar, and beef—three household staples of which Biddy and her friends are extensive consumers—have advanced enormously; flannel and calico, moreover, remaining at about last year's figures. This sudden amelioration in the condition of the dust-pan and tea-kettle sisterhood is accounted for by a principle of political economy, namely, "Prices are regulated by the proportion of supply to demand." The immigration has been large, but the bulk of it is not "thrown upon the market," but shipped, on arrival, directly into the insatiable maw of the Great West.

At the "Labor Exchange," kept open by the Commissioners of Emigration at their head-quarters in Worth Street, there may be found a very large and ill-assorted stock of household functionaries who have just landed, and are allowed to exhibit themselves here gratuitously to employers. Here, however, to use a commercial phrase, "transactions are checked by the large views of holders." This unwashed army of female exiles, while confessing generally to a total ignorance of the very elements of housewifery, refuses to render any description of service at a less figure than "siven dollar," or "achtsen thaler" per month. They are often, however, constrained by the officials to put up with $3 and $4, as they are not allowed to remain if they refuse to work for what they can get. Under the extravagant representations of their American correspondents, the "views" of

immigrants are constantly enlarging, and they will soon be prepared to offer the pleasure of their society to the inhabitants of this continent as an ample equivalent for board and wages. "C'est ridicule!" exclaims the benevolent Frenchman who has charge of the "Exchange," as he labors among his unruly flock in bewilderment and despair. His shoulders have writhed themselves into an inextricable shrug.

The demand for maids-of-all-work is at present chiefly from the country, where they are much wanted at $5 @ $6 per month. Biddy, however, has a deep-seated preference for a city life, and, even after long domestication in the rural districts, she sighs for the leeks and onions of the metropolis. Flirtations with policemen at the area-gate, snug suppers with stray "cousins" in the basement, and similar urban privileges, have a charm for her eyes which far exceeds any of the milk-and-water inducements held out in pastoral poetry. Biddy despises the country, and responds reluctantly to all inquiries for help from that quarter.

We quote the average rates now obtained for female house-servants at the intelligence offices :

	Per Month.
Maids of all work.—Very raw	$4
" " Average	$5
" " Good	$6 @ $7
Chambermaids.—Good	$6
Cooks.—Good	$7 @ $8
" Extra.........................	$12 @ $16
Laundresses	$8 @ $10

The cooks who obtain the higher rates, sometimes reaching $20, are employed mostly in hotels or private families in this city. There is a demand just now for a first-rate article of cook for summer boarding-houses at $12. The "extra" cooks are mostly French and German women, who have obtained their culinary education in the restaurant kitchens, beginning in the humble capacity of scullions, and gradually attaining unto such perfection in the mysterious art as to be able to cause the del-

icate palates of Fifth Avenue to titillate with delight. Five or six years' education in a restaurant, during which period the pupil is supporting herself, will thus often add 75 per cent. to the market value of female labor. The average price paid for totally uneducated female bone and muscle is $60 per year, and board ; the actual value thus paid would be about $150 per annum. It would take about 14 years to bring this bone and muscle up from infancy to a self-supporting point, at an average annual cost, for food and clothing, in Ireland and Germany, of $75. To the product of $75 multiplied by 14, which is $1050, add $50 for cost of landing, and we have $1100 as the total investment. On this, $150 per annum, or about 13 per cent., is returned. Comparing this with the market value of the same class of labor in the old country, we find that the operation of self-shipment has "paid" handsomely.

PATTERN FOR THE HARD TIMES—CARPET REMNANT STYLE.

ANOTHER DITTO—THE SWALLOW-TAIL PATTERN.

CHAT.

THE FEMININE REVELATIONS OF BROADWAY.

A MODEST friend complains that his delicacy is dreadfully shocked, during his daily walks in Broadway, by the free revelations at shop doors and in shop windows of such mysteries of female making-up as no one would venture to disclose by word of mouth, though they are flouted in the eyes and face of every passer-by.

He tells us he is painfully put to the blush at every step he takes, for the whole of Broadway is festooned with skeleton hoops, inflated crinolines, and expanded petticoats. He can not, he says, go into a dry-goods store to buy a pair of gloves, without popping his head (of the impropriety of which he seems duly conscious, as becomes an unmarried man) under a full-blown female skirt, which, hanging from the top of the door, threatens, like a gigantic extinguisher, to catch and envelop his bachelorhood within the mazes of petticoat restraint.

Nor is it only that his modesty is wounded; his imagination, he says, has received an irreparable shock, for he had always hoped to admire our belles as beautiful and complete living totalities, while this unabashed disclosure of details so freely reveals the means of the making-up of our fashionable beauties, that he can only view them as artificial figures, ingeniously constructed, like a Chinese puzzle, out of odd pieces.

Our correspondent is unnecessarily fastidious, perhaps; but we have been somewhat surprised ourselves, we confess, at the free revelations of our Broadway shopmen, who, by-the-by, should have nothing to do with the sale of articles of female apparel and adornment, which should be left to women, who are exposed to so much suffering and temptation for the want of just such employment as is monopolized by those of our own sex.

Did you ever calculate the proportion of city stores exclusively devoted to the wants and caprices of women? Nine-tenths of all Broadway purchases are made by and exclusively for them, and the immense capital of that great mart, with its hundred of millions invested in land, buildings, and stock, may be considered as a perpetual settlement upon our wives and daughters. Here, then, is business enough to justify the employment, in their proper sphere, of thousands of unoccupied women; and we can not imagine how their own sex can possibly utter many of their wants in any other but female ears. Let alone what may be called the necessities of dress and household requirements, which, from their universality, may perhaps be a not improper subject of communication between the sexes, and think of the complicated artifices of fashion and the cunning devices to supply the deficiencies of nature. What must it cost female delicacy to reveal to a smirking, bewhiskered French *coiffeur* the capillary destitution, and to ask for a front, a braided tail, or a dye? How does a feminine anatomy of fashion venture to ask the masculine shopman for those mountains of skirts and mole-hills of padding by which the dead level of nature is varied with the elevations of art? If the ladies can do all this without a rising blush, we think that our correspondent need not be so nice, and might open his eyes, without winking, to the feminine revelations of Broadway.

The Rev. Sydney Smith says that when he "took his Yorkshire servants into Somersetshire, a cider country, they thought that making a drink out of apples was a tempting of Providence, who had intended barley as the only natural material of intoxication.

A blind man is a poor man, and blind a poor man is,
For the former seeth no man, and the latter no man sees.

A correspondent, something new
Transmitting, signed himself X. Q.;
The editor his letter read,
And begged he might be X. Q. Z.

A young lady at a ball was asked by a lover of serious poetry whether she had seen "Crabbe's Tales?"

"Why, no," she answered; "I didn't know that crabs *had* tails."

"I beg your pardon, Miss," said he; "I mean, have you *read* 'Crabbe's Tales?'"

"And I assure you, Sir, I did not know that red crabs, or any other, had tails."

FASHIONS FOR MAY.

A HINT TO DRY GOODS MEN.

The handsome Clerk always attracts the Ladies.

CHARITÉ DANSANTE.

The new moire antique has been sent home, the steel hoop adjusted, the white kids purchased, and before the hundreds of thousands of readers of this *Weekly* will have read our columns, the great Nursery Ball, about which the world of New York has been so long agog, will have been danced out. Thousands, at two dollars a ticket, will, we hope, have been paid into the treasury of the Nursery Hospital—a good object, deserving of all public sympathy—but how many thousands will have been spent upon vanity?

We confess that we have no great liking toward these compromises between benevolence and selfish indulgence. True charity blesses him who gives as well as him who receives. How much of the blessing will fall to the share of the fashionable *figurantes* at the Opera-house on Thursday night is under our means of computation. Paley recommends that we should bestow our alms even upon an unworthy object for the sake of cultivating the sentiment of benevolence; but no moralist that we know of advises charity toward the deserving for the purpose of gratifying our own selfish indulgence. There should be no confusion of motives; if we are to give, let us give without stint; if we are to enjoy ourselves, let us do so within proper bounds, with all our hearts. It is a new form of simony, this dealing in the blessings of Heaven for our own private gain. If you will dance, dance; but do not pretend to be charitable to others while you are only indulgent to yourselves.

DR. FELL AND HIS CURE.

Dr. Fell has published his book, from which it appears that the remedy with which he is supposed to have been so successful in the treatment of cancer is a caustic composed of the chlorid of zinc and of our native blood-root (*sanguinaria Canadensis.*)

CHAT.

BUSY HUSBANDS AND NEGLECTED WIVES.

AN American merchant's house is a place, more or less comfortable, to confine his wife and children in. His own home is in his store or counting-house. He may take an uneasy sleep and a hasty cup of coffee up-town, when he is not running the risk of having his neck broken on a railroad or losing his life in a steamboat, in pursuit of new goods or an absconding debtor; but he reads his newspaper, he smokes his cigar, he chats with his friends, he does the amiable, he takes his dinners, and enjoys himself—in a way of his own—always down-town.

Wives are beginning to complain, and well they may, of the little use they have of their so-called halves, which might be better expressed by some very inconsiderable fraction. Husbands become gradually reduced, after the whole-souled times of the honeymoon, down from the legal marital measurement of one-half to one-fourth, one-eighth, one-sixteenth, until, finally, they reach so small a degree as to be left entirely out of the conjugal calculation. Under such circumstances of reduced fractional connubial endearment, who can blame Mrs. B. if she consoles herself innocently with the good-looking foreign gentleman of leisure, who finds time to dye his whiskers and put on a new pair of lavender kid gloves, at high noon, and give his arm to Mrs. B. to a Thalberg *matinée*, or sympathize with the sighs of "the Bosom" (as Dickens has it, in the Mrs. Merdle of his Little Dorrit), at a morning reception, over its neglect by him who should be that bosom's partner, but who is only the partner of Smith & Co., No. — Pearl Street?

This is the busy season. The spring trade has begun with unusual vigor. New goods have arrived in fearful abundance. The croakers try to frighten us in vain with that old scarecrow—the balance of trade. The bears of finance threaten to garrote the bulls with a monetary pressure. But it is all useless; the spirit of trade is up, and the spring is opening with a promise of expansiveness that will be sure to blossom in a full flower of speculation and expense.

There is no doubt the city is busy—very busy—and you are busy, Mr. B., for customers must be attended to; but with all the pressure of the spring-trade, Mr. B., you are not so busy as you would have Mrs. B. believe. There is no reason for your grumbling that the buckwheat cakes are not ready at 7 A.M., these dull mornings. You are away in a huff without looking over that bill of your wife's, or kissing little Johnny's shining morning face: you can't stop, you are so busy. No! but you can step into Delmonico's, on your way to your daily dry-goods, and compensate yourself very deliberately with a cutlet of mutton and a pint of Bordeaux for the protracted buckwheat cakes of home. Busy as you are, you can take your time with your cigar and that big morning paper, with nothing in it but advertisements and what you might have read, with a great deal besides, at your leisure a week ago in *Harper's Weekly*. Busy as you are, you can afford time to give your neighbor, Smith, half an hour's talk over his new span of horses, and go out with him at lunch-time to eat oysters at Downing's, and wash them down with a bottle of Scotch ale to the health of Mrs. S. "You'll be home to dinner, my dear?" were Mrs. B.'s parting words in the morning. "No, no! it's impossible; I'm too busy!" was your emphatic answer, you'll recollect, Mr. B. Did you time that day's dinner at Delmonico's? Did it take you two or three hours to discuss that elegant spread, with its three courses, dessert, a bottle of *La Rose*, and a ditto of *Mumm?* On the score of taste, we don't object to your preference of *filet de bœuf aux champignons*, commended by the cheering welcome of the broad face of our friend Delmonico, to the cold mutton, and the uneasy and rather sharply-cut peculiarities of Mrs. B. at home. But it is not domestic, Mr. B.—it is not conjugal—it is only taking the "better," and not the "worse," as you solemnly promised you would before the Rev. Dr. Snore.

We would recommend neglected wives to appoint a committee of investigation, to examine into the daily business of their busy husbands. We promise to publish the report free of charge. Institute at once a series of domiciliary visits to Front and Pearl streets, Maiden Lane and Park Place; and if your husbands may not be found there, busy with newspapers, cigars, and scandal, it is just possible, by extending your inquiries, you may catch them equally busy with realizing the bills of fare at Downing's or Delmonico's. Fancy the fluttering of husbands, and the rapid clearing of bar-room and restaurant, at the sudden apparition of the domestic hoops in those quarters! Husbands, in our opinion, might be more busy than they are, and their wives still less neglected. The constantly-widening separation between the companionship and sympathy of the married is one of the greatest dangers to which our social life and morality are exposed. Let us have a little more of the old-fashioned, Darby-and-Joan connubiality. With all its sentimentality, so difficult of appreciation by unattached bachelors and disappointed maids, it is better and safer than the modern system of remote affinities.

LOUIS NAPOLEON ON THE HOOP QUESTION.

We have "assurances worthy of the highest consideration" that the Emperor of all the French, after a very long bed-curtain consultation with the Empress of all the French, came to the profound conviction, that, from the agitation produced in France particularly, and throughout the world generally, by the rumor that Fashion was about unhooping itself, and shrinking into the contemptible proportions of Nature, it was necessary to make a specific allusion in the Imperial speech to the subject. The following sentence was accordingly prepared, as we learn on the best authority, by the Empress Eugénie herself, and delivered by the Emperor with a particular emphasis, and accompanied by a very knowing glance at his royal consort, who stood before the throne, on the occasion, in the fullest amplitude of hoop and skirt:

"The manufacturing portion of the nation has lately been made uneasy by the report that the Government cherishes projects inimical to its development and its prosperity."

This was as strong as the delicacy of the subject would allow, but its force was greatly confirmed by the expansive presence of her Imperial Majesty, whose breadth of hoop was more than enough to counteract the widest-spread rumor of proposed female contraction. *Vive Eugénie!*

POLICE CONSTABLE (*to Boy*). "Now then, off with that Hoop, or I'll precious soon Help you!"
LADY (*who imagines the observation is addressed to her*) "What a Monster!"
[*Lifts up the Crinoline, and hurries off.*

DEMI-SAISON.

PROMENADE TOILETTE,
FOR COUNTRY.

PROMENADE TOILETTE,
FOR CITY.

VERY RÉCHERCHÉ STYLE—À LA BELL-ROPE.

ANOTHER—À LA MOUCHOIR DE POCHE.

OUR FASHION ILLUSTRATIONS.

IN a previous Number (May 23d), we presented to our lady readers a resumé of the principal changes brought about in the Spring and early Summer Fashions. The Illustrations on this page will further exemplify the adaptation of the hints before given to actual costume. A reference to our previous Number will make particular explanations unnecessary here.

FIGURE 1.

HOME EXERCISES.

It has happily become almost unnecessary to prove to Americans the great benefits resulting to mind as well as body from regular physical exercise. It is only, however, within a few years that gymnastic and calisthenic exercises have found a place on the school programmes of our best educational institutions. And most writers on hygiene are content to insist on the necessity of such exercises for the proper *development* of the physical and mental powers, to great extent losing sight of the fact that their pursuit is quite as necessary to preserve in healthful condition the matured powers of body and mind as it was to aid in their proper and graceful development.

If young girls while at school have practiced calisthenics, they almost invariably lay this aside with their studies, and, on entering into social life as young ladies, cease those exercises which have aided so materially in making them the graceful, rosy, buoyant beings they are, or ought to be.

It is a truth not to be denied, and to which the short duration of the health and beauty of American ladies bears sorrowful witness, that these

usual sitting-room and the following articles: A stout broad-backed chair; a stout movable roller, fitted into brass sockets neatly fixed in the door lintels about three inches below the top of the door; a light mattress; a light round staff four and a half feet in length, and half an inch in diameter; a set of light dumb-bells; a set of battle-doors and shuttle-cocks; and an Armstrong's chest-expander. Which outfit may be obtained for about ten dollars or less, and can be stowed away out of sight in any closet.

The sitting-room will be the scene of operations. Premising that most of the exercises which space permits us to denote here are intended to strengthen the chest and abdomen, we will begin by calling attention to Figure 8. Let the person exercising assume a horizontal position; then, extending the arms above the head, raise herself slowly to a sitting posture, as from *b* to *a*. In a similar manner, without moving the lower part of the body, extending the arms as in Figure 8, permit the body to glide slowly from *a* to *b*. Draw a deep breath before each repetition of this movement, as this will contribute materially to the purpose of the exercise, which is to strengthen the muscles of the chest, back, and abdomen. If you have a companion, let her hold your knees firmly, and then, extending your hands, as in Figure 8, you can practice the circular motion denoted by *e d*, in which only the upper portion of the person is to be moved. This is to be performed first from right to left, then from left to right.

A farther extension of the same principle is the chair exercise, as shown in Figure 1. Resting the person upon the hands and feet, move it slowly from the position *b a* to *c a*. This will expand the chest and strengthen the abdominal muscles greatly. It should

FIGURE 2.

to the top of the head; then brought over, so as to hold the staff at *a*; and, lastly, lowered so as to bring the staff on line *c*. In other four motions it is brought back to its first position. The left hand will be used to perform similar motions. This, as well as all other exercises, will be found most beneficial if the performance is divided as above specified, and gone through in regularly-timed succession.

Dumb-bells may weigh from two to four pounds each. They are excellent for expanding the chest, and strengthening all the muscles of the arms, the chest, the abdomen, and the back. In Figure 2 several useful exercises are denoted. The first consists in the alternate extension and drawing back of the arms, as from *a* to its first position. A second motion is from *b*, with arm fully extended, describing a semicircle along the line *b c*. The arms should be kept entirely clear of the body. The same motion is performed with arms drawn in, as from *d* to *c*.

Another series are the circular motions shown in Figure 5. Starting from the points *a*, the dumb-bells meet half way, both before and behind, the body being held as stiffly as possible. Also, the swing from *a*, in the direction of *b* and back, will be found of use.

Armstrong's chest-expander is an India rubber strap, one and a half inch long and one quarter of an inch thick, fitted with convenient handles, as seen in Figure 3. The first exercise is shown in our engraving. The arms are extended along the body, and the strain is in the directions *b* and *c*. When the strap is extended as far as the strength of the arms makes it possible, it should be retained in that position for the space of a minute. As a farther exercise, either hand may then be moved up and down along the line *a d*. A second form of this exercise is obtained by holding the arms out

practiced some time. They will prove highly beneficial.

The game of battle-door and shuttle-cock may be engaged in by one, two, or any given number of persons. It necessitates various active movements of every part of the body and limbs, and will be found, if practiced daily, to have a very beneficial effect, not only upon the physical health, but also upon the spirits of the persons engaging therein. See Figure 4.

We have here given a series of exercises which may be graduated so as to benefit females of every age and condition of health, which are easy of perform-

FIGURE 3.

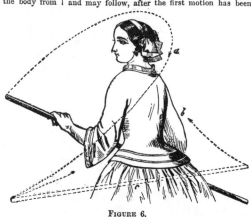

FIGURE 4.

FIGURE 5.

healthful exercises should be continued regularly by all whose pursuits do not otherwise necessitate the needful health-giving stimulus of blood and muscles. The employments of American women, especially of those resident in cities, are so entirely sedentary, that they do continual violence to the laws of nature; and it is only surprising that we see so much of happy health as we do among our female friends.

Many doubtless feel the necessity for calisthenic exercises, but think themselves unable to spare the time; and urge farther the impossibility of attending public institutions if such were in existence, and the impracticability of finding room in a house of moderate dimensions for the paraphernalia of a gymnasium.

As regards the question of time, we shall only say here that exercise is quite as necessary to health as personal cleanliness; and as ladies find time for the bath, and the multifarious duties and pleasures of the toilet, so can they make time for the daily calisthenic exercises. That which may be begun as a duty will very soon become a pleasure-giving habit, which will no more be omitted than any other necessary attention paid to the body.

As for space, and preliminary preparations necessary to be provided in order that the ladies and female children of a family may have the proper degree of daily exercise, all that is needed is the

be used moderately at first, but repeated daily or at regular intervals.

The roller exercise is shown in Figure 7. Besides swinging by the hands, which will bring into play nearly every muscle of the body, the hands should be moved while swinging the body from side to side. Thus, with practice, the hand grasp may be changed to *a*, to *b*, to *c*, and to *d*, and back.

With the staff a number of easy and graceful movements may be performed; all of which tend to strengthen the muscles of the shoulders and the vertebral column, and remedy or prevent the deformity known as round shoulders, at the same time expanding the chest. The chief of these exercises is that shown in Figure 6. The staff is loosely held, the hands being placed about a foot from each end. The body, and more especially the head, must be motionless. The right hand is then raised, first breast high; then

horizontally from the body, and then expanding them as far as the strength of the muscles can overcome the resistance of the India rubber. In a third, the arms are held straight above the head. The last two require more strength than the first, and may follow, after the first motion has been

FIGURE 6.

FIGURE 7.

ance, occasion no undue commotion in the house, take up no otherwise needed space for apparatus, and will be found pleasant—particularly if practiced by a party of three or four persons—and tending greatly to increase a graceful development and carriage of the body, and the general good health and genial spirits of those engaging therein.

There is no good reason why such exercises should not be introduced in every family throughout the Union. There *is* a certainty that, when regularly performed, the health and happiness of the ladies will be lastingly benefited, and their years of usefulness lengthened. What is lost in time will be more than saved in doctors' bills. Those, however, who have the inclination will readily find time.

Where a small party of three or four persons undertake these exercises together, it will be found an excellent plan to have a piano or other musical accompaniment. This will enliven the motions, and make a real pleasure of that which many will for a time look upon as somewhat of a laborious duty. Any simple and regular melody

FIGURE 8.

will be found suitable as an accompaniment. Those exercising should take turns in playing upon the instrument.

The space accorded to us here permits us merely to call attention to this subject. To those who feel sufficient interest in it, we can recommend the perusal of Miss Catharine Beecher's "Physiology and Calisthenics," in which volume they will find the subject of physical exercise treated in a thorough and practical manner.

The urgent necessity of physical exercise can not be too strongly insisted upon. The physical deterioration of the Americans, as a people, is remarked upon by almost every traveler who comes among us. Many blame it upon our climate, which is said to be more exhausting than that of any other country tenanted by civilized people. But the main cause all who have properly investigated the matter know to be the unnatural life led by the greater part of our ladies. In no country in the civilized world do the women of the wealthier classes idle away so much time in amusements positively injurious; nowhere do children show so strongly the effects of the physical neglects of parents.

Will not our American fashionable ladies set a good example, and thus place the practice of "Home Calisthenics" upon a permanent footing in American households?

THINGS WISE AND OTHERWISE.

Too much vinegar spoils the salad.
Gutta Percha is good for the sole.
Ceremonies, like flags, are best waived.
Prejudices and frogs croak loudest in the dark.
With men, as with monuments, position is every thing.
The busy tongue, sooner than not talk, scandalizes.
An English wife and a French cook !—if a man's home is not happy with those blessings, it is his own fault!

There are men, like mines, that do not pay for the working; so, before you select your man, mind he is well worth the plant.

A woman will never acknowledge to a defeat. You may conquer her; you may bring her on her knees; you may wave over her head the very flag of victory; but still she will not acknowledge she is beaten—in the same way that there are Frenchmen who will not admit, to the present day, that they lost the Battle of Waterloo.

Chesterfield was at a rout in France where Voltaire was one of the guests. Chesterfield seemed gazing about the brilliant circle of ladies. Voltaire accosted him:

"My lord, I know you are a judge: which are the more beautiful, the English or the French ladies?"

"Upon my word," replied Chesterfield, with his usual presence of mind, "I am no judge of paintings."

Some time afterward Voltaire, being in London, happened to be at a nobleman's party with Chesterfield. A lady in the company, prodigiously rouged, directed her whole discourse to Voltaire, and engrossed his whole conversation. Chesterfield me up, tapped him on the shoulder, and said:

"Sir, take care that you are not captivated."

"My lord," returned the French wit, "I scorn to be taken by an English craft under French colors."

REMARKABLE CONVENIENCE OF HOOPS FOR YOUNG MOTHERS IN THE COUNTRY.

MILLINER. "Really, Mrs. M——, you look lovely in this hat; it sets off your face so well, and brings out the shape of your head."

NOTHING TO WEAR.

AN EPISODE OF CITY LIFE.

MISS FLORA M'FLIMSEY, of Madison Square,
　Has made three separate journeys to Paris,
And her father assures me, each time she was there,
　That she and her friend Mrs. Harris,
(Not the lady whose name is so famous in history,
But plain Mrs. H., without romance or mystery)
Spent six consecutive weeks without stopping,
In one continuous round of shopping;
Shopping alone, and shopping together,
At all hours of the day, and in all sorts of weather;
For all manner of things that a woman can put
On the crown of her head or the sole of her foot,
Or wrap round her shoulders, or fit round her waist,
Or that can be sewed on, or pinned on, or laced,
Or tied on with a string, or stitched on with a bow,
In front or behind, above or below:
For bonnets, mantillas, capes, collars, and shawls;
Dresses for breakfasts, and dinners, and balls;
Dresses to sit in, and stand in, and walk in;
Dresses to dance in, and flirt in, and talk in;
Dresses in which to do nothing at all;
Dresses for winter, spring, summer, and fall;
All of them different in color and pattern,
Silk, muslin, and lace, crape, velvet, and satin,
Brocade, and broadcloth, and other material,
Quite as expensive and much more ethereal;
In short, for all things that could ever be thought of,
Or milliner, *modiste*, or tradesman be bought of,
　From ten-thousand-francs robes to twenty-sous frills;
In all quarters of Paris, and to every store,
While M'Flimsey in vain stormed, scolded, and swore,
　They footed the streets, and he footed the bills.

The last trip, their goods shipped by the steamer Arāgo
Formed, M'Flimsey declares, the bulk of her cargo,
Not to mention a quantity kept from the rest,
Sufficient to fill the largest sized chest,
Which did not appear on the ship's manifest,
But for which the ladies themselves manifested
Such particular interest, that they invested
Their own proper persons in layers and rows
Of muslins, embroideries, worked under-clothes,
Gloves, handkerchiefs, scarfs, and such trifles as those;
Then, wrapped in great shawls, like Circassian beauties,
Gave *good-by* to the ship, and *go-by* to the duties.
Her relations at home all marveled no doubt,
Miss Flora had grown so enormously stout
　For an actual belle and a possible bride;
But the miracle ceased when she turned inside out,
　And the truth came to light, and the dry goods beside,
Which, in spite of Collector and Custom-house sentry,
Had entered the port without any entry.

And yet, though scarce three months have passed since the day
This merchandise went, on twelve carts, up Broadway,
This same Miss M'Flimsey, of Madison Square,
The last time we met, was in utter despair,
Because she had nothing whatever to wear!

NOTHING TO WEAR! Now, as this is a true ditty,
　I do not assert—this, you know, is between us—
That she's in a state of absolute nudity,
　Like Powers' Greek Slave, or the Medici Venus;
But I do mean to say, I have heard her declare,
　When, at the same moment, she had on a dress
　Which cost five hundred dollars, and not a cent less,
　And jewelry worth ten times more, I should guess,
That she had not a thing in the wide world to wear!

Since that night, taking pains that it should not be bruited
Abroad in society, I've instituted
A course of inquiry, extensive and thorough,
On this vital subject, and find, to my horror,
That the fair Flora's case is by no means surprising,
　But that there exists the greatest distress
In our female community, solely arising
　From this unsupplied destitution of dress,
Whose unfortunate victims are filling the air
With the pitiful wail of "Nothing to wear."

Researches in some of the "Upper Ten" districts
Reveal the most painful and startling statistics,
Of which let me mention only a few:
In one single house, on the Fifth Avenue,
Three young ladies were found, all below twenty-two,
Who have been three whole weeks without any thing new
In the way of flounced silks, and thus left in the lurch
Are unable to go to ball, concert, or church.
In another large mansion near the same place
Was found a deplorable, heart-rending case
Of entire destitution of Brussels point lace.
In a neighboring block there was found, in three calls,
Total want, long continued, of camels'-hair shawls;
And a suffering family, whose case exhibits
The most pressing need of real ermine tippets;
One deserving young lady almost unable
To survive for the want of a new Russian sable;
Another confined to the house, when it's windier
Than usual, because her shawl isn't India.
Still another, whose tortures have been most terrific
Ever since the sad loss of the steamer *Pacific*,
In which were ingulfed, not friend or relation,
(For whose fate she perhaps might have found consolation,
Or borne it, at least, with serene resignation)
But the choicest assortment of French sleeves and collars
Ever sent out from Paris, worth thousands of dollars,
And all as to style most *recherché* and rare,
The want of which leaves her with nothing to wear.
And renders her life so drear and dyspeptic
That she's quite a recluse, and almost a skeptic,
For she touchingly says that this sort of grief
Can not find in Religion the slightest relief,
And Philosophy has not a maxim to spare
For the victims of such overwhelming despair.
But the saddest by far of all these sad features
Is the cruelty practiced upon the poor creatures
By husbands and fathers, real Bluebeards and Timons,
Who resist the most touching appeals made for diamonds
By their wives and their daughters, and leave them for days
Unsupplied with new jewelry, fans, or bouquets,
Even laugh at their miseries whenever they have a chance,
And deride their demands as useless extravagance!

But why harrow the feelings by lifting the curtain
From these scenes of woe? Enough, it is certain,
Has here been disclosed to stir up the pity
Of every benevolent heart in the city,
And spur up Humanity into a canter
To rush and relieve these sad cases instanter.
Won't somebody, moved by this touching description,
Come forward to-morrow and head a subscription?
Won't some kind philanthropist, seeing that aid is
So needed at once by these indigent ladies,
Take charge of the matter? or won't PETER COOPER
The corner-stone lay of some splendid super-
Structure, like that which to-day links his name
In the Union unending of honor and fame;
And found a new charity just for the care
Of these unhappy women with nothing to wear,
Which, in view of the cash which would daily be claimed,
The *Laying-out* Hospital well might be named?
Won't STEWART, or some of our dry-goods importers,
Take a contract for clothing our wives and our daughters?
Or, to furnish the cash to supply these distresses,
And life's pathway strew with shawls, collars, and dresses,
Ere the want of them makes it much rougher and thornier,
Won't some one discover a new California?

And oh, if perchance there should be a sphere,
Where all is made right which so puzzles us here,
Where the glare, and the glitter, and tinsel of Time
Fade and die in the light of that region sublime,
Where the soul, disenchanted of flesh and of sense,
Unscreened by its trappings, and shows, and pretense,
Must be clothed for the life and the service above,
With purity, truth, faith, meekness, and love;
Oh, daughters of Earth! foolish virgins, beware!
Lest in that upper realm you have nothing to wear!

THE FASHIONS.

The warm weather has called forth robes of barège, muslin, and other transparent textures; but dresses of rich silk, nevertheless, maintain their pre-eminence.

Among the most admired bonnets we may mention those of French chip, or of crape, or tulle, goffred, bouillon', or souffl'. Bonnets of very fine leghorn have also been worn. Shawls of black or white lace, and mantelets of silk of various forms, have been very numerous. We have observed several basquines made up of colored silk, the silk serving merely as a lining for the innumerable rows of lace with which these basquines were covered.

We will here briefly describe our illustrations.

Fig. 1. Barège dress with double skirt. The upper skirt is in the tunic style, and is trimmed at each side with ruches of ribbon. The corsage is trimmed in corresponding style, and round the waist is a ceinture tied at one side. The sleeves are in the style of those seen in the portraits of Marguerite de Valois; that is to say, the puffs are separated one from the other by bands. Collar of worked muslin. Bonnet of white tulle, trimmed with flowers and blonde guipure. Mantelet of black silk, trimmed with lace.

Fig. 2. Robe of mallow-colored glacé, with side trimmings representing large leaves formed of ruches of mallow-colored ribbon, edged with narrow black lace. The corsage, which has a basque, is tastefully closed up the front with bows of ribbon. The sleeves have three frills falling one over the other. The collar is of a new shape, called the Ristori, being copied from one worn by the celebrated actress of that name. It is made of rows of lace insertion. Under-sleeves of the same. The head-dress is formed of two short barbes of Brussels lace and tufts of azalea.

Fig. 3. Dress of silver-gray glacé, having the skirt ornamented with side trimmings of pink glacé. The corsage has a basque edged with three frills of pink silk. Sleeves formed of two puffs and two frills, edged with pink. Collar and under-sleeves of Irish point, and the collar fixed in front of the neck by a bow of pink ribbon. Head-dress of pink ribbon and black velvet.

THINGS WISE AND OTHERWISE.

DEFINITION BY A CYNICAL BRUTE.—*The most Delicate Attention.*—Inattention, when a man is talking nonsense, or a woman is talking at all.

A POPULAR DELUSION.—It is an error to suppose that a man belongs to himself. No man does. He belongs to his wife, or his children, or his relations, or his creditors, or to Society in some form or other. It is for their especial good and behalf that he lives and works, and they kindly allow him to retain a certain percentage of his gains to administer to his own pleasures or wants. He has his body, and that is all, and even for that he is answerable to Society. In short, Society is the Master, and Man is the Servant; and it is entirely according as Society proves a good or bad master, whether the Man turns out a good or bad servant.

A lady's maid hooked one of the best of her mistress's dresses the other day, but the affair was passed over because it was done behind the lady's back—so that there was nobody to testify to the fact.

A young gentleman, the other day, asked a young lady what she thought of the married state in general?

"Not knowing, I can not tell," was the reply; "but if you and I would put our heads together, I could soon give you a definite answer."

A coat out at the elbow may be buttoned over a generous heart.

We have lately heard of a minister named Craig, who purchased a whistle, and, when his hearers went to sleep, he emitted from it a very shrill sound. All were awake, and stood up to hear him. "You are certainly smart specimens of humanity," he said, as he slowly gazed at his wondering people; "when I preach the Gospel, you go to sleep; when I play the fool, you are wide awake."

"You flatter me," said a thin exquisite, the other day, to a young lady who was praising the beauties of his mustache.

"For mercy's sake, ma'am," interposed an old skipper, "don't make that monkey any flatter than he is."

An Irishman, who lived in an attic, being asked what part of the house he occupied, answered, "If the house were turned topsy-turvy, I'd be livin' on the first flure."

May Taylor must have worn a Hood when she wrote these lines on "the Vegetable Girl:"

Behind a market stall installed,
    I mark it every day,
Stands at her stand the fairest girl
    I've met with in the bay;
Her two lips are of cherry red,
    Her hands a pretty pair,
With such a pretty turn-up nose,
    And lovely reddish hair.

'Tis there she stands from morn till night,
    Her customers to please,
And to appease their appetite
    She sells them beans and peas.
Attracted by the glances from
    The apple of her eye,
And by her Chili apples, too,
    Each passer-by will buy.

She stands upon her little feet,
    Throughout the livelong day,
And sells her celery and things—
    A big feat, by-the-way.
She changes off her stock for change,
    Attending to each call;
And when she has but one beet left,
    She says—"Now that beat's all."

A handsome woman pleases the eye, but a good woman pleases the heart. The one's a jewel, and the other a treasure.

A MEAN WRETCH.—JUST LIKE 'EM.

MR. JONES. "How pretty your bonnet looks, my dear!"

MRS. JONES. "Lor', Henry, it is quite an old one."

MR. JONES. "That fact constitutes its chief prettiness, my economical love."

It is said of Dean Swift that he preached before the Merchant Tailors' Company at three several anniversaries. The first time he took for his text, "Steal no more!" The members of the company took umbrage at this text. On the following anniversary he chose the words, "A remnant shall be saved!" His audience were more irritated than before. Nevertheless, he began his third sermon as follows: "There were lice in their quarters!"

"Father, I hate that Mr. S——!" said a beauty the other day to her honored parent.

"Why so, my daughter?"

"Because he always stares at me when he meets me in the street."

"But, my child, how do you know that Mr. S—— stares at you?"

"Why, because I have repeatedly seen him do it."

"Well, Julia, don't you look at that impudent man again when you meet him, and then he may stare his eyes out without annoying you in the least. Remember that it always takes two pair of eyes to make a stare."

An Irish lady wrote to her lover, begging him to send her some money. She added, by way of postscript: "I am so ashamed of the request I have made in this letter, that I sent after the postman to get it back, but the servant could not overtake him."

An advertisement lately appeared, headed, "Iron bedsteads and *bedding.*" We suppose the linen must be *sheet*-iron.

FASHIONABLE HATS AND THEIR TRIMMINGS.

NAPOLEON stamped his feet, took an enormous pinch of snuff, and grumbled loudly when he had to pay for thirty-six new bonnets in one month for Josephine. We fear the lords of creation in this latitude will have good occasion about this time to fret and scold too. Fashion never offered so many tempting baits to "our ladies" as at this moment, and they are springing eagerly, like so many trout, at the brightly-colored bits of ribbon and f her dangling from Broadway shop and window.

Every woman knows what is meant by Opening-day; and every man, if father or husband, however innocently unconscious, has it brought, in the course of time, vividly to his comprehension, by a bill to pay. In the middle of this month there is a week sacred to Fashion, and its worshipers do not fail to show their devotion by thronging its temples in crowds, and freely submitting to its exacting demands upon their obedience. From the fifteenth to the twenty-first of September, or thereabout, you will see the streets crowded with these female devotees. Their devotion is of a cheerful kind, as it may well be, for all the penance undergone is suffered vicariously through their husbands' pockets. Fashion has, like other religions, its select places of worship. There is the private chapel in Waverley Place, and the half dozen lesser shrines in and about Broadway, where the St. Lawsons, and Mitchells, and Dugals, and Lentzes, and Harrises, have their niches, prepared to impose the blessings of Fashion upon the heads of their worshipers, in the shape of new bonnets—or hats, as we in the United States insist upon calling them—and receive in return the prodigal offerings of the faithful.

Every duty, social or domestic, must yield to the claims of the opening-days of the fashionable week. No woman would dare to show her head in Broadway or at church if not crowned with a halo of the latest Fall fashion, and how is such a glorification to be secured without the most diligent devotion at the shrines of Fashion? Accordingly the whole week is piously devoted to this importunate duty, and as each shrine is visited in turn, there is not a day without its obligation.

There is no reasoning about woman's devotion to Fashion, for every one knows that it does not necessarily conduce to utility or ornament. No one will pretend, for example, that the coal-scuttle hats of our grandmothers are handsome, as no one will venture to claim that the present little, flimsy head-coverings are useful. What lady of your acquaintance puts on her hat to protect her from the cold, the rain, or the sun? There is not a woman in existence who would not rather brave all the storms of heaven, bare-headed, than expose her fashionable covering to a single drop of rain. A female hat is neither useful nor comfortable, and our ladies know it, and will confess that their

greatest trouble in life is to take care of it. It can't get wet, it can't be exposed to the sun, and it can't be squeezed without being spoiled and becoming unfit for going out, or any thing but being turned over to Lucille the nurse or Bridget the cook. The fashionable female hat is nothing, after all, but a caprice, and, as a caprice, all we insist is that it should not be offensive to taste. Let those who pay for it—fifty dollars, more or less—grumble about the cost; we, as spectators, shall be satisfied if it prove an ornament.

The present style of fashionable bonnet we think,

undoubtedly, an immense improvement in taste upon those old gig-covers in the remote distance of which our beauties of the past used to hide their pretty faces. The fashionable hat of the present day has become more like a head-dress, subordinate, as it should be, to that most beautiful of all ornaments, the hair. With its graceful slope and its flowing trimmings, it blends readily with the flexibility of the long locks which crown naturally the head of woman. It is an approach to the simple and always graceful vail of the Spanish beauty, which falls, ordinarily, in easy folds from the hair-knot behind, whence it can be readily, with a simple movement of the hand, brought forward to interpose a screen before the pretty face it hides and the too importunate gaze of a provoked curiosity.

We are a little too fond of bright and flaunting colors, although, with the clearness of our atmosphere, which brings out every tint in such strong relief, we have less occasion for them than most people. The ladies believe that they are implicitly following the French fashions, but the milliners know better, and are obliged to suit the tastes of their American customers by a very considerable exaggeration, both as to color and form, of the Parisian styles. The neutral tints, for example, are much more in vogue in Paris than with us. The sober grays or the demure browns, however, will be rejected by our beauties for the fiery reds or flashing yellows. The fashionable female hat (and this applies to other articles of American toilet),

too, is much more overloaded with trimming than its supposed French model, and this is done not only to please the taste for what is prominent and flaring, but to gratify the desire for what is costly. We do not know how much Napoleon had to pay for the thirty-six bonnets of Josephine, but we will wager a new Fall hat against fifty dollars (the stakes being about equal) with any fashionable woman in Fifth Avenue, that the Empress's three dozen did not cost as much as a single dozen that we can select of those purchased this week in Waverley Place.

The transitions of Fashion are so frequent and

necessarily gradual, that it is difficult to catch the slight shades of difference between them from season to season. The Fall only varies enough from the Summer hat to justify Fashion in the purchase of a new one. No woman would be less comfortable and less attractive if, for the coming three months, she would forego the expense of that "sweet pet of a Fall hat" she caught a sight of at Mitchell's the other day, and wear nothing but that "old Summer straw." There is hardly any difference between the two. The shapes are about the same, with perhaps, in the Fall hat, a trifle more of a lap forward on the head. They are both made of straw, and the only variation in the trimmings is that the Autumn hat has velvet and flowers, while the Summer one has ribbons and ditto. But ladies judge for yourselves, as now you have eight of the choicest patterns before your eyes stamped by Fashion itself as the perfection of taste and skill. Your own taste can supply the color, whether it be mazarine blue, black, a sober brown, or a brilliant scarlet. If you will take our advice, it will be one of the more quiet tints. The prettiest hat we have seen is a close, variegated straw, trimmed with maroon velvet, and adorned with acorns and oak-leaves, and the smallest dash of that caterpillar-like chenille now so much in vogue. You need not put any lace upon your hat, for it will only add to the cost, and not improve its beauty, in male eyes at least, and particularly just now, when Wall Street is tight, and every one wishes to draw the purse-strings in sympathetic stricture.

FOUR WAYS OF MAKING LOVE.

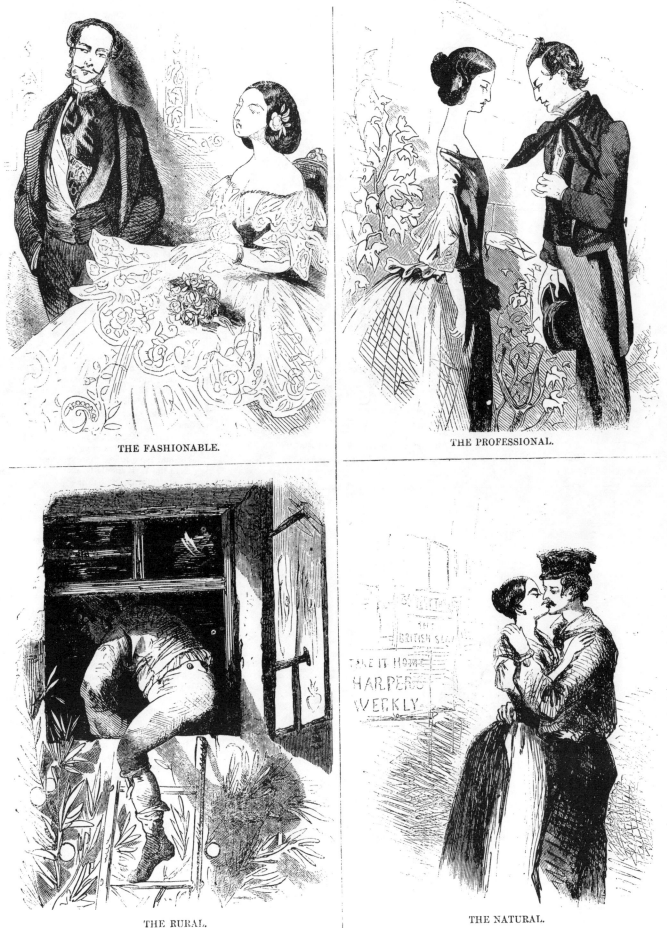

THE FASHIONABLE.

THE PROFESSIONAL.

THE RURAL.

THE NATURAL.

MISTRESS. "Why, Cook, what *have* you been doing with my Hoop?"
COOK. "Hoop, M'm, sure I thought it was a new kind o' Meat Safe!"

It is quite possible to have too much of a Good Thing—as, for example, when you get the Asparagus shot over your favorite Dress Coat with the Silk Facings.

HOUSE-SERVANTS.

AMONG the commodities which the prosperity and the general expansion of the last few years have greatly enhanced in price, one of the most important, though least talked about, is the wages of house-servants. A few years ago, four dollars a month procured the services of a very respectable girl, either as nurse or housemaid, in a city family, and a good cook could be had for six. Now, eight and ten dollars frequently fail to command the same domestics. Mistresses complain that, with large experience and great exertion, they are unable to procure good servants, even at rates of wages which the last generation would have thought utterly absurd and ridiculous. We hear on many sides stories of combinations on the part of registry-offices, etc., etc., to keep up wages beyond their legitimate level.

The truth is, of course, that the demand for good servants is in excess of the supply. The Scotch and English girls who immigrate find better prospects of settlement in life out West than in the sea-board cities; American girls can generally do better than go to service; and thus we in New York are left to the tender mercies of such German and Irish girls as have not the means or the wit to seek a home in a more promising region. Very many of these are not fitted, by their education and their habits, to be good domestics; the extraordinary step in life which they take when they exchange beggary at home for affluence here, does not improve their character; in not a few cases, their first thought, when their mistress has been at the pains to teach them their duties, is to leave her, and make capital elsewhere out of their new acquisitions.

This is the case for the mistresses, and in one point of view it seems hopeless. Certainly no one would hope to see the day when the prospects of the West should be such as to deter immigrants from flocking thither; nobody would desire to see our prosperity checked in order to bring down wages. Nor can any new impulse given to immigration help the matter; for, in proportion to the supply of men and women, the country will advance, and every commodity, including domestic labor, will advance with it. Something perhaps might be done by further encouragement to colored service. Colored women, when properly trained, make excellent house-servants, and were they placed under a rigid discipline at an early period of life, they would no doubt excel in attention, affection, and steadiness, many races from which our present supply of house-servants is derived. It might be worth consideration whether institutions for training young colored girls for domestic service would not answer a useful purpose. We beg to commend the subject to the kind consideration of those who have made themselves conspicuous by their efforts to alter, if not to improve, the standing of the negro race in America.

But let us inquire whether all the difficulty that exists arises from the operation of an economical law, and the perversity of newly imported girls. The relation between mistress and servant is not altogether a one-sided contract; it involves reciprocal and mutual obligations. If the servant owes obedience, faithfulness, and zeal, the mistress as plainly owes kindness, watchfulness, and a judicious superintendence. By the first principles of natural law, a breach of contract on the one side justifies a breach on the other. And if the mistress is faithless to her duty, she can not complain if the servant disregards hers. A mistress, for instance, who devotes the whole of her time to the enjoyments of society, and disregards the concerns of her household, can not be allowed to bewail herself if her servants follow her example, for her charge of them is as clear and as peremptory as their charge of her interests. Nor can a querulous, selfish mistress expect devotion and zeal from persons whom she teaches to dislike her. Satisfactory performance of duty must exist on both sides, or not at all.

The old New England notion that the word servant was degrading, and that a separate servant's table was a thing not to be thought of, has died out in this meridian long since, and it is well so. But some of our fashionable people are drifting into the opposite extreme, with a much more pernicious result. They are now reaping part of the penalty.

WHEN SHALL WE MARRY?

WE know what old Tenpercent will say: "Marry when you can afford it." That is Tenpercent's answer; and he will not let his daughter go on any less easy terms, although he has money enough to support a dozen or more asylums for widows and orphans. His "when you can afford it," according to the expansive views of the times, means something very different from what it did when Tenpercent, in his youth and poverty, took his Polly to be his wedded wife, for better or for worse, to love and cherish; and is something so magnificent, that only the heir of fortune, or the happy holder of a great prize in the lottery of life, after some forty years or more trial of luck, can possibly compass.

We agree with the political economists, for the most part, that it is essential, as a check to pauperism, for a man to consider before he marries whether he has, or is likely to have, the wherewithal to support a family. We do not think it prudent that any one should inconsiderately—like the old woman in the shoe—burden himself or herself with so many children that he or she may be puzzled what to do. This question, however, of affording to marry, has a very wide expanse of solution. Paddy considers himself entitled to the privilege of matrimony when all his worldly goods are comprised in a bellyful of potatoes. Young America must have a brown-stone house, tapestry carpets, and five thousand dollars a year, at least, before he can venture to become a Benedict.

We shall so far give in to the prudent view of the question, as to grant that it is wise to consider the prospects of a youthful suitor for your daughter's hand. But is it wise to be too exacting? Is it not safe to have some faith in character, health, and the devotion of a young and loving heart? Can you not give long or short credits connubially, as you do commercially; and is it not possible that it may turn out equally to your advantage, and that you may secure happiness for your child by the one, as you have fortune by the other? Take your hands out of your pockets, old Tenpercent, and give a filial embrace to Tom Sprightly, that promising young clerk of yours, and intrust to him your daughter (giving them both enough out of your abundance to help them along in life), as you have long since your more dearly-beloved cash on account. Society, we know, matrimonially and otherwise, is inexorable. Nature, too, is inexorable, and has an interest in the question "When shall we marry?" which should be considered.

Leaving out of the calculation three-story brown-stone houses and five-hundred-dollar cashmere shawls, which terribly perplex the question, and indefinitely postpone its solution, we, if asked "When shall we marry?" should answer to the connubially-disposed, be she woman, "Marry at the age of nineteen, or thereabout;" be he man, "Marry at one-and-twenty, or not much beyond." We are looking at the question, just now, only in its physical bearings, and consider our rule as being more especially peremptory amidst the excitements of a highly-inflammatory town life, than in the repose of a comparatively stagnant rustic existence.

The pale faces, *dragged* expressions, meagre frames, and invalid constitutions of our women, have been attributed to their early marriages. This is, however, an error, as is well known to the observant physician, who will tell you that the mischief has all been done previous to matrimony, and that this, if not always a specific, is one of the best correctives of the difficulty. Most female disorders, whatever they may be, which make up three-fourths of the whole nosology, are easily traceable to the "hope deferred" of an unnaturally-excited nuptial longing. The whole tendency of our social habits, especially in the large cities, is to foster what the disorganizing friends of the *Tribune* would call "the passional harmonies" between the sexes.

Look at our boys and girls, still redolent of bread and butter, ogling each other in the street, like so many veteran Chesterfields and Pompadours. Look at them warming in the intimacy of the waltz and the redowa, at the nightly balls of the season, before the very faces of their mammas reddened with sham(e)—blushes of the deepest rouge. Look at them carrying on their coquetries at lecture-room, opera-house, and even within the precincts of home, in the front parlor—however, recollect, with the folding-doors closed. Look at all this precocious development of the connubial instincts—this always thinking of matrimony, and never doing it (according to the Prayer Book, at any rate)—and tell us, old Tenpercent, whether it is safe to put it off until that indefinite future "of being able to afford it" may arrive.

The natural period for the union of the sexes is that epoch when the growth is fully reached. This, of course, varies in individuals and races, but may be set down at an average of about sixteen for the female and eighteen for the male. As, on the approach, and at the time of this consummation of man or woman, there is more or less water of crystallization, if we may use a chemical illustration, which has not yet taken an organic form, or evaporated, it is well to postpone matrimony for two or three years, until the male, as we have already stated, will have reached the age of twenty-one, and the female that of nineteen years.

We know the social difficulties, and we are not disposed to make light of them; but with the artificial notions prevalent, particularly among the wealthier classes in the large cities, these difficulties are made heavier than necessary, and than can be safely borne. Granting that early marriages can not be indulged in with a due regard to prudence, then we should change the whole system of our fashionable habits, which are constantly leading on the young to the altar, not to receive an offering, but to find themselves a sacrifice. The only corrective that we know of for the evils to health and morals, produced by the inordinate pecuniary conditions attached to matrimony by the rich, who can best afford to be generous, and are least so in this respect, would be to put cowls upon our sons and vails upon our daughters, and thrust them within the iron bars of the convent or monastery, that flagellation may beat out the natural Adam of the one, and fasting may starve out the natural Eve of the other. With the present system, we shall only succeed in making rakes of our young men, and puling, invalid spinsters of our young women.

Consider well the fact, that not only is a single life unfavorable to health of body, but even to health of mind, and that both hospitals and lunatic asylums give, in their terrible records, the most emphatic assertion of the dangers of a compulsory celibacy. So much for the physical advantage of early marriages. We shall leave the moral view of the question to be revealed by the preacher, who, perhaps, will tell us, for virtue's sake, "When shall we marry?"

HOOPS AS A LIGHTNING-CONDUCTOR.

"As Mr. JAMES R. M'SHANE was walking out one day last week with his wife, who was attired in the full rotundity of the fashion, they were overtaken by a violent thunder-storm. The gentleman received a severe shock, but the lady escaped uninjured, the steel hoops which expanded her crinoline proving a perfect lightning-conductor. She was terrified and fainted away, however; but here the hoops proved their utility in another direction, and supported her, so that it was impossible for her to fall to the ground."—*Memphis* (Tenn.) *Daily Palladium.*

A WHOOP ABOUT HOOPS.

For when a smitten wretch has seen
  Among the lost in crinoline,
    The one his heart holds dearer,
Oh! what a chill to ardent passion,
To feel that through this hollow fashion
    He never can be nearer!

That instead of timidity drawing near,
And pouring into her thrilling ear
    The flood of his soul's devotion,
He must stand and bellow in thunder tones,
Across half an acre of skirts and bones,
    As if hailing a ship on the ocean.

A Western editor, whose subscribers complained very loudly that he did not give them news enough for their money, told them that if they did not find enough in the paper they had better read the Bible, which, he had no doubt, would be news to most of them.

A wag has truly remarked, that if some men could come out of their graves and read the inscriptions on their tomb-stones, they would think they had got into the wrong graves!

A wealthy but miserly old man, dining down town one day with his son at a restaurant, whispered in his ear: "Tom, you must eat for to day and to-morrow."
"Oh, yes," retorted the half-starved lad, "but I han't eaten for yesterday and the day before yet, father!"

"What are you about, my dear?" said his grandmother to a little boy who was sliding along the room and casting furtive glances at a gentleman who was paying a visit.
"I am trying, grandma', to steal papa's hat out of the room without letting the gentleman see it, for papa wants him to think he's out."

Two country attorneys overtaking a wagoner on the road, and thinking to break a joke upon him, asked him why his fore horse was so fat and the rest so lean? The wagoner, knowing them to be limbs of the law, answered that his fore horse was a *lawyer* and the rest *were his clients.*

"Make yourself an honest man, and then you may be sure that there is one rascal less in the world."

There is more true happiness and genuine comfort in presiding over and enjoying the sweets of a quiet home, than in swaying the destinies and commanding the luxuries of an empire.

"Small thanks to you, Sir," said a plaintiff to one of his witnesses, "for what you said in this cause."
"Ah, Sir," said the conscientious witness, "but just think of what I didn't say."

A DRESS REHEARSAL FOR A SIDE-WALK EXHIBITION.
"One inch higher, Lucy, and you'll be perfectly irresistible."

"These Dresses are very well in their way, but they make us all appear the same size. Why, a Girl might be as thin as a Whipping-post, and yet be taken for a Decent Figure."

OUR LADIES' BOARDING SCHOOLS.

CONSIDERATE MAMMA *to* BOARDING-SCHOOL MISTRESS. "Then the only thing which remains for me to observe, Mrs. BROWN, is, that I hope you will have at least two balls a week; my CARRIE has always been used to that sort of thing, and I couldn't think of depriving her of it at her time of life."

BOARDING-SCHOOL MISTRESS. "Our course of studies, did you say, m'm? It is beautifully systematic and regular. At nine in the morning, prayers, with Signor Pregarvi to overlook the kneeling of the young ladies—difficult thing to kneel gracefully with hoops, you know. At ten, one of our French governesses gives her course of *maintien* and deportment. At eleven, singing in Russian and Portuguese, by two eminent exiled Counts. At twelve, Madame Crinoline lectures on the art of dress, with illustrations from nature. We lunch at one, and the Marquis of Jambon instructs the young ladies in habits of refined eating as practiced in aristocratic circles in Europe. At two, visitors—between you and me, young men whom I engage by the month—in order that my young ladies may be perfect in the art of receiving company. At half past three, Signor Bonaventura reads to the boarders for a quarter of an hour a portion of an Italian romance of the most unexceptionable morality. At four, dressing for promenade, under the eye of Madame Crinoline. At five, promenade. At six, dress for dinner, as before. We dine at seven; and the rest of the evening is devoted to light conversation, under the auspices of a poet, a divine, and an ex-foreign embassador. So you see, our time is pretty well occupied, and we finish our pupils pretty thoroughly."

LADY. "Oh! very thoroughly indeed!"

CHAT.

THE NEW FEMALE METAMORPHOSIS.

FASHION is a cunning jade. While strong-minded females have in vain been bawling long and loud for woman's rights, and with tooth and nail doing their utmost to pull man down from his preeminence, Madame la Mode has quietly slipped, and almost unconsciously, into the prerogatives of the opposite sex. Pulling on the masculine boots, she strides *manfully* through our dirty streets "in spite of wind and weather," and now buttoning herself in a fashionable coat or jacket of the day, she elbows our Broadway dandies with the conscious air of one who would say, "I'm a better man than you." Boots, coat, and ——; *to b continued* must we add, as to an unfinished tale (tail)? So Cham, the great French caricaturist, would seem to think, who thus prophesies pictorially for the present year of 1857.

Our beaux have been lamenting over the disappearance from the fashionable horizon of dress-coats, and it may be some consolation to find them again enveloping the graceful figures of our belles. There may be satisfaction, too, in an economical point of view, to know that the long laid aside swallow-tail, with considerable letting out here and there, may be transferred from the husband's to the wife's wardrobe without a tailor's account, to be added to the already large enough bill of female expense.

Some of our ladies (*laddies*, since they assume the jacket they might be called, which would settle at once the Benton controversy) are a little chary of showing themselves in public, dressed in the new masculine attire. Some think that the jacket should be confined to young girls under sixteen, to whom the new fashion gives a delightful hoidenish, coquettish air, which, it must be confessed, does not sit so well on "fat, fair, and forty." A great many collateral questions have also arisen in regard to the new costume, as, for example, whether it is "the thing or not" to thrust one or both hands into the pockets, for the new coats have pockets both before and behind, sidewise and lengthwise. We have long since had military tailors, clerical tailors, and boys' tailors; now we have ladies' tailors; for it is a fact, which will somewhat startle, we fear, our country readers, that wives and daughters get measured for their cloth jackets by the same masculine snip who cuts their fathers' and husbands' inexpressibles. We have hardly reached yet, however, the extremity of our less fastidious English friends, as may be learned by the following advertisement, which we publish gratuitously from the *Illustrated London News* of December 13, 1856:

LADIES' RIDING TROUSERS,
Chamois Leather, with black feet.
53 Baker Street (near Madame Tussaud's Exhibition).
W. G. TAYLOR (late Halliday).

The men may well revenge themselves by taking to shawls, muffs, and petticoat sacks! "A fair exchange is no robbery."

NEW FALL FASHIONS.

CHARLES. "Why, Mary, what on earth have you got on your head?"

MARY. "This, Charles? Don't you know, Stupid? 'Tis the new Head-Dress—the 'Cloud.' Pretty, isn't it?"

SOMEBODY.

SOMEBODY'S courting somebody,
　Somewhere or other, to-night.
Somebody's whisp'ring to somebody,
Somebody's list'ning to somebody,
　Under this clear moonlight.

Near the bright river's flow,
Running so still and slow,
Talking so soft and low,
　She sits with somebody.

Pacing the ocean's shore,
Edged by the foaming roar,
Words, never breathed before,
　Sound sweet to somebody.

Under the maple-tree,
Deep though the shadow be,
Plain enough they can see—
　Bright eyes has somebody.

No one sits up to wait,
Though she is out so late—
All know she's at the gate
　Talking with somebody.

Tip-toe to parlor door—
Two shadows on the floor—
Moonlight reveals no more—
　Susy and somebody.

Two, sitting side by side,
Float with the ebbing tide.
"Thus, dearest, may we glide
　Through life," says somebody.

Somewhere, somebody
Makes love to somebody,
　To-night.

Curious effect produced by a fashionable lady walking down the aisle of a church.

Mrs. EATON has just been elected Lamplighter by the Jersey City daily papers.
(*Vide* daily papers.)

Die Mode.

Der Bazar

Der Bazar

Part III

The Age of the Bustle

1870–1908

The last few decades of the 19th century were a dynamic period for the United States, as the last frontiers were settled and the industrial revolution spurred urban growth. It was a dynamic period for the American woman, too, with the woman's suffrage and "feminism" movements beginning to make themselves heard. In the Fashion world bustles were in vogue, and many women were taking advantage of their new sewing machines and the availability of paper dress patterns to make their own.

A new family of publications, written for and by women, came into being at this time. The advent of the great mail order house, notably Montgomery Ward in 1872 and Sears & Roebuck in 1894, made it possible for any woman to select her wardrobe from a wide range of reasonably fashionable ready-to-wear clothes at modest prices. And, of course, for those who could afford and appreciate them there were always the latest creations of the great European fashion houses, available from Marshall Field & Company or their eastern equivalents.

The art of advertising had also undergone a dramatic change. At mid century newspaper and magazine advertising had been simply a few sticks of set type, unillustrated and uninspired. By the 1880s and '90s all manner of products were being widely displayed in dynamic, creative presentations, many directed specifically towards women.

The selections on the following pages attempt to capture the varigated flavor of those changing times.

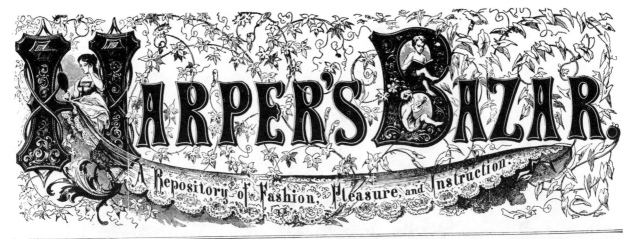

HARPER'S BAZAR.

A Repository of Fashion, Pleasure, and Instruction.

Vol. III.—No. 3.] NEW YORK, SATURDAY, JANUARY 15, 1870. [SINGLE COPIES TEN CENTS.
$4.00 PER YEAR IN ADVANCE.

Entered according to Act of Congress, in the Year 1869, by Harper & Brothers, in the Clerk's Office of the District Court of the United States, for the Southern District of New York.

Bridal and Evening Toilettes.

Fig. 1.—WHITE POULT DE SOIE DRESS WITH HIGH WAIST. The skirt is trimmed with two wide lace flounces; each flounce forms a heading on the upper edge, and is finished with a fold of white satin. The waist, wide sleeves, and sash are trimmed with lace and satin folds in the manner shown by the illustration. Veil of white silk tulle; wreath of orange flowers and blossoms. This dress is cut from the pattern given for the Brown Poplin Dress, Supplement, No. X., Figs. 38–43, *Harper's Bazar*, Vol. III., No. 2.

Fig. 2.—WHITE MUSLIN DRESS WITH HIGH WAIST. The under-skirt is trimmed with three flounces, which are arranged in flat pleats all turned one way. The upper skirt is looped on the sides, and is trimmed, like the waist, with trimming corresponding to that of the skirt. Mechlin tulle veil. Wreath of orange flowers.

BRIDAL, DINNER, AND CHILDREN'S TOILETTES.

Fig. 1.—BRIDAL TOILETTE.—WHITE POULT DE SOIE DRESS WITH HIGH WAIST.

Fig. 2.—BRIDAL TOILETTE.—WHITE MUSLIN DRESS WITH HIGH WAIST.

Fig. 3.—DRESS FOR GIRL FROM 8 TO 10 YEARS OLD.

Fig. 4.—DINNER DRESS WITH SQUARE WAIST.

Fig. 5.—DINNER DRESS WITH DOUBLE SKIRT AND HIGH WAIST.

Figs. 1 and 2.—LOUISE PALETOT. FRONT AND BACK.

Figs. 3 and 4.—DON CARLOS MANTLE FOR ELDERLY LADY.—FRONT AND BACK.

Figs. 5 and 6.—BEATRICE PALETOT. FRONT AND BACK.

Figs. 7 and 8.—DEA PALETOT. FRONT AND BACK.

Figs. 9 and 10.—MARIA PASAQUE.—FRONT AN

Figs. 11 and 12.—Camilla Paletot. Front and Back.

Figs. 13 and 14.—Maria Basque. Front and Back.

Figs. 15 and 16.—Luna Paletot. Front and Back.

Figs. 17 and 18.—Augusta Basque. Front and Back.

Figs. 19 and 20.—Katharina Paletot. Front and Back.

CHOOSING A WIFE.

COBBETT is said to have been first attracted toward the woman whom he afterward married by the vigor with which she whirled a mop. COOKE, the celebrated tragedian, became so enamored of the rump steaks served to him at a certain coffee-house in this city that, in order to perpetuate his enjoyment, he installed the kitchen-maid in his own house as Mrs. COOKE. Both of these women proved excellent wives, though they were by no means equally appreciated. Mrs. COBBETT was always tenderly cherished by that rude demagogue, her husband; but Mrs. COOKE got little but hard knocks in return for her devotion to the drunken actor.

If a man, in these days of delicate and superfine women, wait for a wife until he finds one capable of whirling a mop or cooking a beefsteak, he need be patient, and will probably die a bachelor. Our marriageable girls make no pretension to the rude vigor of a Mrs. COBBETT or the humble skill of a Mrs. COOKE, yet they might possess both, and have none the less beauty of person and delicacy of sentiment. FIELDING's sweet wife could at the same time dress the dinner "and herself as neat as any lady who had a regular set of servants could have done." Mrs. SOMERVILLE, the woman of science, turns readily from the celestial mechanics to the cookery-book, and mixes a pudding with the same accuracy as she solves a mathematical problem. A wise and true woman will always strive to make home attractive to her husband and children. In doing so she is more satis-

factory to herself as well as to others. This we know is not to be done by a mere display of fine feathers and fine airs, which, however bravely they may show abroad, soon droop in the close atmosphere of home.

If our women would give us something more elevated than mere frivolity of dress and manners, in exchange for the solidities of a good dinner, husbands might try to spiritualize themselves so far as to dispense with any thing so gross and material as beef and pudding. If wives would strive to become learned, witty, or wise, men might reconcile themselves to the loss of what they perhaps cling to overfondly, the material comforts of home. If the digestion of their overdone steaks or underdone puddings was facilitated by the piquancy of a *bon-mot*, or the scantiness of an ill-provided dinner made up for by the fullness of learning and philosophy, it is possible that husbands would be less disposed to grumble at the domestic shortcomings of their wives. To expect them, however, to behold with complacency the insolent triumph of chignon and skirt, while their purses and stomachs are alike collapsing, is expecting too much from marital good-nature.

It is far from our purpose to persuade women to make mere household drudges of themselves. We desire that they should aspire to become complete wives, not only capable of fulfilling the lowliest of their domestic duties, but the highest—to cook beef-steaks properly if need be, and to enliven home by their intelligence and elevate it by refinement.

WATTEAU-CASAQUE WALKING SUIT.

THIS elegant street suit consists of two garments—a Watteau casaque and a short skirt. The Watteau casaque is becoming to both large and small ladies, to old and young alike. The entire suit may be of silk or woolen goods, or the casaque may be of black velvet or cashmere over a silk skirt, or of any gray, green, or blue goods over a black skirt. It is also very pretty in Swiss muslin, pongee, or other summer fabrics. When made of silk it should be trimmed with velvet ruffles, or lace and a ruche; for cashmere the trimming is silk ruffles and fringe; for alpaca or beaver mohair, ruffles of the same and silk bands; for Swiss muslin, box-pleatings and Valenciennes lace.

WATTEAU-CASAQUE WALKING SUIT.—[FROM HARPER'S BAZAR, VOL. III., No. 22.]

THE LADY STOCK-BROKERS.

WE give herewith the portraits of Mrs. Victoria C. Woodhull and Mrs. Tennie C. Claflin, the sisters whose recent appearance, under the guise of the firm of "Woodhull, Claflin, & Co., Bankers and Brokers," has attracted so much notice. It is not, indeed, altogether a new thing for ladies to deal in stocks; many have been known to do so in a private way for years, personally or through others; in England Miss Burdett Coutts has remained at the head of the great banking house built up by her predecessors; and in France Madame Welles-Lavalette has occupied a similar position. But for ladies to open an office, and undertake banking and brokerage as a legitimate calling, is a decided innovation.

MRS. TENNIE C. CLAFLIN.—[Phot. by Howell, 867 and 869 Broadway.]

MRS. VICTORIA C. WOODHULL.—[Phot. by Howell, 867 and 869 Broadway.]

NEW-YEAR'S NIGHT—THE LAST CALLER.—[Drawn by W. L. Sheppard.]

HOW TO MANAGE A HUSBAND.

1. If he be a Confirmed Fault-finder, give him Plenty of Reason for being so. This will bring Matters to a Crisis.

2. If he won't do the Marketing himself, Tough Steaks throughout the Week.

3. Make your Kisses infrequent, so that the application of one may Produce what you Desire—a New Dress or Bonnet, etc.

4. If he will Smoke in the House, practice before him the Pleasant Custom of certain Southern Ladies —Snuff-Eating. Once will be found sufficient.

5. If he be fond of Staying Out Late o' Nights, always Sit Up for him, and appear in a State of Nervous Distraction.

6. If he likes to have you Read him to Sleep, propose Taking Turns in that Agreeable Performance.

High Waists, Figs. 1-3.

Fig. 1.—Waist cut heart-shaped in front. This waist is of blue silk poplin, trimmed with bias folds of blue velvet and white lace two inches in width. The bow, belt, and sash are of blue velvet.

Fig. 2.—Pompadour waist and open sleeves of green Chambery; the neck and sleeves are trimmed with a pleated strip of the same material, and with lace two inches and a half wide. The bow, belt, and sash are of green gros grain.

Fig. 3.—Blouse waist of black figured silk tulle. The trimming consists of a ruche of two rows of narrow lace,

MUSLIN AND LACE FICHU.

with the straight edges together, and satin folds. The bow, belt, and sash are of violet velvet. Figs. 38-41, Supplement, give a waist pattern; the dotted line on Fig. 38 gives the edge of the heart-shaped pattern, and the straight line gives the edge of the Pompadour pattern. Figs. 47 and 48, Supplement, give the pattern of the blouse waist.

Muslin and Lace Fichu.

THIS fichu is made of pleated muslin. The trimming consists of Valenciennes edging an inch and a half and three-quarters of an inch wide, and green satin ribbon half an inch and an inch and a quarter wide. Make the fichu of two straight strips of muslin each twenty-four inches long and sixteen inches wide, which are arranged in five upright pleats of equal width, so that the width of a strip shall be six and a half inches on one end, and two inches on the other. In order to secure this result the pleats must lap over further on the narrow side than on the wide one; both strips are then sloped on the wide end till the upper edge of each shall be only seventeen and a half inches long. Sew the pieces together along the sloped sides, and arrange the trimming in the manner shown by the illustration.

Fig. 1.—DRESS WITH HEART-SHAPED CORSAGE.
For pattern see Supplement, No. X., Figs. 38-41.

Fig. 2.—DRESS WITH SQUARE CORSAGE.
For pattern see Supplement, No. X., Figs. 38-41.

Fig. 3.—BLACK TULLE BLOUSE WAIST.
For pattern see Supplement, No. XII., Figs. 47 and 48.

Lace Fichu trimmed with Blue Satin Ribbon.

THIS fichu is made of a three-cornered piece of white Mechlin lace thirty-six inches long and ten inches wide in the middle, and edged with a tulle ruche. The latter is made of a strip of tulle two inches, and another an inch and three-quarters wide, each of which is laid in close double box-pleats. The narrow strip is sewed along the middle of the wide one. Pleat the middle of the back in three upward pleats on the upper part, and trim it, in the manner shown by the illustration, with loops and ends of blue satin ribbon an inch and a half wide. This fichu may be worn with either high or low light dresses.

Kitchen Apron with Bodice.

See illustration on page 29.

THIS white linen apron is trimmed on the edges with a bias strip of linen, two-fifths of an inch wide, stitched on. First cut for the apron part a straight piece of linen thirty inches long, sixty-five inches wide on the bottom, and twenty-nine inches wide on the top; this must be sloped on the sides, and the lower corners slightly rounded off. Turn down the edge two-fifths of an inch on the right side, the top excepted, and stitch on the bias folds. Gather the top to six inches in width, and set it in a double linen belt three-quarters of an inch wide. For the bodice of the apron cut from Fig. 69, Supplement, one piece, stitch a bias strip around the edge, except the bottom, and sew the bodice down on the under side of the belt. Set linen tape on the under side of the bodice, making a sheath for flexible whalebones; this prevents the necessity of pinning the bodice on the waist.

Muslin Kitchen Apron.

See illustration on page 29.

THIS fine muslin apron is both pretty and useful. The original consists of a piece of material thirty-seven inches long, and seventy-three inches wide on the bottom, and twenty-six inches wide on the top: the sides are proportionately sloped, and the lower corners are rounded off. Bind all, except the top, two-fifths of an inch wide with a bias strip of muslin, which is stitched down on the right side. Gather the top to seven inches in width and set it in a straight double muslin binding three-quarters of an inch wide, which is stitched at the distance of a

LACE FICHU TRIMMED WITH BLUE SATIN RIBBON.

fifth of an inch from the top and bottom. On the ends of the binding set two muslin strings three-quarters of an inch wide and fourteen inches long, the ends of which are sewed together. In putting on the apron the loop thus made is thrown over the head. Nineteen inches from the upper edges sew on two hemmed strings of equal width, and each sixteen inches long, which are tied together behind.

Crochet Tobacco Pouch.

See illustration on page 21.

THIS pouch is designed for Turkish tobacco; it may also be used for a purse. It is crocheted with silk twist of various colors, and is lined with thin leather and ornamented with tassels of different colored silks. Fig. 102, Supplement, gives the design and the colors to be used. If it be desired to make the pouch larger, split wool may be used instead of silk. Begin on the under point, and make with violet silk a foundation of six stitches, join this in a round by means of a slip stitch, and work thereon three rounds of single crochet, widening in such a manner that the last round counts twenty-four stitches. In the fourth round begin the design, which here consists only of star-like figures crocheted from the design, Fig. 102, Supplement.

Fig. 1.—JACKET FOR ELDERLY LADY.—FRONT.
For pattern and description see Supplement, No. XI., Figs. 44-46.

Fig. 2.—JACKET FOR ELDERLY LADY.—BACK.
For pattern and description see Supplement, No. XI., Figs. 44-46.

"THESE ARE MY JEWELS."

CORNELIA, MOTHER OF THE GRACCHI.

"I AM TIRED OF DISCUSSING HOUSEHOLD MATTERS; THERE IS NO WORSE THING THAN FOR WOMEN TO SIT DAY AFTER DAY TAKING CARE OF MISERABLE SICKLY, PULING CHILDREN."

SEE REPORT OF PUBLIC MEETING N.Y. CITY.

Fig. 1.—White Tulle Dress with Pink Satin Train.

Fig. 2.—White Tarlatan Dress.

Fig. 3.—India Muslin Dress with Tunic trimmed with Black Velvet Ribbon.

Fig. 4.—Dress with Tunic.

OPERA WRAPPINGS.

Fig. 1.—Embroidered White Cashmere Talma.

Fig. 2.—Crimson Velvet Beaver Mantelet.—Back.—[See Fig. 3.]

Fig. 3.—Crimson Velvet Beaver Mantelet.—Front.

Fig. 5.—WHITE TARLATAN DRESS WITH GREEN POULT DE SOIE TRAIN.

Fig. 6.—BLUE TULLE DRESS WITH TUNIC.

Fig. 7.—PINK GAUZE DRESS WITH PEPLUM.

Fig. 8.—YELLOW TARLATAN DRESS.

Fig. 4.—BEDOUIN FOR YOUNG GIRL. BACK.—[See Fig. 5.]

Fig. 5.—BEDOUIN FOR YOUNG GIRL.—FRONT.

Fig. 6.—BLACK CASHMERE SCARF MANTILLA EMBROIDERED WITH GOLD BRAID.—FRONT.

Fig. 7.—BLACK CASHMERE SCARF MANTILLA EMBROIDERED WITH GOLD BRAID.—BACK.

Ball and Evening Coiffures

Fig. 1.—Chignon of waved hair and long curls. The front hair is combed up over crêpes on the sides. Several short curls lie over the forehead. The hair is adorned with velvet ribbon, feathers, and a bead clasp.

Figs. 2 and 3. This chignon consists of puffs edged on each side with a loop made of three-strand braids (see Fig. 3). The waved front hair is partly combed upward and partly arranged in curls, and the chignon is finished with a few long curls. A velvet flower and leaves complete the coiffure.

Fig. 4.—The front hair is somewhat waved, and combed up as shown by the illustration. The chignon is arranged over crêpes in the form of a large bow, with a few curls on the sides. Red velvet ribbon is wound through the hair as shown by the illustration.

Fig. 5.—This chignon is arranged in curls; the front hair is combed up and arranged in curls back of the ear. Arrange a braid over the front, and ornament with green velvet ribbon.

Figs. 6 and 7.—Chignon of waved hair with three-strand braids on each side; the front hair is partly combed up and partly arranged in puffs. A spray of roses completes the coiffure.

Fig. 5.—COIFFURE WITH GREEN VELVET RIBBON.

Fig. 2.—COIFFURE WITH VELVET FLOWERS.—FRONT.—[See Fig. 3.]

Fig. 1.—COIFFURE WITH VELVET RIBBON AND FEATHERS.

Fig. 4.—COIFFURE WITH RED VELVET RIBBON.

Fig. 3.—COIFFURE WITH VELVET FLOWERS.—BACK.

Fig. 6.—COIFFURE WITH ROSES.—FRONT.—[See Fig. 7.]

Fig. 7.—COIFFURE WITH ROSES.—BACK.

EVENING AND DINNER TOILETTES.

Fig. 1.—Dress with Double Skirt and High Waist of Violet Irish Poplin. The under-skirt is trimmed with three wide folds of violet velvet. The tunic is looped at the side with a violet velvet rosette, and is trimmed with violet velvet and violet silk fringe. Short peplum of poplin bound with velvet. Waist trimmed with velvet folds.

Fig. 2.—Dress of Pink Silk Gauze. The two upper skirts are open at the sides, laid back in revers, and trimmed with black velvet ribbon. Low waist and short puffed sleeves, trimmed with black velvet ribbon. Black velvet belt and bow.

Fig. 3.—Under-skirt of white gros grain. Tunic and low waist of pink poult de soie, trimmed with broad white lace and satin piping. Belt and bow of pink satin ribbon. Rose in hair. Flexible gold chain and medallion on neck.

Fig. 4.—Dress with Double Skirt of Russian Green Satin. The under-skirt is trimmed with a wide, and the upper skirt with a narrow pleated flounce. High waist with ruffles, simulating a square corsage.

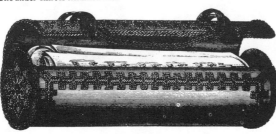

—Embroidered Music-Case.—Open.

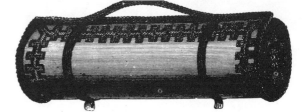

—Embroidered Music-Case.—Closed.

NIGHT-SACQUE FOR GIRL FROM 12 TO 14 YEARS OLD.
For pattern see *Harper's Bazar*, Vol. III., No. 41, Supplement,
No. II., Figs. 4–7. Description in next Supplement Number.

PIQUE BIB WITH LACE
TRIMMING.—FRONT.
For pattern and description see
Supplement, No. IX., Fig. 21.

GIRL'S NETTED
SLEEPING-NET.

Fig. 3.—GIRL'S COLLAR WITH
TRIPLE REVERS.
For description see Supplement.

CHEMISE FOR GIRL FROM 2 TO 4 YEARS OLD.
Description in next Supplement Number.

NIGHT-SACQU
For pattern see Su
Description in

Fig. 2.—CUFF FOR
COLLAR, FIG. 1.
For description see Supplement.

SACQUE FOR CHILD FROM 1 TO 3
YEARS OLD.
For pattern and description see Supple-
ment, No. XXIV., Figs. 71–74.

DRAWERS FOR GIRL FROM 2 TO 4 YEARS OLD.
For pattern and description see Supplement,
No. III., Fig. 3.

Fig. 7.—CHILD'S MUSLIN COLLAR.
For description see Supplement.

UNDER-WAIST FOR GIRL FROM
12 TO 14 YEARS OLD.
For pattern see *Harper's Bazar*,
Vol. III., No. 41, Supplement,
No. XII., Figs. 40–44.
Description in next Supple-
ment Number.

Fig. 1.—GIRL'
PERCALE
For desc
Supp

NIGHT-DRESS FOR CHILD FROM 1 TO 3 YEARS OLD.
For pattern and description see
Supplement, No. XXIII., Figs. 68–70.

Fig. 8.—HEART-SHAPED COLLAR.
[See Fig. 9.]
For description see Supplement.

DRAWERS FOR GIRL FROM 5 TO 7 YEARS OLD.
For pattern and description see Suppl., No. II., Fig. 2.

CHILD'S JACONET FRIL

Fig. 9.—CUFF FOR
COLLAR, FIG. 8.
For description see
Supplement.

SHIRT FOR BOY FROM 8 TO 10 YEARS OLD.
For pattern see Supplement, No. XXVII., Figs. 82–88.
Description in next Supplement Number.

NIGHT-SHIRT FOR BOY FROM 12 TO 14 YEARS OLD.
For pattern and description see Suppl., No. XV., Figs. 29–36.

SHIRT FOR BOY
For pattern and
No. X

BRAIDED PIQUÉ BIB.—FRONT.
For pattern and description see
Supplement, No. X., Fig. 22.

NIGHT-CAP FOR GIRL FROM
6 TO 8 YEARS OLD.
For pattern and description see Supplement, No. XII., Figs. 25 and 26.

SHIRT FOR BOY FROM 10 TO 12 YEARS OLD.
For pattern and description see Supplement,
No. XXVII., Figs. 82–88.

NIGHT-CAP FOR
GIRL FROM 10 TO
12 YEARS OLD.
For pattern and de-
scription see Supple-
ment, No. XIII.,
Fig. 27.

8 TO 10
Figs. 63–67.
number.

SHIRT FOR CHILD FROM 1 TO 3 YEARS OLD.
For pattern and description see Supplement, No. XIX., Figs. 54 and 55.

GIRL'S KNITTED SLEEPING-NET.

Fig. 4.—CHILD'S MUSLIN COLLAR.
For description see Supplement.

PIQUÉ BIB WITH LACE TRIMMING. BACK.
For pattern and description see Supplement, No. IX., Fig. 21.

NIGHT-SACQUE FOR GIRL FROM 10 TO 12 YEARS OLD.
For pattern and description see Supplement, No. XXII., Figs. 63–67.

UNDER-WAIST FOR GIRL FROM 12 TO 14 YEARS OLD.
For pattern and description see Supplement, No. XXI., Figs. 58–62.

DRAWERS FOR GIRL FROM 3 TO 5 YEARS OLD.
For pattern and description see Supplement, No. III., Fig. 2.

Fig. 6.—CUFF FOR COLLAR, FIG. 5.
For description see Supplement.

SACQUE FOR CHILD FROM 1 TO 3 YEARS OLD.
For pattern and description see Supplement, No. XXV., Figs. 75–78.

DRESS FOR CHILD FROM 2 TO 4 YEARS OLD.
For pattern and description see Supplement, No. XXVI., Figs. 79–81.

TTED FRILL.

Fig. 5.—GIRL'S LINEN COLLAR.—[See Fig. 6.]
For description see Supplement.

DRAWERS FOR BOY FROM 2 TO 4 YEARS OLD.
For pattern and description see Supplement, No. III., Fig. 3.

Fig. 10.—LINEN COLLAR WITH TRIPLE REVERS.—[See Fig. 11.]
For description see Supplement.

Fig. 11.—CUFF FOR COLLAR, FIG. 10.
For description see Supplement.

SHIRT FOR BOY FROM 5 TO 7 YEARS OLD.
Description in next Supplement Number.

SHIRT FOR BOY FROM 12 TO 14 YEARS OLD.
For pattern see Supplement, No. XXVII., Figs. 82–88.
Description in next Supplement Number.

NIGHT-CAP FOR GIRL FROM 4 TO 6 YEARS OLD.
For pattern and description see Supplement, No. XIV., Fig. 28.

BRAIDED PIQUÉ BIB. BACK.
For pattern and description see Supplement, No. X., Fig. 22.

EARS OLD.
pplement,

NIGHT-CAP FOR GIRL FROM 12 TO 14 YEARS OLD.
For pattern and description see Supplement, No. XI., Figs. 23 and 24.

NIGHT-SHIRT FOR CHILD FROM 6 TO 8 YEARS OLD.
For pattern and description see Supplement, No. XVII., Figs. 43–49.

Children's Suits, Figs. 1-3.

Fig. 1.—Suit for Boy from 2 to 4 Years old. The blouse and trowsers are of muslin, while the dress is of Scotch plaid trimmed with a revers. Short over-skirt and pockets of black velvet.

Fig. 2.—Suit for Girl from 7 to 9 Years old. The dress is of dark green poplin, trimmed with folds of the same material. The black silk apron is trimmed with velvet ribbon and velvet buttons.

Fig. 3.—Suit for Girl from 6 to 8 Years old. The dress and paletot are of blue satin-faced wool, trimmed with bias folds of black velvet.

Coiffures, Figs. 1-3.

Fig. 1.—Coiffure of White Blonde, Velvet Ribbon, and Roses. This coiffure is made of white blonde two inches and a half wide, which is sewed around a circular piece of stiff lace three inches in diameter; the ends of the lace hang down fifteen inches long behind, where they are joined on one side. Loops and ends of black

velvet ribbon two inches wide and a red rose with buds and leaves complete the coiffure.

Fig. 2.—Coiffure of White Blonde, Lilac Gros Grain Ribbon, and Sprays of Convolvulus. Take a small semicircular piece of stiff lace, edge it with gathered blonde two inches wide, and ornament it, in the manner shown by the illustration, with loops and ends of lilac gros grain ribbon and long and short sprays of convolvulus.

Fig. 3.—Coiffure of Black Lace, Red Gros Grain Ribbon, and Roses. Take an oblong piece of stiff lace and sew gathered black lace two inches and a half wide around the edge, letting it hang down behind. Loops and ends of red gros grain ribbon two inches wide and a spray of red roses complete the coiffure. Finish the front with a pearl clasp.

Fig. 1.—Suit for Boy from 2 to 4 Years old.

Fig. 2.—Suit for Girl from 7 to 9 Years old.

Fig. 3.—Suit for Girl from 6 to 8 Years old.

Fig. 2.—Coiffure of White Blonde, Lilac Gros Grain Ribbon, and Convolvulus.

Breakfast Cap with Pink Silk Ribbon. Back.

Breakfast Cap with Black Velvet Ribbon.

Breakfast Cap with Blue Gros Grain Ribbon.

Breakfast Cap with Green Satin Ribbon.

Cap of Tulle, Lace, and Red Velvet Ribbon.

Fig. 1.—Coiffure of White Blonde, Velvet Ribbon, and Roses.

Breakfast Cap with Blue Satin Ribbon.

Breakfast Cap with Pink Satin Ribbon.

Fig. 3.—Coiffure of Black Lace, Red Gros Grain Ribbon, and Roses.

Breakfast Cap with Lilac Satin Ribbon.

Breakfast Cap with Lilac Gros Grain Ribbon.

Ladies' and Children's Toilettes.

Fig. 1.—SUIT FOR GIRL FROM 4 TO 6 YEARS OLD. Dress with double skirt and square-necked corsage of pink alpaca, trimmed with flounces of the same material. Chemisette of tucked Swiss muslin. Pink ribbon sash and hair ribbon.

Fig. 2.—DRESS OF LILAC POULT DE SOIE, trimmed with a wide flounce and pointed strips of the same material. Tunic slit at the sides and bouffant behind. The waist is cut square in front and edged with Valenciennes; and the sleeves are slashed and finished with tulle and lace under-sleeves.

Fig. 3.—DRESS OF BLACK GROS GRAIN. Mantelet of black velvet, trimmed with wide Chantilly lace and gros grain piping. Black velvet hat trimmed with pink roses and tulle scarf.

Fig. 4.—DRESS WITH TUNIC OF RUSSIAN GREEN SATIN-FACED SERGE. The under-skirt is trimmed with a wide pleated flounce of the same material, and dark green velvet ribbon. The tunic is edged with fringe and velvet ribbon. Dark green velvet belt and bow.

Fig. 5.—SUIT FOR GIRL FROM 6 TO 8 YEARS OLD. Dress of blue poplin, trimmed with three flounces. Black velvet sack trimmed with blue silk braid. Black velvet hat with blue feathers.

LADIES' AND CHILDREN'S TOILETTES.

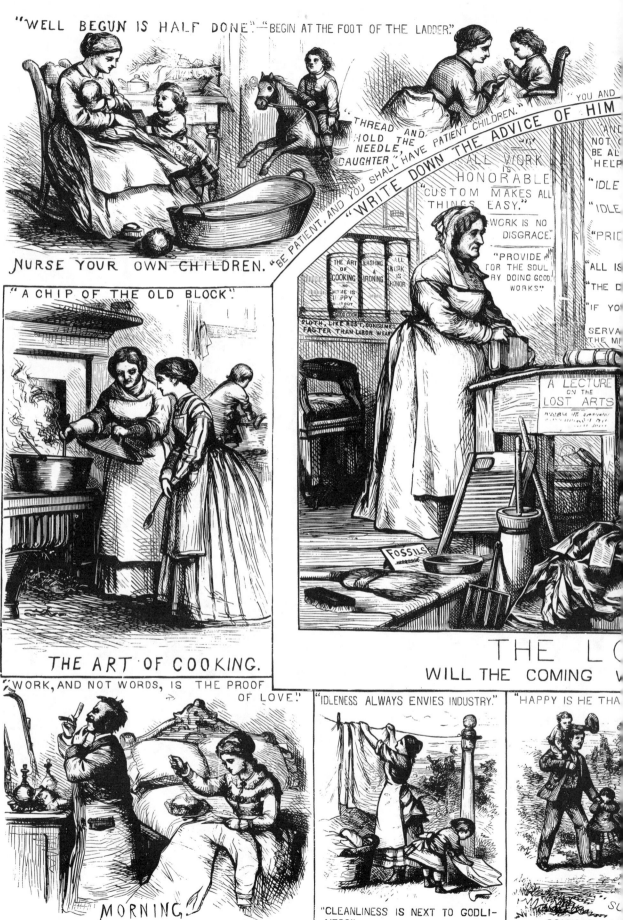

"WELL BEGUN IS HALF DONE."—"BEGIN AT THE FOOT OF THE LADDER."

"THREAD AND HOLD THE NEEDLE, DAUGHTER," HAVE PATIENT CHILDREN."

"WRITE DOWN THE ADVICE OF HIM

"YOU AND

"BE PATIENT, AND YOU SHALL HAVE PATIENT CHILDREN."

ALL WORK IS HONORABLE

"CUSTOM MAKES ALL THINGS EASY."

"WORK IS NO DISGRACE."

"PROVIDE FOR THE SOUL BY DOING GOOD WORKS."

AND NOT BE AL HELP

"IDLE

"IDLE

"PRI

"ALL IS

"THE D

"IF YO

SERVA THE M

NURSE YOUR OWN CHILDREN.

"A CHIP OF THE OLD BLOCK."

THE ART OF COOKING
NO HOME IS HAPPY WITHOUT A GOOD COOK

WASHING & IRONING

ALL WORK IS HONOR

SLOTH, LIKE RUST, CONSUMES FASTER THAN LABOR WEARS

A LECTURE ON THE LOST ARTS

FOSSILS

THE ART OF COOKING.

THE L

WILL THE COMING

"WORK, AND NOT WORDS, IS THE PROOF OF LOVE."

"IDLENESS ALWAYS ENVIES INDUSTRY."

"HAPPY IS HE THA

MORNING.

"CLEANLINESS IS NEXT TO GODLI-NESS."

COMING H

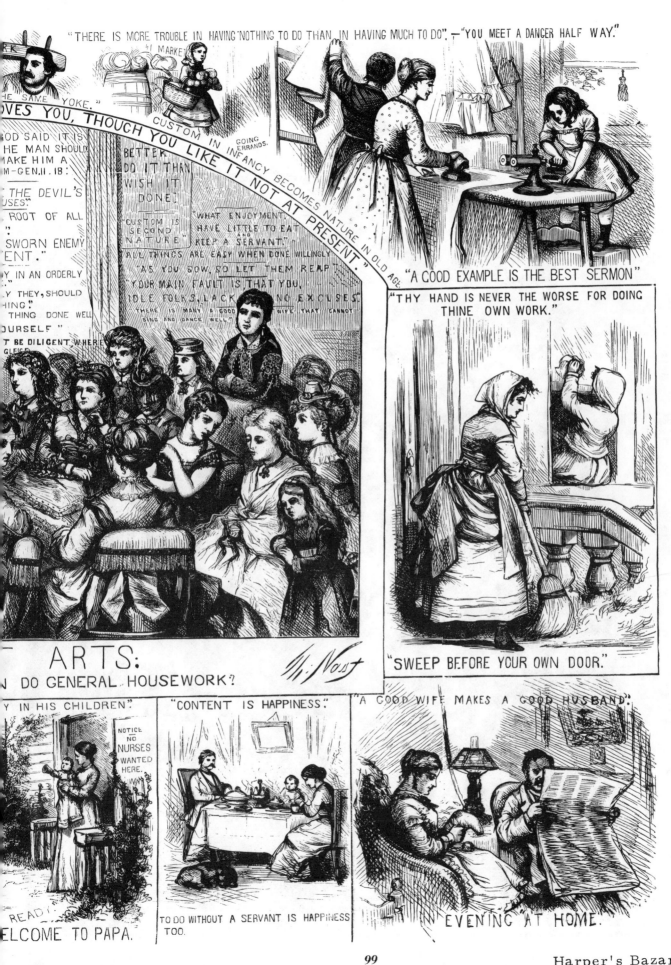

LADIES' SUMMER WRAPPI

Figs. 1 and 2.—Frou Frou Paletot.—Front and Back. Figs. 3 and 4.—Mousquetaire Casaque.—Front and Back. Figs. 5 and 6.—Camelia Paletot.—Front and Back. Figs. 7 and 8.—Watteau Paletot.—Front and Back. Fig. 9.—Gray Cloth Talma. Front.— Fig. 10.—Lucca Casaque. Front.— Fig. 11.—Bianca Front.—

DIAGRAM ON PAGE 356.]

Fig. 12.—NINON PALETOT.   Fig. 13.—TALMA TRIMMED   Figs. 14 and 15.—MEDICI   Figs. 16 and 17.—CAPRICE   Fig. 18.—RUCHE PALETOT.   Fig. 19.—POMPADOUR PALETOT FOR
BACK.—   WITH BLACK VELVET RIBBON.   PALETOT.—BACK AND FRONT.   PALETOT.—FRONT AND BACK.   BACK.—   ELDERLY LADY.—FRONT.—

101   Harper's Bazar

SHORT-BASQUE WALKING SUIT.

A VALUABLE feature of this suit is its graceful basque with half flowing sleeves, as this
garment may be made with trained skirts, or in
conjunction with any other over-skirt pattern.
The whole pattern is a good model for shaded
suits of silk, Irish poplin, pongee, empress cloth,
or cashmere, as the trimming of silk puffs is always a darker shade than the dress. For mourn-
ing suits of tamise cloth or serge, folds are now
used instead of puffs.

EFFECT OF SIMPLICITY.

WHATEVER may be the fashion of woman's dress, there is always an abundance of ill-natured critics to find fault with it.
Our dames evidently try hard to suit every
variety of taste. Their efforts, in fact, never
cease, and they make a new trial at least once
a quarter. Each of the four seasons is sure to
be marked by something novel in feminine costume. The critics must indeed be hard to
please if, in the numberless changes of these
later years, they have not found any thing to
their liking. There has been diversity enough
of form and proportion. We have had waists
which might be grasped within the thumb and
forefinger, peripheries of skirt too broad for an
ordinary street-door, petticoats so short and
necks so low that further compromise with the
primitive fig-leaf was impossible, and trains so
long that they continued to sweep one street
after their wearers had turned the corner into
another. Now it has been all head, and now
all tail, and again the reverse; at one time
towering high, at another crouching low. The
most surprising thing is the readiness with
which these transitions are made. It would
appear that a woman, like a Jack-in-the-box,
could lengthen or shorten, swell or collapse, at
the touch of some hidden spring. Fashion is
certainly endowed with a mysterious power of
suddenly metamorphosing the human being.

A famous French grumbler at what he terms,
forsooth, the caprices and follies of women, says
a great deal has been said about the power of
fashion, but not enough. He accordingly adds
his dictum. We would not venture to quote
it had it not been uttered a long time ago, for
twelve years constitute an age in the history
of fashion. Our dames must bear in mind, in
reading the strictures of the unamiable Frenchman, that what he says was uttered in a comparatively barbaric age, and can not be at all
applicable to the women of these days of advanced civilization.

Look, he tells us, at the portraits of the time
of Louis XV. Pug-noses were the fashion then.
Every woman managed, by some means or other, to have one. Well, at this moment three
yards of hair are the fashion. Every woman
has three yards of hair. It is not a little surprising that women who last week had hardly
a hair to their heads, have now the full length
required. If you meet a woman in society who
appears to be, relatively to those who surround
her, scantily supplied with hair, and has it
simply dressed, you may safely conclude that
she is particularly well furnished naturally, and
that the condition of her neighbor is the reverse. In fact, a woman with a fine head of
hair is alone in such a position that she can
refuse "to dishonor it by a mixture of the false
and contraband." Those who make the greatest show of abundance of locks have the least.

Few seem to be aware of the effect of simplicity in the midst of elaborate and expensive
artifice. Let a young woman with no hair but
her own, and that simply dressed, enter a room
filled with those whose heads are elaborately
built up with a profusion of purchased locks,
and see who will be most admired.

It is a great advantage for a woman, in these
days of artifice, to remain herself, and thus be
unlike every one else. A simple dress, white
or black, will produce the greatest effect when
surrounded by the most gorgeous costumes.
These serve, as it were, as frames for the former, and women are often forced to confess
that they have draped themselves magnificent-
ly, at an immense expense, for no other purpose than to heighten by contrast the beauty
of a rival. In fact, they have been wearing a
dress which is very becoming to—others.

THE VENUS OF MILO; OR, GIRLS OF TWO DIFFERENT PERIODS.

Chorus. "Look at her Big Foot! Oh, what a Waist!—and what a Ridiculous Little Head!—and *no* Chignon! She's no Lady! Oh, what a Fright!"

NEW YORK FASHIONS.

BATHING COSTUMES.

THE bathing season has returned, and bathing suits are again in requisition. A variety of fancy materials are used for these suits, but experience proves that nothing is so good for the purpose as flannel. Twilled flannel sufficiently fine is sold for 50 or 60 cents a yard. Seven or eight yards are required for a well-made suit. White, navy blue, and very dark gray are the most popular colors for suits, as they will endure rough usage. Scarlet suits are gay and pretty at the beginning of the season, but are apt to fade to an undecided pinkish hue. Dark Scotch plaid flannels are chosen by brunettes, who consider the becoming, and require color.

Wiry moreens, and stiff serges that are partly cotton, are commended by merchants for bathing-dresses. They say they do not retain the water, or cling as closely to the person as flannel. These fabrics are made up at the furnishing houses in stripes, plaids, and solid colors. A flannel suit of good quality and well made costs $10; moreen suits, $8; cotton serge, $6; old-fashioned, unsalable materials are made into suits, and sold for $4 or $5.

The trimming for bathing dresses is alpaca braid stitched on flatly, or box-pleated in ruches, or else the garment is scalloped and bound with braid. Bias bands of striped flannel are also used for trimming.

The only novelty in bathing suits is the kilt skirt made in pleats all turned one way, and stitched flatly their whole length. These are heavy when wet, but they conceal the figure, and are more especially becoming to slight ladies. The waist is a Garibaldi, or else a square yoke with the body pleated to a belt. A belted blouse, or a polonaise cut like a long sacque, is the best upper garment for ladies inclined to stoutness. The skirt reaches to the knee or below it. A gay sash knotted at the side adds to its beauty. Very high-necked waists and long close-fitting sleeves are preferred in this country, but foreign ladies leave the arms unencumbered, and free for exercise. Some imported suits have the body and trowsers in one garment enveloping the figure, and shaped like the sleeping drawers worn by children in winter.

The trowsers of all suits are made by the ordinary closed-drawers pattern given in a previous number. They are very full about the hips, are buttoned on the sides, and are pleated to a belt. Make the front of the belt in a deep and broad point, as that does away with the ungraceful fullness. Some trowsers are gathered into a buttoned band at the ankle in Turkish fashion; others are sloped very narrow, left loose, and scalloped. Flannel suits should be made large, to allow for shrinkage. There should be no rough seams left to irritate the skin. Thick seams should be bound on the wrong side. To sew seams that are merely double of the flannel, first make the seam on the outside as if the garment were being made wrong side outward, then turn the garment and sew it in the usual way on the wrong side, inclosing the raw edges of the stuff between the seams and out of sight.

Marine fancies are seen among the prettiest suits. A navy-blue flannel blouse, trimmed with white braid, has a wide, square collar in true sailor shape, with an anchor wrought in the corners. A white moreen suit, similarly made, and trimmed with blue, has no collar, but a blue percale neckerchief is worn loosely around the neck, and tied in a sailor's knot in front like the Ida Lewis scarfs of last season. A pretty suit for a blonde is blue and green checked flannel trimmed with scarlet braid. The braid is box-pleated on the polonaise, and sewed plainly up the outer seams of the trowsers. White moreen and stone-gray flannel, with cherry-colored trimmings, are pretty for dark complexions.

Gentlemen's suits, usually of blue or gray flannel, are made with short belted blouses and trowsers. A white cord is up the outer seams of the trowsers, and flat Hercules braid trims the blouse.

BATHING SHOES, CAPS, AND HATS.

Sandals and pretty straw slippers with cork soles are used abroad for bathing shoes. A ruche of braid trims the top of the slippers, and they are held on by braid strapped across the instep. A yarn moccasin is made by industrious young ladies from directions given in *Bazar* No. 28, Vol. II. The shoe most used is made of common canvas with manilla sole. It is clumsy-looking, but serviceable. as it lets in water but keeps out sand. Price $1 a pair.

Bathing caps of oiled silk, trimmed with braid, and made like those illustrated in this paper, cost $1 50 or $1 75. Many ladies do not use a cap at all, leaving the hair loosely flowing, and tied back by a bright-colored braid. Coarse broad-brimmed straw flats are worn to protect the face from the sun. A string of braid passes over the crown and ties the brim down at the sides. Bags of oil-silk and of twine are used for carrying bathing suits.

MISCELLANEOUS.

The traveling suit that meets with most favor during the present season of journeying is the shawl costume described early in the spring. It consists of a short slashed paletot and very long draped upper skirt, made of a gray wool long-shawl, and worn over a black silk skirt. The simple trimming of this stylish suit is the fringe woven with the shawl. A brown shawl casaque. very long and draped in soft folds, is also much admired with skirts of brown or black silk. The shawl is sold for $8. A paletot and skirt, or a casaque ready-made, cost from $20 upward. These suits are worn with black or brown straw bonnets, and are especially popular with ladies of thirty years of age and more. Younger ladies wear casaques of very thick buff or gray linen over black silk skirts.

A NEW YORK BELLE AT LONG BRANCH.

HOW SHE WENT IN.

HOW SHE CAME OUT.

VENUS RISING FROM THE SEA.

AFTER THE BATH.

BATHING CAP WITH RUCHES.

TATTED ROSETTE FOR CAP.

NET-SHAPED BATHING CAP.

Fig. 1.—BOY'S BLUE
FLANNEL BATHING
SUIT.

Fig. 2.—RED AND WHITE STRIPED
FLANNEL BATHING SUIT (TROWSERS
AND LONG BLOUSE).

Fig. 3.—RED FLANNEL BATHING OR
SWIMMING SUIT (TROWSERS, SHORT
BLOUSE, AND SKIRT).

Fig. 4.—WHITE FLANNEL BATHING
DRESS.

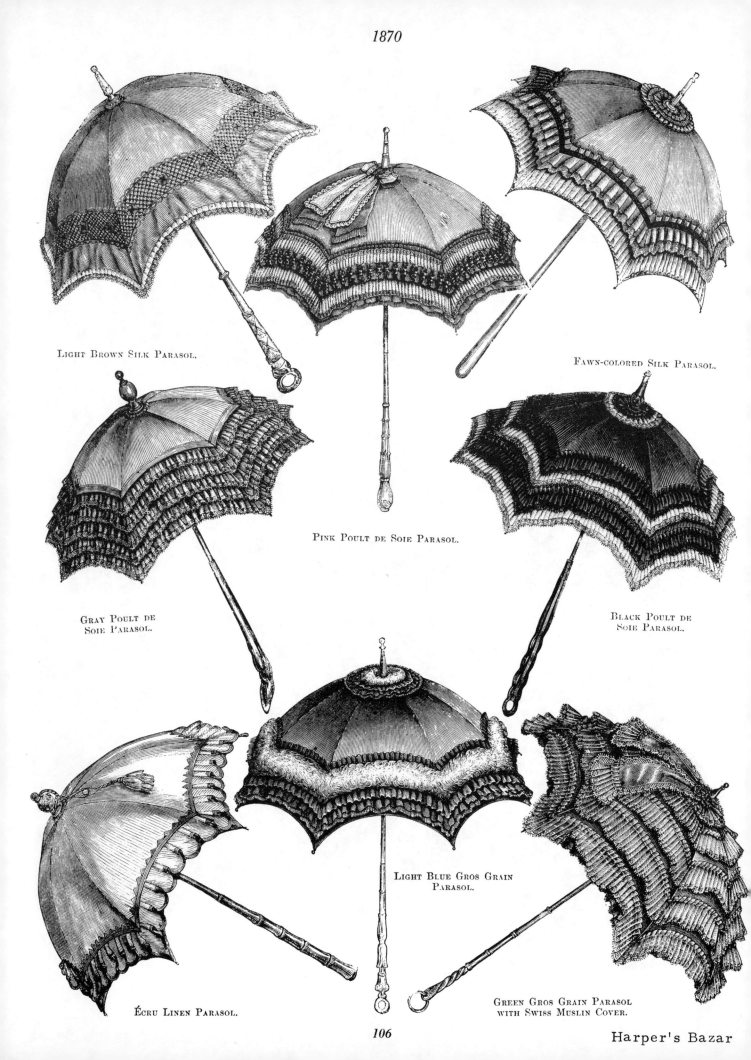

LIGHT BROWN SILK PARASOL.

FAWN-COLORED SILK PARASOL.

PINK POULT DE SOIE PARASOL.

GRAY POULT DE
SOIE PARASOL.

BLACK POULT DE
SOIE PARASOL.

LIGHT BLUE GROS GRAIN
PARASOL.

ÉCRU LINEN PARASOL.

GREEN GROS GRAIN PARASOL
WITH SWISS MUSLIN COVER.

Fig. 1.—Dress with Low Waist of Pink Silk Gauze.

Fig. 2.—Dress with High Waist for Girl from 14 to 16 Years old.

Fig. 3.—Dress with Low Waist for Girl from 14 to 16 Years old.

Fig. 4.—Dress with Casaque of Satin-Faced Serge.

Fig. 1.—Bertha with Sash Ends of Tulle and Satin.

Fig. 2.—Low Blouse Waist with Basque.

Fig. 3.—Black Tulle Blouse Waist.

Fig. 4.—Bertha of Muslin and Blue Satin Ribbon.

lowing 4 violet st. of the preceding round, and from ✳ repeat three times. Finish the four star-like figures here begun in the manner shown by the design, Fig. 102, Supplement. In the middle of the stripe worked with violet silk widen 2 st. between every two star-like figures as far as the 20th round, but in the remaining rounds widen only 1 st. Beside this, from the 20th round work the little foundation figures between the stars which are visible on the design, Fig. 102. After the 30th round, with which the star-like figures are finished, work one round with violet silk without widening, after which cut off the thread and fasten it. Begin the upper part of the pouch on the upper edge (under the open-work part) with violet silk, and a foundation of 152 st., join this in a round, crochet one round sc., and then work according to the design, Fig. 102, beginning from the under edge of it with the first square of the right side edge. 2d round.—✳ 1 black, 5 violet, 1 black, 5 violet, 1 black, 6 violet, 1 yellow, 6 violet, 1 black, 5 violet, 1 black, 5 violet st., and from ✳ repeat three times.—Now crochet 37 rounds with silk according to the design and given colors, but from the 25th round on widen between the black points in such a manner that the 39th round shall count as many stitches as the last round of the under part; then crochet the last round of the under part with the last round of the upper part of the pouch by means of single crochet stitches of violet silk. Along the black points of the upper part crochet the following edge with violet and yellow silk : 1st round of the edge (with yellow silk).—2 dc. (double crochet) separated by 3 ch. in the black st. in the hollow between two black points, 2 dc. separated by 3 ch. in the black st. of the fourth following round (on the outer edge of the point), and so on; on the point of each point the space between the dc. must be somewhat less. 2d round (with violet silk).—5 dc. in every 3 ch. of the former round, always 1 sc. between the dc. 3d round (with yellow silk).—1 sc. in each of the 5 dc. of the former round, after that always 1 sc. between every 2 dc. coming together, so as to embrace the sc. of the former round at the same time. Then crochet with violet silk on the upper edge of the pouch four rounds of open-work dc. ; that is, always alternately 1 dc., 1 ch., and after this an edge like the one just described; but in this case the second round of the edge must be worked with black silk instead of with violet. Now crochet a round of sc. with yellow silk on the foundation stitches on the upper edge of the pouch. Lastly, run two violet silk cords crosswise through the two upper open-work rounds, and fasten the ends with an ornamental covered button.

Fig. 2.—POPLIN WRAPPER.—BACK.
For pattern and description see Supplement, No. I., Figs. 1-4.

Fig. 1.—POPLIN WRAPPER.—FRONT.
For pattern and description see Supplement, No. I., Figs. 1-4.

Lay on the yellow silk, and work off with this the last violet stitch of the third round, ✳ crochet 1 st. (stitch) with the yellow silk, work this off with the violet silk, crochet six violet st. on the following 5 st., work off the last violet st. with the yellow silk which has been continued along on the under side of the work, and repeat three times from ✳. In all the following rounds, as in this one, always work off the last stitch of one color with the thread of the color which is to follow. At the end of the 4th round 6 violet st. on the last 4 st. of the preceding round. 5th round.—Pay on the red silk, ✳ 1 yellow, 1 red, 1 yellow st. on the following 3 st. of the former round (the red st. must come on the first yellow st. of the preceding round), 6 violet st. on the fol-

SOCIAL AFFECTION.

SOCIETY has been aptly compared to a heap of embers, which, when separated, soon languish, darken, and expire ; but, if placed together, glow with a ruddy and intense heat—a just em-

KITCHEN APRON WITH BODICE.—[For pattern see Supplement, No. XXII., Fig. 69.]

MUSLIN KITCHEN APRON.

Fig. 1.—Suit for Boy from 10 to 12 Years old.

For pattern and description see Supplement, No. IX., Figs. 42–54.

Fig. 2.—Suit for Boy from 3 to 5 Years old.

For pattern and description see Supplement, No. X., Figs. 55–58.

Figs. 3 and 4.—Frock for Boy from 2 to 4 Years old.—Back and Front.

For pattern and description see Supplement, No. XII., Figs. 61–63.

Fig. 5.—Suit for Boy from 6 to 8 Years old.

For pattern and description see Supplement, No. XI., Figs. 59 and 60.

Fig. 1.—Dress for Girl from 2 to 3 Years old.—Back.—[See Fig. 4.]

For pattern and description see Supplement, No. II., Figs. 8–12.

Figs. 2 and 3.—Dress for Girl from 6 to 8 Years old.—Front and Back.

For pattern and description see Supplement, No. III., Figs. 13–16.

Fig. 4.—Dress for Girl from 2 to 3 Years old.—Front.—[See Fig. 1.]

For pattern and description see Supplement, No. II., Figs. 8–12.

Figs. 5 and 6.—Dress for Girl from 4 to 6 Years old.—Front and Back.

For pattern and description see Supplement, No. I., Figs. 1–7.

JACONET NIGHT-CAP WITH LACE
TRIMMING.
For pattern and description see Supplement, No. VI., Figs. 22 and 23.

BRIGHTON COLLAR.
For pattern and description see Supplement, No. XXIII., Fig. 70.

GENTLEMAN'S SHIRT.
For pattern and description see Supplement, No. XI., Figs. 36–39.

DIMITY NIGHT-SACQUE.
For pattern and description see Supplement, No. II., Figs. 4–7.

LADY'S CHEMISE WITH YOKE IN VE
For pattern, design, and description

CUFF WITH ROUNDED ENDS.
For pattern and description see Supplement, No. XXVII., Fig. 74.

SERAPHINE CUFF.
For pattern and description see Supplement, No. XXVI., Fig. 73.

PANAMA COLLAR.
For pattern and description see Supplement, No. XVIII., Figs. 61 and 62.

UNDER-WAIST WITH PUFFED
TRIMMING.
For pattern and description see Supplement, No. XII., Figs. 40–44.

KENSI
For pattern and descriptio

SARDOU COLLAR.
For pattern and description see Supplement, No. XIX., Figs. 63 and 64.

LADY'S CHEMISE WITH HEART-SHAPED NECK.
For pattern, design, and description see Supplement, No. X., Figs. 34 and 35.

CRAVAT FOR MORNING DRESS.

JACONET BREAKFAST
CAP.
For pattern and description see Supplement, No. XXVIII., Fig. 75.

JACONET DRESSING-SACQUE.
FRONT.
For pattern and description see Supplement, No. I., Figs. 1–3.

GENTLEMAN'S UNDI
For pattern and des ip
Supplement, N. X
Figs. 49–l.

LADY'S NIGHT-GOWN WITH TURNED-DOWN COLLAR.

LADY'S DRAWERS WITH BAND.

JACONET WRAPPER WITH CAPE.—BACK.

NT LACE EMBROIDERY.
VIII., Figs. 26-28.

EMBROIDERED MUSLIN NIGHT-SACQUE.
For pattern, design, and description see Supplement, No. IV., Figs. 15-17.

JACONET AND LACE NIGHT-CAP.
For pattern and description see Supplement, No. VI., Figs. 22 and 23.

MAGDALA COLLAR.
For pattern and description see Supplement, No. XXI., Figs. 67 and 68.

GENTLEMAN'S NIGHT-SHIRT.
For pattern and description see Supplement, No. XVI., Figs. 52-58.

CUFF WITH SLOPED ENDS.
For pattern and description see Supplement, No. XXIV., Fig. 71.

O. XXII., Fig. 69.

PADDOCK COLLAR.
For pattern and description see Supplement, No. XX., Figs. 65 and 66.

REVERSIBLE CUFF.
For pattern and description see Supplement, No. XXV., Fig. 72.

EMBROIDERED UNDER-WAIST.
For pattern and description see Supplement, No. XII., Figs. 40-44.

KHEDIVE COLLAR.
For pattern and description see Supplement, No. XVII., Figs. 59 and 60.

LADY'S CHEMISE—CLOSED ON THE SHOULDER.
For pattern and description see Supplement, No. V., Figs. 18-21.

CRAVAT FOR MORNING DRESS.

JACONET DRESSING-SACQUE.—BACK.
For pattern and description see Supplement, No. I., Figs. 1-3.

LINEN NIGHT-CAP.
For pattern and description see Suppl., No. VII., Figs. 24 and 25.

JACONET WRAPPER WITH CAPE.—FRONT.

LADY'S MUSLIN DRAWERS—CLOSED AT THE SIDE.

LADY'S NIGHT-DRESS WITH STANDING COLLAR.

OUT OF FASHION.

THE *Bazar* has much pleasure in presenting its lady readers with a few ridiculous Old Fashions, the absurdity of which, when contrasted with the Modern Style, will at once become apparent.

Bar-maid of the Cleopatra period, some years (B C. Before Crinoline); a period at which there was a good deal of waste, notably in the way of melted pearls.

Married Lady in the thirteenth century, with her Sunday Turban on, and Respirator of that epoch; thought at the time to be sweetly pretty. Unmarried Ladies of a flirtish turn wore the Respirator a couple of inches lower.

Another period, after Crinoline had gone out and Feathers had come in with great severity. Ladies were Short-sighted about this time; previously it was not fashionable.

A Buck, Blood, or Dandy of the time of the Regency. At this period gentlemen actually wore blue coats with brass buttons in the evening, and absurdly large shirt-collars. We know much better now.

Magnificent specimen of the Modern Swell; undoubtedly the finest and noblest male creature extant.

A Little Thing peeping out of a window, in the fourteenth century, in Royal Bonnet of that time. Awkward to get in and out of omnibuses, if there had happened to be any!

Here you may see the ridiculous old fashion of yesterday; the high heels and piled-up chignon of our great-grandmothers very properly giving place to the heelless shoe and modest plaited hair, as worn by our mammas when our papas fell in love with them, in 1830 or thereabouts. As to what our daughters are to wear when they grow up we really haven't the time to bother about just at present.

They had a way of wrapping up all that was precious in the fifteenth century, of which this is a specimen. Perhaps some of them might have borne more wrapping up still, with advantage. It's an open question.

DINING-CAR ON THE UNION PACIFIC RAILWAY.

SHOPPING IN BROADWAY.

W.S.L.Jewett.

A FASHIONABLE WEDDING.—[Sketched by Thomas Worth.

THE COMING SEASON

The Dowager's Stud Book

Coming out

Four girls to Commoners
The fifth must have a Coronet

Came out last Season

Not shelved yet

Engines of War

Didn't come out yesterday

A royal Salute

Apropos de bottes

Will conquer or Die

Evening Dress?

Frou-Frou

The Locketomanic

The Gordian

Chignon à la Minerve

FASHIONS TO FOLLOW

Elevators

Receipts.

CHICKEN PILLAU.

Ingredients.—Chicken,
      One-eighth of a pound of salt pork,
      Three cups of rice,   Salt and pepper.

Cut the chicken in rather small pieces; wash clean and put in stew-pan with the pork also cut in small pieces. Cover with cold water, and boil gently till the chicken is tender, then season highly with salt and pepper, and add the rice; let this boil thirty or forty minutes. There should be a full quart of the liquor when rice is added; care must be taken that it does not burn.

BOSTON DROP CAKES.

Ingredients.—One pound of flour,
      Three-quarters of a pound of sugar,
      One-quarter of a pound of butter,
      Five eggs,
      One wineglass of rose-water.

Beat butter and sugar to a cream; add the eggs, well beaten, flower and rose-water. Drop on a floured tin sheet with a teaspoon; sprinkle a few colored sugar caraway seeds on the top.

SOME POPULAR CHRISTMAS GAMES.

"HUNT THE SLIPPER."

"HIDE·AND·SEEK"

"BLIND MAN'S BUFF."

"HEAVY, HEAVY WHAT HANGS OVER."

"PUSSY-IN-A-CORNER"

"CONSEQUENCES"

WEDDING CAKE.

Ingredients.—Twelve pounds of currants,
      Eight pounds of flour,
      Eight pounds of sugar,
      Eight pounds of butter.
      Fifty-six eggs,
      One ounce of nutmegs,
      Half an ounce of cloves,
      Half a pint of brandy,
      One pint of yeast,
      Half a pound of citron,   Saffron.

Mix these ingredients as for any kind of cake; if you desire it to look dark colored, take a little brandy and steep half a teacup of saffron in it, pour the liquid into the cake. If you desire frosting, reserve the whites of eight of the eggs, thicken with powdered sugar, flavor with lemon-juice.

PINEAPPLE PUDDING.

Ingredients.—Grated pineapple,   Sugar,   Butter,
      Five eggs,   Cup of cream.

Peel the pineapple, taking care to get out all the specks and hard parts; grate it, then take its weight in sugar, and half its weight in butter. Rub these to a cream and stir into the apple; add the eggs and cream. Bake in paste in a moderate oven.

NOTHINGS.

Ingredients.—Three eggs,   Saltspoonful of soda,
      Flour.

Beats the eggs; add soda, a little salt, and flour enough to make a stiff batter; roll very thin, and fry in hot lard. Put two together with jelly between.

TIP TOP GINGERBREAD.

Ingredients.—Half a pound of butter,
      Three-quarters of a pound of sugar,
      Seven eggs,
      Three-quarters of a pound of flour,
      Yellow ginger.

Beat butter and sugar to a froth. Add the eggs, one at a time, well beaten; then flour and ginger.

WATER ICE.

Ingredients.—Seven lemons,   Whites of six eggs,
      One quart of water.

Squeeze juice from lemons; add water, and make very sweet with white sugar. Add the whites of eggs, well beaten. Mix together and freeze.

TOMATO OYSTER SOUP.

Ingredients.—Five ripe tomatoes,
      One pint of water,
      Teaspoonful of soda,
      One quart of milk,
      Small piece of butter,
      Two pounded crackers,
      Pepper and salt.

Boil tomatoes in the water and soda; add the milk, butter, pepper and salt. and thicken with the crackers; let it boil, and serve very hot.

FRICASSE OF BEEF.

Ingredients.—Cold roast beef,
      One pint of water,
      Tablespoonful of flour,
      Salt,   Pepper,   Butter.

Put the water into a frying-pan, and, when it boils, add flour, a little butter, pepper and salt; cut the beef in thin slices, put them into the gravy and let them boil five minutes; if you have beef gravy, use it and omit the butter. Serve with boiled potatoes, tomatoes, rice or macaroni, and squash.

SALT FISH IN CREAM.

Ingredients.—Salt Fish,   One quart of water,
      One pint of new milk or cream,
      One spoonful of flour
      Butter and pepper.

Tear the fish into small strips; wash clean and put into a pan with the water. Let it simmer half an hour, pour off the water, and add the milk or cream; when this comes to a boil thicken with the flour. Let it boil five minutes; add a good sized piece of butter and a little pepper.

Receipts.

MARBLE CAKE.

Ingredients.—White part : Two cups of flour,
One and a half cups of sugar,
Half a cup of butter,
Half a cup of milk,
Four eggs (whites only),
Half a teaspoonful of cream of tartar,
Quarter of a teaspoonful of soda,
Spice to taste.
Dark part : Two and a half cups flour,
Half a cup of butter,
One cup of sugar,
Half a cup of molasses,
Half a cup of milk,
Four yelks of eggs and white of one,
Half a teaspoonful of soda,
Half a teaspoonful of cream of tartar,
Cloves, Cinnamon, Mace.

Mix these separately, and drop into the baking pan by tablespoonfuls alternately. Bake two hours; this makes two loaves, and is very nice.

ICING FOR MARBLE CAKE.

Ingredients.—One cup of white sugar,
One egg, white only.

Put to the cup of sugar water enough to dissolve it, set it on the fire and let it boil till it will "hair;" beat the white of the egg to a stiff froth; pour the heated sugar on the egg and stir briskly until cool enough to stay on the cake. It should not be put on till the cake is nearly or quite cold. This will frost only the top of the loaves; if more is needed, double the ingredients.

CURRANT JELLY.

The currants should be ripe and fresh picked. Put them on to the fire with only water enough to prevent burning; let them stew gently till they turn white, strain them through a sieve. To one pint of juice add a pound of sugar, boil it half an hour, then put a spoonful on a plate and set on ice; if boiled sufficiently it will stiffen in five minutes, if it does not stiffen boil longer, try it every five minutes. When done, strain through a *very* fine sieve or coarse muslin into glass jars, set them in the sun two days, then tie paper over them.

PICCOLOMINI CAKE.

Ingredients.—One cup of butter,
Two and a half cups of sugar,
Four eggs, One cup of milk,
Four cups of flower,
Half a teaspoonful of soda,
One teaspoonful of cream of tartar.

Beat butter and sugar to a cream; add eggs beaten to froth, then milk, with the soda dissolved in it. Put cream tartar dry into the flour, season with rosewater and nutmeg or extract of almond. Is a delicate cake, and very nice.

RASPBERRY VINEGAR.

Ingredients.—Three pounds of raspberries,
One quart of white wine vinegar,
One pound of white sugar,

Put the vinegar to the berries, and let it stand three days; then strain it, and to each pint of the juice add a pound of white sugar; let this boil a few minutes, skim it, let it cool, then bottle. Nice *cider* vinegar is as good as wine. A refreshing drink for a sick person. Two tablespoonfuls in a tumbler of water is sufficient.

TOMATO CHOW-CHOW.

Ingredients.—Six large, ripe tomatoes,
One large onion, One green pepper,
One tablespoonful of salt,
Two tablespoonfuls of brown sugar,
Two cups of vinegar.

Peel and cut fine the tomatoes, chop fine the onion and pepper; add salt, sugar, and vinegar. Stew gently one hour.

BAKED BLUE FISH.

Ingredients.—Salt pork, Bread crums,
Parsley, Pepper, Salt, One egg.

Make a dressing of two cups of bread crums, a little salt pork cut fine, parsley, pepper and salt, and one egg. Mix this all together, and stuff the body of the fish and sew it up. Fry a very little pork a nice brown; add half a teacup of hot water, lay the fish into the baking-pan, dredge well with flour, and baste with the pork fat; dish the fish, then add a little water, flour, and butter; let it boil, and turn over the fish.

STRAWBERRY SHORT CAKE.

Ingredients.—One cup of sour milk,
One-third of a teaspoonful of soda,
One-quarter of a teaspoonful of salt,
Two tablespoonfuls of butter.

Mix these, and bake in a quick oven. While baking, take a pint and a half of strawberries; mash them fine. When the cake is baked, split in two, and butter each part. Put on a layer of sugar, then strawberries, then sugar, then the top of cake, and serve immediately.

DESIGN FOR A COUNTRY HOUSE.

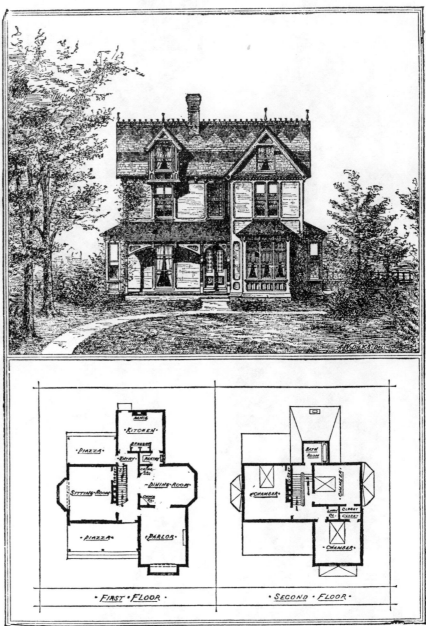

This plan, though adapted to moderate wants, has every convenience. The arrangement presents several good features. Though a small house, it makes a good show by having the greatest length on the front. The front and rear piazzas; the isolation of the sitting-room, always insuring its coolness; the rear entry, giving access to all parts of the house without going through the rooms, will be fully appreciated. There are six bed-rooms and bath-room, all properly lighted and ventilated. The house is heated by heater in cellar. It is of frame, with roofs of black and pale-green slate. It will cost from $2500 to $3000, according to the finish. All information, estimates, etc., will be furnished by

A. W. DILKS, Architect,
307 Walnut St., Phila.

Fig. 2.

Fig. 6.

Fig. 1.

Fig. 5.

Fig. 7.

Fig. 8.

Fig. 9.

Fig. 10.

Fig. 12.

Fig. 11.

Fig. 14.

Fig. 13.

Fig. 17.

Fig. 15.

Fig. 16.

Fig. 20.

Fig. 18.

Fig. 19.

LADIES' PARIS FASHIONS.

DESCRIPTION OF PLATES.

No. 1.—Young lady's ball dress. The corsage is cut low and square at the neck, trimmed with a full ruche of tulle, which also forms the sleeves. It has a shirred, pointed plastron at the centre-

3.—FRONT OF RED FLANNEL DRESS.

front, and the lower part is shaped into a point at the front and back. A full drapery is attached to the corsage at the left side, and a scarf drapery covers the right edge, and this is draped upon the former, under a bouquet of flowers. The draperies are edged with lace. The skirt trimmings consist of horizontal puffings, two lace ruches, and a box pleating at the foot.

5.—SURAH AND LACE EVENING CORSAGE.

No. 2.—Ottoman velvet and brocaded faille dinner dress. The corsage with a square medicis collar, stiffly lined and wired to keep in position, opens square upon the chest, with two revers formed by the two sides of the collar, which continue along the front opening. The lower part shapes into a point at each side, with a scarf drapery passing underneath, and draped very full at the back. The plain skirt of brocade is slashed at the sides, showing the under part entirely pleated. The cuffs are plain, like the brocade skirt, but the trimming at the sides and back of the corsage is plain.

Nos. 3 and 4.—Front and back of red flannel dress trimmed with black velvet ribbon. The front and back

1.—YOUNG LADY'S BALL DRESS.   2.—OTTOMAN VELVET AND BROCADED FAILLE DINNER DRESS.

of body are pleated to the plain yoke. Narrow collar and cuffs and sash tied at the centre-back.

No. 5.—Surah and lace evening corsage. This is of pale blue surah, with full paniers of the same material pleated over the lower part of the corsage. A short lace-edged drapery is set at the centre-back between the paniers. The corsage is laced at the back, and the bertha trimming at the low neck is of pleated blue tulle lace and ribbon. A long spray of dark red poppies

with foliage starts from the right shoulder and crosses the front diagonally with the end falling upon the left panier. This corsage is worn with a skirt of blue tulle and lace, also trimmed with clusters of the same flowers as those upon the corsage.

No. 6.—Surah and tulle evening corsage. This corsage of pale yellow satin is worn over a surah dress of the same tint, richly ornamented with

Spanish lace. It shapes into a point at the centre-front, and into three at the back, the two side points being very much longer than the centre one. The bertha neck trimming is of shirred tulle with a heading at the top; following the tulle are two sprays of flowers, one for front, the other for back. Tulle pleating edges armholes.

No. 7.—Myrtle green cloth and velvet basque. The back is cut like an ordinary basque, the front is pleated and joins to a plain yoke. Panier

4.—BACK OF RED FLANNEL DRESS.

drapery is secured to the lower edge, the joining covered by a velvet scarf knotted at the front.

No. 8.—Dress for girl from three to five years. Pale blue cashmere is the dress material, the trimming is of blue and white checked silk, and edging of pale blue embroidery on a white foundation. The double-breasted fronts close with pearl buttons. Narrow pleating edges bottom of dress.

No. 9.—Dress for little girl. The materials are Scotch tartan plaid and plain olive green cheviot.

6.—SURAH AND TULLE EVENING CORSAGE.

The kilt skirt is made with a box pleat at the centre-front. The plastron of the same goods buttons along the centre. The jacket of cheviot is bordered with a pleating, and has pointed revers and cuffs. These and the jacket edge are trimmed with soutache.

No. 10.—Shirred capote for young lady, of surah and lace. The box-pleated brim is raised in a point at the front. The edge of the crown is shirred in a wide band to have the fullness form a large puff. Triple alsacien bow of velvet at the front of the crown; strings of same.

7.—MYRTLE GREEN CLOTH BASQUE.

8 AND 9.—DRESSES FOR LITTLE GIRLS.

10.—SHIRRED CAPOTE.

Happy Hours

LADIES' PARIS FASHIONS.

DESCRIPTION OF PLATES.

Nos. 1 and 4.—Toilette for young girl, with blouse corsage; skirt of pale rose-colored veiling. The first flounce is shirred. Above this are three flounces of embroidery, headed by a puffed flounce. The overskirt is of the plain veiling, and falls behind in two points. Blouse corsage of gros-grain or ottoman velvet. Round belt and steel buckle.

Nos. 2 and 5.—Costumes for the seaside. The skirt of No. 2 is composed of three wide flounces and two small ones; they are formed of pleatings of bronze satin, alternating with plain bands of pale-green surah. Cuirasse corsage of the pale-green with a shell pleating of lace and bronze satin; shoulder cape with a First Consul collar, held in very tightly on the chest with a knot of the same. Round hat of bronze straw, lined with bronze satin; bronze satin ribbons around the crown and cluster of roses on the front. The other costume, No. 5, is a checked taffetas dress, white and brown overskirts, and round waist with shirt covered with plain foulard embroidery. Belt and ribbon of brown velvet.

No. 3.—White nainsook dress, for child of five or six, trimmed with embroidery.

Nos. 6 and 8.—Front and back of surah and crepe dress for young lady. Skirt of cream-colored surah trimmed at the bottom with a pleating, surmounted by a puffing; the latter does not continue on the back breadths, which are covered by a silk drapery. The rest of the draperies, both back and front, are of cream-colored English crepe; large cluster of pink flowers and knots of cream-colored ribbons at the side; pointed corsage of surah, with a fichu and shirred chemisette of crape; sleeves of the same, made of a puffing and pleating; cluster of pink flowers on the left shoulder.

No. 7.—Evening corsage. This pretty corsage of ecrue grenadine is made up over a rose-colored silk lining. A garland of roses of different colors forms a plastron, and heads the lace ruffling on the elbow sleeves.

WHIPPED CHILDREN.

Some women cuff their children out of pure laziness. It is so much easier to box little Johnny's ears than to tell him why he should not do this or that. It is so much less troublesome to slap Hannah Ann for breaking something than it is to teach her how to use it so that it shall not be broken. Punishment of the flesh for the sins of the soul or the errors of the mind is a simple relic of barbarism, even if it is done because the person who punishes thinks it a duty to use stick or switch or whip or slipper on the tender skin of some little child. It never made a boy better yet, and it only crushes the spirit of a girl. You may repeat "Spare the rod and spoil the child" as often as you like; blind beating of the little ones does not carry out the idea, which is, that you must not let them go to destruction for want of reproof or admonition. It is a moral rod that is meant, not one of birch or willow. Men love the fathers whose "You must not" was law; the mothers whose "I'd rather you would not" was a barrier not to be overleaped. But a cruel, unexplained beating has turned the heart of many a child from its parent for ever. Walking through a village street, I saw an illustration of this one day. Some furious cattle were being driven up the road beyond. Two boys started out of their gates, anxious, as boys always are, to be in the midst of danger. One mild woman called out gently: "Don't go, Tom. You might get hurt; and at least you would make me anxious." Her boy came back and said: "I shouldn't get hurt, but I don't want to worry you, mother." After the other boy came a furious little woman, with a switch, crying: "I'll beat you to a jelly when I catch you, Jim!" but she did not catch him. As for little girls born in respectable families, where they see nothing very wrong, they will follow their mothers as lambs follow the parent sheep. If she will only patiently tell them what to do, they will do it; and when they are tired, or have their feelings hurt, and seem to cry without reason, the way is to talk to them, find out what they are thinking, what powerful little reason or terror moves them, and explain it away. Whipped children are miserable little creatures, who make the whole house unhappy. Remember that before you switch your boys or slap your girls.

PAPER FLOWERS.

The Best Paper Flower Outfit contains over 60 samples of paper, Book of Instructions, Made Flowers, Patterns, also Material for making 12 flowers. Mailed on receipt of 25c. 25 Sheets best Imported Paper assorted colors for 50c.

MADISON ART CO., Madison, Conn.

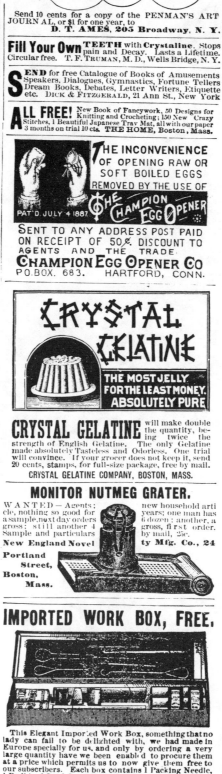

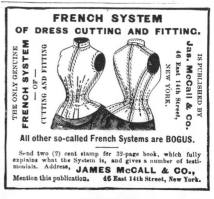

AFFLICTION.

It is by affliction that the heart of man is purified, and that the thoughts are fixed on a better state. Prosperity, alloyed and imperfect as it is, has power to intoxicate the imagination, to fix the mind upon the present scene, produce confidence and elation, and to make him who enjoys affluence and honors forget the hand by which they were bestowed. It is seldom that we are otherwise than by affliction awakened to a sense of imbecility, or taught to know how little all our acquisitions can conduce to safety or to quiet.

1 AND 4.—COSTUME WITH BLOUSE CORSAGE.

3.—DRESS FOR LITTLE GIRL.

2 AND 5.—SEASIDE TOILETTES.

6.—FRONT OF SURAH AND CREPE DRESS.

7.—EVENING CORSAGE.

8.—BACK OF SURAH AND CREPE DRESS.

Happy Hours

EVERY-DAY DRESSES, GARMENTS, ETC.

BY EMILY H. MAY.

No. 1—Is a walking-costume, of self-colored nun's-veiling, in a very delicate shade of pearl-gray. Albatross, pongee, or sateen would be equally suitable material for this model. The

No. 1.

skirt has a deep kilted flounce, (say eighteen inches.) The tunic has an apron-front, edged with lace or open-worked embroidery, and the back is simply draped to form irregular puffs. The basque is quite long and close-fitting, like a coat, buttoning on the right side with small bullet-shaped buttons. The edge of the basque, the rolling collar, and cuffs are trimmed to correspond with the skirt. A plaited vest, with close standing collar, is fitted to fill in the open neck of the basque made by the rolling collar; or, if preferred, a plain round plaited waist with tight sleeves may be added to this costume for house-wear; and for the street, the coat-basque worn over the plain waist. A belt, with rosette and long loops of satin ribbon two inches wide, will be required to finish the round waist. Any of the embroidered sateen robes, made after this

model—as it is simple—would be more stylish than the elaborate designs which usually come with such dress-patterns. Eight, nine, or ten yards of double-fold goods will be required.

No. 2—Is a costume suitable for either house or street. Our model calls for a surah silk skirt of electric-blue, (silk skirts, with overdress of cashmere, or other soft woolen material, are the latest novelty,) with overdress of summer cashmere of precisely the same shade. The skirt is kilted from a yoke, which just escapes the point of the basque; over this, from the waist of the

No. 2.

yoke, the side panels of the cashmere are arranged plaited in wide plaits at the waist, and all these six wide plaits fulled into a narrow point at the end of the panel, as seen in illustration. One width of the cashmere is slightly puffed to fill in the back drapery. A wide open guipure muslin embroidery edges the front of these panels, turning the point, and is lost under the back drapery. A closely-fitting basque, pointed back and front,

with close sleeves, has cuffs and deep collar made of the embroidery. Plain self-colored sateen, made up in this style, trimmed with Hamburg or open-worked embroidery, would be equally stylish, although not so elegant. Maroon sateen, with écru embroidery, or dark-blue, with white embroidery, would be very effective. Seven yards of surah silk for skirt, and six yards cashmere, will be required. Three and a half yards, of four inches wide embroidery for panels and cuffs; one and a quarter yards of wider for collar, or two yards of the four inch, using two rows, shaping the collar over a paper pattern, cut to fit.

No. 3—Is a dressy breakfast-costume, of white nainsook, linen lawn, or any white goods having sufficient body to lay in kilts for the trimming of the skirt. A plain round skirt, with a deep flounce, kilted, reaching to the knee, is all of the skirt. Two flounces of embroidered muslin head this kilted flounce. The long basque, or matinée, as it is called, is made tight in the back, and not entirely so in front. The length

No. 3.

of it is adjusted so that the embroidered flounce which edges it may exactly meet the upper one on the skirt. This requires careful cutting, fitting, and trimming. Some modistes put all three flounces upon the matinée. A row of the embroidery is put on down the front in a full ruffle, so that it may fall in a jabot. Pockets, collar, and edge of sleeves trimmed with the em-

lace, and tied with crimson or pale-pink ribbons, or else one of those cheap pongees trimmed with écru embroidery or lace—ribbons of the same color or contrasting. Twelve to fifteen yards of embroidered ruffling. Ten yards of yard-wide material.

No. 4—Is a morning wrapper, of flannel or cashmere, of any useful color. The form is Princess, and half-fitting. The ornaments are either braiding or appliqué. Lace or em-

of gold braid, laid on a foundation of the cashmere, shaped to fit. Tiny gilt buttons ornament both sides of the plastron. The right side buttons over. The sleeves are trimmed to correspond, and ornamented with buttons. Collar standing, covered with rows of the braid.

No. 6—Is a pretty little costume, for a girl of four to six years, made of white piqué. The ruffles which trim the skirt are of nainsook, and are mounted upon a petticoat-waist. The little coat-basque cuts off in front, at the top of the second ruffle, ending in square coat-tails at the back. Ball buttons of pearl or ivory are the only trimmings. A deep linen collar and cuffs are worn with this costume. For the seaside or mountains, make of navy-blue or white flannel.

No. 7.—Pelisse, for a baby of two to three years. Cashmere, flannel, or piqué, trimmed with open-work English embroidery. A simple sacque, with deep collar.

No. 8—Is a blouse-dress, for a child of three years. Made of Turkey-red twill or flannel, and trimmed with black braid, it is a most useful garment for a child to play about in. Made of cashmere or white flannel, and trimmed with black velvet ribbon, it is a very stylish and dressy costume. It is simply a skirt plaited into a yoke, and belted at the waist; being tied loosely by a sash made of the material, and trimmed to match.

No. 4.

No. 6.

No. 8.

broidery. A two-inch-wide ribbon ties the collar, and a wider one is tied loosely from the side seams at the waist, also a bow and ends at the back. The sleeves in our model are slightly gathered at the wrist, edged with the embroidery, and tied with the ribbon. A close sleeve, with a simple cuff of the embroidery, we would prefer. For a more elaborate breakfast-toilette, we would suggest black surah silk, trimmed with Spanish

broidery may be used for trimming, if preferred.

No. 5—Is a corsage of cashmere, with plastron. The corsage is of marine-blue cashmere,

No. 5.

No. 7.

cut with a long point in front and a petite basque in the back. The plastron is composed of rows

No. 9.—Sailor-frock, of blue serge, for a boy of three years. Kilted skirt. The sailor-waist has a deep collar, edged with red or pale-blue braid. Cuffs to match.

No. 9.

STRAW BONNET.

LACE FICHU.

WAIST FOR HOUSE-DRESS.

HOUSE-DRESS: FRONT AND BACK.

STRAW BONNET.

FRONT OF MANTELET.

BACK OF MANTELET.

HOUSE-DRESS. WALKING-DRESS.

COLLARETS.

SPRING STYLE FOR WALKING-DRESS.

CHILDREN'S FASHIONS FOR MARCH.

CHILD'S STRAW HAT.

CHILDREN'S FASHIONS FOR APRIL.

CHILDREN'S FASHIONS FOR JULY.

BATHING-DRESSES. STRAW HAT.

BONNETS.

NEW STYLES FOR SUMMER DRESSES.

Peterson's Magazine

EVERY-DAY DRESSES, GARMENTS, ETC.

BY EMILY H. MAY.

No. 1—Is a simple and stylish model for a costume of pongee or nun's-veiling. The skirt is kilted into a yoke, fitting the waist and hips. The tunic is arranged to simulate a polonaise; opens in front, and is gathered up high on the

No. 1.

sides; the fullness at the back is slightly puffed and made to come out between the side-seams of the basque. The basque is pointed in front, rounding up towards the sides, and then curves into a short point at the side-back seams, where it is left open for three inches, for the drapery of the back to be pulled through. The back of the basque forms a postillion. The trimming for this costume is of guipure embroidery (white), which is laid on flat, being sewed on the under side and then turned up on the material. The fronts and sides of the tunic are trimmed, but not the back. Cuffs, collar, and fronts of the waist are arranged to correspond. At the point of the basque in front, two loops, with long ends of satin-faced velvet ribbon of the same color as the material, or of a contrasting color, are tied in a bow. Nine to ten yards of nun's-veiling, double-fold, or pongee, which is generally sold by the piece of nineteen or twenty yards. A piece will be required, as it is narrow. Six yards of embroidery, one dozen buttons, two and a half yards of velvet ribbon.

No. 2—Is a dressy and becoming model for a foulard or summer silk, also suitable for a grenadine or embroidered muslin. The skirt has three inches back, forming the puff, as seen in the illustration; from this the fullness is looped back, forming paniers. The back is very bouffant, and arranged in irregular puffs. A deep fringe of silk edges the tunic as far as the sides. The basque is pointed back and front. The trimming on the front of the waist is made and put on: gathered into a point, to fit the waist; this is fastened in place on the right side. The dress buttons underneath; hooks and loops, or several pins, will keep the other side in place. The

No. 2.

collar and cuffs are of plain or brocaded velvet. Twenty yards of twenty-four-inch-wide foulard will be required, or twenty-five of eighteen-narrow box-plaited ruffles, each two and a half inches deep when completed; these are put on just to touch each other. The fullness forming the puffed tunic is sewed on to the seam of the upper ruffle and then turned up, forming a slightly drooping puff all round. This is gathered into a deep yoke at the waist, the same as would be used for a kilted skirt. The tunic is gathered lengthwise, with four or five rows of gathers close together, then another, two

inch summer silk—wider material, of course, in proportion—three yards of fringe, one dozen buttons.

No. 3.—For a young girl from fourteen to sixteen years, we have here a stylish toilette of checked woolens or checked sateen. A kilted skirt, with an apron overskirt, which is trimmed across the front with white Hamburg or guipure embroidery. The waist is gathered into a yoke, and then into the waist both back and front. The yoke is trimmed with the embroidery to simulate a deep sailor's collar. The basque skirt is plain, and cut to fit in front and over the hips; in the back three double box-plaits are arranged; this is trimmed with the embroidery all round, and where it joins the waist a black velvet ribbon ties in front, as seen in the illustration. This basque skirt fastens at the left side under the first box-plait. Cuffs to match. Twelve to fourteen yards of double-fold goods, or ten to twelve yards of yard-wide material, such as sateen. This is a very suitable model for a wash-dress, other than sateen, gingham, zephyr cloth, etc.

No. 4—Is quite a novel design for a combination costume. Our model calls for cashmere and brocaded silk. Grenadine, plain and brocaded, we think would be equally suitable. First there is the kilted skirt of the cashmere, with a box-plait down the front. This is arranged on a yoke, as we have described above. The drapery is arranged to form an irregular tablier, the plain cashmere beginning at the point on the right side, under the basque; from under this the

No. 3.

brocade is arranged, forming a petite tunic; this meets the drapery of the back, as may be seen in the illustration. The pointed basque has a plastron of the brocade down the front, and the cuffs are also of the brocade. The basque may be either pointed in the back, or finished with two double plaits forming a habit-postillion—this is altogether a matter of taste. Two yards of brocaded silk, ten yards of cashmere, will be required. Of grenadine or single-width goods, sixteen to eighteen yards will be required.

No. 5.

No. 7.

No. 4.

No. 6.

No. 6—Is a costume suitable for either boy or girl of three years. Made of flannel, cashmere, linen, or checked gingham. The elongated waist is made to fit the figure neatly; the back is plain, with coat-seams. The fronts have a plastron gathered and fitted upon the waist. A box-plaited skirt is attached to the waist, and a wide sash ties in a bow at the back.

No. 8.—For a boy of four to five years, we have the short pants, with plaited blouse. A belt of the material, or a leather belt, is worn over the blouse. Tiny buttons are the only trimming. The back is box-plaited, as the front —without the buttons, of course.

No. 8.

No. 5.—For a little girl of four years, we have plaited skirt and waist plaited into a yoke. Over this fitted the little jacket, which is turned back with an embroidered edge. A wide sash of the material forms the belt, and ties in a large bow at the back, holding the sides and back of the jacket in place. A deep linen collar and cuffs are worn with this costume. Make of flannel, cashmere, or wash-goods.

No. 7.—For an infant of two to three years, we give a model for a piqué dress. Princess in front, with a plaited back. Hamburg or English embroidery trims the front: two rows, turning back from the buttoned front; the same passes around the edge of the garment, over a narrow plaited ruffle of nainsook. Wide sailor collar, cut in three deep vandykes at the back, with cuffs to match. A wide ribbon sash completes this costume.

1.—COIFFURE.

2.—DRESS FOR GIRL.

3.—DRESS FOR GIRL.

LADIES' PARIS FASHIONS.

DESCRIPTION OF PLATES.

Nos. 1 and 4—Two new styles of hair-dressing.

No. 2.—Cashmere and velvet dress for little girl. The jacket is made of bronze velvet. The bouffant and skirt of pale blue cashmere.

No. 3.—Cashmere dress for little girl. The vest revers, sash and cuffs can be made of a different colored cashmere or of satin.

No. 5.—Costume of golden brown, dahlia or plum-colored repped wool. False skirt covered with a pleated skirt. Tablier draped in a shawl point, and raised very high near the hips. At the back is a small *pouf* coquettishly draped. Gypsy jacket. The fronts open widely, and are fastened only at the neck. They are trimmed by a small round cord forming brandebourgs. Buttons terminate each one of these. The side forms of the back are slightly extended, and fasten over the box-pleated back in the same manner. Red velvet collar, cuffs and Swiss belt.

Nos. 6 and 7.—Front and back of dress for small child, of ecru embroidery over a colored silk slip. The front is shirred at the neck and at the bottom of the waist. The back has four pleats. The bottom of the dress is trimmed with a flounce of embroidery, and the same embroidery is used to form a collarette and tablier. A wider ribbon forms a belt, with knots on each side.

No. 8.—Striped wool dress. False skirt of silk, bordered with a taffetas pleating. Cloth jacket fitted behind and loose in front. The basque forms in the centre a triple pleat. The sides have small extensions which lie over on the centre forms, and are fastened there by buttons. Small turned-over collar and pockets on the chest and sides. Long sleeves with cuffs simulated by rows of mohair braid. Braid ornaments all the edges of the jacket.

———

A pretty way to make a table-spread is to have a border on two sides only. Suppose the spread to be of crimson felt, the border should be of plush or velvet or of velveteen, or even satin. Each block should have a different design embroidered or painted on it; the corner which has no border may be ornamented with embroidery. The entire spread should have a large, handsome cord or a flat braid around it at the edge. Here is afforded opportunity for the display of much ingenuity. Some of the blocks may be of crazy or mosaic patchwork and the others of plain material.

A girl's every-day toilet is a part of her character. The maiden who is slovenly in the morning is not to be trusted, however fine she may look in the evening. No matter how humble your room may be, there are eight things it should contain: a mirror, washstand, water, soap, towel, hair, nail and tooth brushes. These are just as essential as your breakfast, before which you should make good use of them. Parents who fail to provide their children with such appliances, not only make a mistake, but commit a sin of omission. Look tidy in the morning, and after the dinner work is over improve your toilet. Make it a rule of your daily life to "dress up" for the afternoon. Your dress may, or need not be, anything better than calico; but with a ribbon or flower, or some bit of ornament, you can have an air of self-respect and satisfaction, that invariably comes with being well dressed. A girl with sensibilities cannot help feeling embarrassed and awkward in a ragged, dirty dress, with her hair unkempt, if a stranger or neighbor should come in.

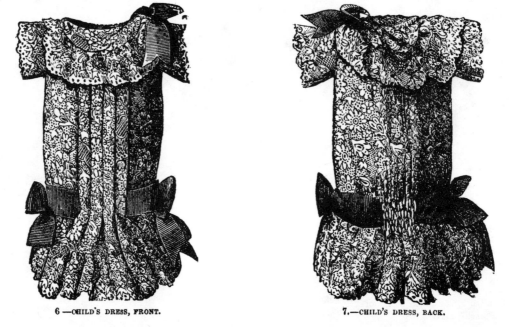

6.—CHILD'S DRESS, FRONT.

7.—CHILD'S DRESS, BACK.

5.—REPPED WOOL COSTUME.

4.—COIFFURE.

8.—STRIPED WOOL DRESS.

Moreover, your self-respect should demand decent apparel for your body. You should make a point to look as well as you can, even if you know nobody will see you but yourself.

One of the new fancies is called the soutache skirt, and consists of any cloth lower skirt covered as far as it is visible below the drapery by lengthwise rows of mohair braid sewed on one edge to throw it in high relief, placed near together, though not quite touching, and giving glimpses of the foundation skirt beneath. At the foot a border of braid is formed with points at the upper edge, while the lower edge is ravelled in fringe. The over-skirt is then without trimming, and is usually a simple apron drapery. The border of points and fringe is the trimming for the basque, and for the short, half-loose jacket added for the street.

Pale gray, prune-color, and maroon, are the colors worn by mothers at the wedding of their daughters, and these dresses are of plain velvet or the heaviest ottoman silk, with cords as thick as knitting-needles, for the basque and train, while the front and side breadths are satin of the same shade completely covered with flounces of old lace, either point d'Alencon or the fine black Chantilly lace.

Happy Hours

[FOR THE LADIES' HOME JOURNAL.]

SUMMER FASHIONS.

Dainty Dresses for Outdoors and Evening Wear. Novelties in Bodices and Summer Wraps.

BY JENNY JUNE.

There are many charming features of the present fashions, which are well adapted to the season, and especially becoming to the young. One is the use of simple materials, in fine stripes, and checks; another the return to simpler forms; and a third the substitution of natural (artificial) flowers, in place of the tinselled rubbish, which was for a time employed as a substitute. The delicate spring-like coloring too, is a matter for congratulation. The glaring reds and yellows are toned down, or have disappeared altogether. Soft shades of yellow are used, but in cooler and fresher combinations, with pale blue, or wood brown. Spring green, in lettuce, cress, and moss shades, appears in thin summer materials, as ornamentation, united with cool greys, fawns, and soft browns, reproducing atmospheric tones, and open-air effects; where there is sufficient intelligence, and knowledge of color, to work up available resources to the best advantage.

There is nothing striking that is not bad in street dress, the predominating influence being, exactly as it should be, quiet and practical. Young girls reserve the short cloth jackets, in fine check, or plain cloth, unlined, untrimmed, and only faced interiorly with silk, for cool morn-

ing wear in the country, over the cambric, gingham, batiste, or flannel gowns, which form the staple of the summer wardrobe. Trimmings have not disappeared, but they have become less elaborate, and less conspicuous. Dull wax beads are used for bordering, pearls, and delicate combinations of color, for open sprays; which show the silk beneath. The fine summer wools are trimmed with silk galloons, which have looped edges, and narrow ribbons are employed in the form of rosettes, and clustered loops; or panels, with gathered ends, which form a point, and is finished with a rosette.

The revival of the habit chemisette, or plaited vest, has had an instantaneous success because it is found so useful and becoming. In one, or another, it is universally adopted, some having it inserted as an integral part of the bodice, others

having several made independently, of foulard, or crepe, and ribbon, of ribbon, and lace, and the like, so that they can be adapted to any dress.

The outdoor garments for summer street wear, have grown smaller by degrees, until there is little left of them. The newest are mere capes, which fall an inch, or more short of the line of the waist, but have quite long ends in front, or they are made with narrow, fitted basque back, a shoulder cape for sleeve, and loose fronts. Most of them are masses of bead work, wrought into the meshes of silk netting which forms the open ground plan.

White embroidery, and white lace, are no longer used upon colored cottons, the work is

done in white, and colors upon the material. Some of it is executed in raised work, some in open work, some in solid color, some in varied colors, and some in different shades of one color, or in combination of a color with white

The study in grey and brown, which is given under the title of a "Summer Walking Dress," is copied from a batiste, the skirt of which is composed of brown stripes, and cluster lines of grey, and white. The overskirt and basque are checked, in the same colors, and the full vest is of soft silk, in lines of yellow, and brown. The cuffs and collar are of nut-brown velvet. The hat of crinoline, is of grey, striped with brown, and trimmed with brown velvet, and lilacs in the

natural color. The drapery is of the simplest, and falls in a series of natural ripples from the sides, which are turned back from the front. The back may be arranged with or without a *pouf*; the effect of the latter being to depress the centre, and throw the fulness more to the sides. There is a difference which should be noted this season, in the length of the sleeves.

For several years they have been very short, so that the arms must either be covered with very long gloves, or exposed to the roughening effects of sun, and wind. It is not always possible to wear long gloves, and often looks like an affectation, while for the majority, is useless extravagance. This year the sleeves are cut a more natural length, arms are better protected, and gloves do not need to be so long.

The application of drawn work to linen is shown in a pretty costume which a young lady wears who is evidently taking her little fox terrier for an airing. The detail of the work is given below, the spaces showing where ribbon, or velvet may be run in to add to the effectiveness of the work. The square mesh is usually about an inch and a-quarter in width, and is placed over a color, unless threading the diamond with narrow ribbon or silk cord, is preferred.

The model as here given, is of cream linen lawn. The overskirt falls straight all round. It is tucked in front, very finely, and bordered down

the sides, with three rows of drawn work, through which black velvet is run. Collar, and sleeves are finished to match. The chemisette is tucked to match front, only still more delicately, a bow of ribbon uniting the collar, at its points, and dividing the tucked vest, into upper and lower parts. The sailor hat is of coarse straw, is bound with black velvet, and trimmed with lettuce green ribbon, with double picot edge. The gloves, and parasol, are both of a very faint, and charming shade of lettuce green. The parasol, is covered with open, embroidered muslin.

The "tucked" bodice gives an idea of the uses to which tucking is put, and the new application of pinked, or what is called "flower" ruching, to indoor dressing. This pretty bodice is made of soft silk, or muslin, in any soft shade of forget-me-not blue, yellow, terra-cotta red, tinted white, or black. It is simply tucked to form a yoke, to mould the waist, and shape the top, and bottom of the sleeves. The finish is with pinked-out ruching of the material, except when made of

muslin, then it is with ruching, or looping of ribbon, or gathering of narrow (doubled) lace. It is a most useful little bodice for afternoon wear, with white skirts, and in black, or grey pongee, may be worn under a mantle, for the street, or in traveling.

Another pretty design, more suitable for dressy purposes than the preceding, is the "Cora" jacket. It is made in cloth, cashmere, Bengaline, *pean de soie*, plush, or velvet; lined with silk, and edged with dull wax beads. The model from which our illustration is drawn, is of golden brown plush, lined with pale yellow silk, and edged with dull, yellow wax beads. It is worn over a dress of India mull, with high, full waist, and long, full

sleeves, which show below the upturned cuff of the jacket. Two yards of plush, and two yards of silk will make it, and a few strings of rather large wax beads.

Some of the prettiest of the spring, and early summer costumes are of vicuna cloth, trimmed with moire antique, and having full vest of china crape, or surah. All the gray shades, from fawns to steel, are in favor; the watered silk matching the cloth, but the vest may be cress, or lettuce green. Cowslip yellow, a new and delicate combination with grey, or coral pink. Moire antique is used in combination with wool, and for the high collars, cuffs, *revers*, bands, stripes, panels, and the like, very much as velvet has been for two years past. It has not however, displaced velvet entirely.

Striped materials are as much in vogue as ever for tennis, croquet, and outdoor games. They are very simple, consisting of a rather short skirt, and "Garibaldi" bodice, which should be made of a plain material, or a narrower stripe than that of the skirt. The true Garabaldi bodice, is a loose blouse waist, cut long, so that the fulness which is gathered into the belt, falls over it. If the bodice is striped, the cuffs, and collar, are of a

plain material in the color of the stripe. There is no ruffle, flounce, or drapery upon the skirt, which may be simply gored, laid in perpendicular tucks across the front, and gathered at the back. A new idea this season, is the placing of square pockets at the sides of the skirt; and employing them instead of drapery to hold the back in position. They are useful, as well as effective, and render an apron with pockets unnecessary.

The dainty evening dress of sprigged muslin, will go straight to the hearts of all young lady readers. So inexpensive too, and so easily made. The skirt is perfectly plain, slightly gored, hemmed, and gathered straight, the fullness, of course, massed at the back, and only just enough of it distributed in front and upon the hips to make it hang well. There is no other draping, no looping, no bunching, and no overskirt; nothing but a panel at the left, formed of three sash ends of wide ribbon, graduated in length, gathered upon the ends, and attached by rosettes at unequal distances, to each other, and to the skirt. The bodice is round, and low, and finished with a little heading of lace, and ribbon; and the arms and neck. There are no sleeves, but the gloves come nearly to the top of the arms.

The design can be made much more expensive. The underdress may be of silk, with narrow plaitings upon the edge. Over this two skirts of silk tulle, one plain, the other dotted with silver, or sprigged with embroidery. The edge of the upper one finished by hand, with dots, and button-hole stitch, in filoselle. The ribbon may be silk, or satin, or moire, but it must match the sprig if this is in color, and the rosettes must exactly match the ribbon.

The new summer wraps are very small, and revive many old ideas. They are very short on the ack, and either form a sort of pelerine cape, with square ends in front, or a fitted basque back, with half sleeves, which are often composed wholly of falls of lace, or lace intermingled with ribbon loops. Many of the capes, and smaller mantles are composed wholly of jet, or jetted silk, woven in an open work, and showing pendant attachments. Others are in-wrought with lace, as in the jetted mantle, which we illustrate, and which is finished short across the back, and with no un-natural height, or fulness upon the shoulders.

The Lace Wrap is one of the prettiest, and most becoming of out-door garments for summer. It is of beaded lace, and jetted galloon. The back

is basque shaped, the fronts somewhat loose, but slightly gathered in, and the sleeves loose also, so

that a certain amount of fullness is gathered into the armholes, and the wrists, which are finished like the neck, front, and lower edge, with a ruching of lace, in which narrow loops of galloon are set.

Narrow ribbons, and galloons with looped edges, are among the newest, and most fashionable styles of ornamentation. The narrower the galloons, the closer the loops, the more there is of them in a series, the better, and more distinguished the design.

SEE HERE, GIRLS.

Girls, don't marry a man for money, position, or anything but love. Don't do it, if you want to live to a good old age and be happy. You may think that money can bring you all you desire, but it can't. That is where you are mistaken. It can buy a good many things, but it can never purchase contentment for your heart or happiness for your soul. It may bring temporary smiles to your face, but it will leave great shadows in your heart. Don't think that I would advise you to marry a worthless fellow, just because you imagine you love him. A refined, good, intelligent woman should never marry a vulgar, ill-bred man. No, no, never unite yourself to any one who is not a man in the truest meaning of the word. Neither could I advise a woman to marry a man who had no visible means of supporting her, but for heaven's sake don't marry a millionaire or a king, if you don't love him. It will not do. People have tried it time and again, only to find it a miserable failure. It may do for a while. You may revel in gilded halls, and be lost in the giddy rounds of pleasure, but a time will come when these things will be a hollow mockery to you. There will be "aching void" the world can never fill. Sometimes mothers are to blame for the unhappiness of their daughters. They teach them that respect for their husband and lots of "boodle" are infinitely to be preferred to that foolishness called love. That would do very well if life had no waves of trouble, but it takes something more than simple respect to make two hearts cling together in the hour of adversity. A woman that turns her back upon wealth, and takes the man of her choice may miss some of the luxuries of life, but she will be happy. Don't marry a dude. Better get you a monkey. It is cheaper and a great deal nicer. Don't fool with that class of animals. They generally wear a $10 hat on a ten cent brain, and the woman who takes one of these chaps will get left about as bad as the southern confederacy did at Appomattox.

EARLY EDUCATION.

America opens to her people on all sides, avenues of learning such as are enjoyed by few other countries. Her colleges, schools, (public and private) seminaries and academies are unnumbered, and that thing which makes the man or woman, more surely than anything else, save natural disposition, is to be had almost for the asking, if he has but time to ask.

Among us, however, there be many who, by reason of necessity, have lacked the time in early years, to obtain the "*early* education" so desirable. Later in life, when "easy circumstances" have made education possible, the work has been taken up, with perhaps fair results. But unfortunately, so constituted is the human mind, that with all the "book learning" one may acquire, the habits of early training or want of training will display itself in one's speech, unless one's particular faults are pointed out, and one strives specially against them. And nothing so immediately classifies the speaker as the manner in which he expresses what he has to say. A man is none the less a *good* man, a woman none the less a lovable, pleasant woman, because the grammar of each is faulty; because the sentences are ill-expressed. But why not add one more element of attractiveness?

Many of the bad habits of conversation, are *merely* bad habits—the result of a *carelessness* of speech more than anything else. There are many people, however, who really do not know how hair-like is the line between correct and incorrect speech. Nor is either class aware how the *little* faults affect the hearer; nor how the really refined, intelligent hearer at once classifies those around by their methods of speech.

Last winter, a gentleman was quite attracted by the appearance of a lady in a railway station. A bright, pretty-looking, pleasant-faced woman; an uncommonly attractive woman, bearing that in her manner and surroundings which betrayed wealth and refinement. Nothing flashy in the elegant sealskin coat; nothing gaudy in the expensive bonnet. Nothing about her but what a refined and intelligent gentlewoman should be and have. But alas!

A friend came up, and her first replies betrayed her, hopelessly:

"Did he, what did he do it *fur*? O my! Ain't that *terrible*! Naow ain't that awful!" she answered to some remark, in that nasal tone that makes the hearer shudder.

It was enough! The gentleman left; for there is nothing that will dispel an enchantment as some such thing as this.

It was with a view to correcting just such errors as these, and many others equally unsuspected by the speaker, that "Mildred's Conversation Class" was written; and it was to meet the demand for the back numbers of these very popular papers, that they were reprinted in book form. In their present shape they form a manual that should be in the hands of every woman who desires "Ease in Conversation," or "Hints on Grammar."

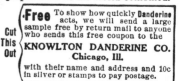

THE PRACTICAL HOUSEKEEPER.

[For the Ladies' Home Journal.]

BILL OF FARE FOR THANKSGIVING DINNER.

BY ELIZA R. PARKER.

Thanksgiving being a festal day that recalls old fashioned and homelike memories more fully than any other in the year's calendar, it should be the aim of housekeepers to serve such dishes as are associated in the minds of all with the days of their childhood, and remembrances of Grandmother's Thanksgiving dinners. And this may be done, with the addition of some more modern delicacies that gives the housewife an opportunity of displaying her skill in the art of cooking.

If the accompanying bill of fare be found too elaborate, it may be modified to suit the convenience of each household. The exercise of a little forethought and good management will enable the wife and mother burdened with many cares to prepare much of the dinner beforehand, and render the labor of the day much less.

Most pies are the better for being kept a day or two. The cake will improve with age. The pudding may be made, and warmed over for dinner, and the ices frozen the evening before.

A THANKSGIVING DINNER.

Raw Oysters.
Turtle Soup.
Boiled Fish. Anchovy Sauce.
Boiled Potatoes.
Roast Turkey. Giblet Sauce.
Chicken Pie.
Celery. Cranberry Jelly.
Mashed Potatoes. Turnips. Sweet Potatoes.
Roast Venison. Stuffed Ham.
Cauliflower. Squash. Boiled Onions.
Baked Salsify.
Celery Salad.
Thanksgiving Pudding.
Pumpkin Pie. Mince Pie.
Chocolate Ice Cream.
Thankgiving Cake. Neapolitan Cake.
Angel Cocoanut Cake.
Crackers. Cheese. Pickles.
Fruit.
Coffee.

Raw Oysters. Drain the oysters well, sprinkle with pepper and salt, and set on ice an hour before serving. Put on half shells with slices of lemon. Serve little thin slices of buttered brown bread with the oysters.

Turtle Soup. After cutting off the head, let the turtle hang for four or five hours with the neck downwards to bleed, then separate the two shells with a knife, being careful to remove the entrails whole. Cut the meat in several pieces, take the green fat and lay aside separate from the meat. Boil the shells and remove the mu-

cilage that adheres to the shells, and put in a dish. Put the head fins, heart and liver in a saucepan with a pound of ham, a dozen cloves, a bunch of sweet herbs and a sliced onion. Cover with the liquor in which the shells were boiled, and let cook gently till the meat is thoroughly done. Cut the meat into squares, melt half a pound of butter, thicken with flour, add to the liquor, boil gently for half an hour, strain, pour over the meat, add the green fat, the yolks of a dozen hard boiled eggs, the juice of two lemons and a tablespoonful of Cayenne pepper. Serve.

Boiled Fish. Anchovy Sauce. Wash the fish in cold water, wipe dry and rub with a little salt and lemon juice, wrap in a thin cloth, sew the edges, and put in a fish kettle. Cover with boiling water, add a tablespoonful of salt, and simmer gently, allowing eight minutes to every pound of fish. As soon as done take up the fish, remove the cloth, turn on a plate and garnish with slices of lemon. Serve with anchovy sauce.

Boiled Potatoes. Pare the potatoes, cover with cold water, boil gently until they are done. Pour off the water and sprinkle salt over them: then take each potato up in a clean warm cloth, with which press out all of the moisture; turn carefully into a dish and set before the fire, cover with a cloth until ready to send to the table.

Roast Turkey. Giblet Sauce. Select a fat young turkey. Singe and wash. Lard with fat bacon, fill with rich bread dressing, well seasoned. Lay a greased paper over the turkey and put in a deep pan with a teacup of boiling water, set in the oven, baste frequently. Roast for an hour and a half, then sprinkle with salt and pepper. When done the surface should be a rich brown.

To make sauce, boil the heart, liver and gizzaro in two quarts of water for two hours, take up, chop and return to the gravy with a spoonful of flour; season with pepper and salt, pour in the pan in which the turkey was cooked and stir. Serve in gravy boat with fried oysters.

Chicken Pie. Take two young chickens, cut up and boil tender, mince one small onion, put in the saucepan with the chicken, season with butter, salt and pepper. Beat two eggs and add to the liquor with a cup of cream. Line a tin pan with rich biscuit dough. Pour in the chicken, cover the top with rich pie crust and bake brown.

Sweet Potatoes. Boil and slice. Put in a deep pan a layer of sweet potatoes and a layer of butter and sugar until the pan is full. Set in the oven to brown. Sift sugar and nutmeg over the top.

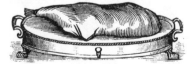

Roast Venison. Wipe the venison with a dry, coarse cloth. Lard with salt pork, sprinkle with salt, place in a baking pan with a teacup of boiling water and two ounces of butter; roast before the open fire, or bake in a very hot oven. Baste often. Bake one hour for every three pounds of meat. Just before dishing, pour in a teacup of vinegar, add two tablespoonfuls of currant jelly and a tablespoonful of grated cracker to the gravy. Serve with currant jelly.

Stuffed Ham. Boil a ham. Do not skin. Take one pound of bread crumbs, half a pound of butter, one teaspoonful each of ground

cloves, nutmeg, ginger, mace, celery salt, with half a teacup of sugar, two tablespoonfuls of mustard and six well beaten eggs. Mix well and moisten with cream. Gash the ham deep while hot, fill in with the dressing. Rub over with the white of an egg, sugar and grated cracker. Set in the oven to brown.

Cauliflower. Trim off the outside leaves and boil in salt water. Make sauce of an ounce of butter and a tablespoonful of flour melted together, thinned with a pint of soup stock, seasoned with salt and pepper. Pour over the cauliflower.

Squash. Cut the squash in halves, scrape out the soft part and seeds, put the halves in the oven and bake half an hour. Serve in the shell.

Baked Salsify. Boil tender and mash, season with salt, pepper and butter. Put in a baking dish. Beat an egg in a cup of cream, to which add a cup of stale bread crumbs. Put in the oven and bake brown.

Celery Salad. Take six heads of celery; wash and wipe dry; cut in small pieces in a salad bowl. Mix the yolk of one egg, a teaspoonful of mustard, a little salt and pepper and the juice of a lemon with two tablespoonfuls of water. Beat all together, pour four ounces of olive oil in drop by drop, to which add a small spoonful of hot water. Pour over the celery.

Thanksgiving Pudding. Take a pound of stale cake cut in slices, and lay in the bottom of a pudding dish. Cover with half a cup each of stoned raisins, chopped citron, candied cherries, chopped figs and blanched almonds, put another layer of sliced cake on top, pour a pint of milk over, with six beaten eggs, and a pint of sugar. Steam one hour and serve with currant jelly sauce.

Thanksgiving Cake. Two and a half pounds of flour, in which mix three teaspoonfuls of baking powder, two pounds of butter, three of sugar, eighteen eggs, half a pound of beaten almonds, one grated cocoanut, a teacup of preserved lemon peel, and two tablespoonfuls of lemon extract. Bake in a moderate oven for three hours. When cool ornament handsomely with bon bons.

Neapolitan Cake. One cup of brown sugar, three eggs, half a cup of butter, half a cup of molasses, half a cup of strong coffee, three cups of flour, one teaspoonful of baking powder, one cup of raisins and one of currants; a teaspoonful each of cinnamon, cloves and mace; bake in jelly cake pans. For white part take two cups of sugar, one of butter, three of flour, half a cup of milk, a teaspoonful of baking powder and the whites of four eggs; bake in jelly pans and put together alternately with dark, spreading icing flavored with vanilla between. Ice the top.

Angel Cocoanut Cake. Two cups of sugar, half a cup of butter, three of flour, one teaspoonful of baking powder, whites of eight eggs, and half a cup of milk. Flavor with vanilla. Bake in jelly cake pans. Spread the top of each with thick icing, then the bottom; let dry and sprinkle thickly with cocoanut. Ice all over and sprinkle with cocoanut.

MADAME ROWLEY'S TOILET MASK

The following are the claims made for Madame Rowley's Toilet Mask, and the grounds on which it is recommended to ladies for Beautifying, Bleaching and Preserving the Complexion:

First—The Mask is Soft and Flexible in form, and can be Easily Applied and Worn without Discomfort or Inconvenience.

Second—It is durable, and does not dissolve or come asunder, but holds its original mask shape.

Third—It has been Analyzed by Eminent Scientists and Chemical Experts, and pronounced Perfectly Pure and Harmless.

Fourth—With ordinary care the Mask will last for years, and its VALUABLE PROPERTIES Never Become Impaired.

Fifth—The Mask is protected by letters patent, and is the only Genuine article of the kind.

Sixth—It is Recommended by Eminent Physicians and Scientific Men as a SUBSTITUTE FOR INJURIOUS COSMETICS.

Seventh—The Mask is a Natural Beautifier, for Bleaching and Preserving the Skin and Removing Complexional Imperfections.

Eighth—Its use can not be detected by the closest scrutiny, and it may be worn with Perfect Privacy, if desired.

Ninth—The Mask is sold at a moderate price, and is to be PURCHASED BUT ONCE.

Tenth—Hundreds of dollars uselessly expended for cosmetics, lotions, and like preparations, may be saved its possessor.

Eleventh—Ladies in every section of the country are using the Mask with gratifying results.

Twelfth—It is safe, simple, cleanly and effective for beautifying purposes, and never injures the most delicate skin.

Thirteenth—While it is intended that the Mask should be Worn During Sleep, it may by applied WITH EQUAL GOOD RESULTS at any time to suit the convenience of the wearer.

Fourteenth—The Mask has received the testimony of well-known society and professional ladies, who proclaim it to be the greatest discovery for beautifying purposes ever vouchsafed to womankind.

COMPLEXION BLEMISHES

May be hidden imperfectly by cosmetics and powders, but can only be removed permanently by the Toilet Mask. By its use every kind of spots, impurities, roughness, etc., vanish from the skin, leaving it soft, clear, brilliant and beautiful. It is harmless, costs little, and saves its user money. It prevents and removes wrinkles, and is both a complexion preserver and beautifier. Famous Society Ladies, actresses, belles, etc., use it.

VALUABLE ILLUSTRATED TREATISE, WITH PROOFS AND PARTICULARS,

—MAILED FREE BY—

THE TOILET MASK COMPANY,

Send for Descriptive Treatise }

1164 BROADWAY,

{ Send for Descriptive Treatise.

NEW YORK.

☞ Mention this paper when you Write.

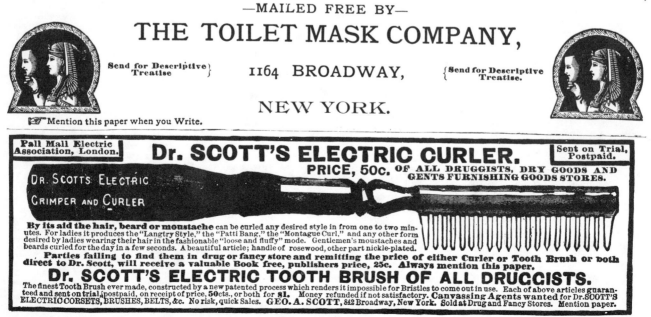

Paris and New York Fashions
by Constance Astor Choate

Spring Millinery.

The buyers just back from Paris are showing flowers; roses in strange hues—unknown in nature, but nevertheless approved by the model-designers—are in vogue. In these faint pinks with shaded effects that reflect purple tints, vivid greens, black, violet and pansy shades, are most prominent on the models.

Giant pansies, in most natural shadings, are used en aigrette from a base of green foliage. Again, large, upstanding sheaves of small pansies, mounted in two piquets, which are placed back to back, rise from a round base of pansy foliage.

Fuchsias in brilliant colorings of pink and red, or in the natural tints of red and white, red and purple are novelties of the moment and are more odd than tasteful.

Nasturtiums in vivid orange and yellow colorings appeal strongly to some of the leading designers, who use them in a variety of methods—laid around drooping brims, as aigrettes and in the revived cachepeigne.

Pale-blue forget-me-nots are also much en evidence, the method of their employment being to mount them in large, round, star-like form around a centre of white calyx. Two of these are mounted on flower stems, and are used as aigrettes.

Turquoise-blue being a strong lead in the Paris models, the myosotis, which reflects this hue, is in request.

Violets are not in such pronounced favor this season.

Feathers and Fantasies.—The reports under this head are to the effect that ospreys are much in request and certainly higher in price, the demand from England and America being very great.

There are many new forms of mounting them, the most popular being that known as the cross mount, in which shorter ospreys outspread from the base of upstanding mounts.

New Blouse. (Plaid silk, and velvet ribbons. Could be made of plaid wool, using braid, and a frill of silk in place of the lace.)

and a coarse plait hat brim will be frequently seen enveloped in a cloud of the finest silk tulle in the same or a contrasting tint.

Ribbons.—Ribbons are scarcely the most prominent feature of the models which are showing in the Paris salons, but where they do appear they are mostly of a plain but

New-style Sailor.

rich make. A very choice thing in novelty ribbons is a make which shows a rich velvety bloom on its surface, the groundwork being a fine quality epingle.

English Walking-hat.

Mousseline and gauze are very evident in some of the newest makes, and as the season progresses we are very certain to see a liberal use made of these. In some of the designs a good effect is made by a method of crossbars or checks in which the lines run across the design instead of longitudinally.

Straw Plaits and Fibres.—Wondrously beautiful as regards both lightness of texture and delicacy of coloring are the straw fibres coulisse or plisse, which are already starting on a great run in London, Paris and New York.

An instance may be quoted of a straw canvas of the lightest make in a soft shade of rose or turquoise very finely crinkled, the width being much in its favor. This often measures twenty-one to twenty-four inches, and it can be readily imagined that this can be used for an infinite variety of purposes—par exemple, for full crowns, and —most useful of all—for the new "Tyre" brim. Again, its delicacy permits its successful employment as chou or coquille, as may be desired.

A new toque has a brim formed of large bows of triple loops of coarse plait, and tie-overs of the same, four of these forming the brim.

Laces.—Fine lace in white, creme and champagne tints, makes a very frequent appearance in the new models, in which it is most often seen as a plisse, or gathered lining, under the brim of a fancy straw hat.

feather set in a strass buckle and forming an aigrette.

A very original model noted one day this week was a black toque of crinkled bass plait with three steel buckles in front, an Alsatian bow with a cluster of silk roses at the back, and a very handsome cluster of brush osprey, the centre upright and the two sides flowing. A black bonnet on a similar principle as the toque, had a very handsome piquet of cross osprey curled and a curled base of a different kind of osprey. —Millinery Record.

Fashionable Colors.

Nickel and silver-grays, castor-brown and all the "mode" shades of light tinted suede "tan" gloves, several shades of army and china-blues, and mignonette-greens predominate in the new dress-goods. Black will be worn a great deal, and black-and-white combinations will be popular. All the new shades are "soft" not hard in tint, and harmonies instead of sharp contrasts prevail.

The Skirt.

Some time ago the lining and the skirt material were no longer attached. The lining—of silk for best dresses—was tight and narrow, while the outside material was allowed to hang in loose and graceful folds. This proved the advancing step toward the draped skirt. And this, a return fashion of about twenty years ago, is already here, even to the apron front trimmed with a double ruffle or frill of the material all around its lower edge. It is to be hoped the befrilling and befurbelowing will not keep on increasing; the labor, and consequent expense of the dressmaking must naturally increase at the same rate.

Spring Fancies.

The solid-color, plain-surfaced goods are more likely to be in good taste than the variety of plaids likewise on the counters.

The introduction again of mousseline de soie, gauze, or barege, as it is likewise called, is a great help in preparing dressy toilettes for the summer. They are always light and airy-looking, and of course retain their good looks much longer than wash goods. Another novelty of the season is the supreme moire, a watered satin.

Black still abides as a piece de resistance.

Wash waists are most frequently in fine check ginghams, tucked with few or many tucks across the front, thereby simulating a yoke.

The brush-edging for the bottom of skirts has quite superseded the much advertised "bias velveteen." This is really durable, and outlasts the dress. It is easily put on, needing only two rows of sewing.

The "skirt elevators" that are on the market, bode ill for the walking-skirt. It seems after reveling in the comfort of the past few years, women never can be so stupid as to submit to the train again except for evening dresses.

Ruchings for the neck continue. Two very pretty new ones appear. The knife-plaited full puff of chiffon is soft and fluffy, while the pin plaits of mousseline de soie in dull Roman stripes are rich.

Earrings.

Earrings, it is said, are once more making their appearance in the "upper circles" of society. It is there, of course, that fashions are set; so in time, they will probably become common.

To make these barbaric little ornaments popular, the jewelers are contriving the most sensible little attachments, by which earrings can be comfortably worn, and no cruel hole forced through the under lobe. From the top of the ring, a threadlike gold hoop passes up into the hollow of the ear in front, and at the back a little gold foot lies against the tender lobe with a firm yet not annoying pressure. Thus the ornament is hung on safely and painlessly.

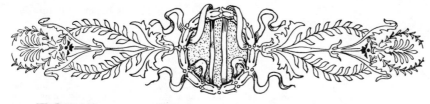

PARIS and NEW YORK FASHIONS
By CONSTANCE ASTOR CHOATE.

Fashions for Early Fall.

The correspondent of a large importing house, writing from Paris, has this to say concerning fashions for fall and early winter:

A decided reaction from puffed sleeves and bouffante effects has set in and the present tendency is to greater simplicity and slightness, all draperies and trimmings being so disposed as to give the figure a graceful, slight and lissom appearance.

Sleeves will be narrower and plainer than ever, the vogue of a mannish coat sleeve seeming to be a foregone conclusion.

Velvet will be the material "par excellence" this autumn. Later on we shall see the loveliest shades of green and mauve for ball and dinner dresses. For tailor gowns, smooth faced cloths and broadcloths will prevail.

Bride's Traveling Costume. Dove-colored faced cloth braided with gray and silver.

A strong effort will be made to revive the Louis XVI. coat, with rounded fronts and long, narrow, tailed backs. This coat, in plain huntsman's green, has already made its appearance at early hunts, and its introduction confirms the early rumor that frock coats and cutaways would become a feature of new cloth gowns.

The stiffening is all to be taken out of skirts, which will cling closely to the form, and be even longer than formerly.

The three-piece costume, consisting of frock coat, or cutaway, with vest and skirt, will be introduced as soon as the weather is sufficiently cool to warrant wearing this warm suit. Every woman who has tried them knows that a tailor-made gown with its many padded places and heavy linings, is not a summer costume, and a three-piece, tailor-made dress at once suggests snow, ice, and furs.

New silks will show many novel designs, the most popular will be printed warp taffetas, in which the floral figures take on a wavy, indistinct outline which blends admirably with the plain ground; another handsome weave is the Pompadour flower sprigged grosgrain, in which the flower has the appearance of being embroidered upon a heavy, black satin duchesse. Tucked silks, following out the furore for bayadere effects which was introduced in the spring, will be used somewhat, but they are destined to become common and enjoy a questionable vogue for ready-made waists and suits.

Other rich silks which will not come into too general use because of their high price —the average being $7.50 a yard, and from this upward indefinitely—are Persian and Ottoman weaves. These, with the corded silks, such as were in vogue twenty-five years ago, will be much used for elaborate

dinner and ball gowns, fancy waists and for lining opera cloaks and carriage wraps.

As to trimmings, fringes are to be employed upon costumes and capes. It is easily understood that with the introduction of fringes, the reign of the plain skirt is over. Entire dresses of black silk knotted fringes are being made, with embroidered garlands of flowers in colored silks. It is also certain that fur will be more popular as a trimming than even at the close of last season when it enjoyed such a vogue. Pipings of fur will be used to trim entire costumes, skirts and outside coats; the usual mode of decoration being pipings headed by braid in plain rows or scroll patterns.

Schoolgirl's Jacket. (Design from Best & Co., New York.) Reefer of blue serge, double-breasted, buttoned high at neck, rolling collar, sleeve and around bottom trimmed with heavy black braid. 11 to 19 years.

Buttons are and will continue to be among the favored trimming. There are some in dull gold, in crystal and gold, and in rounded pearl of the size of a boot button Elaborate sets of buttons are now designed and sold by jewelers, and often come as high as $50 for a set of six buttons. Some are enormous, and in many instances perfect works of art. Upon some of the capes and fancy coats, there are large buttons in wood, with painted portraits of the beauties of the seventeenth and eighteenth centuries, copied from old miniatures.

Cashmeres, crepes and those other soft, clinging materials which drape naturally in graceful folds about the figure, will come forth in the autumn, and are bound to have an immediate vogue, affording as they do an easy transition from the regime of the foulard, which has entrenched itself so firmly in feminine fancy, that its wearers will rejoice to make a change so gradual and acceptable as that from foulard to cashmere.

The most decided change in any fashion will be in millinery. Just as we have become accustomed to the forward tilted hat with its bristling wings and hanging gardens of flowers, lo, capricious fashion gives the new head-dress a pat with her fickle hand, and behold, every new shape not only sets well above the forehead, but the brims turn deliberately back with a saucy flare, and seem to say, "How is this for a change?" Chenille braided effects are shown in early models, the prevailing style being "Victoria flats" faced with chenille braid in various patterns. The imported models now displayed at strictly "private openings" show a marked tendency to deep brown shades, combined with magenta, pink and purplish red. As the season advances, the brown will become richer and darker, until golden browns and seal browns will take precedence over other colors. Azure, or natural blue, gray, castors, and some green, especially the shade known as

reseda green, will obtain. Let the woman who expects to buy only one new gown beware the purple gown.

Velvet is the feature of new hats and toques, and is already seen upon every stylish model. Feathers, rather than quills, appear on new importations. A characteristic of the lavishness with which plumes will be used is that where heretofore three plumes have usually been grouped together, now four or five are used—never less than four, upon the smallest toques.

Velvet ties that do not tie, and buckles galore give brilliancy and variety to this season's millinery.

Schoolgirl's Jacket. (Design from Best & Co., New York.) Reefer of good-quality cloth, coat black, large collar, trimmed with braid. 11 to 18 years.

Another novel feature is faced wings. One charming model which was of dove-colored velvet was trimmed with pale-gray wings faced with deep-blue wings; the only other decoration being loops of gray velvet, faced with blue velvet, stitched five times about the edges.

The fashion of stitching velvet is quite new, and is developed in stitched velvet crowns, loops and bows; ribbon having no place in fashionable millinery this season.

Petunia-colored flowers will be much worn on brown toques, and all plumes are worn erect. Brown will predominate in millinery as in dress goods, and will afford a welcome relief from the season just closed when so many distressingly unbecoming shades—burnt-orange, turquoise, lavender and trying black-and-white combinations were braved by the plainest and most sallow-faced women.

❦ ❦ ❦ ❦

THE NEW GIRL'S WEAKNESS.

Madame Sarah Grand, herself one of the newest of new women, finds upon her return to England, after a sojourn in France, that the "new girl" of to-day compares badly with her continental sister, and sums the situation up, briefly, as follows:

"In return for all that society concedes to her in the way of education, physical training and independence, she should at least show a desire to please. She has a great objection to disagreeable people, yet she takes no trouble to make herself agreeable. When she is out of temper she does not conceal the fact. In her home life she is apt to be selfish, and in society she is only genial when it suits herself. She walks with a stride and there is a want of becoming deference to people older than herself which is particularly unlovely, and proclaims her at once underbred and ungenerous. Ungenerous, in that she accepts privileges bestowed upon her but offers nothing in return, and cultivates none of the gentler graces and dignity with which women can add so much to the beauty of life."

If the modern girl would be a success in her time she would do well to remember, for her own sake as well as that of others, that

"* * manners are not idle, but the fruit
Of loyal nature and of noble."

NEW WAIST EXERCISES.

In Edward Bellamy's "Equality," the gymnasium visits are compulsory for all young people, until such time as the constitution and the body are "set," but the old folks continue going just the same, thinking they are never too old to reap the benefits of it.

From the internal economy of the woman, her waist muscles are apt to become flabby and weak, and the consequence is that about middle life she is apt to lose her symmetry of form, and the lower part of the body is larger in proportion to the chest and bust than it ought to be.

The following new waist exercises are both pleasant in the using, and persevered in, they prove beneficial in the results.

Rest the weight on the left foot. Swing the right foot round in front of it, resting on tiptoes. Raise the arms slowly, the left one highest. Lift the right foot from the floor. Push up and out with the left hand, and down and out with the right one. Keep in position four counts.

Repeat on reverse feet. Repeat with the feet placed out in front, and then push upward and back. Repeat with the feet placed back. Then push forward and up.

Practice the dance movement. Hold the dress up on each side. Place the right foot in front, bending the body back. Cross the foot to the left, bending the body forward. Repeat the same with left foot. These exercises are generally recommended to be taken at night. If the brain has been principally worked all day, well and good; but if the body is fatigued they seem to me to be then out of time.

I think the best time is before breakfast, in moderate weather at an open window, taking long breaths the while. The lungs get thus filled with oxygen, which is passed on to the blood. Rising a few minutes earlier is well repaid by the vigor that is experienced.

Spring Styles.

It always seems and really is incongruous to be talking of spring styles in dress when winter envelopes everybody and everything. But the fashions in fabrics for spring were not only designed but manufactured months ago, and although styles for making will continue to be evolved till spring is fairly here, still the general designs are already pretty clearly established.

The best way for a young man to begin who is without friends or influence is first, by getting a position; second, keeping his mouth shut; third, observing; fourth, being faithful; fifth, making his employer think he would be lost in a fog without him, and sixth, being polite.—Russell Sage.

Bonnets.

There is a strong attempt to introduce the enormous bonnet of the beginning of the century. They used to be called coalscuttles. Wood-baskets would be a good name for them. On children's heads, I see them in the fashion-plate. Heavy, cumbersome and unwieldy they look, and yet they do not act as a sunshade to the little face. With regard to following the fashions, the old poet Pope's rule still holds good.

"Be not the first by whom the new is tried,
Nor yet the last to lay the old aside."

Fashion's Fancies.

"Leghorn flats" will be worn again this year, but the shape will be decidedly narrower than the style in vogue last year. The hats are bent up at each side and much bent in at the back, and are worn well over the face. The tops are covered with flowers and veils, but the major part of the trimming is at the back and under the edge of the upturned sides. The trimming in the back extends quite low and will rest upon the hair.

Both capes and jackets will be worn, though jackets will be more popular for general wear. However, for very dressy occasions or for traveling capes will be much worn, the style for the former being very elaborate creations of lace, silk ribbons and feathers, while the latter are heavy homespuns, meltons, beavers, etc., either plain or plaided with bright-lined hoods. A stylish cloth cape shown in a New York window is made of gendarmes blue-face cloth cut circular shape and trimmed with rows of the inch white moire ribbon headed by narrow black-velvet ribbon, pleated on in full ruffles beginning at the edge of the cape and extending nearly to the neck. The high slashed collar was faced with white moire and the edge trimmed with velvet ribbon. Wide moire ties edged with ribbon and finished with pompons of velvet ribbon finish this very stylish cape which is lined with black silk. Any one who can

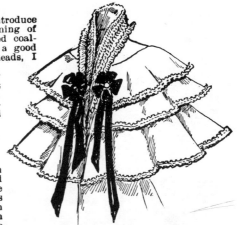

Smart Spring Wrap for Matrons.

Latest Design in Boudoir Gowns.

Then sprinkle powdered cloves over it and wrap securely in newspaper, being careful that the paper does not break. Place this package in a clean, carefully aired and dusted pasteboard box, which should be placed in a trunk or some cool, dry closet.

The cleaning of the fur is the most important essential. If it is packed away dusty or soiled it is more likely to contain also moth eggs which will later breed in spite of other precautions. Cloves impart a delightful odor and are just as effective as camphor or the repulsive moth balls. The main thing is to put furs away before the eggs are laid, and where the moths cannot reach them.

The Chatelaine Novelty.

This novelty consists of three long, slim, crystal bottles with gilt screw tops, encased in silk of any color. These are attached to a hook with ribbons, the hook being slipped on to the belt, and the whole to be worn at the church, to the theatre, or when calling, as they contain sal volatile, (an ammonia preparation,) cologne, and salts. This does seem like going back to the dark ages. It reminds me of some pretty young ladies I remember as a child, who always carried to church what their mother called their "praying apparatus,"—a bottle of smelling-salts! Twenty years later, when they were all married and gone it was discovered why they needed this. Their family pew in an old country church, hundreds of years old, was exactly over the family vault of some titled grandees, who resided formerly in the parish. Some one or other must have been buried without the leaden coffin, for the effluvia rising into the pew was discovered to be most dangerously poisonous. After gaining permission from the family, the parish authorities hermetically closed up the vault; and since then the "praying apparatus" has not been needed by the occupants of the pew.

To Renovate Stockings.

A much more sensible and useful novelty, is the manufacture of the separate feet of stockings. When your stocking feet wear out, and become past darning, and even patching, the legs still remaining good, there is yet "a way out." For ten cents in cotton either black or unbleached, detached feet can be purchased from the Racine Knitting Co., Department O., Racine, Wisconsin. For fifteen cents, woolen ones can be had. Four or five sizes of each kind.

A Charming Party Frock.

The oddest and prettiest of all the dresses worn at a recent party, says a woman in the Boston Globe, was of ivory Liberty satin, very light and clear in texture and with a wonderful luminousness. It was made over pale-pink taffeta, which showed through the satin plainly, making the whole look like a tinted seashell. It was trimmed with openwork, showing the pink taffeta beneath and also with point d'esprit tulle.

COIFFEUR FOR EVENING DRESS.

Sleeves for Afternoon-Dress.—One is tight-fitting of brown velvet; the lower part is cut in square tabs and fixed down to the outer seam of sleeve under fancy buttons; the last tab is left hanging from the wrist, and trimmed with wide lace falling over the hand. Another is of green broche and is tight-fitting; the wrist is trimmed with a piece of the broche put round the sleeve, and drawn through a paste buckle, leaving a full loop to stand out at the back; pleated chiffon finishes the edge of sleeve, and falls over the hand.

Zouave.—A stylish zouave is of dark blue stet cloth lined with silk, and trimmed across the fronts and at the edge with narrow bands of white cloth, machine-stitched; turn-down collar edged with white; tie of dark blue silk with pointed ends.

Fashionable Sleeves.—A close-fitting sleeve of fancy blue silk with butterfly drapery at the top has a wide ribbon brought from the shoulder down centre of sleeve, forming a large bow at the elbow and again at the wrist. Another has a tight lining; the material is put on plain from the wrist nearly to the elbow; from there it consists of a series of folds lined with silk; the cuff is tabbed and turned up with corners of velvet fastened by buttons.

Trimming for Bodice.—A new Paris gown has a deep belt of silvery-gray silk striped in black; it crosses over at the back, the ends being brought up to the busts in front, finished with large rosettes.

Vest.—On a smart London frock the vest is of red Amazon cloth and is tight-fitting; the fronts are trimmed across with black military braid, revers and collar also edged with braid; it is fastened down the front with fancy black buttons.

Breakfast-Jacket.—The jacket is of a pink and green plaid woolen material; it is made very full; a belt of green velvet is placed round the waist, passing under the back and front widths, leaving them loose; the zouave is of green velvet fastening in the centre of front under a large fancy button; collar and cuffs to the bishop sleeves also of green velvet.

Invalid's Jacket.—The jacket is of fine white flannel striped in mauve, and has a deep full basque; a piece of the flannel, edged with a band of mauve velvet, is placed across the shoulders, and held together in front by thick white cords and fancy buttons; outstanding collar and wide corselet-belt of mauve velvet; the latter is trimmed across the front with cords and buttons; bishop sleeves, with cuffs of velvet.

The Way to Lace a Corset.

If you wear corsets do you lace them properly? There should be two laces, one reaching from the top to the waist-line, one from the waist-line to the bottom. The corset should fit properly and should be laced comfortably, each lace being tied at the waist-line; this prevents either half of the corset opening wider at the expense of the other. Corsets fastened with one lace invariably spread over the hips and contract about the bust, thus ruining the figure. Laces should never be tied above the waist as they wear out the corset if so tied. They should be tied at the waist-line in the back.

A Becoming Sleeve.

Long sleeves are now preferred by many ladies to short ones, in low-necked dresses, especially for dinner parties. If prettily made, they are generally more becoming than arms without gloves. Our illustration is of pale amber silk, dotted with mauve; the top is trimmed with two full double pleatings of amber chiffon; the mitten-cuff is finished with a kilting of chiffon. This style of finishing off the wrist is very becoming to the hands especially if they are not beautiful. In challie with plaitings of silk this would be a pretty sleeve for an at home toilet. It is equally appropriate for summer silks trimmed with plaitings of silk muslin.

Dressing Jacket.

The illustrated dressing jacket is a useful and simple shape for a dressing jacket, being quite loose, and tied in with a belt of ribbon. The shaped collar and cuffs are edged with lace, and hanging lace finishes the sleeve. It may be made of either flannel or silk or muslin.

New Dress Skirt.

The skirt in the illustration is cut with a narrow front piece, and then the selvedge is used for the side seam. There is besides only one seam in the centre of the back, but the skirt is so cut as to leave the sides much flatter than they have been while the back has two box pleats. Only a narrow stiffening is required in the hem. The breadths may be lined, or the skirt may be seamed up unlined and hung over a foundation skirt lining. A narrow trimming on the front seams makes the wearer look taller, and is therefore especially desirable for stout figures.

New "Petticoat Bodice."

The "petticoat bodice" or corset cover illustrated in another column is an extremely simple shape. It consists of two pieces—back and front—and the sleeve. The latter is gathered top and bottom and put into a narrow band. The front finishes with a point at each side, where a tape is stitched, crossed at the back and tied in front. It can be made half high, like the illustration, or low.

Party Dress for Girl of Fourteen.

This sweet little frock is made of pink accordion plaited silk with a Marie Antoinette fichu of cream chiffon. The band about the square neck, the sleeves and the belt are of passementerie, studded with imitation rubies. Pink cream Suede gloves, pink silk stockings and pink Suede kid slippers complete the lovely toilet.

A far less costly, but very pretty gown could be modeled after this using girlish muslins for the gown, and pretty ribbons in place of the jeweled bands of galon.

The longer I live, the more deeply am I convinced that that which makes the difference between one man and another—between the weak and powerful, the great and insignificant, is energy—invincible determination—a purpose once formed and then victory or death.—Fowell Buxton.

THE CORRECT USE OF FURS
By Isabel A. Mallon

FUR is always becoming and always has about it an air of luxury. The golden-brown furs are given the vogue this season, mink and its many imitators being especially fancied. This fur, and by this I mean mink, is one that cuts desirably into pipings, allowing sufficient skin to be sewed by, and yet the line of fur, though narrow, looks full and achieves the effect desired. Black fox, blue fox, skunk and seal are in vogue, and where one has many gowns, the gray velvet costume elaborately decorated with chinchilla is considered most elegant. The fur of the skunk is an extremely pretty brown, but one must beware of getting it wet for a disagreeable odor is almost always perceptible when it dries.

THE MODE OF DECORATING

ON coats, deep collars that curve in and stand up high on the shoulders are liked, and if no other fur trimming is put upon them, then cuffs reaching to the elbow

COAT OF CLOTH AND FUR (Illus. No. 1)

are the proper finish. Quite often, however, a piping will outline the jacket, and then several rows of the fur in pipings will decorate the sleeves. On silk or brocade coats the collar is usually of fur with a lace frill over it, while a lace jabot extends to the waist, and pipings of fur and frills of lace are on the cuffs. On gowns fur trimming is very simply applied.

THE SHORT COAT

THE long, fur-lined, fur-trimmed wrap permits little ingenuity in the arrangement of the fur upon it. That it is the inner lining, that it is about the throat, down each side of the front, and, where there are sleeves, constitutes the cuffs, fully describes the only disposition possible on the long garments. Of course, they are most artistic looking, and by the choice of becoming fur are made to give to the wearer an air of magnificence. In golden-brown, crimson and dark blue serge, as well as in the various rich brocades, the long cloaks are trimmed with fur in the manner described, though they are not always lined with it.

On the short coats fur is very generally used, and many odd arrangements are noticed. The brown cloth coat, shown in Illustration No. 1. is cut after the fashion of a frock one and reaches to below the knees. It has a collar of black fox cut after the shawl fashion, which permits to be seen, like a tiny vest, a section and high collar of mink. The sleeves are full at the top and shape in to the wrist where they are trimmed with five rows of mink piping. A belt of the cloth starts at each under-arm seam, is piped with mink and is caught in the centre with a silver-gilt buckle. The edge of the coat is piped with the fur. The hat is a toque of brown velvet, trimmed with mink head and tails, and worn very far back on the head.

Another short coat, which is of gray cloth, has a high collar and a flaring collar of chinchilla, while its only other decorations are the deep cuffs of the fur and the fancy steel buttons that decorate each side of the front.

SMART ETON JACKET (Illus. No. 2)

A VERY STYLISH JACKET

THE smartest of the Eton jackets is pictured in Illustration No. 3. The regulation, close-fitting shape is developed in sealskin, and it is made more feminine and more becoming by having a high shawl collar of black fox and flaring revers that come far down on the corsage at each side. These, of course, tend to make the shoulders look broader and the waist smaller. The sleeves, which are very full, shape in to the arm at the elbow and are entirely of sealskin.

A very smart Eton jacket is of brown cloth, with sleeves, collar and revers of mink. Another, intended only for visiting and carriage wear, is of white ermine, with its trimmings and sleeves of sealskin. A green cloth is made rich looking by trimmings of black fox, and a silver-gray by those of chinchilla.

ABOUT BUYING FURS

IN buying furs especially for trimming, go to a first-class place, inasmuch as the furs that are apparently sold for such cheap prices are usually found lacking. Frequently they have not been taken care of during the summer, and the moth has made his home among the hairs, and in a short time you will find your gown or skirt continually covered with them, and wherever you sit, or whoever may be near, will also suffer from this rain of loose fur. If a good effect is produced by an imitation fur, buy it, but examine it well. Mink is particularly well imitated, and as the real fur is quite expensive it may be taken for granted that on nine out of ten gowns the fur has never been acquainted with that sharp-looking little animal whose head just now is of so much value. The imitations of ermine are never good, and therefore not to be thought of. Astrakhan is sufficiently low in price to permit any one getting a gown trimming to have the real article itself. By-the-by, in speaking of laces and furs, I forgot to mention that over the deep fur capes, those reaching far below the waist, it is considered in perfectly good taste to wear a shoulder cape of lace. Usually one of the sharply-pointed designs is chosen for this purpose.

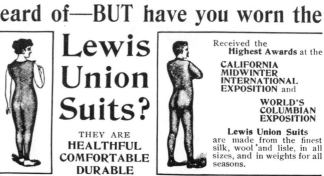

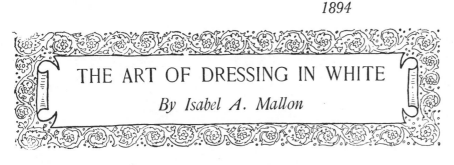

THE ART OF DRESSING IN WHITE

By Isabel A. Mallon

WHEN wearing a white gown thought must be given to the becomingness of the shade, for, after all, there are as many tints in white as in other colors ; the one that may suit the pale blonde is absolutely unbecoming to the rosy brunette. Dead white, which has a glint of blue about it, is seldom becoming to any one. It brings out the imperfections of the complexion, tends to deaden the gloss of the hair, and dulls the brightness of the eyes. The white that touches on the cream or coffee shade is undoubtedly the most artistic and best suited to the general woman. However, in choosing it one must be careful not to get too deep a tone, which is apt to look not quite dainty, and to give the impression of a faded yellow, rather than a cream white. White gowns are usually counted

A DAINTY MUSLIN FROCK (Illus. No. 2)

as expensive, the fact that they soil so easily and necessitate visits either to the laundry or the cleaners that cost much, being the reason given for their so-called expensiveness. Yet with care one may be worn an entire season.

A WHITE PIQUÉ GOWN

A WHITE piqué gown is shown in Illustration No. 1. The skirt, which is quite plain, is made after the flaring five-gored fashion, which fits smoothly about the hips and front, and has the fullness laid in box-plaits at the back. With this is worn a white silk blouse, having a turned-down collar and deep cuffs, and over it a Zingara jacket of piqué made double-breasted and closed with enormous white pearl buttons, three only being necessary. The jacket collar is faced with olive green velvet, and the cuffs are of the velvet, with three of the large pearl buttons set upon each. The silk cuffs of the blouse come below the piqué sleeves, which are large and very wide, even at the wrists. The belt is a folded one of green velvet, with a pearl buckle in front. A tie of white silk is arranged in a stiff bow, and shows from under the collar of the blouse. With this frock is worn a sailor hat of dead white straw, with high bows of green velvet at the back and a band of white satin ribbon about the crown. The gloves are white undressed kid, and the parasol is of green velvet with a white handle. If one did not care to use velvet for the trimming upon such a gown as this, moiré, which is greatly in vogue, could be substituted for it, but as a contrast is desired between the blouse, the gown proper and its trimmings, the preference is given to velvet.

A DAINTY MUSLIN GOWN

MUSLIN, which always makes a dainty-looking gown, is to be preferred when it is embroidered. The embroidered material does not cost much more, and the little figures upon it tend to give it a body, which is most desirable, as the fabric will not then so easily wrinkle and grow stringy. For wear under a muslin skirt I would advise two thin skirts of lawn prettily trimmed with frills of the same, unless, indeed, one should be fortunate enough to possess a white silk skirt. The frock pictured in Illustration No. 2 is made with the usual flaring skirt, and has for its decoration two frills of the material edged with a rather coarse lace, each flounce having a row of insertion set in, the width of material between the insertion and edge being a little over one inch. The upper flounce is draped at regular intervals and caught with a rosette of white satin ribbon.

MATERIALS AND TRIMMINGS

THIS summer laces and ribbons are noted on thin white gowns, while velvet and silk are used upon the thicker ones. Chiffon, crêpe, muslin, plain and embroidered, light-weight silks are the thin whites most in vogue, while cloth, piqué and heavy linen are the preferred thicker ones. Linen, which is rather newer than piqué, has one disadvantage : it creases easily, and I do not think it stands laundering as well as does the heavy corded fabric.

A WHITE PIQUÉ GOWN (Illus. No. 1)

Piqué is greatly liked when made up after the tailor designs. The jacket which last year was called the Eton, but is now known as the Zingara, is one of the favored models. The long frock coat is also developed in piqué, but it is only suited to the girl who is tall and slender, the full, flaring skirt making a short figure look awkward. Of the ribbons used velvet and satin are given the preference. The ones noted are imperial purple, petunia, olive green, moss, and where a frock is to be worn in the evening or for driving, white matching the material, pale rose, blue and Nile green are also seen. When the heavier stuffs are developed in simple styles, sashes of velvet are liked, and then the collar and cuffs, and frequently the sleeves, are of that fabric. Of course, when velvet is used in combination with piqué it is never supposed that the gown will be laundered. Shoulder capes, as well as belts and sashes, made of velvet, may be worn with any summer gown.

THE GAME OF GOLF FOR WOMEN

by John Gilmer Speed

GOLF, the great national game of Scotland, has become both popular and fashionable in England, and is likely soon to be held in high favor in America. Those who are ignorant of the game beyond that it is of Scottish origin, and who have only the vague idea of it that "shinney" sticks and balls and holes are employed in playing it, usually smile in a good-natured and superior way when it is mentioned, just as an accomplished gourmet would smile if he were told that haggis was good to eat. "Good for a Scotchman to eat," the gourmet's smile would say as plainly as uttered syllables. And so the ignorant sportsman would be apt to speak of the ancient and royal game of golf. But in reality there was never a more fascinating nor a more healthful game invented than golf, and the sooner it becomes popular in America the better it will be for all of those who fall under the spell of its charm. In writing about the humors of the game Mr. Gladstone's Parliamentary adversary, Mr. Balfour, has said : "Consider, for instance, the fact that while the performers at other games are restricted within comparatively narrow limits of age, golf is out of relation with no one of the seven ages of man. Round the links may be seen in endless procession not only players of every degree of skill and of every social condition, but also of every degree of maturity and immaturity. There is no reason, in the nature of things, why golf should not be begun as soon as one can walk, and continued as long as one can walk."

NOW, if very young children and very old men can compete in golf, finding both pleasure and healthful exercise in it, why should it not be played also by women? As a matter of fact, women play the game both in Scotland and England, and to some extent in this country, where the game is as yet known at but few places. Prominent among these places are Yonkers, New York ; Shinnecock Hills, on Long Island, and Newport, Rhode Island. It is quite likely, however, that before the winter of this year it will be played in half a hundred neighborhoods, and where it is once introduced it is likely to flourish permanently. Tennis, being both fast and furious, is a game exclusively for young people who are both strong and agile. To be able to walk and to have the free use of the arms is all that golf primarily requires.

THERE is, it must be said, a vast difference between good playing and bad, but even the bad player feels from the very first time that he tries to drive the ball from the "tee" that he can improve with a little patience and practice. And what is more he does improve. All of the golf authorities are agreed that if a boy or girl begin playing at ten years of age and keep it up for half a century, at the end of that time the player should make the best score ever by him or her achieved. It is a matter of record that the most famous professional golfer in Scotland, old Tom Morris, keeper of the links at St. Andrews, made the best score of his life on his sixty-fourth birthday. This can be said of no other game with which I have acquaintance. The advantage of it, and specially with reference to women players, is too obvious to argue. Another advantage is this : golf can be taken up even in late middle life by both men and women, and such players will be gratified to observe that their play improves quite steadily with practice. With golf links in every neighborhood there is no reason why the middle-aged woman should fasten herself in a rocking-chair and consent to be regarded by the youngsters around her as antiquated at forty-five. Instead of that, with firm tread, she can, with her golfing club, follow her ball from link to link, renewing her beauty and

POSITION OF A "HIGH LOFTING STROKE"

her youth by exercise in the open air.

IT will not be easy to explain golf so that it may be understood by those who have never seen it played. But by means of the accompanying diagram I shall endeavor to explain briefly. The grounds on which the game is played are called links, each distance between holes being a link. The object of the game is to drive a small gutta-percha ball one and a half inches in diameter from hole to hole until the full course be covered. The player doing this in the least number of strokes is the winner. For the purpose of driving the ball there are various clubs, some twelve in number, fashioned so as to do what is desired. Chief among these are the driver, the cleak, the niblick, the lofter, the spoon and the putter. These clubs are carried by a lad technically called a "caddie," whose other duties are to keep track of the ball after a stroke, so that it may not be lost, to keep the score of strokes, and also to give advice as to any particular stroke or club. No one save the "caddie" is permitted to advise the player. The game is played by sides—one against one, or two against two. When there are two on each side the game is called a foursome. Each hole is about four inches in diameter, and these are surrounded by a few yards of smoothly-prepared grounds called putting greens. Near by each hole is a place called the "teeing ground." In our diagram the first "teeing ground" is "A," and the first hole

"B." Now, at the beginning of the game the player takes a handful of earth and makes a little mound above the turf. This mound is called the "tee," and on this the ball is placed. Now the player makes the first drive, sending the ball as far as possible toward "B," six hundred feet away. For fear of misunderstanding it is well, perhaps, to say just here that there is no general rule for laying out golfing links. The topography of the ground must be considered, and the distance between holes regulated as much by the hazards the player will encounter as by anything else. But the distance between holes should never be less than four hundred and fifty feet, as a good driver can send his ball that far with one stroke. Now return to the diagram. The player has driven the ball toward "B," and the first stroke probably takes the ball somewhere near the stone wall that intervenes. Now judgment must be used as to what club to use. If the player is tolerably close to the wall the lofter will be selected so as to strike the ball high into the air and so clear the wall. If the ball is very close the spoon may be used, but if there is space enough for a second long drive then the cleak or niblick will be employed. Having cleared the wall the player approaches the "putting green" around the hole "B." Once within the green the putter is used and play made for the hole. If it require more than two strokes to make the hole from within the green the player will be more than amiable if he preserve an easy temper.

POSITION FOR "THE DRIVE"

HOLE "B" having been made the score of strokes required to achieve this result is noted and the ball removed to "teeing ground" "C," whence it is driven toward hole "D," and the proceedings just described repeated till all of the links have been covered and the hole at "S" has been made. Once around the course of the links as shown in this diagram would be short of a mile, though, to be sure, the player would, in all probability, have walked a mile and a half in going the course. This would make a very short course, so with such links very likely a game would consist of three times around. Therefore, over such links in each game a player will have walked something like four miles and a half, and this will not have been on a paved street or dusty roadway, but over grassy fields with fences here and there and every now and then, perhaps, a brook. Walking is capital exercise, but an objectless walk to the majority of persons seems more like labor than sport. But the walking a golfer does is purposeful, and therefore never tiresome ; but when five or six miles have been covered by a stout person, a trifle short of breath, and specially if the course be a good deal up and down hill, that player when the last hole has been made will be apt to conclude that he or she has been doing something. And if the score shows that the player has improved since the last game then the wholesome fatigue will be doubly grateful and the next golfing day be looked forward to with pleasurable anticipations.

The history of golf is so lost in antiquity that even so erudite a scholar and patriotic a Scot as Andrew Lang failed in his efforts to trace its origin. He believes that the Scots six hundred years or so ago got the idea from some foreign game and then developed it to what it is now. Of its antiquity there can be no doubt.

THE links at St. Andrews are the most famous in existence, and there Mary Stuart played after the death of Darnley. For centuries the rules of golf were not codified, but were handed down from generation to generation with the dignity of traditions and the authority of established customs. But in more recent years, and rather for the benefit of foreign than Scotch players, the laws of the links at St. Andrews have been formulated and printed. I have only seen these rules in the golf volume of the Badminton Library, but they have probably also been printed in other books. The rules are simple and easily understood by

POSITION AT "TOP OF SWING"

any one who has once seen the game, but to the totally uninitiated they appear to be hopelessly unintelligible. For that reason I do not in this paper go into detail.

The etiquette of the game is also well established, and therefore there is little or no excuse for angry disputes in the course of a game. For instance, ten, twenty or even thirty parties may be going over the course at the same time. There might be interferences between these parties were not the etiquette well understood, for it is frequently the case that the players who started from the "teeing ground" first may be slow or meet with misfortune, while all may go smoothly and quickly for those behind. In such a case the slow or unfortunate players make way and wait till the luckier players have gone ahead. Then, again, etiquette requires that the players ahead shall be warned that a ball that might strike one of the players is about to be driven. Were these customs not established by long usage there might occasionally something disagreeable happen in a game, for there are times in the game when the temper of an unlucky player is most sorely tried. Mr. Balfour says that in England and Scotland bad language is not as frequently heard in a game of golf as it once was. He says:

"Deeds, not words, are required in extreme cases to meet the exigencies of the situation, and as justice, prudence and politeness all conspire to shield his opponent from physical violence it is on the clubs that, under these circumstances, vengeance most commonly descends. Most players content themselves with simply breaking the offending weapon against the ground."

THE fact that in playing this game men lose their tempers and make ridiculous spectacles of themselves, and the further fact that not all of them are always restrained in their language, are the reasons, I fancy, which induced Andrew Lang to say that there are "excellent reasons for objecting to the flutter of petticoats on the green." Such reasons are no reasons at all against the presence of women in games of golf, but an argument in favor of their playing with the men, for their presence would

ON THE "PUTTING GREEN"

restrain a man both in language and in deeds, and such restraint would be a good thing for all concerned. One of the rules of the game is that after the ball is in play it shall not be touched with anything other than the club, and that each time it is so touched a stroke shall be added to the score. It is the general testimony of golf authorities that there is nothing that so strains a person's integrity as the obeying of this rule. The temptation to touch the ball with the foot and put it into a better position for a good stroke is said to be too great for some players to resist. These authorities also agree in saying that a man who once yields to this temptation is irretrievably lost, and that his capacity to be honest in golf is as hopelessly gone as the power of a sheep-killing dog to stop taking his mutton on the hoof. These authorities recommend not betting heavily with such offenders, but in other regards not to pay any attention to their play.

THIS is another feature of the game that women would do much toward reforming. A gallant gentleman will not cheat a woman, and a woman at all worthy of consideration will not cheat any one at all. The only arguments against women playing golf are to the effect that they may in one way or another interfere with the play of men. This I have shown to be untrue, and I trust I have also said enough about the fascination of the game and its suitableness for women to induce many to try it. Nine out of ten of those who try it once will keep up their play if they live within easy reach of any golfing links. And as golfing links can be established easily in every country neighborhood, places to play will probably be accessible to nearly all women so soon as the beauties and charms of the

game become to be known and appreciated.

The practical instruction needed in locating a course and playing the game should be easily accessible in every part of America. Nearly all Scotchmen, not from the great cities such as Glasgow and Edinburgh, know the game, and some such amiable person can pretty surely be found almost anywhere. And such a one may be depended upon to teach with enthusiastic pleasure his great national game, which bids fair soon to belong to the whole world. So charming, innocent and healthful a game is worthy of the strongest possible encouragement.

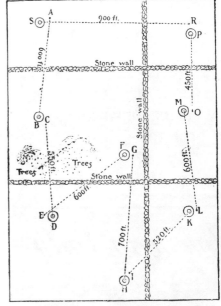

DIAGRAM OF A GOLF LINKS

THE CHINESE LAUNDRY TICKET

By John Hubert Grensel

ROBABLY not one person in a
thousand understands the true
interpretation of the Chinese
laundry ticket.

The Celestials have a system
of their own. It is based on
the many gods and goddesses of the laundry.
Although the system is a very complicated
one seldom does a Chinese laundryman
deliver a package of washing to the wrong
person. Furthermore, if the ticket is lost
the chances are that you will not get your
linen, unless you be a particular friend of
the proprietor. Instances are on record
where an American has gone to court to
force the Chinese to yield up the washing,
but the judge was not convinced that the
case of the white man was a good one.

THIS SAYS "HEAVEN, NO. 17, WAH LEE"

The Chinese laundryman at the beginning of each week makes out a batch of
checks, in duplicate, to be used as wash
tickets. He selects the name of some god
or goddess, or of some object, as the sun,
the moon or the stars. To this name he
prefixes a number, as "Moon, No. 1,"
"Moon, No. 2," and so on. In the space
between the two legends—for the signs are
repeated twice—he has his own name, as,
for instance, "Wah Lee."

When a customer takes a bundle of washing to the laundry the Chinese, first tearing
a ticket in two in a ragged fashion, puts
one-half on the packet for reference, the
other half he gives as a receipt to the
person who has brought the package of
laundry. It must be presented when the
laundry is demanded, and no fears need
be entertained that the package of clean
clothes will not be forthcoming, for the
Chinese are scrupulously exact in these
matters, and seldom or never make mistakes.

The Chinese check herewith given is a
correct representation of a laundry ticket or
check. Such checks are in use in all laun-
dries managed by the Chinese. The three
hieroglyphics on the left say, "Heaven,
No. 17," the three on the right say the
same. In the middle is the name of the
proprietor of the shop, "Wah Lee."

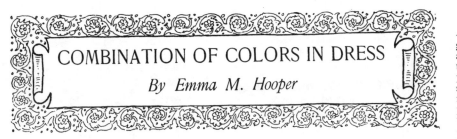

COMBINATION OF COLORS IN DRESS
By Emma M. Hooper

HE dress of one color will be an exception this season and from three to four colors and materials will be the general rule. Nearly every gown worn shows cherry, bluet—cornflower blue—or black in some form, just as nearly every bit of dress goods said to be fashionable gives at least traces of brown, tan, navy or bluet, dark green or black. It is both fashionable and economical to wear a kind of a Joseph's coat of many colors, but the combination of these colors would form an unknown book to those patching the coat many years ago, therefore it will be well for those persons who have an eye for color to cultivate it.

USING CHERRY AND BLUET

WHAT is called cherry or cerise should really be styled reine, pivoine or Jacqueminot, as they are on the French color cards, being very pinkish-reds that are not becoming to bright red hair or florid complexions. The French are successful with this because they use only a touch of it in a costume, as a crush collar on a black, navy, bluet, brown or dark green dress, or at the most a collar and belt, which will also renovate any half-worn gown of last year. Velvet is preferred for these accessories in the plain or miroir—ironed to give the looking-glass effect—though satin is also much worn for such additions to a gown. Bluet is used just as cherry is, and one trims the other as well. A very stylish gown of bluet cloth has braces or suspenders from the front to the back of the belt of black satin ribbon No. 12, overlaid with a band of open jet insertion and a belt of the same tied in a bow of two upright loops and two long ends, each end having another bow half way to the end. The round waist, leg-of-mutton sleeves and untrimmed bell skirt, four yards wide, need only a crush collar of cherry velvet to complete them. A black silk-warp Henrietta skirt made six yards wide, with flaring gores forming flutes or godet plaits all around the bottom, each plait being held by elastic straps, is worn with a round waist of bluet satin: The full leg-of-mutton sleeves, crush belt and braces (cut bias, two inches wide and faced with crinoline) are of black satin or gros-grain, and the crush collar having swallow-tail bows at the back and sides is of bluet or cherry velvet.

REMODELED GOWNS

IT is the easiest season to make over in. Cut waists off round, add a crush collar of red or blue, and a belt to match either the collar or dress of velvet, satin or ribbon; then add very full sleeve puffs or new leg-of-mutton sleeves, a pair of the largest needing four yards of twenty-inch silk, of velvet, velveteen, satin duchesse or gros-grain. A V-shaped vest covered with appliqué figures of white lace guipure, a yoke of the same effect or a full soft vest of chiffon drooping low over the belt like a Fédora front of ten years ago are among the new trimmings. Since jet returned there are Vandyke points for yokes, braces

that end as a fringe in front over the bust, draped corsage ornaments from shoulder to shoulder, girdles, etc., that are stylish and dressy on woolen and silk dresses. The loose fronts are made of silk muslin or chiffon. To widen skirts insert side panels of velvet or silk, or if for a house gown cut down the centre and insert a front of velvet. Lace is chiefly worn as a flat border on house dresses, as girdles, yokes, in separate figures or appliqués on silk and velvet yokes and vests, and as entire bodies or waists fitted smoothly over a silk lining, and with silk sleeves and skirt of the same or a second color, using guipure lace. Jetted nets are used as full vests and yokes, and in soft drapings over a silk lining for a waist; if the net is very thickly jetted it is drawn plainly over the waist lining. As so many colors and materials are allowed renovating a costume becomes of small account. Brown may be trimmed with black satin ribbon braces and belt and bluet velvet collar and V, the latter covered with white lace appliqués. Green of a dark shade has a touch of black in jet braces and belt, a light green chiffon vest in accordion plaits and a collar of rose velvet. A mixed navy and green suiting has collar of cherry velvet and vest and belt of navy Liberty satin, a soft imported satin of very high lustre at one dollar to two dollars and fifty cents a yard, that is used for costume accessories and odd waists. Brown ladies' cloth has a girdle and yoke of cream guipure lace in points edged with narrow mink fur and laid on yellow satin .

PREVAILING STYLES

THE four-yard bell skirt having a godet back has been described many times. It must be lined with grass or hair cloth at the back to hold the plaits in position, and straps of elastic are also placed across the plaits at the belt and ten inches below. Then have a bias facing of canvas fifteen inches deep and a binding of bias velveteen. Get a decent quality of the latter and sew it on so that it is a mere trifle below the edge of the dress fabric after turning it up; baste carefully and your binding will set smoothly. The leg-of-mutton sleeve may be moderately full, using three yards of twenty-inch silk, or if the very large size, requiring four yards. Unless of very slimpsy goods sleeves are not lined with any stiffening—at the most lawn or thin crinoline will do. A new sleeve extends at the top of shoulder to the collar like a plaited tab; another one has two rows of shirring up the centre, throwing the fullness out on either side like the wings of a butterfly. Still another one has the lower part from the wrist to the elbow wrinkled like a mousquetaire glove from gathers along the inner seam. Round waists abound with only side and shoulder seams in the outside material. Some are plaited and yoked like a cotton shirt waist, others are pulled plainly over the lining, and others have much of the fitting done with tiny plaits at the waist-line, back and front. Where the figure absolutely forbids a round waist a pointed corsage is worn or one pointed in front and with added coat skirts or basques on the sides and back. This is a favorite style of the English tailors.

THE IMPORTANT BLACK SILK

AS they are named black silks are now ranked : satin duchesse, peau de soie, gros-grain and all reps, small-figured satin and taffeta. Moiré is still worn, but as trimming on a skirt, as a waist of it adds years to any one wearing it. While black silks are again in complete favor they are not like the all-black gowns of a decade past. Now it is the exception not to find them combined with a collar and plastron of bright color or a skirt and sleeves and waist of a vivid red or striking blue, green, etc. Chiffon, lace, jet, ribbon and velvet are the trimmings worn. Cherry is particularly fashionable on black, followed by bluet, yellow, pink, leaf green and mauve. The black silk skirt has become a standard institution to wear with odd silk waists and thus get several changes apparently out of one. These skirts are of speckled or plain satin duchesse, moiré, gros-grain, or of surah in accordion plaits if the wearer be of a slender figure. The skirts are of a bell shape, with godet back, and are from four to five yards wide, except those in accordion plaits that should be ten yards wide before plaiting them. They are untrimmed, or if the wearer is very short and stout the side and front seams are covered with a band of jet beads and spangles about three-quarters of an inch wide. With such skirts a black ribbon belt is worn, or a crush belt of the colored silk waist material, or one like the velvet collar if such an addition is liked. The waist may be checked, plain, striped or figured satin, taffeta, surah or filmy chiffon draped over silk. Such a costume is worn to the theatre, concerts, calling, small evening entertainments, for evenings at home, and at informal dinner parties, etc.

YOUNG LADIES' BLACK SILKS

THE skirt will be like those described, and large leg-of-mutton sleeves that have four yards of material in them. Round waist of cherry, bluet, yellow, green or mauve satin or gros-grain, with a crush collar of velvet of the same color. Braces of jet only, or of the black silk covered with jet. Loose Fédora front dropping in French fashion over the front of the belt of black jetted gauze. Another style shows a yoke of tucked chiffon, black over cherry silk, and a cherry velvet collar. Below the yoke is draped a jet corsage ornament finished with a fall of "rain" fringe. Others have a yoke or collar of jet Vandykes with bead, spangle and nailhead effects over a colored silk yoke, as one of bluet chiffon forming puffings between each point. A French model shows the upper part of the silk waist slashed to show a colored lining beneath and the slashes edged with narrow jet ; in some cases the sleeves are slashed to correspond. Belts of velvet, silk, jet or ribbon are worn. The jet girdles are very dressy with jet braces, draped corsage ornaments or yokes. Partly-worn black silk gowns can be re-modeled by adding new sleeves and a yoke, for instance, of black chiffon over colored silk, using a low, round bodice and skirt of the black silk, belt of ribbon having ends, etc. If the skirt is too narrow add side panels and leg-of-mutton sleeves of moiré, figured gros-grain or satin. Round waist of the old material, loose plastron of jetted black chiffon, crush collar and belt of cherry, mauve or bluet velvet. A very striking trimming is a yoke and girdle of colored velvet or satin overlaid with white guipure lace in appliqué figures. It is a good plan for those of limited wardrobes to have the gown made up plainly and wear detachable belts and collars and made-up neckwear, as chiffon and lace collarettes, yokes, plastrons, crush collars or fichus of lace or chiffon.

Bleached Cotton Flannel.

Per yard.
4520 Bleached Cotton Flannel, width 24 inches.................................$0.06½
Price for full piece of about 58 yards, 6¼ cents per yard.

4522 Bleached Cotton Flannel, width 26 inches, per yard.................................08½
Price for full piece of about 58 yards, 8¼ cents per yard.

4524 Bleached Cotton Flannel, width 26 inches .10
Price for full piece of about 57 yards, 9½ cents per yard.

4526 Bleached Cotton Flannel, width 28 inches, .12
Price for full piece of about 55 yards, 11¼ cents per yard.

4528 Bleached Cotton Flannel, heavy weight, width 28½ inches.................................14
Price for full piece of about 55 yards, 13¼ cents per yard.

Cotton Flannel—Continued.
4530 Bleached Cotton Flannel, width 29½ inches, extra heavy.................................$0.15½
Price for full piece of about 54 yards, 15 cents per yard.

Colored Cotton Flannel or Drapery Plushes.

Used for Portieres, Wall Hangings, Linings, etc.

Per yard
4550 Colored Cotton Flannel, old gold, medium and navy blue, olive, wine, cardinal, scarlet, drab or brown, 25½ inches $0.09
Price for full piece of about 54 yards, 8½ cents, per yard.

4554 Colored Cotton Flannels, high colors, blue, scarlet, garnet, brown, slate, pink, drab and gold, 27 inches 12½
Price for full piece of about 55 yards, 11¼ cents per yard.

Drapery Plushes—Continued.
4556 Heavy Cotton Plushes, 28 inches wide: plain colors: Cardinal, scarlet, wine, pink, claret, blue, drab, slate, brown, old gold.......$0.15
Price for full piece of about 55 yards, 13 cents per yard.

Fancy Colored Cotton Plush.

4560 Colored Cotton Flannel, black striped or checked with scarlet, old gold checked with black, width 27 inches... ....$0.10
Price for full piece of about 56 yards, 9½ cents per yard.

Use the William Clark Co.'s "N-E-W" Six Cord Spool Cotton.

LADIES' AND CHILDREN'S SUIT DEPARTMENT.

Ready Made Wrappers and Tea Gowns; dresses made to order. Styles absolutely correct and up to date.
NOTE.—We cannot furnish samples of wrappers or other ready-made garments. Samples of any garments which we quote to measure and make up in our custom department will be cheerfully sent upon request.
SPECIAL.—*We can make to order any dress shown in the Standard Fashion Catalogue.* Samples of dress materials and any information desired will be furnished upon request.
Write for our Special Dressmaking Catalogue No. E, mailed free of charge.
See our Special Catalogue E for rules for measurement.
Ready made wrappers, gowns and dresses are made in the following scale of sizes only:
Bust, 32 in. Length, 54 in. Bust, 38 in. Length, 58 in.
Bust, 34 in. Length, 56 in. Bust, 40 in. Length, 58 in.
Bust, 36 in. Length, 56 in. Bust, 42 in. Length, 58 in.

5600 Ladies' Ready Made Wrappers, made of dark prints; new styles; lined waist, belt, full sleeves, wide ruffle over shoulders and forming pointed yoke.
Each.........................$0.59
Per doz.....................6.65

5600

5602 Ladies' Ready Made Wrappers, made of indigo blue prints, small and medium figures, lined waist, large sleeves, belt, wide ruffle over shoulders and forming yoke.
Each.... ....$0.69
Per doz 7.85

5604 Ladies' Ready Made Wrappers, made of fast black prints, medium and small white figures and stripes, lined waist, belt, large sleeves, wide ruffle over shoulders and forming yoke, Wateau back.
Each $0.85
Per doz...................9.75

5602-4-6

5610

5610 Ladies' Ready Made Wrappers, made of high grade novelty chintz, black grounds with small neat floral designs in colors, lined waist, belt, Wateau back, large sleeves and wide cape ruffle over shoulders, trimmed with handsome 2-inch cream lace, the prettiest garment ever made for the price.
Each............$1.25
Per doz......—...14.25

5611 Ladies' Ready Made Wrappers, made of best quality American indigo prints, blue grounds with neat white figures, yoke, collar and cuffs of plain indigo blue cloth trimmed with narrow fancy braid in blue and white, has lined waist, belt, full front and Wateau back and shoulder ruffles.
Each.................$1.25
Per dozen... ..... 14.25

5611

5614 Ladies' Wrapper, made of Domett outing flannel in narrow stripes; medium colors, lined waist, belt, full back, large sleeves and wide ruffle over shoulders, forming yoke.
Each..................$1.40
Per dozen............16.25

5614-16

5616 Ladies' Ready Made Wrapper, made of plain fast black Henrietta sateen, lined waist, belt, Wateau back, large sleeves, wide ruffle over shoulder, forming yoke. Same style as above.
Each......... ....$1.45
Per dozen...........16.85

5618 Ladies' Wrappers, made of cashmere de laine in dark grounds with floral stripes in bright contrasting colors, entirely new; has lined waist, belt, Wateau back, leg of mutton sleeves, circular ruffle.
Each......... .....$1.50
Per dozen...........17.45

5618-20-22-24

5620 Ladies' Ready Made Wrappers, made of new dark striped ginghams; same style as above.
Each.........................1.50

5622 Ladies' Ready Made Wrappers, made of printed flannelette; handsome figured stripes in dark colors. New goods. Same style as above. Each.........................1.50

5624 Ladies' Ready Made Wrappers made of cashmere flannelette; ·fleeced back, dark grounds printed in bright mixed floral and Persian designs. Style same as above. Each,,......1.89

5606 Ladies' Ready Made Wrappers, made of best American indigo blue prints, same style as above.
Each...........$0.85
Per doz 9.75

5608 Ladies' Ready Made Wrappers, made of best qualcan indigo blue or fast black and white prints, lined waist, large sleeves, belt, wide cape ruffle over shoulders, Wateau back, ruffle and collar trimmed in narrow feather stitching.
Each...........$0.98
Per doz........11.25

5608

5612 Ladies' Wrappers, made of high grade novelty chintz; black grounds with small figures or dots in white or colors, such as gold, blue, etc., lined waist, belt, Wateau back, large sleeves, wide ruffle over shoulders forms pointed yoke, ruffle trimmed with two rows white rickrack braid.
Each.............$1.10
Per dozen.. .....12.80

5612

5626 Ladies' Ready Made Wrappers, made of dark figured sateen; black grounds with small bright printed designs, lined waist, belt, Wateau back: new cape front trimmed with cream lace inserting, large sleeves.
Each.............. ......$1.75

5626

5627 Ladies' Ready Made Wrappers, made of medium and dark colored Persian striped flannelette, cashmere twilled surface with fine soft fleece on inside; lined waist; wide ruffle over shoulder, tapering to waist line in front and back; large drop sleeves and belt. Each.............$1.50

5627

5628 Ladies' Ready Made Wrappers, made of English cashmere; half wool. Colors: Navy blue, cardinal, wine or black; lined waist, full Wateau back, loose front held to form with small strap, large drop sleeves, embroidered collar and two rows embroidery, scroll design worked in the material the entire length of front. Each.............$3,50

5628

5629 Ladies' Ready Made Wrappers, made of half worsted brocaded suiting, ruffle of the same material forms yoke front and back, large sleeves with ruffle at elbow; Wateau pleat from yoke; lined waist. Colors: Navy blue, tan, cardinal, light gray, brown, wine, myrtle or black. Each......$2.75

5630   **5632-34**

5630 Ladies' Ready Made House Wrappers, made of striped English flannelette, medium colors, pointed yoke and full back, held to the form with belt of the same material, revere front, raised shoulders, full ruffled sleeves. Each.....$2.25

5632 Ladies' Ready Made House Wrappers, made of fast black Henrietta sateen, full back and front shirred at collar, lined waist, raised shoulders. Each....................... 2.25

5634 Ladies' Ready Made Wrappers, same style as above, but made of small figured or striped black and white sateen. Each 2.50

Ladies' Tea Gowns.
Made to measure.

5650   **5652**

5650 Ladies' Tea Gowns, made of best English cashmere; black, cardinal, wine, navy or sapphire blue, full front and back, lined throughout, large gathered sleeves, wide revere front, worsted braid trimming on collar, reveres and sleeves. Each........ ....$5.00

5652 Ladies' Tea Gowns, made of best English cashmere, black, wine, cardinal, navy or sapphire blue, light blue or pink, lined throughout, tight fitting waist in back with Wateau pleat from yoke, loose front, leg of mutton sleeves, epaulet shoulders and ruffle across front and back. Each...................... 5.00

5654 Ladies' Tea Gown, made of all wool reversible serge, fine twill, lined throughout, has large puff sleeves, wide ruffle and collar trimmed with narrow silk ribbon, full Wateau pleats in back from collar. Colors: Cardinal, wine, navy blue or black, or any other seasonable colors. Each.....................$6.50

5656 Ladies' Tea Gown, made of new illuminated twill suiting, lined throughout; has large sleeves, close fitted back and loose front held to figure with half belt, velvet butterfly front and collar trimmed with tinsel braid. Colors: Wine, cardinal, navy, myrtle, brown or tan. Each $6.75

5558 Ladies' Tea Gown, made of fine French Henrietta; lined throughout handsomely shirred front and back, ruffled collar full coat sleeves with ruffle shirred in arm hole, full Wateau back, full front trimmed with silk ribbon to match. We can furnish all seasonable shades. Ea..$9.00

Children's and Misses' Dresses.

5680 Little Girls' Dresses, made of best staple gingham; small checks in navy blue, brown, or pink, with white; yoke of white all over tucking; trimming of white Hamburg edging. Ages, 2 yrs,, 3 yrs., 4 yrs., 5 yrs.
Each.......................................$0.69

5682 Little Girl's Dress, made of small checked baby flannel, in pink, light blue, tan, scarlet or gray. The daintiest fabric you ever saw. Round yoke, wide circular ruffle, full bishop sleeves.

Ages....	1 yr.	2 yrs.	3 yrs.	4 yrs.	5 yrs.	6 yrs.
Price...	$0.75	$0.95	$1.00	$1.10	$1.20	$1.30

5684 Little Girl's Dress, made of printed flannelette, in scarlet and black only. Small neat designs in black on scarlet grounds; full front with girdle, wide sash at back, full bishop sleeves; girdle, cuffs, collar and bottom of skirt trimmed in all wool black hercules braid.
Ages—
2 yrs. 3 yrs. 4 yrs. 5 yrs. 6 yrs. 7 yrs. 8 yrs. 9 yrs.
Price—
$1.25 $1.35 $1.45 $1.55 $1.75 $1.95 $2.15 $2.35
Age, 10 years, $2.50

5686 Little Girl's Dress, made of English cashmere, half wool, wide pointed ruffle over shoulders to waist line forming V front and back; lined throughout; full bishop sleeves, cuffs, collar and ruffle in fancy silk braid, made in all seasonable colors.

Ages..2 years.	4 yrs.	6 yrs.	8 yrs.	10 yrs.	12 yrs.
Price.. $1.75	$2 10	$2.45	$2.80	$3.15	$3.50

5688 Little Girls' Dress, made in same style as above, but of fine finished, all wool flannel suiting; lined waist only.

Ages....2 yrs.	4 yrs.	6 yrs.	8 yrs.	10 yrs.	12 yrs.
Prices.. $1.90	$2.20	$2.50	$3.00	$3.50	$3.65

5692 Misses' Dress, made of English Cashmere, half wool, lined throughout, has round yoke formed by wide military cape ruffle extending across shoulders, full balloon sleeves, empire belt, collar, cuffs, ruffle, and bottom of skirt trimmed with worsted hercules braid. We can furnish all seasonable colors.

Ages....	12 yrs.	13 yrs.	14 yrs.	15 yrs.	16 yrs.
	$5.00	$5.25	$5.50	$5.75	$6.00

5694 Misses' Dress, same style as above, made of fine all wool serge. All the staple and new shades.

Ages.....	12 yrs.	13 yrs.	14 yrs.	15 yrs.	16 yrs.
	$6.00	$6.25	$6.50	$6.75	$7.00

5696 Misses' Dress, made of new novelty suiting, wool bourette effects, combinations of dark colors intermixed. Waist is made over fitted lining. Three box pleats are formed of the material in the back and front below a shapely yoke of velvet in shade to harmonize with goods. Epaulets above shoulders ripple prettily over the leg-o'-mutton sleeves, narrow belt, new gored skirt. Color effects are in brown, green, wine or gray.

Ages.........	12 yrs.	13 yrs.	14 yrs.	15 yrs.	16 yrs.
Price.........	$5.50	$5.75	$6.00	$6.25	$6.50

Ladies' Newport Suits.

See note under department heading for scale of sizes.

5700 Ladies' Newport Suit, ready made, consists of jacket and skirt to be worn with shirt waists. Jacket is made with Tuxedo back, large leg-o'-mutton sleeves, wide revers in front, double stitched seams, inside seams bound, gored skirt, very full and wide, deep turned hem at bottom. Made of good looking and serviceable repellent cloth, in navy blue or black.
Per suit. $4.90

5702 Ladies' Newport Suit, same style as above. Made of strong repellent cloth, Collar, cuffs and bottom of skirt trimmed with black worsted hercules braid. Colors, black or navy blue only.
Per suit........$5.50

5704 Ladies' Newport Suit, same style as above, made of heavy all-wool storm serge, trimmed with two rows of folded satin rhadame on collar, cuffs and bottom of skirt. Colors: Black or navy blue only. A stylish and splendid wearing suit. Per suit.......................... ....$5.95

Montgomery Ward & Co.

18764 Marcello, Misses' Hat. English felt, satin wire edge, trimmed with large bows of fancy wide silk ribbon, jet pin and fancy feather colors: navy, brown, ecru and black. Each..... $2.35

18772 Orchid, English felt, satin wire edge, trimmed with silk velvet, large steel buckle, bows of silk ribbon, fancy feather and jetted aigrettes; colors: brown, ecru, navy and black. Each $2.50

18774 Margery, English felt, satin wire edge, trimmed with bows and rosettes of velvet and fancy wide silk ribbon, bunch of three tips, velvet face trimming; colors: brown, navy and ecru; no black. Each $3.00

18776 Windsor, black velvet with jet edge and fancy jet crown. trimmed with fancy black brocaded ribbon and rosette of colored satin ribbon, bunch of black jetted tips and aigrettes. $3.00

18776

18778 Iona Fur Felt Bonnet, jet edge and velvet fold, trimmed with silk velvet bow, wide satin ribbon rosettes, jetted pompom and aigrettes, velvet ribbon ties and bow. .Colors: Brown, navy and black. Each............ $3.25

Each.

18780 Odette, wool felt, best quality, trimmed with large bows and rosettes of fancy wide silk ribbon, jet buckle and bunch of fine black jetted cocque feathers. Colors: Brown, navy, ecru, with ribbon to match, or in black trimmed with colored fancy ribbon. Please state what color ribbon is desired when ordering black hat................. .... $3.25

18782 Empress, Large Black Silk Velvet Hat, jet edge, puffed velvet with fancy jet crown and band, trimmed with two black ostrich half plumes and bows and rosettes of colored and black satin ribbon. Please state color of ribbon preferred. Each............................... $5.25

18784 Toreador, Wool Felt, best quality, trimmed with silk velvet, wide fancy silk ribbon, jetted fancy feather, and face trimming of silk velvet and jet pins. Each...................... $3.35

We sell more SEWING MACHINES
than any other house in the world.
Why ?

18786 Tonquin, Wool Felt, best quality, jet edge, trimmed with silk velvet, wide satin ribbon bows and rosettes, fancy bird ornament. Colors: Brown, ecru, navy and black. Each $3.40

Each

18788 Deering, English felt satin wire and jetted edge, trimmed with wide silk moire ribbon, four jetted birds, aigrettes and jet rings; comes in black only $3.65

Each

18790 Ivanhoe, wool felt, best quality, with fancy felt edge, trimmed with wide all silk ribbon, large gilt or steel buckle, bird, jetted quills and aigrettes. Colors: Brown, ecru, navy and black $3.50

Each

18792 Graphic, wool felt, best quality, felt braid edge, trimmed with large bows and rosettes of wide silk ribbon, six black birds, fancy jetted feathers and two fancy jet pins. Colors: Brown, navy, ecru with ribbon to match, black with fancy colored ribbon. State color of ribbon preferred.................................... $4.25

Ladies' Dongola Oxfords.

52107 Ladies' Bright Dongola Kid Lace Oxford, Picadilly toe, long perforated patent leather tip, very attractive and dressy; flexible soles; sizes, 2½ to 7; width, C, D, E and EE. Per pair........$1.40 Weight, 12 oz.

52108 Ladies' Dongola Oxford Patent Leather Tip, with turn sole, all solid, and a very neat and dressy shoe for summer wear. Sizes 2½ to 8; widths, C, D, E and EE. Per pair...........$1.25 Weight, 12 oz.

Housekeepers' Delight.

52109 In this Oxford we give you better value for the money than any other shoe. It is made from a good plump grade of Dongola kid, patent leather tip, all solid and very good style; made to give excellent wear; sizes, 2½ to 8; widths, D, E and EE. Weight, 14 oz. Per pair...................$1.00

Common Sense Oxfords.

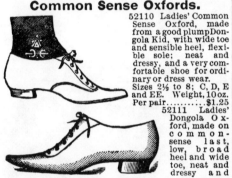

52110 Ladies' Common Sense Oxford, made from a good plump Dongola Kid, with wide toe and sensible heel, flexible sole; neat and dressy, and a very comfortable shoe for ordinary or dress wear. Sizes 2½ to 8; C, D, E and EE. Weight, 10 oz. Per pair..........$1.25

52111 Ladies' Dongola Oxford, made on common-sense last, low, broad heel and wide toe, neat and dressy and bound to insure comfort; slipper or turn sole; sizes, 2½ to 8; widths, D, E and EE. Price, per pair...$1.65 Weight, 13 oz.

The Elite.

52112 This is a new departure in the line of stylish footwear. The stock in this shoe is of a very fine selection of Dongola, French tannage, very soft and durable. This being the first season for this very stylish Congress, we look for a large sale on same. The accompanying cut represents this very accurately. It has a very neat patent leather stay up the front and a light turn sole with thin edge, and a medium heel, which makes a very comfortable and stylish dress shoe. Sizes, 2½ to 7, C, D, E, EE. Weight, 11 oz. Per pair......$2.75

The Juliet.

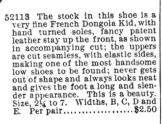

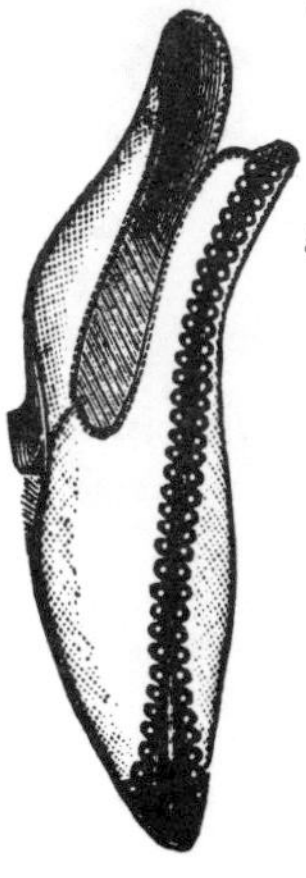

52113 The stock in this shoe is a very fine French Dongola Kid, with hand turned soles, fancy patent leather stay up the front, as shown in accompanying cut; the uppers are cut seamless, with elastic sides, making one of the most handsome low shoes to be found; never gets out of shape and always looks neat and gives the foot a long and slender appearance. This is a beauty. Size, 2¼ to 7. Widths, B, C, D and E. Per pair..................$2.50

The Old Reliable.

52119 Ladies' Pebble Goat Oxford, medium toe and heel, special value; sizes, 2½ to 8; widths, DE and EE. Weight, 15 ounces............$1.10

52120 Ladies' Dongola Oxford, machine sewed, neat looking, soft and pliable, ladies' favorite; sizes, 2½ to 7; full width. Weight, 14 ounces.. 1.10

52122 Ladies' Pebble Grain Newport Tie, all solid and well made, for rough wear; sizes, 2½ to 8, regular width ....$0.90 Weight, 16 ounces.

Ladies' Toilet and House Slippers.

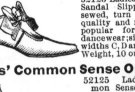

52123 Ladies' Kid Strap Sandal Slipper, hand sewed, turn sole, extra quality and finish, very popular for house or dance wear; sizes 2½ to 7; widths C, D and E..$1.60 Weight, 10 ounces.

Ladies' Common Sense Opera.

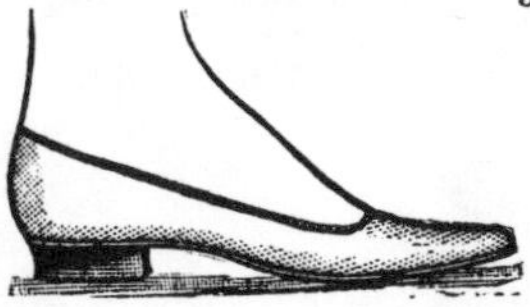

52125 Ladies' Common Sense Opera Slipper, made from a light soft Dongola stock, common sense heel and toe; light slipper sole, making a very durable and comfortable house slipper. Size, 2½ to 7; widths, C, D and E. $1.25

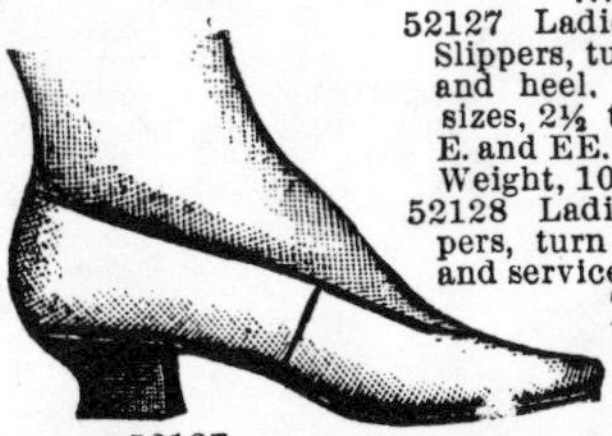

52127 Ladies' Kid Opera Slippers, turn sole, opera toe and heel, soft and pliable; sizes, 2½ to 7; widths, C, D, E. and EE. Per pair....$1.35 Weight, 10 ounces.

52128 Ladies' Kid Opera Slippers, turn soles, well made and serviceable; sizes, 2½ to 7, full width $1.00 Weight, 10 oz.

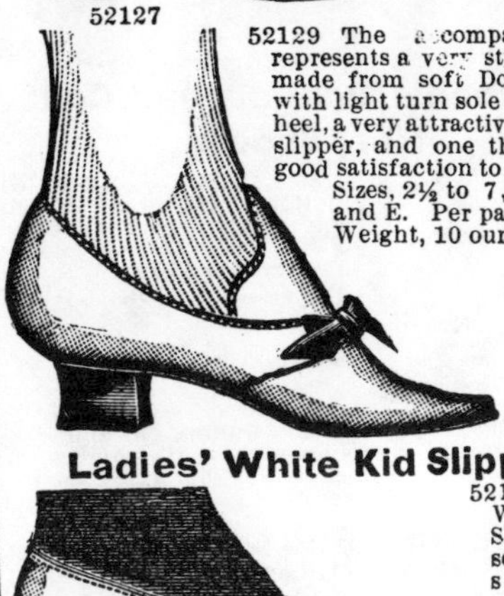

52129 The accompanying cut represents a very stylish slipper made from soft Dongola stock, with light turn sole and medium heel, a very attractive and sightly slipper, and one that will give good satisfaction to the wearer. Sizes, 2½ to 7, widths, C, D and E. Per pair....$1.40 Weight, 10 ounces.

Ladies' White Kid Slippers.

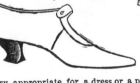

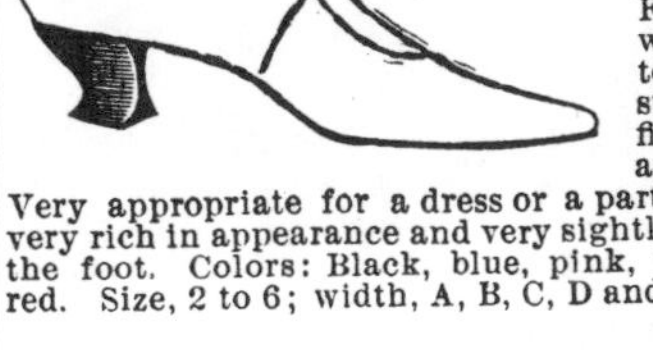

52130 Ladies' White Kid Slippers, hand sewed, turn soles, fine quality and finish; sizes, 2½ to 6, width, C, D and E........$1.50 Weight, 8 oz.

Ladies' Satin Slippers.

52131 Made from genuine Satin; open toe, hand-turned sole, French heel, with strap buttoning across instep; light and fine; made in assorted colors.

Very appropriate for a dress or a party slipper; very rich in appearance and very sightly when on the foot. Colors: Black, blue, pink, white and red. Size, 2 to 6; width, A, B, C, D and E $2.00

52132   52136
Per Pair.

52132 Ladies' Glove Kid, 3 point slipper, turn soles, low flat heels, soft and pliable, easy on the feet, and very desirable for house wear; sizes, 2½ to 8; width, D, E and EE. Weight, 12 oz ..$1.00

52136 Ladies' Pebble Goat Buskin Slippers, old ladies' style, best quality; sizes, 3 to 8, full width. Weight, 11 oz....................... 1.00

52137 Ladies' Pebble Goat Buskin Slippers, flannel lined; warm and comfortable; sizes, 3 to 8; full width. Weight, 12 oz..................... 1.00

52139 Ladies' grain slippers, damp proof, sewed, strong and durable for out or indoor wear, all solid; sizes, 3 to 8; full width. Weight, 15 oz.....................$0.75

52141 Ladies' Serge Buskin Slippers, turn soles, low flat heels, fine quality; sizes, 3 to 8; full width. Weight, 8 oz 90

52142 Ladies' Serge Buskin Slippers, medium grade; sizes, 3 to 8, full width.....................65

Ladies' Carpet Slippers.

Weight, 10 ounces.

52143 Ladies' Brussels Carpet Slippers, best quality, bound and stayed; sizes, 3 to 8, full width..   .35

"The German" Slipper.

Weight, 15 ounces.

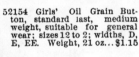

52144 Ladies' German Slipper, heavy cloth, embroidered toe, leather foxing; nothing better for wear and for comfort, no equal; see 52497 for men's; sizes, 3 to 8; full width.........................$0.90

Girls' Wear.

Weight, 14 ounces.

52145 Girls' Bright Dongola Kid Button, opera last, flexible single soles, genteel and dressy, for fine wear; sizes, 12 to 2; widths, C, D, E.......$2.00

52147 Girls' Pebble Goat Button opera last, extra quality and finish, machine sewed; sizes, 12 to 2; widths D and E. Weight, 16 oz...$1.65

52148 Girls' Domestic Kid Button; good style, quality and finish, machine sewed; sizes, 12 to 2; widths, D, E, EE..$1.75 Weight, 14 oz.

52145

52153 Girls' genuine Dongola Kid, button, opera last, single soles, medium weight, machine sewed worked buttonholes; a good fitting, serviceable shoe at rock bottom price; sizes, 12 to 2; full width. Weight, 12 oz $1.25

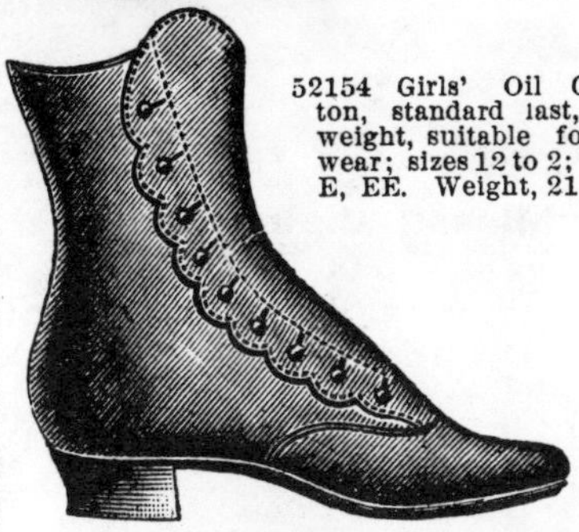

52154 Girls' Oil Grain Button, standard last, medium weight, suitable for general wear; sizes 12 to 2; widths, D, E, EE. Weight, 21 oz...$1.15

Girls' Glove Grain Spring Heel.

Weight, 18 oz.

52161 Misses' Glove Grain spring heel, button, oil-tanned, strong and durable for every day service, Sizes, 12 to 2; full widths. Per pair.-..... ......$1.45

Misses' and Children's Goat Shoes.

Weight, 11 to 14 oz.

52162 Misses' and Children's Genuine Tampico Oil Goat, spring heel. These shoes are made of the very best material, with solid leather counters and insoles, the wearing qualities being first-class, and at the same time making a neat, dressy shoe.   Per pair

Sizes, 6, 6½, 7, 7½ ....$0.90 Sizes, 8, 8½, 9, 9½, 10 10½ 1.15. Sizes, 11, 11½, 12, 12½, 13, 13½ Per pair.....$1.50 Sizes, 1, 1½, 2, Per pair....$1.65

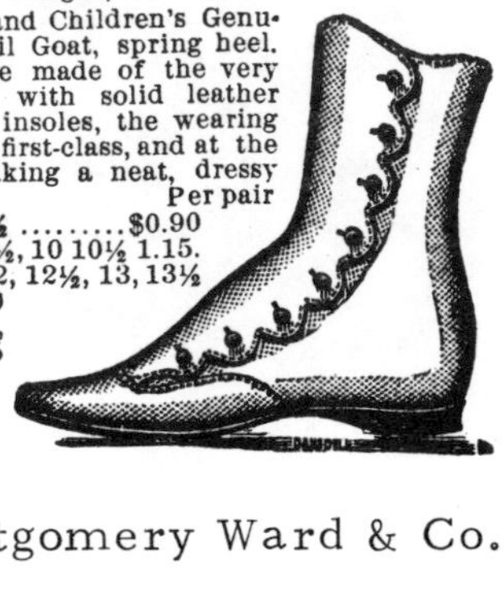

Montgomery Ward & Co.

Misses' and Children's Tan Colored Shoes.

Weight, 11 to 14 oz.

52164 Made from a very fine selection of Russet tan-colored goat skin. Spring heel, flexible soles, all solid, and a shoe that will give excellent good service, as the stock is very soft and pliable and at the same time tough, wearing equally as well as a much heavier shoe. Made over a very neat spring heel last. They require no blacking or oiling, and for light summer wear they are considered cool and very dressy. Sizes, 8, 8½, 9, 9½, 10, 10½. Widths C, D, E.....$1.25
Sizes, 11, 11½, 12, 12½, 13, 13½, 1, 1½ and 2. Widths, C, D and E.......................... 1.65

Misses' Heavy Calf Polish.

Weight, 22 to 25 oz. Per pair.

52166 Misses' Oil Grain Polish, pegged, double soles, damp proof; nothing better for wet weather use; sizes, 13 to 2..............................$1.10
52167 Misses' Bright Grain Polish, pegged, double soles, strong and solid; sizes, 13 to 2............ 1.00
52169 Misses' Custom All Calf Polish, hand pegged, double soles, warranted; sizes, 13 to 2...... 1.50
52170 Misses' Calf Polish, pegged, double soles, well made and solid throughout; sizes, 13 to 2 ..1.25
52172 Misses' A Calf Polish, pegged double soles, stout and heavy; for hard wear; sizes, 13 to 2.. 1.00

Misses' Tan-Color Oxfords.

52174 This shoe is made from Tan Goat skin, is very neat and dressy, with tip, and the prevailing style for the coming season. Spring heel only. Sizes 12 to 2; width, C, D, E; per pair, ...$1.25
Weight, 10 oz.

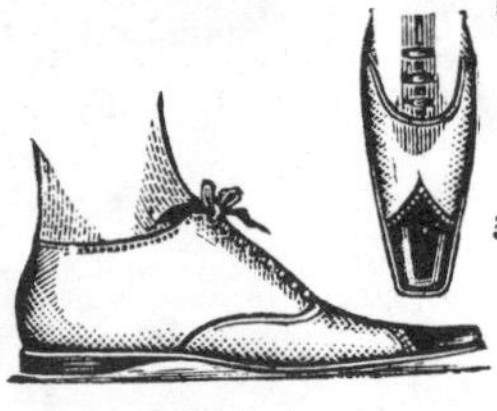

52178 Misses' Dongola Tie, machine sewed, single sole, with heels, light and fine; sizes, 13 to 2; widths, D and E.. ....$1.25
(Weight, 10 oz.)
52179 Misses' Dongola Spring Heel Oxford, machine sewed, good style and quality; sizes, 11 to 2; widths, D and E..................$1.25

Misses Grain Ties.

52180 Misses' Grain Ties, straight last, sewed strong and solid; sizes 13 to 2 .... .80

Misses' and Chidren's Dongola Spring Heels.

Weight, 11 to 13 oz.

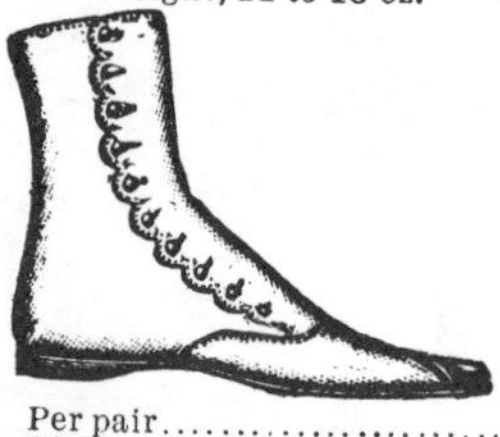

52181 This shoe is made from a fine selection of Dongola kid, with patent leather tip and square toe, which adds greatly to the appearance. The bottoms are of solid sole leather, also the counters, which are a sure guarantee of a good wearing shoe. Misses' sizes, 1, 1½, 2. Widths, C, D and E.
Per pair...$1.75
Girls' sizes, 11, 11½, 12, 12½, 13, 13½. Widths, C, D and E. Per pair........................ 1.55
Children's sizes, 8, 8½, 9, 9½, 10, 10½. Widths, C, D and E.. 1.25

Weight, 9 to 14 oz.

52182 Misses' and Children's Glazed Dongola Kid, spring heel, plain toe. This shoe is designed for general wear, also for dress, being made from a good selection of stock; the bottoms and counters are of solid leather, and in appearance the shoe is perfect; we can recommend this shoe as being a good wearer.

Per pair.
Misses' sizes, 1, 1½, 2. Widths, C, D and E.......$1.55
Girls' sizes 11, 11½, 12, 12½, 13, 13½. Widths, C, D and E.. 1.40
Children's sizes, 8, 8½, 9, 9½, 10, 10½ Widths, C, D and E.. 1.25
Children's sizes, 5, 5½, 6, 6½, 7, 7½. Widths, C, D and E.. .95

M. W. & Co.'s School Shoes.

We wish to call your special attention to our celebrated school shoes, numbers 52183, 52184, 52185. These shoes are warranted by us. We have the fullest confidence in their wearing qualities, and our increasing sales for the past 18 years demonstrate that that confidence is shared by our customers.

Weight, 11 to 18 oz.

52183 Child's Pebble Grain School Shoe, button, double sole, spring heel, sole leather box tip toe, worked buttonholes; all solid and warranted.

						Per pair.
Sizes, 5,	5½,	6	6½	7	7½	........$0.95
Sizes, 8	8½	9	9½	10	10½	.... 1.15
Sizes, 11	11½	12	12½	13	13½	.... 1.30
Sizes, 1	1½	2				.... 1.60

52184 Child's Pebble Grain School Shoe, button, double sole, low flat heels, sole leather box tip toes, worked buttonholes; all solid and warranted.

Weight, 12 to 20 oz.

						Per pair
Sizes, 5	5½	6	6½	7	7½	........$0.95
Sizes, 8	8½	9	9½	10	10½	.... 1.15
Sizes, 11	11½	12	12½	13	13½	.... 1.30
Sizes, 1	1½	2				.... 1.60

52185 Child's Pebble Grain School Shoe, front lace, double soles, low flat heels, sole leather box tip toe, straight cut top; very desirable for boy's wear.

Weight, 16 to 20 oz.

						Per pair.
Sizes, 8	8½	9	9½	10	10½	...........$1.15
Sizes, 11	11½	12	12½	13	13½	.... 1.30
Sizes, 1	1½	2				.... 1.60

Children's Dongola and Goat Heel Shoes.

52186 Child's Dongola Kid Button, machine sewed, single sole, worked buttonholes; neat fitting and stylish; sizes, 8 to 11.
Per pair.......................$1.15
Weight, 10 ounces.

52188 Child's Bright Goat Button, medium weight, worked buttonholes, sewed; suitable for every day and dress wear (see 52186 for style); sizes 8 to 11. Per pair........................ 1.15

Children's Red Goat Shoes.

Weight, 6 ounces.

52189 This shoe is made; from genuine red tanned goat, spring heel, turn sole, with tassel, the very latest color in children's shoes, making a very neat and sightly shoe. Sizes, 4 to 8.
Per pair.....................$0.80

Children's Tan Shoes.

Weight, 6 ounces.

52190 This shoe is made from Tan Goat skin, which is very neat and stylish, and at the same time, serviceable; with spring heel, worked buttonholes. Sizes, 4 to 8.
Per pair................. $0.80
Sizes, 1 to 5, no heel.
Per pair........................ .65

Children's Dongola Shoes.

Weight, 6 ounces.

52191 Child's Dongola Kid Button, hand sewed, turn sole, spring heel, worked buttonholes and tassel, six button; sizes, 4 to 8.
Per pair.............................$0.70

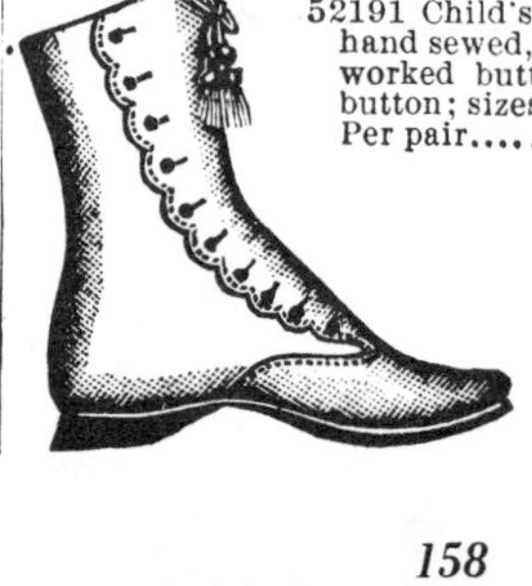

Children's Goat Shoes.

Weight, 6 ounces.

52192 Child's Bright Pebble Goat Button, hand sewed, turn sole, spring heel, worked buttonholes and tassel, neat and serviceable; sizes, 4 to 8..$0.70
52193 Child's Pebble Goat Button, spring heel, turn sole with sole leather tip toe, light weight and durable, for every day wear; sizes, 4 to 8.... .75
Weight, 9 ounces.

52195 Child's Bright Grain Button, with heels, single sole, neat and serviceable; sizes, 5 to 8. Price...................$0.60

Children's Red Goat Oxfords.

Weight, 5 to 8 ounces.

52196

52196 This is the prevailing color for the coming season in children's shoes. Made from genuine red goat skin, with spring heel, very neat and dressy. Sizes, 8, 8¼, 9, 9½, 10, 11. Per pair.......$0.98
Sizes, 5, 5½, 6, 6½, 7, 7½. Per pair................. .75

Children's Dongola Oxfords.

Weight, 8 ounces.

52197 Child's Kid Oxford Tie, flexible sole, spring heels, fine quality, sewed; sizes, 8 to 11. Per pair.$0.88
52198 Child's Kid Oxford Tie, fine quality, turn soles, with spring heels, sewed; sizes, 4 to 7½... .75
Weight, 5 ounces.

Children's Tan Color Oxfords.

Weight, 5 to 8 ounces.

52199 Child's Tan Oxford, made from a genuine Goat Skin, soft and pliable, with turn sole and spring heel; very dressy for the little ones. Sizes, 8½, 9, 9½, 10, 10½, 11.
Per pair...$0.90
Sizes, 5, 5½, 6, 6½ 7, 7½, 8. Per pair...... ... .75

For Hard Knocks.

Weight, 16 ounces.

52200 Child's Custom All Calf Front Lace Shoes, hand pegged, double sole, warranted; sizes, 8 to 12.
Per pair.................................$1.15
52202 Child's Calf Front Lace Shoes, double sole, tipped, strong and heavy, pegged; sizes, 8 to 12.
Per pair.........................$1.00
52203 Child's Oil Grain Front Lace Shoes, tipped, double sole, damp proof, pegged; sizes, 8 to 12 Per pair...............................$0.90

Infant's Red Shoe.

Weight, 4 ounces.

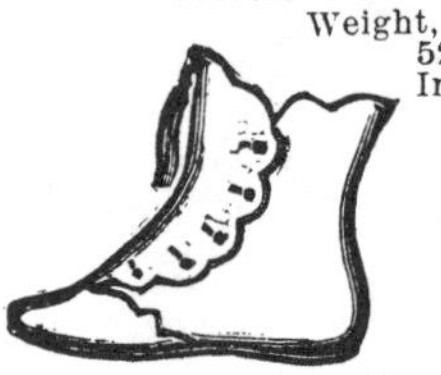

52204
Infant's Red Shoe, worked buttonhole and tassel, turn sole, no heel, fine quality and latest color. Sizes, 1 to 5.
Per pair................$0.65

Infants' Dongola Shoe.

Weight, 4 ounces.

52205 Infants' American French Kid Button, worked buttonholes and tassels; flexible, turn soles, sewed, no heels; sizes, 1 to 5.........................$0.75

52206 Infants' Kid "Fat Baby" Shoe; button-worked buttonholes and tassel light and fine, made especially for thick, fat feet; no heels. Sizes, 1 to 5.
Per pair..........$0.65

Per pair.
52207 Infants' Kid Button, turn sole, sewed, worked buttonholes and tassels, no heels; sizes, 1 to 5..$0.60
52208 Infants' Pebble Goat Button hand-sewed, turn sole, no heels, sole leather tip toe; sizes, 1 to 5.. .55
52209 Infants' Kid Button, turn sole, well made, no heels, sizes, 1 to 5.............................. .45
52210 Infants' Pebble Goat Button turn soles, no heels, durable; sizes, 1 to 5........................ 40

Infants' Soft Sole Shoes.

Weight, 2 ounces.

52212 This shoe is made from genuine French kid with kid sole, nothing finer for an infant; sizes, 0, 1, 2, 3. Per pair........................$0.35
The same style, only in Dongola kid; sizes, 0, 1, 2, 3. Per pair.. .25

Coming Styles
DESIGNED BY THE
GREAT COSTUMERS
OF
EUROPE

PARIS - - - - - E. FELIX
LONDON - DEBENHAM & FREEBODY
BERLIN - - - - JULES BISTER
FRANKFORT A/M - ULLMANN & STRAUSS
BRUSSELS - - - HIRSCH & CIE
THE HAGUE - - - M. A. VOGELS
ST. PETERSBURG - A. IZAMBARD

VIENNA - - - - CH. DRECOLL
TURIN - DE GASPARI, ROSA E TORTA
FLORENCE - - - EMILIA BOSSI
MOSCOW - - MAISON E. MINANGOY
GLASGOW - SIMPSON, HUNTER & YOUNG
DUBLIN - - - - - - MANNING
LIVERPOOL - GEO. HENRY LEE & CO.

An Introduction to the Modelers

❦❦❦

There are presented herewith short sketches of the European leaders of fashion whose designs are reproduced in this book. They are so well known to the wealthy and fashionable ladies of this country that a reminder only is necessary. They are mentioned so as to give assurance to American patrons that they can rely upon the information given as being correct.

M. Félix of Paris is so well known that it seems almost unnecessary to say that at least there is not a more famous costumer in the world. His costumes, which are the most radical known. are adopted by the Royalty of Europe, the Théâtre Français, and the Vaudeville, and we Americans view them every year on our own stage. Twelve years ago, when Mme. Sarah Bernhardt first came to America, all her scenic costumes were designed by Félix, and those who remember the eulogies bestowed on her gowns can hardly fail to perceive that they were the work, not of the artist alone, but of the master. The high esteem in which he is held may be gathered from the fact that the Paris Exposition (1900) Committee has granted him the sole concession to erect a building on the grounds, and there display a history of Women's Costume, showing all the epochs of dress from ancient days to the present.

While in London, if one asks, "Which is the greatest house for general costumes?" he will invariably receive the reply, "Debenham & Freebody," and this in the face of the fact that it is an enormous wholesale and retail establishment, which has been in existence for more than a century, and has spread its wholesale houses to New York, Paris, Melbourne, Sydney, and Brussels. The firm's artist, "Pilotelle," who designed the costumes contributed by them. is the most famous artist of London in this especial line.

Hirsch & Cie. of Brussels (also of Amsterdam, Cologne. Dresden, and Hamburg) are costumers to the Court of Belgium. The house was founded in 1869, and employs in Brussels alone over a thousand employes on gowns, coats, and fur trimmings for ladies. M. Hirsch was decorated by the Queen of Belgium with the order of "Leopold." The house received gold medals at the National Exposition of Brussels in 1880, the International Exposition of Amsterdam in 1883, and the International Exposition of Antwerp in 1885.

Jules Bister occupies the head position as costumer at Berlin; he is "fournisseur" to the Imperial Court, to the ladies of honor, to four monarchial courts of Germany, and to most of the resident ambassadors at the German capital.

Ullman & Strauss of Frankfurt-am-Main are a firm of the first rank in that great city of finance. The house is one of the youngest and most progressive of Europe, and makes a specialty of jackets, adopting the "genres" of Vienna fashion.

The house of M. A. Vogels has been in existence for over sixty years, and is the firm, "par excellence," of The Hague, the residence capital of Holland. Among its patrons are the Royal Court and principal families of Holland.

Alfred Manning of Dublin enjoys a reputation second to none in Great Britain. The house was established by his father sixty years ago, and the son spent years with the leading costumers of Paris and London before taking up his father's affairs, which he has enormously developed. In addition to the names mentioned on his pages of illustrations. he counts among his clientèle the greatest nobility of Great Britain, and such artists as Patti, Melba, Nordica, Albani, Scalchi, Langtry, Nilsson and many others.

The Maison Izambard of St. Petersburg has been in existence many years, and makes a specialty of court costumes, which are all of the same pattern and colors at the Russian Court when worn by the ladies of honor to Her Imperial Majesty. M. Izambard presented to the writer, while at St. Petersburg, a photograph of the costume worn by the present Dowager Empress at her coronation at Moscow; this costume was the creation of M. Izambard.

Ch. Drecoll of Vienna is the greatest costumer of Austria; his clientèle embraces the Austrian Court and the nobility, and his tailor-made costumes are sent to all parts of Europe and America, where they are used as models; in fact, it is he who makes Vienna famous for tailor-made dresses. The establishment is one of the most elegant in Europe.

De Gaspari, Rosa e Torta occupy a handsome establishment on the grand square of Turin, Italy, and have a great reputation; they are costumers to the Queen of Italy, the Queen of Saxony, and the Dowager Duchesses Elizabeth of Genoa, Isabelle of Genoa, and the Imperial Dowager Duchess d'Aoste Bonaparte.

The house of Emilia Bossi of Florence, Italy, is the representative one of that beautiful city, and counts among its patrons some of our wealthiest and best known American families residing there.

The Maison Minangoy (à Judeune) of Moscow, Russia, is a magnificent and extensive house. It was founded in 1850, and executed many commissions for the Empress at the time of the coronation of Alexander II in 1856. The house attained its pinnacle of fame in 1883, at the time of the coronation of Alexander III. A whole page could be devoted to a description of the ateliers of this great institution, where even hand-made lace and lingerie of the finest order are made in the house itself. Some idea of its size can be gathered from the fact that there are forty-seven windows on each floor.

The firm of George Henry Lee & Co. of Liverpool is owned by Alderman T. W. Oakshott, and his two sons, Arthur and T. D. Oakshott, are joined in the management; the house is well known on this side of the water, and is especially famous for novelties in riding habits and tailor-made gowns, although these compose a small part of the business, which is an exhaustive one.

Simpson, Hunter & Young of Glasgow have been established nearly half a century; it is a representative Scotch house, of high reputation and refined taste, its clientèle extending throughout Great Britain.

To the Royal Court of Holland.

POMPADOUR.

This costume is of " pompadour " material—a wool and silk cream colored " fond,"
with flowered crêpe de chine. The corselet is of cream colored crêpe de
chine. The crêpe de chine "ruche" around the throat is trimmed with
lilac ribbons of the same shade as the flowers. The sleeves
are of the same material as the skirt, and bordered
with a ruche of crêpe de chine and ribbon.

(M. A. VOGELS, The Hague.)

Marshall Field & Co.

EVENING GOWN.

In pale blue pompadour satin with pale pink chiffon
and écru Bretonne lace.

Simpson Hunter & Young.

(SIMPSON, HUNTER & YOUNG, Glasgow.)

Marshall Field & Co.

Fournisseur
à La Princesse de Chimay.
La Duchesse de Maillé.
La Duchesse d'Uzes.
La Duchesse de Luynes.
La Comtesse de la Rochefoucault.
La Vicomtesse de Greffulhe.
La Duchesse de la Torre.
Madam Sarah Bernhardt.
Miss Ada Rehan, et au Théatre
Français du Vaudeville.

EVENING GOWN.

Skirt of mauve silk, embroidered at hem with design in same shade. Tight-fitting bodice of plum-colored velvet. Light yellow gauze draperies caught about the bodice with bouquets of flowers, and falling as a sash on the skirt. Stiffened lace forms revers and Stuart collar. Small sleeve of pleated mauve and yellow silk.

(E. FELIX, Paris.)

Marshall Field & Co.

PROMENADE COSTUME.

Brown cloth; full skirt edged at hem with rows of narrow gold braid; waist
forming jacket from back seams, and striped diagonally with rows
of gold braid finished by tiny brass buttons; white silk
vest embroidered with gold; white silk cravat.

(CH. DRECOLL, Vienna.)

Marshall Field & Co.

ROBE DE VISITE.

Of taffeta chiné; small roses of several delicate colors on porcelain blue
ground; the waist of cream embroidery appliqued on black
gauze. Revers of porcelain blue velvet; collar
and jabot of mousseline Nil.

De Gaspari, Rosa e Torta

(DE GASPARI, ROSA E TORTA, TURIN.)

Marshall Field & Co.

PROMENADE TOILETTE.

In novelty goods of mixed wool and silk impressed in a "chain" design of variegated
colors.   Godet skirt; waist covered mousseline-de-soie of dark shade; the trimming arranged to form a fichu; small godet basque with ribbon girdle
tied in a knot and falling in long ends on the skirt; sleeves, as
the model shows, with ruffle of mousseline-de-soie bows
of ribbon; draped collar with bow in the back.

AUX DES PASSAGES, LYONS,

Tollis Kenzinger

Administrator

Marshall Field & Co.

By special appointment to Her Majesty
The Queen of Roumania
and the Irish Court.

To H. M. The Queen of England.
H. R. H. The Princess of Wales.
H. R. H. The Duchess of York.
H. R. H. The Princess Louise.

STREET GOWN.

Fawn-shot poplinette principally constitutes this gown. The bodice, of white silk
brocaded with mauve and yellow flowers, hooks invisibly in front under the
folds, and is finished at the waist by a wide band of white grass-lawn
embroidered with colored flowers and gold thread and spangles.
A yoke-like collar of poplinette falls over the bodice in
front and back, and epaulettes of the same goods
adorn the shoulders. Collar and epaulettes
are trimmed with small paste buttons.

Alfred Manning

(ALFRED MANNING, Dublin.)

Marshall Field & Co.

TOILETTE DE CÉRÉMONIE.

Brocaded satin of varied shades; godet skirt; corsage back cut in one piece; trimming of ivory satin and embroidery; revers in front forming epaulettes; center of the front of mousseline-de-soie pleated very fine; belt of satin with gilded galloons, the same galloons on corsage forming "Brandebourgs;" godet basque; tight lower sleeve extending and gathering full upper sleeve; top of sleeve not too bouffant.

AUX DES PASSAGES, LYONS,

Marshall Field & Co.

"VIVIA."

This street gown is made of green cloth. The skirt is entirely plain. The
basque fits snugly everywhere except in the back, where it falls
in two short box pleats. It is richly hand braided and
trimmed and faced with Persian lamb.

(GEORGE HENRY LEE & CO., Liverpool.)

Marshall Field & Co.

VISITING COSTUME.

The skirt in black satin duchesse, quite plain. The corsage in rose pink peau de soie with deep tabbed collar in old guipure studded with jet. Belt of green and pink shot velvet. Hat en suite.

(DEBENHAM & FREEBODY, London.)

Marshall Field & Co.

New Winter Styles

17T2022
Velour Plush
$18.50

17T2027
Velour Coating
$13.95

17T2017
Pannette Cloth
$19.95

17T2032
Fancy Mixture
$10.98

Women's and Misses' Fall and Winter Coat. Made of velour plush, which is woven of fine cotton yarn in a thick, dense pile surface having a bright lustrous finish, giving it the appearance of a silk velvet. It is made in one of this season's most becoming styles, showing the full loose back and belted front. The coat is beautifully trimmed with large rolling collar, which may be worn fastened up snugly around the neck, and pocket lapels of a heavy mohair plush with gray and black markings to resemble the real chinchilla fur and is very silky and furlike in appearance, trimming the coat very beautifully. Lined throughout with durable flowered sateen and is about 48 inches long. Sizes, 34 to 46 inches bust measure. **State size.** Average shipping weight, 6 pounds.

17T2022—Black.
17T2023—Navy blue.
17T2024—Brown.
17T2025—Green.
17T2026—Burgundy.

Price,
each **$18.50**

Women's and Misses' Fall and Winter Coat. Material is a serviceable wearing, heavy fabric that is about 80 per cent wool and the balance cotton. Coat is about 48 inches long. The back is cut straight and full and finished at each side with button trimmed plaits. The front is fastened with large fancy buttons and wide belt. The convertible collar, which may also be worn buttoned high up, close around the neck, is of velour plush, matching the lapels on the pockets. For a low priced coat, we consider this style one of our best values. It is unlined, comes in sizes 34 to 46 inches bust measure. **State your size when ordering.** Average shipping weight, 5½ pounds.

17T2027—Black.
17T2028—Dark navy blue.
17T2029—Dark brown.
17T2030—Dark green.
17T2031—Dark Burgundy.

Price, each . . . **$13.95**

Women's and Misses' Fur Cloth Coat. For the woman who desires an extra heavy Winter coat that will give exceptional wear we recommend this particular style, which has all the appearance of a fur coat. It is woven of bright, glossy mohair with a short, hairy nap, and has a bright silky finish. This style is one of the popular models for this season. Made with the loose, full back, belted fronts and has extra large collar of Kit Coney fur in color gray. Collar may also be worn fastened up snugly around the neck. Coat is about 48 in. long, has large, fancy patch pockets button trimmed and is lined throughout with a durable wearing mercerized sateen. May be ordered in sizes 34 to 46 inches bust measure. **Give size when ordering.** Average shipping wt., 6½ lbs.

17T2017—Black.
17T2018—Navy blue.
17T2019—Brown.
17T2020—Green.
17T2021—Burgundy.

Price,
each **$19.95**

Fall and Winter Coat of Dark Mixture Cloth. This is one of the new and attractive models for this season. It has the straight, loose cut back which hangs in large, soft folds, and the material is a very heavy, fancy mixture cloth showing a plaid design. It contains about 50 per cent wool and the balance cotton. We consider this an exceptional value at the price quoted. The collar, which may also be worn open in regular coat style, is of velour plush to match the deep turnback cuffs. The fronts are finished with wide belt and slash pockets, button trimmed, and fasten with velour plush covered buttons. Coat is unlined, about 48 in. long and comes in sizes 34 to 46 inches bust measure. **State size when ordering.** Average shipping weight, 6 pounds.

17T2032—Dark mixture.

Price, each . . **$10.98**

| ROUND BOA MADE OF GENUINE THIBET, RICH AND DRESSY **$7.50** | MARTEN SCARF LINED WITH FINE SQUIRREL ONLY . . . **$15.75** | GENUINE MINK SCARF LINED WITH FANCY SQUIRREL **$16.75** | LADY JANE SCARF, MADE OF GRAY SQUIRREL .... **$6.75** |

No. 17P1098 VERY STYLISH LADIES' BOA, made of genuine thibet, 70 inches long. Colors, black or white.

Price............... **$7.50**

If by mail, postage extra, 30 cents.

No. 17P1099 LADIES' DOUBLE SCARF, made of genuine marten. Upper part of garment is made of all marten and tab part is lined with fancy squirrel, finished with six rich tails at bottom. Silk ornaments and silk cords in front. Cords are finished with two extra tails. Color, very dark brown only. Price....... **$15.75**

If by mail, postage extra, 35 cents.

No. 17P1101 LADIES' SCARF. Made of genuine mink, 45 inches long not including tails. Lined with fancy squirrel lining, finished with six tails at bottom and two extra tails on silk cords in front.

Price.............. **$16.75**

If by mail, postage extra, 26 cents.

No. 17P1103 LADIES' FLAT SCARF. Made of genuine squirrel, 35 inches long, very full around neck. Trimmed with six tails around bottom. Silk cords in front with two extra tails to match. Lined throughout with gray satin. Strictly up to date.

Price.................... **$6.75**

If by mail, postage extra, 25 cents.

FLAT SCARF MADE OF EXTRA FINE SELECTED GRAY SQUIRREL, **$13.75**

No. 17P1107 STRICTLY UP TO DATE AND STYLISH GARMENT. Made of very fine selected squirrel skins, shaped around neck and shoulders. 80 inches long. Rich silk ornaments in front, pointed tabs, lined throughout with fine gray satin. Exceptionally good value.

Price,

$13.75

If by mail, postage extra, 30c.

BEAUTIFUL FUR SET, MADE OF FINE GRAY SQUIRREL, **$19.50**

No. 17P1109 LADIES' BEAUTIFUL FUR SET. Made of genuine squirrel, all selected skins. About 65 inches long. Lined throughout with fancy light squirrel. Trimmed with six tails to match at bottom. Silk cords in front finished with fur ornaments. Muff is the very latest flat shape and is lined with satin. Sets like this usually sell for from $25.00 to $30.00 more than what we ask for it. Our special price, **$19.50**

Postage, 40 cents.

THE KATHERINE, MADE OF SELECTED GRAY SQUIRREL, **$9.50**

No. 17P1105 LADIES' FLAT SCARF. Made of genuine squirrel, about 60 inches long. Lined with fancy light squirrel, finished at bottom with six fur ornaments. Silk cords in front finished with two extra tails. Very latest shown in furs this season.

Price,

$9.50

If by mail, postage extra, 30 cents.

LADIES' FUR COATS OR SACQUES

In the past we had so many requests for driving coats, that we decided to show a full and complete line. Up to this year we were unable to sell them, because we could not get the prices down cheap enough, but this year we have succeeded in buying raw material in large quantities and are in position to sell these goods cheaper than you can buy them elsewhere. You will do us a great favor by comparing these goods with goods shown in your own town or with goods shown in catalogues of other firms and you will find our prices are far below those shown by others, and if you were able to see the quality and make of the garments, you would surely be convinced that they are the best that money can buy. The quality, workmanship, trimmings and materials are far superior than those shown by other firms. We carry a large stock of these and can fill orders promptly. Sizes from 32 to 44 inches bust. State bust measure. The sizes in these coats run larger than on plain cloaks. When ordering be sure to state if measure is taken over a waist, dress or outer garment. No extra sizes.

THE CHEAPEST COAT FOR THE MONEY. NO ONE CAN UNDERSELL US .. $15.75

No. 17P951 LADIES' STORM COAT OR DRIVING COAT. Made of Chinese Mokio dog. 36 inches long. Shawl collar made of Australian opossum. Lined throughout with quilted sateen. Double breasted front, loose back. Color between a very dark brown and black, almost black.

This driving coat at $15.75 is a splendid garment; very serviceable; a quality that would cost you $20.00 to $25.00 in the exclusive fur store. Price...$15.75

STORM COAT WITH NUTRIA COLLAR AND CUFFS $18.95

No. 17P953 LADIES' STORM OR DRIVING COAT. Made of Chinese Mokio dog. Shawl collar and cuffs made of South American beaver otherwise called nutria. Loose front and back. Double breasted style. Lined throughout with quilted sateen. The shape of the collar on this coat can be seen better in illustration of No. 17P951. We take special pride in the values we are offering in these garments. Price.............................$18.95

OUR BLACK ESKIMO DOG STORM OR DRIVING COAT, 36 INCHES LONG .. $21.75

No. 17P955 LADIES' STORM FUR COAT. Made of Eskimo dog, which looks very much like a flat medium long hair Astrakhan. 36 inches long. Loose back and front. Shawl collar made of South American beaver, otherwise called nutria. Lined throughout with black sateen. Price............................$21.75

BULGARIAN LAMB DRIVING COAT ... $24.85

No. 17P957 LADIES' STORM COAT. Made of Bulgarian lamb. Very curly, 36 inches long. Loose back and front. Shawl collar made of South American beaver otherwise called nutria. Lined throughout with quilted mercerized sateen. Black only. Price....$24.85

GENUINE WOOL SEAL STORM COAT, NEAT AND SERVICEABLE $27.50

No. 17P959 LADIES' STORM FUR COAT. Made of fine wool seal, 40 inches long. Large storm collar and lapels, double breasted front. Lined throughout with mercerized sateen. For shorter garment see following description. Price....................$27.50

No. 17P960 LADIES' COAT. Same style as above. 30 inches long. Price....................$21.50

SILVER WOMBAT SACQUE.

No. 17P963 LADIES' STORM FUR COAT. Made of silver wombat, 36 inches long. Nutria collar and cuffs. Lined with mercerized sateen. Price....................$26.50

WALLOBY STORM COAT.

No. 17P965 LADIES' WALLOBY FUR COAT. Nutria collar and cuffs. 36 inches long. Lined with quilted mercerized sateen. Price....................$25.75

FINEST RACCOON COAT FOR THE LEAST MONEY.

No. 17P967 LADIES' STORM FUR COAT. Made of natural raccoon. As the variety of raccoon is so great that we cannot show one particular style, we have decided to make to order just as our customers desire it. We can furnish them from $55.00 to $85.00 made in same style as above garment, 36 inches long according to quality of fur. You can rest assured that we will give you the best values for the money and you can safely send us your order, stating amount you wish to pay for coat and we will make it according to your special measure within ten days after we receive your order. Price............$65.00 to $100.00

$27.50

No. 17P969 LADIES' FUR STORM COAT. Made of genuine hair seal. This fur is very short and has a beautiful luster. It is as rich looking garment as any other fur coat. Very neat in appearance and perfect fitting, 36 inches long. Has a nutria collar and cuffs. Lined throughout with quilted sateen. Price.............$27.50

Sears, Roebuck & Co.

JUST THE THING IN COLLARLESS EFFECT $5.75

UP TO DATE IN STYLE AND RIGHT IN PRICE $5.95

ENTIRELY NEW. THE RAGE OF THE SEASON $6.50

OUR ADVERTISED QUEEN LOUISE COAT $5.75

No. 17P649 LADIES' JACKET. Made of all wool Montagnac cloth. Very nobby and stylish coat made in latest collarless effect, neatly trimmed with kersey straps around the neck and in front, and finished with a velvet square as shown in illustration. Has a loose back and double breasted front. Stylish sleeves. Lined throughout with sateen. Color, black only.
Price.................$5.75

No. 17P651 LADIES' JACKET. Made of very fine all wool kersey cloth, 27 inches long. Loose back and loose front. Collarless effect. Trimmed with kersey around neck, finished with velvet. Front, bottom and sleeves are neatly trimmed with fancy braid. Newest style puff sleeves. Very sensible garment, stylish and up to date. Color, black only.
Price................$5.95

No. 17P653 LADIES' JACKET. Made of all wool Montagnac cloth, 26 inches long. Loose back and double breasted front. Double shoulder cape, neatly trimmed with satin folds. Similar trimming around bottom of jacket, reaching from front to back. Velvet collar, double breasted front, new sleeves and turnover cuffs. Lined throughout with black mercerized sateen. Color, black only.
Price................$6.50

No. 17P655 LADIES' MONTE CARLO JACKET. Made of all wool kersey cloth. Loose back and loose front. Collarless effect. Neatly trimmed with kersey straps in front. This jacket can be worn buttoned, or open as illustration shows, as it has a facing of satin, trimmed with fancy braid. Turnover cuffs, bishop sleeves. Lined throughout with mercerized sateen. Colors, black or castor.
Price................$5.75

A VERY POPULAR FUR TRIMMED MONTE CARLO .. $6.75

No. 17P657 LADIES' JACKET. Made of good quality kersey, 26 inches long. Loose back and front. South American beaver (nutria) collar. Double breasted front. Corded several times around bottom. Puff sleeves, pointed cuffs. Lined throughout with mercerized sateen. Exceptional good garment for the money, and is the cheapest fur trimmed garment shown. Colors, black or castor.
Price..........$6.75

PERFECT MODEL, ORIGINAL IN STYLE, ALL WOOL KERSEY, ONLY.... $7.95

No. 17P659 LADIES' JACKET. Made of all wool kersey cloth, 26 inches long. Loose back, double breasted front, coat shaped collar and lapels, pearl buttons. Neatly corded on sleeves in front and back and all around the bottom. Very fine jacket. Our illustrations will show you exactly how the garments appear. No more stylish goods can be had at any price. Color, tan only.
Price $7.95

CLOTHES HANGERS.

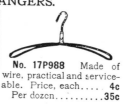

No. 17P987 Made of hardwood, smoothly finished. Price, each, 3c Per dozen..30c

No. 17P988 Made of wire, practical and serviceable. Price, each.... 4c Per dozen........35c

Sears, Roebuck & Co.

LADIES' CAPES

Capes are very popular this season again, and no wonder, since they are so handy and serviceable. No trouble to fit—they are warm—if in a hurry you won't have to stop to put on a tight fitting coat or jacket. We furnish these in the following sizes: 32 to 44-inch bust measure, 13 to 17-inch neck measure. When ordering, please give catalogue number, color, bust and neck measure.

LADIES' CAPE, 27 INCHES LONG ONLY . . . $2.75

No. 17P823 LADIES' CAPE. Made of kersey cloth, 27 inches long. Full sweep. Lined with mercerized sateen. Large storm collar. Color, black only. Price...**$2.75**

SEE PAGES

1 to 4, How to Order and How to Measure.

DON'T FORGET

to Give Size in Ordering.

VERY FINE BOUCLE CLOTH CAPE, with FUR TRIMMING.. $2.98

No. 17P825 LADIES' CAPE. Made of all wool, heavy weight boucle cloth, 30 inches long. Large storm collar. Thibet fur edging around collar and in front. Lined throughout with mercerized sateen. The material alone is worth a great deal more than we ask for the entire cape. We bought the cloth at an exceptionally low price, and thus are able to sell for less than the regular price of material. Color, black only.
Price.........**$2.98**
State bust and neck measure.

TRIMMED KERSEY CAPE FOR $3.75

A REGULAR $5.00 RETAIL CAPE.

SPECIAL VALUE IN GOLF CAPE $3.75

KERSEY CAPE WITH CORDING FOR $4.75

NO BETTER STYLES TO BE HAD AT ANY PRICE.

No. 17P827 LADIES' CAPE. Made of good quality kersey cloth, 30 inches long, very full sweep. Nicely ornamented with satin folds in front as shown in illustration. Large storm collar. Lined throughout with black mercerized sateen. Color, black only.
Price..........................**$3.75**
State bust and neck measure.

No. 17P829 LADIES' GOLF CAPE. Made of all wool fancy plaid back material, 24 inches long. Top part of cape, flounce and hood in back made with plaid side out. Fringes to match around the hood. Very good value for the money. Colors, black, blue, brown, or Oxford, with fancy plaid backs.
Price..........................**$3.75**
State bust and neck measure.

No. 17P831 LADIES' CAPE. Very stylish. Made of good quality heavy weight kersey cloth, 30 inches long. Large storm collar. Neatly trimmed with fancy cording and silk stitches in front and all around the bottom. Three rows of stitching all around the cape. Lined throughout with black mercerized sateen. Nothing better in the market for the price. Color, black only. Price....................**$4.75**

Sears, Roebuck & Co.

LADIES' WAISTS.

WAIST SIZES are from 32 to 42 inches bust measure unless otherwise stated in the description. No extra sizes to be had except in silk goods. When ordering, state catalogue number, color desired and number of inches around bust.

N EVER before have we been able to show such a large and varied assortment of ladies' waists, or have we been able to get together such an attractive lot of styles. There is not a waist shown in this entire line that does not embody style and elegance, and our prices are based on the cost of material and labor with but our one small percentage of profit added. The illustrations will give you some idea of the appearance of these handsome garments.

| SATEEN WAIST FOR .... 69c | ATTRACTIVE AND PRETTY SATEEN WAIST. OUR PRICE .... 89c | A PERFECT BEAUTY IN SATEEN WAISTS, ONLY .... 98c | FAST BLACK WAIST, TRIMMED WITH SATEEN STRAPS .... $1.19 |

No. 31P232 LADIES' WAIST. Made of fast colored sateen. Entire front is corded. High standing soft finished collar, new sleeves and soft finished cuffs. Back corded from shoulder to waist. Colors, black, blue or red. Sizes, 32 to 44 inches bust measure.
Price.................... **69c**
If by mail, postage extra, 21 cents.

No. 31P234 LADIES' WAIST. Made of good quality mercerized sateen. Front is tucked and finished with straps and small buttons. Back tucked from yoke to waist. Soft finished high standing collar and cuffs. Color, black only. Sizes, 32 to 44 inches bust measure.
Price.................... **89c**
If by mail, postage extra, 21 cents.

No. 31P236 LADIES' WAIST. Made of good quality mercerized sateen. Entire front tucked to pointed yoke. Embroidered sateen strap forming the yoke and plaits from yoke to bottom of waist. High standing soft finished collar. Tucks in back from shoulder to waist. New sleeves, soft finished cuffs. Colors, black or red. Sizes, 32 to 44 inches bust measure.
Price.................... **98c**
If by mail, postage extra, 22 cents.

No. 31P238 LADIES' WAIST. Made of fine quality mercerized sateen. The entire front is trimmed with clusters of tucks and finished with straps of same material forming yoke. Clusters of tucks in back from neck to waist. High standing soft finished collar, new sleeves and soft finished cuffs. Color, black only. Price.............. **$1.19**
If by mail, postage extra, 22 cents.

| OUR BRILLIANTINE WAIST IS AN EXTRAORDINARY VALUE FOR ... $1.48 | THIS STYLISH BRILLIANTINE WAIST ONLY... $1.89 | VERY APPROPRIATE FOR MOURNING. MADE OF SICILIAN WITH A FINE LUSTER .... $1.98 | SHIRRED EFFECTS IN WAISTS ARE CONSIDERED TO BE JUST THE PROPER THING .... $2.98 |

No. 31P246 LADIES' WAIST. Made of good quality brilliantine. Front finished with side plaits. Several clusters of tucks in back from neck to waist. High standing soft finished collar, new sleeves and soft finished cuffs. Colors, black or white. Sizes, 32 to 44 inches bust measure. Price **$1.48**
If by mail, postage extra, 20 cents.

No. 31P248 LADIES' WAIST. Made of good quality brilliantine. Front is finished with black and white embroidery and tucks as shown in illustration. Large pearl buttons. Several clusters of tucks in back from neck to waist. High standing soft finished fancy collar, new sleeves and soft finished cuffs. Color, black with black and white with white and black embroidery. Price.... **$1.89**
If by mail, postage extra, 18 cents.

No. 31P250 LADIES' WAIST. Made of good quality brilliantine. Front is finished with folds and side plaits as shown in illustration, trimmed with large cloth covered buttons. Plaited back from neck to waist. High standing soft collar with tabs. Plaited sleeves and soft finished cuffs. Color, black only. Price.... **$1.98**
If by mail, postage extra, 20 cents.

No. 31P252 LADIES' WAIST. Made of good quality brilliantine. Yoke is beautifully shirred. Plaited back from neck to waist. Very full sleeves shirred at top and soft finished cuffs. Soft finished high standing collar. Colors, black or cream.
Price **$2.98**
If by mail, postage extra, 25 cents.

Sears, Roebuck & Co.

EVENING WAIST MADE OF FINE TAFFETA SILK IN THE PRETTIEST SHIRRED EFFECT WHICH IS THE RAGE OF THE SEASON **$5.95**

THIS GRAND LACE WAIST CANNOT BE DUPLI-CATED ANYWHERE FOR OUR PRICE **$5.75**

No. 31P338 LADIES' WAIST. Made of good quality taffeta silk. Front is trimmed with straps of same material and shirring finished with small silk buttons. Seam down center of back from neck to waist. Soft finished collar with pretty tie. Very full sleeves trimmed like front of waist. Fancy turnover cuffs. Colors, black, white or light blue.

Price...... ....**$5.95**

If by mail, postage extra, 25 cents.

No. 31P340 LADIES' BEAUTI-FUL ALL OVER LACE WAIST. Lined throughout with white china silk. Front and lace collar are trimmed with silk ribbon and ornaments. Latest sleeves with soft finished cuffs. Colors, white with light blue or pink ribbon trimmings.

Price **$5.75**

If by mail, postage extra, 30 cents.

Ladies' Silk Shirt Waist Suits.

It is important to know that shirt waist suits have been and are worn by the ladies of society. Everywhere you turn in the large cities, you will find that shirt waist suits are worn extensively. It answers for the same purpose as the dress, and is more comfortable. It always looks neat and always up to date. The skirt or the waist can be worn with another skirt or waist, just as you like, and that way you have a variety of things to wear, while in reality it's only one article. Our prices are so low that it enables anyone to own one. When ordering use the measurements same as if a suit was ordered. Sizes, 32 to 42-inch bust, 22 to 28-inch waist and 37 to 44-inch long skirts.

SHIRT WAIST SUIT OF TAFFETA ONLY **$11.75**

THIS MOST STYLISH SUIT OF PEAU DE SOIE WITH PLAITED WAIST AND SKIRT FOR ONLY **$13.50**

THIS SUIT IN HEIGHT OF FASH-ION. MADE OF VERY FINE TAFFETA SILK .. **$14.95**

No. 31P342 LADIES' SUIT. Made of good quality taffeta silk, consisting of waist, skirt and silk belt. Waist is finished with tucks and open work stitches as shown in the picture. Tucks and slot seams in center of back from neck to waist. High standing turnover collar with tabs. Full bishop sleeves and turnover cuffs. Collar and cuffs trimmed with open work stitches. Skirt finished with side plaits all around and several rows of stitching around bottom. Facing of same material. Unlined. Color, black only.

Price **$11.75**

If by mail, postage extra, 60 cents.

No. 31P344 LADIES' SUIT. Made of good quality peau de soie consisting of waist, skirt and silk belt. Waist is finished in front with plaits and tucks. Slot seam down center of back from neck to waist. Fancy high standing collar with double tab. Trimmed with silk buttons. New sleeves with narrow cuffs. Skirt made with side plaits all around terminating in kilts at bottom in graduated effect. Several rows of stitching all around bottom. Facing of same material. Skirt unlined. Color, black only.

Price **$13.50**

If by mail, postage extra, 60 cents.

No. 31P346 LADIES' SUIT. Made of good quality taffeta silk, consisting of waist, skirt and silk belt. Front of waist elaborately finished with tucks and silk straps as shown in picture. Tucked yoke in back. Trimmed with silk straps and silk buttons. Straps from yoke to waist in back. High standing soft finished collar with tab. Stylish sleeves and cuffs trimmed with straps of same material. Skirt made with stitched lapover seams terminating at bottom in kilts in graduated effect. Stitched several times around bottom. Facing of same material. Color, black only. Price.**$14.95**

If by mail, postage extra, 60 cents.

Sears, Roebuck & Co.

LADIES' SUITS

WE ARE SHOWING extremely attractive styles this season in ladies' tailor suits. Ladies' tailor suits will be as popular as ever this season, and we have succeeded in combining style, fit and elegance in these goods with extremely low prices. Our tailor suits are not to be compared with the ordinary run of these goods, as shown in the ordinary catalogue. The suit you get from us will have a distinctiveness in appearance, a style and fit that you cannot get from your home dealer or from any other mail order house, such a suit as can be had only from fashionable city man tailors, and there at two to three times our special price. If you give us careful measurements, we will guarantee perfect fitting garments. A tailor suit is practically worthless unless it fits nicely, and in this particular feature of good fitting tailor suits we know that the suits we are offering this season excel any other make of goods on the market.

THE FOLLOWING SUITS have been most carefully selected from all the manufacturers' lines that have been offered to us this season, each and every number is a special value, a stylish and fashionable garment, and as to selection, it is simply a matter of price, as to how much you care to invest in a tailor suit.

IN ORDERING state number of inches around bust, around waist and the length of skirt in front. We furnish these suits in the following sizes: 32 to 42 inches bust measure, 22 to 29 inches waist measure, 37 to 44 inches length of skirt; measure the skirt from the bottom of the waist band. Sizes different than regular will be made to order at an advance of 20 per cent above the price quoted in catalogue. It takes ten to fourteen days to make special garments.

If desired, we will send samples of the cloth of which these tailor suits are made although you can order satisfactorily direct from our descriptions, and it is really not necessary to send for samples.

OUR TAILOR MADE SUIT .. $5.50

SPECIAL TAILOR MADE BLOUSE SUIT, FOR.... $5.98

NORFOLK WALKING SUIT OF FANCY MATERIAL, ONLY................. $7.35

No. 31P2 Ladies' Tailor Made Suit. Consisting of jacket and skirt. Made of good quality repellent cloth. Jacket made with coat shape collar and lapels, fly front, bishop sleeves, turnover cuffs. Lined throughout with mercerized sateen. Plain tailor made skirt, lined throughout with spun glass lining, interlined at bottom and bound with velvet. Colors, black, blue, gray or brown.

Price..................... **$5.50**

Not mailable.

No. 31P4 Ladies' Tailor Made Suit. Consisting of blouse and skirt. Made of repellent cloth. Double breasted front, coat shaped velvet collar and lapels, pointed sleeves and velvet belt. Lined throughout with mercerized sateen. Skirt, tailor made, lined throughout with spun glass lining, interlined around bottom with crinoline, and bound with velvet. Colors, black, blue or Oxford gray.

Price..................... **$5.98**

Not mailable.

No. 31P6 Ladies' Norfolk Suit. Consisting of jacket and skirt. Made of all wool snow flake material. Jacket is made double breasted front, coat shaped collar and lapels. Strap trimmings in front and back. No lining in jacket. Facing of same material. Walking skirt made with side plaits all around and kilt plait in center of front. No lining in skirt. Several rows of stitching around bottom. This is a walking suit and we can furnish in lengths from 38 to 44 inches. Colors, black or blue with white dots or sprinkled effect. Price................. **$7.35**

Not mailable.

LADIES' DRESS SKIRTS.

FANCY FIGURED MAN-CHESTER SKIRT............ **$1.35**

No. 31P100 Ladies' Dress Skirt. Made of black fancy figured Manchester cloth. Lined throughout with percaline, interlined at bottom. Color, black only.

Price........................**$1.35**

If by mail, postage extra, 32 cents.

NEAT AND NOBBY, WITH FOLDS, AS SHOWN IN ILLUSTRATION....... **$3.35**

No. 31P107 Ladies' Dress Skirt. Made of habit cloth Very neatly trimmed with folds of same material, bound with taffeta. Several rows of stitching all around bottom. Skirt unlined. Colors, black or blue.

Price........................**$3.35**

If by mail, postage extra, 45 cents.

WHEN ORDERING please state catalogue number, color, waist measure and length in front from waist to bottom of skirt.

Regular sizes, 37 to 44 inches length, and 22 to 29 inches waist. Sizes different than these must be made to order at an advance of 20 per cent over the catalogue price. It takes about 10 to 14 days to make a special garment. No specials made in Nos. 31P100, 31P102 and 31P104. Green, blue, brown and castor colors are very stylish.

RICHLY TRIMMED WITH CORD-ING AND SATIN FOLDS, LINED THROUGHOUT WITH SPUN GLASS, ONLY....... **$3.50**

No. 31P108 Ladies' Dress Skirt. Made of good quality repellent cloth. Very attractive and stylish design. Neatly trimmed with satin folds and several rows of cording. Lined throughout with spun glass lining, interlined at bottom and finished with velvet binding. Colors, black, blue or brown. At $3.50 this skirt is a wonder of value and is equal to any skirt sold others as high as $5.00. No handsomer style skirt was ever before offered or that combines as much style and elegance for so little money. In this catalogue we cater to the very finest class of trade as well as to those who wish to buy inexpensive garments and if you intend to wear fashionable garments you will make no mistake in ordering from this book. We give you the benefit of the city styles, the most approved fashions. Price........**$3.50**

If by mail, postage extra, 55 cents.

REPELLENT SKIRT IN THE LATEST COLORS.... **$2.75**

No. 31P102 Ladies' Dress Skirt. Made of repellent cloth. Neatly trimmed with satin fold as shown in illustration. Lined throughout with percaline, interlined with crinoline and bound with velvet. Colors, black, blue mixed, dark brown, dark red, green mixed or gray. These colors are very stylish this season. Price........**$2.75**

If by mail, postage extra, 50 cents.

MADE WITH A DROP SKIRT, AND ONLY **$3.25**

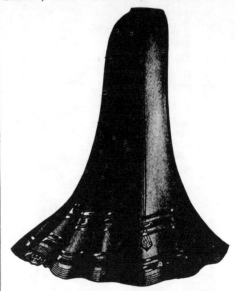

No. 31P104 Ladies' Dress Skirt. Made of good quality repellent cloth. Flounce trimmed with several rows of stitched satin folds, finished with tabs and small buttons. Several rows of stitching all around bottom. Drop skirt made of spun glass material with fluted ruffle. Colors, black only.

Price........................**$3.25**

If by mail, postage extra, 50 cents.

Sears, Roebuck & Co.

No. 38P899 Ladies' High Grade Drawers made of fine soft finish nainsook, has insertion of fine Hamburg embroidery, an umbrella flounce of 5-inch fine open work swiss embroidery, beautiful pattern. Open style only. Price $1.48
If by mail, postage extra, 8 cents.

$1.39

No. 38P902 A Very Strikingly Pretty Umbrella Style Drawers of high grade nainsook; Vandyke flounce trimmed with Point de Paris lace, wide insertion to match. Open style only. Draw strings.
Price..(If by mail, postage extra, 9 cents).. $1.39

LADIES' LONG CHEMISES SKIRT LENGTHS.
32 TO 42 BUST MEASURE.

$1.48

No. 38P710 A Very Pretty Combination Chemise made of a fine grade of lawn; low round neck, insertion of torchon lace and narrow ribbon in front, trimmed all round front and back with one row of feather stitch braid, also edged with torchon lace; has lawn ruffle in front with one row of torchon lace insertion with wide edge to match; armholes trimmed with feather stitch braid and torchon lace edging, has a wide lawn flounce at bottom with torchon lace insertion and edging to match.
Price................... $1.48
If by mail, postage extra, 11 cents.

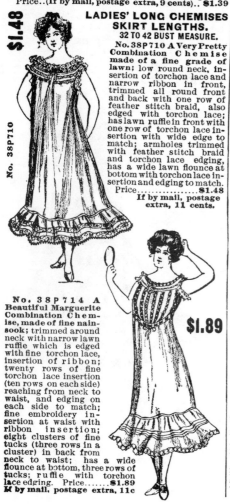

$1.89

No. 38P714 A Beautiful Marguerite Combination Chemise, made of fine nainsook; trimmed around neck with narrow lawn ruffle which is edged with fine torchon lace, insertion of ribbon; twenty rows of fine torchon lace insertion (ten rows on each side) reaching from neck to waist, and edging on each side to match; fine embroidery insertion at waist with ribbon insertion; eight clusters of fine tucks (three rows in a cluster) in back from neck to waist; has a wide flounce at bottom, three rows of tucks; ruffle with torchon lace edging. Price...... $1.89
If by mail, postage extra, 11c

TROUSSEAUX, CONSISTING OF FOUR PIECES—GOWN, SKIRT DRAWERS AND CORSET COVER.

We offer the four following most extraordinary values in Bridal Sets that will at once commend themselves to everyone familiar with fine muslin wear. They have been gotten together with a view of furnishing the very best goods possible and yet at prices within the reach of everyone. Read these descriptions carefully, note the material, the make, the finish—and note OUR PRICES.

Send us your order with the understanding that if the set when received is not perfectly satisfactory, all and more than we claim for it, you are at liberty to return it to us and we will return your money. Be sure to give bust measure.

$4.35

Sizes, 32, 34, 36, 38, 40, 42 inches bust measure.

Fine Cambric Trousseau of four pieces, consisting of gown, skirt, drawers and corset cover, all with matched embroidery.

Gown has a yoke with two rows of embroidery insertion on each side with three tucks between and insertion down center. Wide Hamburg embroidery trimming around the front and embroidery at neck and sleeves to match. Fine herringbone braid trimming.

Skirt has a double flounce Hamburg embroidery on lawn ruffle. Has a dust ruffle.

Drawers have a Hamburg embroidery flounce, with insertion of embroidery with six tucks. Yoke band. Open style. Very neat drawers.

Corset cover has four rows of Hamburg embroidery insertion., with cluster of tucks on each side, trimmed with fine embroidery around neck and armholes. Do not fail to give bust measure.
No. 38P908 Price, entire set of four pieces. $4.35
If by mail, postage extra, 45 cents.

OUR $5.98 TROUSSEAU OUTFIT.

$5.98

A Trousseau fit for an American queen made of fine cambric, of four pieces, gown, skirt, drawers and corset cover. All made with matched point de Paris lace. Sizes, 32, 34, 36, 38, 40, 42 inches bust measure.

Gown is made Empire style, fine grade of cambric, fancy revers, which are trimmed all around with fine point de Paris insertion and lace 4 inches wide. Bosom has one row of insertion and one row of fancy ribbon insertion, also with a 4-inch lace. Sleeves have an insertion of ribbon and 4-inch lace.

Skirt is made of fine cambric, has a lawn flounce which is made V shape all around and trimmed with 4-inch lace. Above this are two rows of point de Paris lace insertion all around flounce. Has a dust ruffle which is also trimmed with 4-inch lace.

Drawers are made of very fine cambric (open), has lawn ruffle with one row of point de Paris insertion and trimmed at bottom with lace to match.

Corset cover is made of fine cambric, low round neck edged with lace, three insertions of point de Paris lace. Armholes trimmed with lace to match. Do not fail to give bust measure.
No. 38P910 Price, entire set of four pieces. $5.98
If by mail, postage extra, 45 cents.

NAINSOOK OR SILK TROUSSEAU OUTFITS.
Our $16.50 Silk Trousseau Outfit.

$16.50 Silk

$8.65 Nainsook

An exceedingly pretty lace trimmed trousseau, made of fine nainsook, or china silk consisting of four pieces, gown, skirt, drawers and corset cover, all trimmed with matched fine duchess lace. Sizes, 32 to 42 inches bust measure.

Gown made slip over style (very newest), with low round neck trimmed with lace. Beading and ribbon insertion in front forming a bow in front. Five insertions in front alternating with folds; elbow sleeves with two V insertions, beading ribbon insertion and 3-inch lace edge.

Skirt made French style, entire flounce is 20 inches deep, trimmed all around bottom with fine duchess lace insertion alternating with narrow torchon lace insertion, above which there are seven fine pin tucks, triangle pieces between each lace insertion, giving flounce a wide flare; edged all around bottom with 3-inch lace. Has dust ruffle. No. 38P911 flounce and triangle pieces made of lawn. No. 38P912 flounce and triangle pieces made of silk.

Drawers made umbrella style, has a 5-inch flounce made of duchess lace insertion alternating with torchon lace insertion triangle pieces between each lace insertion, giving flounce a wide flare. 2-inch lace edge (open style only), draw strings. No. 38P911 made of lawn triangle pieces. No. 38P912 made of silk triangle pieces.

Corset Cover, trimmed very prettily; low round neck, trimmed with lace, beading and ribbon insertion, armholes trimmed with lace, four rows of fine duchess lace insertion in front, alternating with narrow torchon lace, each side edged with 2-inch duchess lace; trimmed around waist with lace edge to match beading and ribbon insertion. Exceptionally good value. Both same style but made of either nainsook or China silk.
No. 38P911 Price, entire set of four pieces made of nainsook................ $8.65
No. 38P912 Price, entire set of four pieces made of china silk.............. $16.50

LADIES' FLANNEL UNDER-WEAR.

We call special attention to this class of goods. Combined with our low prices you will find in our flannel wear, first class workmanship, material and trimming, full lengths and widths, every number is splendid value. Sizes are 14, 15 and 16 in neck, in proportion as follows:

Bust	32-34	36-38	40-42
Neck	14	15	16

Order by neck measure.
For Muslin Gowns see page 80.

42 Cents Buys a 75-Cent Flannel Gown.
No. 38P913 Ladies' Flannel Gown, made in plaids and stripes, in blue or pink colors. Turn down collar. Yoke in front and back. Price................... 42c
If by mail, postage extra, 10 cents.

42c

69c

No. 38P944 Ladies' Gown, made of good outing flannel, double yoke back and front trimmed across bosom with braid, collar and cuffs of solid color flannel to match. Colors are pink or blue stripes. Price...... 69c
If by mail, postage extra, 11 cents.

No. 38P3230 $4.95

No. 38P3231 $3.25

No. 38P3235 $3.50

No. 38P3228 $3.98

No. 38P3226 $3.25

No. 38P3232 $4.95

No. 38P3233 $2.45

No. 38P3227 $3.48

No. 38P3229 $4.25

No. 38P3234 $2.95

GIRLS'
TWO-PIECE BLOUSE SAILOR SUITS.
AGE 6 TO 14 YEARS.

No. 38P3226 GIRLS' TWO-PIECE BLOUSE SUIT. Made of cheviot serge; large sailor collar, trimmed with soutache; silk embroidered ornament on vestee; tie made of same material as in dress; collars and cuffs trimmed with soutache to match; dress lined with cambric; deep hem at bottom. Colors, navy blue or garnet. Price **$3.25**
If by mail, postage extra, 32 cents.

No. 38P3227 GIRLS' TWO-PIECE BLOUSE SUIT. Made of all wool cheviot serge. Has very pretty sailor collar, trimmed back and front alike with three rows of soutache and small pearl buttons; tie made of same material as in dress; collar tie and cuffs trimmed with soutache to match; silk embroidered ornament on vestee; dress lined with cambric; deep hem at bottom. Colors, navy blue or garnet. Price **$3.48**
If by mail, postage extra, 34 cents.

No. 38P3228 GIRLS' TWO-PIECE BLOUSE SUIT. Made of good quality storm serge. Has large sailor collar, trimmed with five rows of silk soutache; silk embroidered ornament on vestee; taffeta silk tie; pearl buttons; collar and cuffs trimmed with five rows of soutache to match; dress lined with cambric; deep hem at bottom. Colors, navy blue or garnet. Price.........**$3.98**
If by mail, postage extra, 36 cents.

No. 38P3229 GIRLS' TWO-PIECE BLOUSE SUIT. Made of all wool storm serge. Has very pretty sailor collar trimmed with braid and two rows of white stitching, embroidered silk stars on corners, embroidered silk ornament on vestee, taffeta silk tie, pearl buttons, new bishop sleeves, two rows of braid and stitching on collar and cuffs. Colors, navy blue or garnet.
Price.................(If by mail, postage extra, 36 cents.)...........**$4.25**

No. 38P3230 GIRLS' TWO-PIECE BLOUSE SUIT. Made of all wool Venetian cloth. Has a very pretty sailor collar trimmed both front and back alike with six rows of soutache and taffeta silk corners with embroidered emblems, pretty silk embroidered design on vestee, black taffeta silk tie, pearl buttons, new bishop sleeves, collars and cuffs trimmed with five rows of soutache, dress lined with cambric. Colors, navy blue or garnet. Price **$4.95**
If by mail, postage extra, 34 cents.

No. 38P3231 THE NEW PETER THOMSON TWO-PIECE SAILOR SUIT. Made of all wool cheviot serge. Has large sailor collar trimmed with 6 rows of soutache. Inside vestee and left sleeve trimmed with silk embroidered emblem, flannel band on right sleeve, yoke and plaids on blouse, tie made of same material as in dress, collar and cuffs trimmed with soutache to match dress, lined with cambric. Color, navy blue. Price................ ....**$3.25**
If by mail, postage extra, 34 cents.

No. 38P3232 GIRLS' TWO-PIECE BLOUSE SUIT, Peter Thomson style. Made of all wool storm serge. Large sailor collar with rows of braid, vestee made of blue all wool storm serge with silk embroidered emblem, also on left sleeve, flannel band on right sleeve, full blouse with yoke and pocket on left side, silk tie, braid on cuffs, skirt lined with cambric. Color, navy blue only.
Price **$4.95**
If by mail, postage extra, 34 cents.

GIRLS' AND MISSES' SKIRTS.
WAIST MEASURE, 22 TO 26 INCHES; LENGTHS, 31 TO 37 INCHES.

No. 38P3233 GIRLS' OR MISSES' SKIRT. Made of heavy weight cheviot (unlined). Flounced, with exception of front gore, three plaits all around flounce, two straps each trimmed with cloth covered buttons as in skirt, all lap seams. Colors are black or gray mixture.
Price...................(If by mail, postage extra, 32 cents.).........**$2.45**

No. 38P3234 GIRLS' OR MISSES' SKIRT. Made of heavy weight novelty cheviot, (unlined). Extra very neatly designed skirt, straps of same material as in skirt covering front seams, each strap piped with flannel to match skirt also cloth covered buttons, lap seams, rows of stitching around bottom. Colors are new blue or gray with fancy mixtures.
Price......................(If by mail, postage extra, 34 cents.).............**$2.95**

No. 38P3235 GIRLS' OR MISSES' SKIRT. Made of all wool ladies' cloth, neatly trimmed with eight narrow strips of taffeta silk alternating with four wider strips, each, trimmed at bottom with silk ring, lined with mercerized percaline, bound around bottom with velveteen. Colors, black or royal blue. Price...........................**$3.50**
If by mail, postage extra, 22 cents.

INFANTS' WEAR DEPARTMENT

INFANTS' OUTFITS.

Those two outfits represent extraordinary value and the pieces, if bought separately in retail stores, would cost you double our price.

WE CALL SPECIAL ATTENTION TO OUR TWO INFANTS' OUTFIT SETS

as described on this page. One outfit consists of 22 and the other set has 24 pieces and you will find that if you bought the pieces separately, the total cost of either set would be nearly double our price. We only illustrate a few of the many pieces in these sets.

INFANTS' OUTFIT, CONSISTING OF 22 PIECES, FOR $5.95.

These sets have been carefully selected with a view of offering a complete outfit at the very lowest price, such as you would pay nearly twice as much for elsewhere. In these sets you will find, as described below, nearly everything that baby needs to wear, thus doing away with the making of different selections of the so many different articles for the baby's wardrobe.

1 Very Dainty Long Cambric Robe, embroidery down front and around bottom.
1 Muslin Day Slip, square yoke made of fine embroidery insertion, wide hem at bottom.
2 Muslin Night Slips, fancy yoke of embroidery and herringbone braid.
1 Domet Flannel Wrapper, embroidered around collar and down front.
1 Cambric Long Skirt, with three fine tucks around bottom.
1 Cambric Long Skirt, with two clusters of tucks (three tucks in a cluster), Hamburg embroidery around bottom.
1 Long Skirt, made of fleeced canton flannel.
1 Long Canton Skirt, fleeced, stitched around bottom with silk.
1 All Wool Flannel Shawl, beautifully embroidered with silk on corners.
2 Bibs, honeycomb pattern, edged all around with lace.
1 Patented Pinless Diaper, made of absorbent cloth.
1 Rubber Diaper (white).
1 Silk Bonnet, beautifully embroidered with silk.
1 Pair All Wool Knit Bootees, very closely knitted with fine all wool zephyr.
1 All Wool Knitted Sacque, trimmed with tassels.
1 Flannelette Sacque, stitched all around collar, down front and cuffs with mercerized twist.
2 Bands, made of canton flannel.
2 Pinning Blankets or Barrior Coats, made of cream color canton flannel.
No. 38C1740 Price for complete outfit, 22 pieces.....................**$5.95**

A HIGH GRADE INFANTS' OUTFIT, CONSISTING OF 24 PIECES, FOR $11.75.

Very dainty slips, skirts, sacques, etc. This set must be seen to be appreciated as the articles are such that the faint descriptions given do not do them justice.

1 Beautiful Cambric Robe, handsomely trimmed with cambric in front, with satin ribbon insertion, wide embroidery ruffle around bottom.
1 Fine Nainsook Day Slip, a very pretty round yoke, made of all over lace followed with a lace ruffle, beautifully trimmed around bottom with two lace insertions and wide point de Paris lace edge to match.
1 Muslin Night Slip with embroidery forming a yoke. Wide hem at bottom.
1 Muslin Slip, yoke trimmed with tucks and embroidery insertion, wide hem at bottom.
1 Domet Flannel Wrapper, collar, down front and sleeves stitched with silk. Satin ribbon bow at neck.
1 Fine Nainsook Skirt (matched to day slip), trimmed with two lace insertions and wide edge. Two clusters of fine tucks.
1 Cambric Long Skirt, trimmed around bottom with three tucks and hem.
1 All Wool (cream color) Flannel Long Skirt, with cambric bodice.
1 All Wool Flannel Shawl, cream color, handsomely embroidered on one corner in flower design.
3 Bibs, Honeycomb Pattern, trimmed with lace. Pocket and teething rings.
1 Bib (quilted) with lace edge.
1 Pinless Diaper, made of good quality birdseye absorbent cloth.
1 Rubber Diaper (white).
1 Stockinet Diaper.
1 Silk Bonnet, handsomely embroidered with silk and lined with Japanese silk.
1 Pair of Bootees, made of all wool zephyr very closely knitted.
1 Pair of Bootees, made of silkatine, very closely knitted. A high class bootee.
1 All Wool Knitted Sacque, very closely knitted zephyr. Crocheted edge around collar, front and sleeves.
1 All Wool Flannel Sacque, stitched with silk. Very pretty and stylish.
2 Bands, made of all wool flannel. Silk stitched.
1 Pinning Blanket or Barrior Coat, made of all wool flannel, cambric bodice.

No. 38C1746 Price for above high grade set, consisting of 24 pieces...**$11.75**
Should any additional pieces be required, select same from the following pages of infants' wearing apparel, and include with your order.
See Index for baby books, with handsome illustrations, in which records can be made of the chief events of baby's life.

INFANTS' LONG SLIPS.

Note the Lengths and Sweeps in Our Infants' Slips.

An Infant's Long Cambric Slip for 18 Cents.

No. 38C1750 Infants' Long Slip. Made of cambric, neck and sleeves trimmed with cambric ruffle, front trimmed with wide embroidery, giving a yoke effect, deep hem at bottom. Length, 31 inches, sweep, 50 inches. Price.....................18c
If by mail, postage extra, 7 cents.

No. 38C1754 Infants' Long Slip. Made of good muslin; yoke in front and back; yoke in front is trimmed with 8 tucks and insertion of embroidery, cambric collar and cuffs, wide cambric tie strings, and deep hem at bottom. Length, 32 inches; sweep, 48 inches. Price.....................25c
If by mail, postage extra, 8 cents.

Infants' Slip with Fancy Yoke, 39 Cents.

No. 38C1756 Infants' Long Slip, made of cambric. Has very neat pointed yoke trimmed with two insertions of neat embroidery, alternating with three clusters of fine tucks, two plaits in back; neck and sleeves trimmed with embroidery. Nice hem at bottom.
Wonderful value. Price..........39c
If by mail, postage extra, 7 cents.

Our 45-Cent Fancy Yoke Muslin Slip.

No. 38C1758 Infants' Long Slip, made of good quality muslin, embroidery ruffle around collar, fancy yoke in front, provided with a wide strip of embroidery, four rows of tucking in front with embroidered insertion, extra wide hem on bottom. Length, 33 inches; sweep, 54 inches. Price.....................45c
If by mail, postage extra, 6 cents.

Lace Trimmed Infants' Slip, 50 Cents.

50c
No. 38C1760 Infants' Slip, made of nainsook. Very neat yoke with insertion of narrow lace alternating with clusters of fine tucks. Yoke followed with lawn ruffle which is edged with valenciennes lace, back of yoke trimmed with six clusters of three fine tucks, neck and sleeves trimmed with lace to match. Price.....................50c
If by mail, postage extra, 8 cents.

48c
No. 38C1762 Infants' Long Slip, made of soft finish nainsook, very neat square yoke trimmed with numerous rows of fine baby tucks and hemstitching. Trimmed each side of yoke with fine embroidery, yoke and back also trimmed with numerous rows of fine tucks and hemstitching, neck and sleeves edged with neat pattern of fine Swiss embroidery, deep hem at bottom. Price..........48c
If by mail, postage extra, 6 cents.

Our 75-Cent White Cambric Slip.

75c
No. 38C1764 Infants' Long Slip, made of cambric. Yoke, back and front with numerous rows of fine tucks, followed with herringbone braid, embroidery insertion in front. Epaulets of Swiss embroidery. Neck and sleeves trimmed with valenciennes lace. Trimmed around bottom with three fine tucks and edged with 4½-inch Swiss embroidery. Price..75c
If by mail, postage extra, 7 cents.

Very Neatly Trimmed Slip at 75 Cents.

No. 38C1766 Very Neat Long Slip, made of fine nainsook. Has a very pretty circular yoke (back and front alike), trimmed with numerous rows of fine hemstitched tucks. A ruffle all around yoke (front and back), made of fine Swiss embroidery, hemstitched collar and cuffs, deep hem at bottom with hemstitching.
Price, 75c
If by mail, postage extra, 8 cents.

Child's Flannel Skirts.

No. 38P1150 Child's Skirt, made of fleeced shaker flannel, with cambric bodice. Embroidered around the bottom with silk. Price.....35c If by mail, postage extra, 5 cents.

48c

Child's Skirt for 48c.

No. 38P1154 Child's Skirt, made of wool cream colored flannel with cambric bodice, fancy ruffle of the same material all around the bottom. Very neat and desirable. Price.....48c If by mail, postage extra, 5c.

Child's Cambric and Nainsook Skirts.

1, 2 and 3-year-old children.

18c

No. 38P1158 Child's Skirt, with muslin bodice, made of white cambric, three rows of tucking around the bottom. Price.....18c If by mail, postage extra, 3c.

45c

No. 38P1162 Child's Skirt, made of good quality nainsook, with cambric bodice, three rows of narrow tucking around the bottom and one row of embroidered cambric. Pearl buttons in back. Price.....45c

If by mail, postage extra, 3 cents.

Nainsook Skirt.

No. 38P1166 A Very Pretty Child's Skirt, made of nainsook, with bodice Has four rows of fine tucks and trimmed with Valenciennes lace around bottom. Price.....48c If by mail, postage extra, 6 cents. For children 6 months, 1, 2 and 3 years of age.

48c

75o

75-Cent Value.

No. 38P1170 Child's Skirt with bodice, made of a very high grade nainsook, trimmed with two clusters (four rows in a cluster), of fine tucks, with an insertion of fine Valenciennes lace. Trimmed around bottom with Valenciennes lace to match. Price.....75c

If by mail, postage extra, 6 cents.

CHILD'S FRENCH DRESSES.

Ages, 1, 2, 3 and 4 years. Scale of measurements giving lengths of dresses in proportion: Age 1, length 20 inches; age 2, length 21 inches; age 3, length 22 inches; age 4, length 24 inches.

75c

No. 38P1174 A Pretty Child's Dress; made of fine nainsook; has two ruffles of embroidery insertion extending from neck to flounce, and twelve rows of tucks; yoke trimmed with herringbone braid and nainsook embroidery, ruffle extending over shoulders; neck and sleeves trimmed with a lawn ruffle and herringbone braid and one row of hemstitching; has a wide nainsook flounce with deep hem. Exceptionally good value. Color, white only. Price.....75c

If by mail, postage extra, 8 cents.

98c

No. 38P1178 A Very Stylish Child's Dress, made of fine white nainsook; trimmed in front with ten plaits; yoke has embroidery insertion and trimmed with herringbone braid, ruffle all around yoke in front and back; eight plaits in back extending from shoulders to flounce; wide lawn flounce with deep hem, herringbone braid at top of flounce; sleeves and neck trimmed with herringbone braid and embroidery edge. Price.98c

If by mail, postage extra, 7 cents.

$1.65

No. 38P1179 A Very Pretty Child's French Dress made of white sheer lawn insertion of embroidery at neck, also embroidery ruffle followed with herringbone braid, a 3-inch embroidery ruffle extending over shoulders to back, embroidery cuffs and waistband to match, a cluster of three tucks at bottom edged with 3-inch swiss embroidery. Sizes, 1, 2, 3 and 4 years. Color, white only. Price.$1.65

If by mail, postage extra, 8 cents.

$1.98

No. 38P1183 A Handsome Child's French Dress; made of fine white cambric; has a very pretty V yoke in front with three insertions of 1-inch embroidery alternating with clusters of three fine tucks, beading and ribbon insertion, herringbone braid and embroidery around neck. Embroidery ruffle over the shoulders; four clusters of fine baby (three tucks in each cluster) tucks to waist line. Cuffs with embroidery insertion and ruffle, embroidery waistband; trimmed below waistband with three embroidery ruffles. Four clusters (three in each cluster) of fine tucks in back from neck to waistband. Exceptionally good value. Price.....$1.98

If by mail, postage extra, 10 cents.

SILK DRESSES.

$2.25

No. 38P1184 A Very Pretty and Jaunty Child's French Dress; made of China silk; has a very pretty yoke trimmed with four rows of Point de Paris lace insertion alternating with beading, giving yoke an allover lace effect. Neck trimmed with lace followed with beading and ribbon insertion; trimmed all around yoke both front and back with 3-inch lace to match, followed with beading and ribbon insertion; has four clusters (three in each cluster) of fine tucks on back from neck to waistband, sleeves trimmed with lace and beading, waistband of beading and ribbon insertion, trimmed all around the bottom with beading and 3-inch lace. Colors, pink, cream or light blue. Price.....$2.25

If by mail, postage extra, 10 cents. See children's bonnets on page 93 to match these pretty dresses.

$2.48

No. 38P1185 An Exceedingly Pretty Child's French Dress; made of China silk. Very pretty yoke front and back, yoke in front with Point de Paris lace, insertion, alternating with beading, giving yoke an allover lace effect. Neck trimmed with lace followed by beading and ribbon insertion; yoke with 2-inch lace ruffle followed with beading and ribbon insertion. Sleeves trimmed with beading and ribbon insertion; ten fine tucks from neck to waistband on back, trimmed around bottom with narrow beading, 1-inch insertion and 2-inch lace edge to match. Colors, cream, pink or pale blue. Price.....$2.48

If by mail, postage extra, 10 cents. See children's bonnets to match on pages 93 and 94.

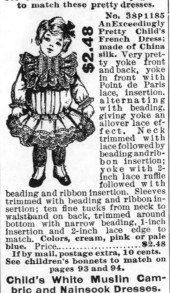

Child's White Muslin Cambric and Nainsook Dresses.

Ages, 6 months, 1, 2 and 3-year-old Children.

23c

No. 38P1186 Child's Dress; made of good quality cambric, ruffle around neck and fancy yoke in front with 5-inch cambric embroidery, hemmed with herringbone braid. Price.23c If by mail, postage extra, 5 cents.

42c

No. 38P1190 Child's Dress; made of white muslin, fancy yoke in front with insertion and tucking, and wide ruffle all around yoke over shoulder and ruching in the back, edged with torchon lace, wide hem on bottom. Ages, 6 months, 1, 2 and 3 years. Price.....42c

If by mail, postage extra, 6 cents.

CHILD'S WHITE CAMBRIC DRESSES.

These dresses are for Children 6 months, 1, 2 and 3 years of age.

Our 48-Cent Child's Dress.

48c

No. 38P1193 Child's Dress; made of white cambric, circular yoke in front, trimmed with tucks and embroidery insertion, Ruffles of embroidery around the neck and yoke embroidery cuffs, three tucks around bottom with 1 and ½-inch embroidery edge. Color, white only. Price.....48c

If by mail, postage extra, 8 cents.

Only 75 Cents for this Child's Dress.

75c

No. 38P1198 Child's Dress; made of high grade cambric. Embroidered ruffle around the collar and tucked yoke in front, ending in a point, with embroidered cambric all around the front and back. Embroidered cambric around the sleeves. Very neat and stylish. Ages, 6 months, 1, 2 and 3 years. Price...75c

If by mail, postage extra, 6 cents.

Here is a Pretty Dress for 75 Cents.

75c

No. 38P1199 Very Pretty Child's Dress; made of white cambric, circular yoke in front, trimmed with two embroidery insertions and tucks, ruffle in front of 2-inch embroidery, neck and sleeves trimmed with embroidery to match, two plaits in back. six tucks at bottom and edged with 4-inch embroidery. Price.....75c

If by mail, postage extra, 9 cents.

98 Cents Buys This Nainsook Dress.

98c

No. 38P1202 Child's Dress; made of good quality nainsook, torchon lace trimming around the collar on yoke and sleeves, and one row of Valenciennes lace insertion on skirt and a wide Valenciennes lace edge to match around bottom. Yoke handsomely trimmed with herringbone braid in front as well as in back. Two rows of triple tucking all around the skirt at bottom. Ages, 6 months, 1, 2 and 3 years. Price.....98c

If by mail, postage extra, 6 cents.

89c

No. 38P1203 Child's Dress; made of white cambric, a very pretty circular yoke trimmed in front with embroidery insertions and tucks, embroidery ruffle around the yoke neck and sleeves trimmed with embroidery, trimmed with six tucks at bottom and insertion of open work embroidery and edged with 4-inch embroidery to match. Color, white only. Exceptionally good value. Price.....89c

If by mail, postage extra, 10 cents

CHILDREN'S FUR SETS.

A splendid selection of splendid values. These sets make Christmas presents that are sensible and delight the hearts of the little ones. When ordering state age of child, and if large or small for age.

No. 17P1205 Child's Fur Set. Made of white coney with black coney dots as shown in illustration. Consisting of muff and scarf attached to muff which reaches around the neck. For 2 to 6 year old children.

Price.............. **69c**

If by mail, postage extra, 11 cents.

No. 17P1207 Child's Fur Set. Made of white lamb. Consisting of muff and scarf. Muff has a purse, small fur head and silk bow in front. Silk bow on scarf. For **3** to 8 year old children.

Price............... **98c**

If by mail, postage extra, 15 cents.

No. 17P1209 Child's Fur Set. Made of white lamb and angora. Muffs trimmed with angora edge, purse on top and satin bow. Collarette is edged with white angora and lined with satin. For 3 to 8 year old children. Price......... **$1.25**

If by mail, postage extra, 15 cents.

No. 17P1211 Child's Fur Set. Made of American squirrel, consisting of muff and small collarette. Satin ribbon in muff to fasten around neck. Small purse on muff. Collarette lined with sateen.

Price.............. **$1.19**

If by mail, postage extra, 13 cents.

OUR $2.98 FUR SET.

OUR $1.39 FUR SET.

ONLY $1.45 FOR THIS $2.50 FUR SET.

No. 17P1213 Child's Fur Set. Made of imitation mink, otherwise called blended muskrat, consisting of muff and small collarette. Muff is trimmed with purse and small head in front and satin bow. Collarette is trimmed with four tails and lined with satin. For 4 to 10 year old children. Price, **$2.98**

If by mail, postage extra, 19 cents.

No. 17P1215 Same style as above. Made of South American beaver or nutria.

Price...................... **$2.98**

If by mail, postage extra, 17 cents.

No. 17P1217 Child's Fur Set. Made of white angora, consisting of muff and small collarette. For 3 to 8 year old children.

Price.......................**$1.39**

If by mail, postage extra, 25 cents.

REFER TO OUR COMPLETE Department of Muslin Underwear for Ladies, Misses and Children and include these goods with your order.

No. 17P1219 Child's Fur Set. Made of white coney with black dots. The muff has purse on top and small animal head and satin bow. Large collarette edged with white angora all around, lined with satin. For 5 to 10 year old children. Price..... **$1.45**

If by mail, postage extra, 20 cents.

Please Show This Catalogue To your friends who might be interested. We will appreciate it.

Sears, Roebuck & Co.

CHILD'S LONG COAT WITH DOUBLE CAPE AND TAB FRONT . . . $3.65

SPECIAL VALUE, NONE BETTER FOR THE MONEY. OUR PRICE . . $3.98

A PRACTICAL AND SERVICEABLE COAT, MADE OF ALL WOOL COVERT CLOTH, . . $4.75

HEAVY WEIGHT ZIBELINE, NICE AND WARM . . $4.50

No. 17P779 CHILD'S LONG COAT. Made of good quality heavy weight melton cloth. Double breasted front, double shoulder cape finished with two tabs in front; turnover cuffs and bishop sleeves, pocket flaps and belt in back; collar, shoulder cape, cuffs and pocket flaps are piped with velvet. Colors, tan with green piping, and blue with red piping. State color when ordering. Price **$3.65**

See Pages 1 to 4 how to order and how to measure.

No. 17P781 CHILD'S LONG COAT. Made of all wool beaver. Double breasted front and facing of same material. Velvet piping in front, extending all the way to back. Loose back caught in a belt, fancy turnover cuffs, bishop sleeves; very neat, clean and serviceable garment, and we can highly recommend it. Style, quality and price make this one of the best garments in the catalogue and we can highly recommend it. Color, blue with red velvet piping. Price. **$3.98**

No. 17P783 CHILD'S LONG COAT. Made in the newest double breasted blouse effect. Is trimmed with two straps in front and one in center of back, piped with blue and white silk cord. Similar trimming in back and on belt which reaches all around the coat. Turnover cuffs and bishop sleeves. Facing in front of same material. Very handsome and nobby garment, good value for the money. Coat is made of good weight zibeline cloth. Colors, military blue or green. Price **$4.75**

No. 17P785 CHILD'S LONG COAT. Double breasted front, made of good quality heavy weight zibeline cloth. Double shoulder cape of which the upper is finished with tabs in front. Turnover cuffs, bishop sleeves, loose back caught in belt. Velvet piping on the cape and ornamented with silk passementerie. Colors, blue or red. Price **$4.50**

DON'T FORGET TO GIVE SIZE IN ORDERING.

ATTRACTIVE EMBROIDERY ON SLEEVE, FOR THOSE WHO WANT STYLE, $4.95

No. 17P786 CHILD'S LONG MILITARY COAT. Made of good quality all wool zibeline cloth. Double breasted front, buttons up to the neck. Silk star embroidered on collar, and anchor on the left sleeve only. Turnover cuffs, latest sleeves. Facing in front of same material. Neatly finished with brass buttons. Box back. Strictly up to date and stylish garment. Color, blue only. Price.. **$4.95**

CHILD'S MELTON CLOAK, FOR $2.75

No. 17P787 CHILD'S DOUBLE BREASTED COAT. Made of heavy weight melton. Shoulder cape neatly trimmed with fancy velvet and fancy cord. Similar trimming on sleeves. Loose back and loose front. Facing in front of same material. Very nobby garment. Colors, blue or red. Price.. **$2.75**

CHILDREN'S COATS. We make these coats in the following lengths and sizes:

| Ages...... | 4 | 6 | 8 | 10 | 12 | 14 |
| Lengths... | 24 | 26 | 28 | 30 | 32 | 34 |

This refers to all numbers from 17P787 to 17P817.

ATTRACTIVE AND NOBBY, SPLENDID VALUE, FOR $3.50

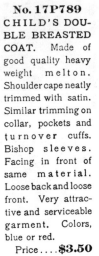

No. 17P789 CHILD'S DOUBLE BREASTED COAT. Made of good quality heavy weight melton. Shoulder cape neatly trimmed with satin. Similar trimming on collar, pockets and turnover cuffs. Bishop sleeves. Facing in front of same material. Loose back and loose front. Very attractive and serviceable garment. Colors, blue or red. Price **$3.50**

Skirts of Fashion

Following are descriptions of skirts shown on opposite page.

31 T 8955—Navy blue.
31 T 8956—Black.
EACH
$6.65

THE WOMAN WHO WANTS A SKIRT THAT IS LOW PRICED and yet showing the late fashionable style features will find this a good selection. The material is a firmly woven PANAMA, nearly one-half wool, balance cotton, which can be depended upon for good service. Skirt is slightly gathered all around at waist and finished with a detachable button trimmed belt. The attractively shaped pockets are trimmed with arrowheads, soutache braid in buttonhole effect and buttons. A very distinctive and popular feature of this pretty skirt is the braid trimming in the elaborate design shown. Average SWEEP, 64 inches. For sizes furnished see size paragraph on this page. **When ordering be sure to state measurements required.**

31 T 8960—Green.
31 T 8961—Navy blue.
31 T 8962—Black.
EACH
$4.79

YOUTHFUL SMARTNESS AND UP TO DATE STYLE are displayed in this skirt for misses. Made of half wool and half cotton SERGE, which will give good service. Skirt is shirred all around at waist in becoming fullness under the detachable belt, which is trimmed with buttons and soutache braid. A very attractive feature is seen in the fine pin tucks on bottom of skirt and on pockets, which are also trimmed to match belt. Average SWEEP, 62 inches. A most desirable skirt and a very good value at the price asked. Furnished in **misses' or junior sizes**, from 22 to 28 inches waist measure, proportionate hip measure and from 34 to 38 inches front length. **When ordering state waist and hip measures, also front length of skirt.** Average shipping weight, 2 pounds.

31 T 8825—Black.
31 T 8826—Navy blue.
31 T 8827—Brown.
EACH
$12.95

FASHION SPEAKS IN EVERY LINE OF THIS BEAUTIFUL SKIRT, one of the season's newest models. Just the style and material that fashionably dressed women desire for best wear. The SATIN is of good quality and has a beautiful high luster. Skirt is further enriched by fine pin tucking on bottom of the side tunics, a very fashionable feature. Note the trim and graceful figure lines given by the straight panel front and yoke effect at sides. Back is designed to match front, with a two-piece button trimmed loose belt. Back panel is slightly shirred at waist under belt. Skirt closes invisibly at left side of back. Average SWEEP, 72 inches. For sizes furnished see size paragraph on this page. **When ordering be sure to state measurements required.**

31 T 8965—Blue.
31 T 8966—Taupe.
31 T 8967—Brown.
EACH
$13.75

"SILVERTONE" VELOUR IS USED IN THIS NEW AND FASHIONABLE MODEL. This material is very popular and a favorable skirting in the making of high grade garments. The gray artificial silk mixed with the all wool yarns effects a beautiful silvery sheen. Fashionable straight lines distinguish this model which is slightly shirred all around at waistline. It displays the popular tailored trimming of pin tucks and a new feature is the button trimmed tuck seam at left side, which ends in open slit extending a few inches above the lower edge. Slashed pockets. The detachable belt is also trimmed with pin tucks and buttons. Back is laid in two box plaits at waist which fall free below. Average SWEEP, 50 inches. Furnished in waist measure from 23 to 28 inches only. For other measurements see size paragraph on this page. **State measurements required.**

31 T 8970—Smoke gray.
31 T 8971—Navy blue.
31 T 8972—Black.
EACH
$11.50

THIS SMART VELVETEEN SKIRT HAS A DISTINCTIVE STYLE ALL ITS OWN, remarkably good looking, dressy and appropriate in simplicity of design. You may wear it on almost any occasion and feel correctly dressed, for this lustrous VELVETEEN resembles velvet in appearance and will give good wear. This skirt is prettily shirred all around at waistline, giving soft and graceful figure lines. Has a detachable belt which fastens in front. The pockets are a very distinctive feature, trimmed with cord loops and buttons. Back is shirred under belt. Average SWEEP, 60 inches. For sizes furnished see size paragraph on this page. **When ordering be sure to state measurements required.**

SIZES The Women's Skirts shown on this and opposite page can be furnished in **women's regular sizes** only, from 23 to 32 inches waist measure, with the exception of styles 31T8965, 31T8975 and 31T8980, which can only be furnished from 23 to 28 inches waist measure, (see descriptions), proportionate hip measure and 36 to 42 inches front length. See description of 31T8960 for sizes of **misses' skirts. State waist and hip measures,** also front length. For simple measuring instructions see order blank in back of catalog. Av. shpg. wt., 2 pounds.

31 T 8975
Chiffon
Panama
$8.95

31T8980
Serge
$7.98

31T8830
Silk and
Cotton Poplin
$5.48

31 T 8980—Navy blue.
31 T 8981—Black.
EACH
$7.98

SMART STYLE, GOOD WEARING MATERIAL AND EXTRAORDINARY VALUE are combined in this stylish skirt. Made of ALL WOOL DOUBLE TWISTED WARP SERGE, which is well known for the excellent service it gives. In every detail it is typical of the latest styles and displays the straight lines which are such a marked feature of the new Fall and Winter skirts. This model is enriched by the slanting rows of tailor braid and the close rows of buttons on the overlapping fold at side, which ends in open slit toward bottom. Shirred all around at waist and finished with a detachable button trimmed belt. Inverted pockets at right side with novel bow tab. Average SWEEP, 52 inches. Furnished in waist measure from 23 to 28 inches only. For other measurements see size paragraph on this page. **State measurements required.**

31 T 8830—Black.
31 T 8831—Navy blue.
31 T 8832—Copenhagen blue.
EACH
$5.48

A VERY NEAT, NOBBY MODEL FOR WOMEN. The material, a silk and cotton POPLIN, possesses a rich, lustrous finish and with its soft, clinging texture is especially appropriate to bring out the pretty design and gives graceful figure lines. Note how attractively the skirt falls from the shirred waistline and the pretty style touch shown in the smartly folded belt of self material, which is trimmed with buttons. The pockets, with tassel and button trimming, further enhance the beauty of this garment. Average SWEEP, 63 inches. Furnished in women's regular sizes only, from 23 to 32 inches waist measure, proportionate hip measure and 36 to 40 inches front length. **When ordering be sure to state measurements required.**

31 T 8975—Navy blue.
31 T 8976—Black.
EACH
$8.95

THIS STYLISH SKIRT FOLLOWS THE TREND OF THE NEWEST FASHIONS. It embodies very pleasing style features and is designed on long straight lines that make it becoming to almost any type of figure. Made of ALL WOOL CHIFFON PANAMA, a good weight and very durable material. Note the trim hip lines given by the fine pin tucks and the novel tucked pockets which are trimmed with buttons. Wide tucks also trim the bottom of the skirt all around. Detachable button trimmed belt. Back is also trimmed with pin tucks to match front. Average SWEEP, 53 inches. Furnished in waist measure from 23 to 28 inches only. For other measurements see size paragraph on this page. **State measurements required.**

LADIES' WRAPPERS.

SIZES ARE FROM 32 to 44 inches around bust. They are made only in one length. We do not alter wrappers. If garment is a trifle long it is very easy to make it shorter. **When ordering, state catalogue number, size and color desired. No extra sizes in these garments.**

49c

69c

69c

89c

No. 31C4101 LADIES' WRAP-PER. Made of calico. Lined to waist with cambric. Trimmed with braid around the collar. Colors, black, blue, gray or red with fancy figures. **State color and size when ordering.**

Price.....................49c
If by mail, postage extra, 25 cents.

Always state Catalogue Number, Color and Size when ordering.

No. 31C4104 LADIES' WRAP-PER. Made of printed calico. Nicely trimmed with fancy braid around the collar, in front and over the shoulder capes. Lining of cambric to waist only. Wide flounce around the bottom. Colors, black, gray, blue or red with fancy figures. **State color and size when ordering.** Price.........69c

If by mail, postage extra, 28 cents.

No. 31C4107 LADIES' WRAPPER. Made of flannelette. Neatly trimmed with braid on collar and shoulder capes. Plaits in back from neck to waist. Cambric waist lining. Flounce bottom. Colors, black, blue, gray or red figures. You could not buy the material in this wrapper and make it up yourself for 69 cents. You will be surprised at the value we give at this low price. Dealers cannot buy these wrappers at this figure in wholesale lots. Be sure to include one of the great value wrappers with your order. Price............................69c
If by mail, postage extra, 30 cents.

No. 31C4110 LADIES' WRAPPER. Made of good quality printed calico. Nicely trimmed with fancy braid around the collar, shoulder capes which reach from front to back forming a yoke. Wide flounce around the bottom. Braid trimming on the sleeves. Lining of cambric to waist only. Colors, black, blue, gray or red with fancy figures. **State color and size when ordering.** Price 89c

If by mail, postage extra, 30 cents.

89c

89c

89c

95c

No. 31C4113 LADIES' WRAPPER. Made of good quality printed calico, fancy braid trimming around the collar, shoulders and in front forming a yoke. Shoulder capes scalloped and trimmed with embroidery cording. Plait in back from yoke to waist. Wide flounce around the bottom. Lining of cambric to waist. Colors, black, blue or red with fancy figures. **State color and size when ordering.**
Price 89c
If by mail, postage extra, 30 cents.

No. 31C4116 LADIES' WRAPPER. Very neat, made of percale, neatly trimmed with fancy colored strap of same material, forming yoke in front. Nice ruffles all around the shoulders, reaching from front to back. Wide flounce around the bottom, trimmed with strap of fancy braid. Lining of cambric to waist. Colors, black, blue or red with white polka dots. **State color and size desired when ordering.**
Price 89c
If by mail, postage extra, 30 cents.

No. 31C4119 LADIES' WRAPPER. Made of percale. Collar, front and shoulder capes are trimmed with one inch wide fancy embroidered braid. Wide flounce around the bottom with braid trimming. Lining of cambric to waist only. Large shoulder capes. Colors, black, blue, gray or red, with fancy figures. **State color and size desired when ordering.**
Price 89c
If by mail, postage extra, 30 cents.

No. 31C4122 THIS NEAT WRAP-PER is made of percale in black and white checks. Very neat. Collar and front trimmed with fancy braid, forming a yoke in front and back, trimmed with fancy braid. Shoulder capes. Colors, black or white checkered patterns.
Price... ....95c
If by mail, postage extra, 28 cents.

LADIES' AND MISSES' SATEEN WAISTS.

No. 31C3702 LADIES' WAIST. Made of black mercerized sateen. Plaits in front. Trimmings of straps of same material, pouch sleeves and neat cuffs. Splendid value for the money. Standing detachable collar. Color, black only.
Price...........................**49c**
If by mail, postage extra, 18 cents.

No. 31C3705 LADIES' STYLISH WAIST. Made of good quality mercerized sateen. Trimmings of embroidery. Plaits of same material and tucks on yoke. Bishop sleeves. Embroidery on cuffs. Standing detachable collar. Color, black only.
Price...........................**75c**
If by mail, postage extra, 20 cents.

No. 31C3708 LADIES' WAIST. Made of good quality sateen. Yoke front on the bias, made of tucks and plaits. Similar trimmings from yoke to waist. Entire garment is nicely tailored. Large sleeves. Detachable collar. Four plaits in back. Color, black only.
Price...........................**89c**
If by mail, postage extra, 20 cents.

No. 31C3711 LADIES' WAIST. Made of very good quality fast black mercerized sateen. Round yoke, made of two rows of openwork lace, trimming to match in front. Plaits from yoke to waist on both sides in front. Standing detachable collar. Plaits in back, bishop sleeves. Buttons at the side and shoulder. Color, black only.
Price...........................**85c**
If by mail, postage extra, 20 cents.

No. 31C3714 VERY PRETTY WAIST. Made of good quality silk finished sateen, nicely tailored. Stylish front, small extensions over shoulders. Trimmings of small pearl buttons and side plaits. Standing detachable collar, large sleeves, fancy cuffs. Plaits in back from neck to waist. Colors, black, blue, red or brown, with white polka dots. Please state color when ordering. Price...........**89c**
If by mail, postage extra, 20 cents.

No. 31C3717 THIS ELABORATE WAIST is made of good quality sateen, pointed yoke in front, trimmed with self covered buttons and shirring from yoke to waist. This effect is very pretty. Detachable standing collar, fancy turnover. Large sleeves. Tucks and side plaits in back. Colors, black, red or castor. State color when ordering.
Price...........................**89c**
If by mail, postage extra, 20 cents.

No. 31C3720 VERY NOBBY WAIST. Made of good quality black sateen, yoke front made of tucks, and fancy embroidery forming the yoke. Other trimmings are side plaits in front, on the sleeves and four in back. Colors, black, red or light brown (castor). State color when ordering.
Price...........................**89c**
If by mail, postage extra, 20 cents.

No. 31C3723 ONE OF THE NEWEST WAISTS in good quality fast black sateen. Yoke front. The entire front is fluted and plaited making it very full, something that a well dressed lady will appreciate. Large sleeves, Plaits in back from neck to waist. Color, black only.
Price...........................**89c**
If by mail, postage extra, 20 cents.

No. 31C3726 LADIES' WAIST. Made of fast black mercerized sateen, nicely embroidered all over with soutache, three plaits from both sides at shoulder, and stitched front. Standing detachable collar. Wide plaits in back. Bishop sleeves. Color, black only.
Price...........................**98c**
If by mail, postage extra, 20 cents.

No. 31C3729 THIS STRICTLY TAILORMADE WAIST is made of fine imported mercerized sateen. Yoke in front is tucked all over and trimmed with straps of same material. Plaits in front from yoke to waist and tucks from neck to waist. Pouch sleeves, standing detachable collar. Several rows of tucks in back from neck to waist. Colors, black, dark red or cadet blue. Price...........**$1.15**
If by mail, postage extra, 20 cents.

LADIES' COLORED WAISTS.

No. 31C3732 LADIES' WAIST. Made of gingham, nicely tailored. The entire front is tucked and plaited. Standing detachable collar, fancy turnover. Large sleeves tucked at the cuffs. Two plaits in back. Colors, blue, tan or oxblood. State color when ordering.
Price...........................**49c**
If by mail, postage extra, 15 cents.

No. 31C3735 VERY PRETTY WAIST. Made of good quality lawn. Entire front is tucked and plaited. Standing detachable collar, large sleeves, two plaits in back. Colors, black with white, brown with white, or white with black polka dots. State color when ordering.
Price...........................**49c**
If by mail, postage extra, 15 cents.

No. 31C3738 LADIES' WAIST. Made of good quality striped lawn, nicely tailored. Front trimmed with pearl buttons and side plaits. Detachable crushed collar, fancy turnover. Full sleeves, neat cuffs and two plaits in back. Color, white with black stripes.
Price...........................**49c**
If by mail, postage extra, 15 cents.

No. 31C3741 THIS TAILORED WAIST is made of good quality mercerized gingham. Entire front is side plaited. Standing detachable collar, fancy turnover. Large sleeves, two plaits in back. Exceptionally good value. Colors, blue or tan with fancy figures. State color when ordering.
Price...........................**75c**
If by mail, postage extra, 18 cents.

No. 31C3744 SPECIAL VALUE IN LADIES' WAIST. Made of good quality fancy figured novelty cloth, nicely tailored. Entire front is side plaited and trimmed with three open work medallions. Detachable collar finished with bow of same material. Large sleeves. Four plaits in back. Strictly up to date. Color, all white with small black figures. Price, **95c**
If by mail, postage extra, 18 cents.

LADIES' SILK JACKETS.

SIZES FROM 32 TO 42 INCHES AROUND THE BUST.

These Jackets are very dressy and are very popular. Many of these styles have no lining and are very light weight.
They are cut full and are to be worn loose. Be sure to state color and size when ordering.

No. 17C2774 THIS ILLUS-TRATION represents silk blouses in different styles, some with collars, some collarless, some with shoulder cape effects, etc. We want to close these out and therefore reduce the price below cost and will sell them, as long as they last, for $2.98. Every one of them is a better garment than picture shows; materials are black taffeta or peau de sole silk. Always state size wanted when you order.
Price....................$2.98
If by mail, postage extra, 25 cents.

No. 17C2775 LADIES' JACKET. Made of good quality silk peau de sole, 23 inches long, sailor collar, leg of mutton sleeves, fancy turnover cuffs. Neat satin bow in front. Loose back and loose front. Jacket is not lined. Colors, all black or black with white trimmings.
Price...............$3.75
If by mail, postage extra, 25 cents.

No. 17C2776 LADIES' JACKET. Made of good quality all silk peau de sole, 23 inches long, large sailor collar, loose back and loose front, leg of mutton sleeves, fancy turnover cuffs. Richly trimmed with cream colored lace and medallions around the collar and on sleeves. Very neat. No lining. Color, black, with cream colored trimmings. Price......$4.50
If by mail, postage extra, 25 cents.

No. 17C2777 LADIES' JACKET. Made of good quality all silk peau de sole, 25 inches long. Loose back and loose front. Large fancy collar. Leg of mutton sleeves, fancy turnover cuffs. Trimmings of silk braid. Bow in front made of peau de sole and trimmed with silk braid. Strap of same material around the bottom. No lining. Color, black only.
Price.................$4.95
If by mail, postage extra, 25 cents.

No. 17C2778 LADIES' MONTE CARLO JACKET. Made of fine taffeta silk, 24 inches long. Large shoulder cape, neatly trimmed with black and white silk braid. Plaits in back and in front, full sleeves, turnover cuffs, trimmed with braid to match. Lined with mercerized serge from neck to yoke in back only. Color, black only. Price.. ....$4.95
If by mail, postage extra, 23 cents.

No. 17C2779 VERY PRETTY LADIES' JACKET. Made of good quality all silk peau de sole, 30 inches long, double breasted front, loose back. Collarless effect. White satin around the neck, trimmed with black silk soutache. Leg of mutton sleeves, fancy cuffs, trimmed with white satin and silk soutache. The back is made with box plaits in center and side plaits, finished with belt. Fancy crochet buttons. No lining in this jacket. Facing in front of same material. Color, all black with black and white trimming around neck and cuffs.
Price.................$6.50
If by mail, postage extra, 35 cents.

No. 17C2780 LADIES' NOBBY COAT, 25 inches long. Made of fine taffeta silk. Loose back and loose front. Collarless effect. Cape over shoulders. Full sleeves and fancy turnover cuffs. Silk ornaments in front and satin strap across the shoulders. Lined throughout with mercerized sateen and heavily interlined. Very neat coat; good value for the money. Color, black only. Be sure to give size when ordering.
Price....................$5.75
If by mail, postage extra, 55 cents.

No. 17C2781 HAND-SOME LADIES' JACKET. Made of fine peau de sole silk, 30 inches long, large collar, bishop sleeves with fancy turnover cuffs. Loose back and loose front. The back is made with an inverted plait. Collar and cuffs are trimmed with lace braid and lace protruding from the cuffs. No lining in this coat. Colors, all black or black with cream colored trimmings. State color and size when ordering.
Price................$6.95
If by mail, postage extra, 40 cents.

No. 17C2782 THIS PRETTY PLAITED JACK-ET, is made of very fine taf-feta silk, loose front and box back. Leg of mutton sleeves with fancy turnover cuffs. Back is plaited and is finished with belt that reaches to front. Very stylish garment. Trimmings are silk soutache and fancy silk braid around the collar in front, forming a yoke in back; belt and cuffs. No lining in this jacket. Colors, black or brown. State color and size when ordering.
Price.................$6.50
If by mail, postage extra, 40 cents.

No. 17C2783 LADIES' COAT, 25 inches long, loose back and loose front. Large collar, stylish puff sleeves with fancy turnover cuffs. The collar is trimmed with lace braid and lace all around. Similar trimming at the cuffs. Jacket lined throughout with romaine silk. Very neat. Colors, all black or black with cream lace. State color and size when ordering.

Price................$7.50
If by mail, postage extra, 45 cents.

No. 17C2990 THIS BEAUTIFUL SHIRT WAIST SUIT OR DRESS, is made of fine figured lawn. Consists of handsome shirt waist, richly trimmed with cream colored medallions, Yoke effect front. Narrow velvet ribbon in front on waistband, around yoke and belt. Pretty sleeves. Detachable collar. Side plaits in back from neck to waist. Skirt nicely tailored,with flounce effect, trimmed with velvet ribbon and embroidered medallions. Colors, pink or blue, with fancy figures. **State color when ordering.** Price............**$2.98**
If by mail, postage extra, 30 cents.

No. 17C2991 THIS ELEGANT LADIES' SHIRT WAIST SUIT, made of good quality white linen, strictly tailored, consists of nice shirt waist, of which the yoke front is richly tucked and trimmed with openwork embroidery insertion. Detachable collar. Side plaits on the sleeves and side plaits in back from neck to waist. The skirt is trimmed to match, with tucks and embroidered insertion. Nicely tailored and made very full. Color, white only.
Price.......................**$3.25**
If by mail, postage extra, 35 cents.

No. 17C2993 ONE OF THE PRETTIEST SHIRT WAIST SUITS SHOWN. Made of very fine madras cloth. Consists of a stylish shirt waist with plaits, white piping, and circular embroidery trimmings. Very full sleeves, side plaits in back from neck to waist. The skirt is nicely made with side plaits all around. Very full. Special value, strictly up to date. Colors, blue or ecru (light shade of tan), with trimmings to match.
Price.......................**$3.98**
If by mail, postage extra, 40 cents.

No. 17C2994 THIS BEAUTIFUL SHIRT WAIST SUIT OR DRESS. Made of very fine dimity in beautiful Dolly Varden pattern. Consists of handsome shirt waist with circular yoke in front, large shoulder cape neatly trimmed with lace insertion. Large sleeves made with fancy cuffs also trimmed with lace. Round yoke in back. This waist buttons in back only. The skirt is made very full on double flounce style. Lace insertion over each flounce. Very pretty; good value. Color, white with rose or violet figures. **State color when ordering.** Price............**$3.75**
If by mail, postage extra, 35 cents.

No. 17C2995 THIS HANDSOME SHIRT WAIST SUIT OR DRESS is made of very fine Luzon Ponge. It consists of a beautiful shirt waist, made with fancy circular yoke. Shoulder cape trimmed with lace insertions, and side plaits in front from yoke to waist. Full sleeves, fancy cuffs. Stylish collar. Yoke in back. This waist buttons in back only. The skirt is extremely stylish, has a double flounce, nicely trimmed with lace insertion and shirring over each flounce. Very handsome. Color, tan (champagne color) only. **State color when ordering.** Price....... ....**$4.95**
If by mail, postage extra, 40 cents.

SAILOR SUITS

ARE VERY POPULAR AND WE SHOW A BEAUTIFUL LINE OF THEM. They are especially adapted for young ladies. Sizes from 32 to 38 inches around the bust, 36 to 44 inches length of skirt, and 22 to 30 inches around the waist.

— STATE COLOR AND SIZE WHEN ORDERING. NO EXTRA SIZES. —

No. 17C2997 MISSES' WASH SUIT. Made of tan grass cloth. Consists of skirt and sailor blouse made with a large sailor collar. White dickey in front embroidered with an anchor. Anchor embroidery on right sleeve. The collar and bow in front are bound in red. Belt of same material with a postilion back. Skirt is trimmed with red piping on side plaits on each seam. For 14, 16 and 18-year old young ladies, measuring 32, 34 and 36 inches around the bust, respectively. Skirt lengths, 36 to 40 inches, only. Color, tan only, with red trimmings.
Price.......................**$1.95**
If by mail, postage extra, 35 cents.

No. 17C2998 THIS PRETTY SAILOR SUIT is made of good quality madras cloth, consists of nice sailor waist with large collar with inlaid front or dickey. Stylish sleeves. Plaits on cuffs and on waist in front. Embroidered anchor on the dickey and on the sleeves. Skirt is nicely tailored, and very full. French seams all around. Wide hem around the bottom. Bow of the same material in front. Colors, blue or oxblood.
Price.......................**$2.35**
If by mail, postage extra, 35 cents.

No. 17C3000 THIS HANDSOME SAILOR SUIT is made of good quality linen finished percale. Consists of stylish sailor waist with inlaid front, otherwise called dickey. Trimmings of white cording on the front and around the collar, as well as on the cuffs. Large sleeves. Embroidered anchor in front and silk embroidered eagle on the sleeves. Silk stars on the collar in back. Skirt is nicely tailored, made with side plaits and trimmed with three rows of cording-around the bottom. Color, blue with white trimming.
Price.......................**$2.98**
If by mail, postage extra, 35 cents.

No. 17C3003 THIS HANDSOME SAILOR SUIT is made of fine grass cloth. Consists of blouse sailor waist with large sailor collar, richly trimmed with three rows of cording. Tie in front of same material. Pointed yoke effect. Cord trimming on the sleeves, on the tie and around the collar. Large sleeves. Silk embroidered anchor in front and eagle embroidered on the sleeves. The skirt is nicely tailored and is made with side plaits all around, trimmed around bottom with three rows of cording. Color, tan only, with red trimmings.
Price.......................**$2.25**
If by mail, postage extra, 35 cents.

No. 17C3004 HANDSOME SUIT. Made of good quality white linen. Stylish collar trimmed with straps of same material, side plaits in front, neat cuffs, large sleeves. Silk embroidered anchor on inlaid front and American eagle embroidered in silk on sleeves. Silk embroidered stars on the collar. Very rich. Skirt is nicely tailored and has side plaits all around with wide hem around the bottom. Beautiful garment, strictly up to date, and we can highly recommend it. Color, white, with light blue or red silk embroideries.
Price.......................**$3.50**
If by mail, postage extra, 40 cents.

Sears, Roebuck & Co.

GIRLS' OR MISSES' SKIRTS.

THESE SKIRTS ARE MADE FOR YOUNG LADIES FROM 8 TO 16 YEARS OF AGE, sizes 24 to 36 inches length of skirt, 22 to 27 inches waist measure. We do not make these garments in any other sizes. For sizes larger than these, please make selections from our ladies' skirts. When ordering, state age, weight, length, number of inches around waist and the color wanted.

$1.35

No. 31C3480 MISSES'SKIRT. Made of good quality melton cloth, side plaits all around, foot plaits around the bottom. Facing of same material. Colors, blue or brown.
Price.......................... **$1.35**
If by mail, postage extra, 25 cents.

$1.75

No. 31C3483 MISSES' SKIRT. Made of good quality fancy striped melton, wool finish, trimmings of straps of same material and satin folds. Several rows of stitching around the bottom. Colors, blue or brown with fancy stripes.
Price..(Postage extra, 28c)...**$1.75**

$1.65

No. 31C3486 MISSES' SKIRT. Made of wool finish melton cloth. This skirt is richly corded and embroidered with soutache. Colors, brown or blue.
Price...... ....**$1.65**
If by mail, postage extra, 30 cents.

$1.95

No. 31C3489 MISSES' SKIRT. Made of good quality wool mixed melton cloth, nicely tailored with side plaits and French seams. Kilt plaits on the front gores at the bottom. Fancy gore in front is piped with different color broadcloth. Trimmings of fancy metal buttons. Colors, military blue with red piping or brown with green piping. Price...**$1.95**
If by mail, postage extra, 30 cents.

$2.19

No. 31C3492 MISSES' SKIRT. Made of good quality fancy mixed melton cloth, side plaited all around. Kilt plaits around the bottom. Trimmings of self covered buttons. Colors, gray, blue or brown, with fancy stripes.
Price........................**$2.19**
If by mail, postage extra, 30 cents.

$2.35

No. 31C3495 VERY PRETTY UP TO DATE GARMENT. Made of good quality Sicilian cloth, side plaited all around and finished with kilt plaits around the bottom. Nicely tailored. Colors, blue, brown or red.
Price **$2.35**
If by mail, postage extra, 30 cents.

$2.75

No. 31C3498 MISSES' SKIRT. Made of all wool broadcloth, well tailored, richly trimmed with taffeta silk folds as shown. Facing of same material. Very attractive and pretty. Colors, all black, blue with black trimming, cardinal with black trimming or brown with brown trimming.
Price..(Postage extra, 30c)..**$2.75**

$2.95

No. 31C3501 MISSES' SKIRT. Made of good quality Sicilian cloth, accordion plaited all around, made very full. Colors, blue, brown or red.
Price... ....**$2.95**
If by mail, postage extra, 30 cents.

$2.98

No. 31C3504 THIS UP TO DATE HANDSOME MISSES' SKIRT is made of good quality Sicilian cloth, the entire skirt is side plaited all around. The plaits are stitched down tight around the hips forming a yoke and open below the yoke, making the skirt very full. Colors, red, blue or brown. Price....................**$2.98**
If by mail, postage extra, 40 cents.

$2.98

No. 31C3507 MISSES' SKIRT. Made of all wool cheviot, made with wide box plait and side plaits kilted all around the bottom. Trimmed with small metal buttons. Colors, black, blue, brown or red.
Price........................**$2.98**
If by mail, postage extra, 40 cents.

$3.55

No. 31C3510 THIS PRETTY TAILOR MADE MISSES' SKIRT is made of all wool covert cloth, very newest design this season, is side plaited all around, forming kilts around the bottom. Colors, castor or oxford.
Price........................**$3.55**
If by mail, postage extra, 40 cents.

$3.98

No. 31C3514 MISSES' SKIRT. Made of very fine all wool fancy mixture, tailor made, trimmed with side plaits and straps of same material and kilt plaits around the bottom, also fancy metal buttons to match. green broadcloth piping around the squares on the side gores. Colors, castor or gray mixtures. Price...**$3.98**
If by mail, postage extra, 40 cents.

LADIES' TWO-PIECE DRESSING SACQUE SUITS.

Comfort and Style Combined in These Garments.
Sizes, 32 to 44 inches bust measure. Skirt length, 38 to 44 inches. Always give bust measure and skirt length.

No. 38C1250 Ladies' Two-Piece Dressing Sacque Suit, made of percale. Sacque made with pointed yoke, plaits in back, turndown collar and full fashioned sleeves. Skirt made extra full with wide flounce and heading; has hem at bottom. Colors, black and white, blue and white or red and white, with neat figures. Price........98c
If by mail, postage extra, 24 cents.

No. 38C1254 Ladies' Two-Piece Dressing Sacque Suit, made of fine percale. Sacque made with a yoke, has wide printed collar with ruffle, full fashioned sleeves. Skirt made nice and full with wide flounce and heading; deep hem at bottom. Colors, black and white, blue and white or red and white figures. Price, $1.25
If by mail, postage extra, 27 cents.

No. 38C1258 Ladies' Two-Piece Dressing Sacque Suit, made of fine percale. Sacque trimmed with fancy braid and small pearl buttons; collar and cuffs trimmed to correspond. Skirt made nice and full with wide flounce and heading; deep hem at bottom. Colors, black and white, red and white or blue and white, with neat designs. Price...$1.48
If by mail, postage extra, 27 cents.

LADIES' KIMONAS.

Wonderful Values in these Comfortable Garments.
Sizes, 32 to 42 inches bust measure.

Figured Lawn Kimona, Only 20 Cents.

No. 38C1262 Ladies' Kimona, made of figured lawn. Yoke back and front, border of white lawn, sleeves trimmed to match. Colors, white ground with black, blue or pink figures. Price........20c
If by mail, postage extra, 9 cents.

Fancy Dimity Kimona, Only 39 Cents.
No. 38C1263 Ladies' Kimona, made of fancy dimity. Yoke back and front stitched with white tape, white lawn border with sleeves trimmed to match. Colors, black, blue or red figures, excellent value. Price........39c
If by mail, postage extra, 10 cents.

Fancy Dotted Swiss Kimona, Only 55 Cents.
No. 38C1264 Ladies' Kimona, made of fancy dotted Swiss. Yoke back and front, border made of white lawn, with sleeves trimmed to match. Colors, white with black or blue fancy figures in stripes. Price........55c
If by mail, postage extra, 11 cents.

Extra Fine Quality Figured Lawn, Only 85 Cents.
No. 38C1265 Ladies' Kimona, made of fine quality figured lawn. Yoke back and front, has white lawn shawl collar, and kimona sleeves trimmed to match. Excellent workmanship. Colors, black and white or blue and white figures. Price............(If by mail, postage extra, 10 cents)...........85c

A Lawn Kimona Only 25 Cents.

No. 38C1266 Ladies' Lawn Kimona. Yoke back and front, made with a border, and sleeves bordered to match. Colors, white with blue border or blue with white border. Price....25c

If by mail, postage extra, 10 cents.

Trimmed With Hemstitched Tucks, Only 48 Cents.

No. 38C1268 Ladies' Lawn Kimona. Yoke back and front trimmed with six hemstitched tucks, shawl collar with hemstitching. Kimona sleeves trimmed to match. Colors, white, with pink collar or blue with white collar. Price........48c
If by mail, postage extra, 10 cents.

LONG KIMONAS OR NECLIGEES.

Very handy house garments. Sizes, 32 to 42 inches bust measure.

Long Kimona of Figured Lawn Only 79 Cents.

No. 38C1280 Ladies' Long Kimona, made of figured lawn. Has yoke back and front, border reaching to bottom made of white lawn. Sleeves trimmed to match. Deep hem at bottom. Colors blue or pink grounds with fancy designs, or black with white figures. Price........79c
If by mail, postage extra, 16 cents.

Lace Trimmed Long Kimona Only 98 Cents.

No. 38C1282 Ladies' Long Kimona, made of dimity. Has fancy pointed collar which is trimmed with point de Paris lace, border of white lawn reaching to bottom with deep hem at bottom. Kimona sleeves trimmed to match. Colors are black and white or blue and white floral design. Wonderful value. Price.....98c
If by mail, postage extra, 19c.

Kimona or Lounging Robe, Made of Heavy Fleeced Flannel.

No. 38C1288 Ladies' Long Fancy Kimona or Lounging Robe, made of fine fleeced flannel. Full shirred yoke, has border of fancy silk, hem at bottom, this is a very handy and practical house garment. Colors, blue or pink grounds with fancy floral designs. Price....$1.98
If by mail, postage extra, 32 cents.

Long Kimona, Made of Cotton Crepon.

No. 38C1292 Ladies' Long Kimona. Made of fine cotton crepon, full shirred yoke, both back and front, has border of sateen in neat Persian effects, kimona sleeves trimmed to match. Colors, red, pink or pale blue. Price....$1.48
If by mail, postage extra, 17 cents.

Short Kimona, Made of Cotton Crepon, Only 98 Cents.

No. 38C1294 Ladies' Short Kimona, made of good quality cotton crepon. Same style as No. 38C1292. Colors, pink or pale blue. Price...98c
If by mail, postage extra, 11 cents.

LADIES' BATH OR LOUNGING ROBES.

A very handy garment for after the bath or lounging. Bust measures, 32 to 42 inches.

No. 38C1298 Ladies' Bath or Lounging Robe; made of all wool elderdown, sailor collar, trimmed with two rows of satin ribbon on back of collar and one row on each side. Ribbon embroidered with silk, collar edged with satin, ribbon bow at neck, two silk loops, cuffs to correspond to collar, finished seams throughout, all wool girdle, fitted back, 3¼ yards sweep, hem at bottom. Give bust measure. Colors, cardinal or pale blue. Price... ....$3.98
If by mail, postage extra, 49 cents.

LADIES' AND MISSES' BATHING SUITS.

32 to 42 Bust Measure.

No. 38C1301 Ladies' Bathing Suit with attached bloomers, made of good quality alpaca. Large sailor collar trimmed with three rows of soutache down the front and detachable skirt trimmed around waistband and bottom with three rows of soutache to match, wide hem. Colors, black or navy blue. Price..... $2.25
If by mail, postage extra, 17 cents.
Always give bust measure.

No. 38C1303 Girls' or Misses' Bathing Suits, ages from 8 to 16 years. Same style as No. 38C1301, with attached bloomers and detachable skirt. Color, navy blue with white trimmings. State age desired.

Price.......................$1.69
If by mail, postage extra, 15 cents.

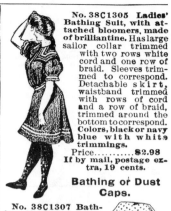

No. 38C1305 Ladies' Bathing Suit, with attached bloomers, made of brilliantine. Has large sailor collar trimmed with two rows white cord and one row of braid. Sleeves trimmed to correspond. Detachable skirt, waistband trimmed with rows of cord and a row of braid, trimmed around the bottom to correspond. Colors, black or navy blue with white trimmings. Price............$2.98
If by mail, postage extra, 19 cents.

Bathing or Dust Caps.

No. 38C1307 Bathing or Dust Caps, made of sateen, pure rubber lining. Has rubber band to make cap fit perfectly around head. Keeps the hair dry. Colors, blue or red, with white polka dots.
Price, each.....$0.23
Per dozen.......... 2.50
If by mail, postage extra, each 4c.

No. 38C1309 Bathing Cap, made of pure rubber, plaid lining. The correct thing to wear when bathing. Rubber band to make it fit perfectly around the head; keeps the hair dry. Color, black only. Price, each........$0.12
Per dozen..................... 1.25
If by mail, postage extra, each 4c.

No. 38C1311 Bathing or Dust Caps, made of pure transparent gum rubber, tape and inserted with rubber, making cap fit perfectly around head. These caps are also very useful as dust caps when house cleaning, etc. Colors, tan or black. Price, each..... $0.25
Per dozen........ .... 2.80
If by mail, postage extra, each, 4c.

LADIES' GINGHAM, SATEEN AND WHITE LAWN APRONS.

Kitchen Aprons at nearly the cost of material.

No. 38C1452 Ladies' Gingham Kitchen Apron, in blue, brown or pink stripes or checks. Size, 30 inches long, 33 inches wide. Extra good value.
Price.............9c
If by mail, postage extra, 4 cents.

No. 38C1454 Ladies' Gingham Kitchen Apron. Size, 34 inches long, 42 inches wide. Material used in these aprons costs nearly as much as we charge for apron already made up. Colors, brown, blue or pink stripes or checks. Price....................14c
If by mail, postage extra, 5 cents.

No. 38C1456 Ladies' Large Gingham Aprons, the best gingham. Hemmed at bottom, long strings in back. Colors, blue or brown checks. A good, reliable apron. Size, 38 inches long, 54 inches wide. Price..........25c
If by mail, postage extra, 5 cents.

Ladies' Bib Apron.

No. 38C1458 Ladies' Gingham Kitchen Apron, made with a bib. Length from waist band, 36 inches. Width, 44 inches. Our price is merely the cost of material only. Colors, blue or pink stripes or checks. Price, 20c
If by mail, postage extra, 6 cents.

Fast Black Sateen Apron 23 Cents.

No. 38C1460 Ladies' Fine Quality Black Sateen Aprons. Very desirable as a work apron, does not require frequent washing and always looks neat. Made full and long; hemmed; with one pocket. The quality sold elsewhere at 35 cents. Price....23c

If by mail, postage extra, 5 cents.

18-Cent White Lawn Apron.

No. 38C1462 Ladies' White Lawn Apron, 34 inches long, 39 inches wide. Wide hem at bottom and wide strings. Very good value.
Price..........15c
If by mail, postage extra, 6 cents.

≡ MUSLIN UNDERWEAR DEPARTMENT ≡

OUR MUSLIN GOODS are made under our own supervision, under the most approved sanitary conditions, and with the result of the best class of workmanship. Each garment is carefully examined as to stitching, 15 to 18 stitches to an inch in our garments. Widths, lengths, sizes, buttons and buttonholes, all undergo a careful inspection before being accepted, thus insuring our customers well made and stylish muslin wear.

READ OUR DESCRIPTIONS as to materials and trimmings. All trimmings, such as laces, embroideries, etc., are of the newest patterns and the daintiest effects, and our styles, workmanship and low prices will surely please everyone who patronizes this department. Send us your order with the understanding that if the goods are not perfectly satisfactory when received, you can return them to us at our expense and your money will be refunded to you.

MUSLIN UNDERWEAR OUTFITS.

FOR THE CONVENIENCE OF CUSTOMERS and also to save them money, we have gotten up two complete muslin underwear outfits, very carefully selected, consisting of all the necessary and best style of garments which we offer in complete sets of fourteen pieces. These outfits are already put up in sets and we cannot make any changes. If you buy one of these outfits, you will be getting remarkable value, for the price is less than you would pay for the individual pieces of the same quality bought separately. We are making very low and close prices on the complete outfits. Our profit is only a very slight margin on the cost of the complete outfit (not on the separate pieces) and is a smaller per-centage of profit, than we could accept if we were pricing each individual garment. We save the handling expense and we give you the benefit of this in the low price. To sell the same number of muslin garments separately would mean a greater handling expense, because each item would have to be picked from stock, handled and packed. In this outfit, everything is complete and we handle the complete outfit, thus one handling as against fourteen (14 garments).

We strongly advise you to order one of these outfits. You will get a complete muslin underwear wardrobe at a price unheard of before. Don't fail to include one of these outfits for your supply of muslin underwear, and such additional pieces as you require can be selected from the following pages.

OUR $4.95 MUSLIN UNDERWEAR OUTFIT, CONSISTING OF FOURTEEN PIECES.

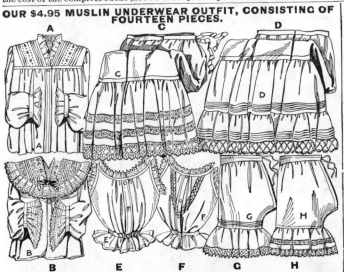

A **Two Gowns** made of muslin, yoke trimmed with tucks and insertion.

One Gown made of cambric, very pretty yoke with torchon lace insertions, hemstitching, tucks, beading and ribbon insertion, lawn ruffle with lace edge to match.

C **One Underskirt** made of cambric, wide lawn flounce with two insertions of torchon lace with edge to match, made with a dust ruffle.

D **Two Underskirts** made of cambric, has 7-inch lawn flounce tucked four times, lawn ruffle with four tucks and edged with torchon lace, has dust ruffle.

E **Two Corset Covers** made of cambric, neck and armholes trimmed with torchon lace.

F **Two Corset Covers** made of cambric, two insertions of torchon lace, neck and armholes trimmed to match.

G **Two pair Drawers** made of muslin, trimmed with three tucks, has 4-inch cambric flounce edged with valenciennes lace.

H **Two pairs Drawers** made of muslin, has cambric flounce, one insertion of torchon lace with edge to match. Be sure and give bust measure and skirt length.

Total, fourteen pieces.

No. 38C100 Price, for entire set of fourteen pieces.................$4.95

For Bridal Outfits with matched trimmings, see pages 932 and 933.

OUR GREAT MUSLIN UNDERWEAR OUTFIT OF FOURTEEN PIECES FOR $7.65.

A **Two Gowns** made of muslin, square neck and yoke trimmed with rows of hemstitched tucks, embroidery insertions and cambric ruffle.

B **Two Gowns** made of cambric, yoke with two insertions of torchon lace, beading and ribbon insertion, lawn shoulder epaulets edged with torchon lace, neck and sleeves trimmed with lace to match.

C **One Underskirt** made of cambric, lawn flounce trimmed with four tucks and four insertions of neat valenciennes lace, lawn ruffle with four tucks and lace edge to match. Entire flounce is 18 inches deep; has dust ruffle.

D **One Underskirt** made of fine cambric, lawn flounce with eighteen insertions of 2-inch point de Paris lace, lawn ruffle with 2-inch insertion and 3-inch edge to match, made with a dust ruffle.

E **Two Corset Covers** made of cambric, trimmed with four insertions of torchon lace and two clusters of four tucks, neck and armholes, with lace to match.

F **Two Corset Covers** made of cambric, three rows of torchon lace insertion, neck trimmed with lace followed with beading and ribbon insertion, armholes trimmed with lace to match.

G **Two pairs Drawers** made of cambric, has lawn flounce with two insertions of torchon lace with edge to match.

H **Two pairs Drawers** made of cambric, trimmed with two clusters of three tucks and 5-inch embroidery ruffle.

Total, fourteen pieces. Sizes, 32 to 42 inches bust measure. Skirt lengths, 38, 40 and 42 inches. Be sure and give bust measure and skirt lengths.

No. 38C101 Price, for entire set of fourteen pieces, only..........$7.65

Bridal Outfits with matched trimmings on page 933.

LADIES' MUSLIN, CAMBRIC AND NAINSOOK GOWNS.

SIZES, 14, 15 AND 16 INCHES NECK MEASURE.

In proportion as follows: { 14-inch neck, 32-34-inch bust / 15-inch neck, 36-38-inch bust / 16-inch neck, 40-42-inch bust }

For extra size gowns see pages 933 and 934.

39c

No. 38C102 Ladies' Gown, made of muslin, hubbard style, yoke trimmed on each side with one row of open embroidery and six tucks, making a total of twelve tucks in yoke, neck trimmed with cambric ruffle, sleeves also trimmed with cambric ruffle to match. Price, 39c. If by mail, postage extra, 15 cents.

50c

No. 38C103 Very Serviceable Gown, made of muslin. Solid tucked yoke, each tuck hemstitched, lawn ruffle around neck and sleeves with hemstitching. Made extra full.

Price.................50c

If by mail, postage extra, 15 cents.

49c

No. 38C104 Wonderful bargain. Ladies' Gown, made of muslin. Empire style. Bosom trimmed with lace insertion and wide embroidery edge. Lapels trimmed with lace insertion with wide ruffle. Sleeves trimmed with cambric ruffle.

Price.................49c

If by mail, postage extra, 15 cents.

No. 38C113. Ladies' Gown, hubbard style, made of a good quality muslin, fancy yoke trimmed with beading and ribbon inserting, with two rows of torchon lace insertion alternating with two clusters of fine tucks; the V-shaped neck is edged with wide torchon lace, sleeves trimmed with a torchon lace to correspond.

Price......65c

Postage extra, 15 cents.

No. 38C125 Ladies' Gown, empire style, made of good quality muslin, collar made of insertions of embroidery with wide ruffle of open work embroidery, bosom trimmed with beading and ribbon insertion, wide embroidery ruffle to match collar, sleeves trimmed with embroidery to match; deep hem at bottom.

75c

Price...........75c

If by mail, postage extra, 15 cents.

48c

No. 38C121 Ladies' Muslin Gown, high neck yoke both back and front; nine rows of tucks (each hemstitched) on each side of the yoke in front, alternating with four embroidery insertions, lawn collar and cuffs with one row of hemstitching.

Price, 48c

Postage extra, 15c.

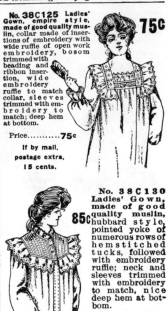

No. 38C130 Ladies' Gown, made of good quality muslin, hubbard style, pointed yoke of numerous rows of hemstitched tucks, followed with embroidery ruffle; neck and sleeves trimmed with embroidery to match, nice deep hem at bottom.

85c

Price......85c

If by mail, postage extra, 16 cents.

CHILDREN'S CLOAKS.

CHILDREN'S DRESSES. AGES, 1 TO 5 YEARS.

$1.98

21c **25c** **75c** **98c**

No. 38C4164 Child's Military Cloak, made of fine all wool flannel. Has wide military collar trimmed with flannel in contrasting color, followed with gilt braid and three small gilt buttons; collar trimmed with braid to match; full fashioned sleeves; cloak trimmed with large gilt buttons and interlined with wadding and lined with sateen. Colors, royal blue or cardinal.
Price.................$1.98
If by mail, postage extra, 34 cents.

No. 38C4700 Child's Dress. Made of good quality washable gingham. Hubbard style, revers on each side trimmed with fancy braid and trimmed in center with embroidery, sleeves trimmed with novelty braid to match, hem at bottom. Colors, blue or pink checks. Price, each.....$0.21
Per dozen............. 2.40
If by mail postage extra, each, 8c.

No. 38C4704 Child's Dress, made of gingham. Solid color yoke trimmed with three rows of fancy braid, ruffle edged with wash lace, hem at bottom. Colors, pink or blue, in checks or stripes.
Price, each............$0.25
Per dozen............. 2.85
If by mail. postage extra, each, 10c.

No. 38C4712 Child's Dress, made of fancy check suiting. Cashmere yoke trimmed with two rows of soutache and small pearl buttons, ruffle all around yoke. Dress lined throughout with cambric. Deep hem at bottom. Colors, fancy checks, blue or red predominating.
Price.....................75c
If by mail, postage extra, 20 cents.

No. 38C4716 Child's Dress made of cashmere. Hubbard style. Fancy circular yoke. Trimmed with tucks and baby ribbon. Plaited ruffle all around yoke and edged with two rows of baby ribbon. Collar and cuffs have two rows of stitching. Lined throughout with cambric. Deep hem at bottom. Ages, 1 to 5 years. Colors, royal blue or wine.
Price.....................98c
If by mail, postage extra, 19 cents

═══CHILDREN'S FRENCH DRESSES. AGES, 2 TO 6 YEARS. ═══

$2.48

39c **45c** **48c** **89c**

No. 38C4167 Child's Cloak, made of good quality velvette. Has wide shoulder cape, neatly trimmed with five medallions, followed with fancy braid, also squares of sateen trimmed with soutache. Collar and cuffs trimmed with fancy braid. Fancy gilt buttons. Interlined with wadding and lined with sateen. Color, black with fancy trimmings.
Price.....................$2.48
If by mail, postage extra, 33 cents.

No. 38C4730 The New Suspender Dress, made of chambray. Suspenders made of same material as in dress, and edged with wash lace. Collar and cuffs edged with wash lace, full blouse, hem at bottom. Ages, 2 to 6 years. Colors, royal blue or red (oxblood).
Price, each............$0.39
Per dozen............. 4.50
If by mail, postage extra, each, 10c.

No. 38C4732 Child's Lawn Dress, very neat yoke made of white striped lawn, the fancy bertha neatly trimmed with valenciennes lace and edged with neat wash lace, sleeves trimmed to match, collar edged with lace, hem at bottom. Ages, 2 to 6 years. Colors, pale blue, tan or pink.
Price.....................45c
If by mail, postage extra, 9 cents.

No. 38C4734 Child's Dress, made of good quality wash gingham; trimmed with three box plaits back and front, made to button on side and trimmed with white pique. Newest style plaited sleeves belt of same material as in dress, white pique collar. Ages, 2 to 6 years. Colors, blue or pink.
Price.....................48c
If by mail, postage extra, 12 cents.

No. 38C4738 Newest Style Suspender Dress. Body made of white lawn, neatly trimmed with six plaits. Skirt made of good quality percale, with belt to match. Suspenders trimmed with row of white pique and edged with neat embroidery; collar and cuffs edged with embroidery to match; deep hem at bottom. Ages, 2 to 6 years. Colors, pink or blue stripes. 89c
If by mail, postage extra, 10 cents.

98c **$1.15** **98c** **$1.48** **75c** **$1.10**

No. 38C4742 Child's Sailor Dress, made of chambray. Very neat sailor collar trimmed with two rows of white tape, white pique dickey. Full blouse trimmed in back and front with three box plaits; tie, cuffs and belt trimmed with white tape. Box plaited skirt with deep hem at bottom. Ages, 2 to 6 years. Colors, blue or tan.
Price.....................98c
If by mail, postage extra 12 cents.

No. 38C4746 Child's Dress, made of chambray. Very neatly trimmed in back and front with six plaits, dress made to button on side. Neatly trimmed with two rows of white tape. Collar and belt trimmed to match. Newest fashioned sleeves trimmed with ten rows of white tape. Ages, 2 to 6 years. Colors, blue or tan.
Price.....................$1.15
If by mail, postage extra, 12 cents.

No. 48C4750 Child's Dress, made of chambray. Has wide sailor collar, neatly trimmed back and front with box plaits. with belt trimmed with two pearl buttons, newest fashioned sleeves with plaits. Full plaited skirt, with deep hem at bottom. Ages, 2 to 6 years. Colors, blue or tan. Price.....98c
If by mail, postage extra, 12 cents.

No. 38C4754 Very Pretty Dress, made of fine dimity, in very neat floral effects. Round yoke, trimmed with clusters of tucks alternating with three insertions of neat embroidery; the very neatly designed bertha is edged with embroidery, neck and sleeves trimmed to match. Full blouse and also trimmed with embroidery. Ages, 2 to 6 years. Colors, neat stripes in blue or pink with floral design.
Price............$1.48
If by mail, postage extra, 11c.

No. 38C4758 Child's Dress, made of fancy checked suiting. Trimmed with two cashmere straps, each with two rows of soutache and small pearl buttons. Collar and cuffs trimmed with two rows of soutache. Very full blouse. Dress lined throughout with cambric. Deep hem at bottom. Ages, 2 to 6 years. Colors, fancy checks, with blue or red predominating. Price...75c
If by mail, postage extra, 20c.

No. 38C4762 Child's Dress, made of cashmere, plaited front. Fancy stitched strap at left side, trimmed with embroidered silk emblem. Collar, cuffs and belt with two rows of stitching plaited back. Dress lined throughout with cambric. Deep hem at bottom. Ages, 2 to 6 years. Colors, navy blue or wine. Price.$1.10
If by mail, postage extra, 18 cents.

Sears, Roebuck & Co.

CHILDREN'S COATS.

FOR 6 TO 14-YEAR OLD CHILDREN.   FOR SMALLER SIZES, SEE PAGES 948 AND 949.

We carry a very extensive line and we are in position to suit everybody.   Our array of styles and colors is magnificent.   We can please the little ones at prices that will astonish you.   When ordering, always state age and bust measure, also color you desire.

No. 17C2892 CHILD'S REEFER JACKET. Made of all wool ladies' cloth, circular cape, double breasted front, loose back finished with a belt. Trimmings of white soutache, with fancy lace braid around the cape. Puff sleeves, fancy turnover cuffs. Facing of same material. Colors, blue, Havana brown or red. State color when ordering.
Price...**$1.48**

If by mail, postage extra, 20 cents.

No. 17C2901 CHILD'S REEFER. Made of all silk peau de soie, double breasted front, loose back finished with a belt. Shoulder capes. Puff sleeves with turnover cuffs. Trimmings of silk rings on the shoulder capes. White silk stitching and white silk cord around collar, cape and cuffs. Pearl buttons. Lined throughout with light blue sateen. Color, black only, with trimmings as described. Price.............**$3.50**

If by mail, postage extra, 20 cents.

No. 17C2910 CHILD'S THREE-QUARTER COAT. Made of all wool good weight cheviot, double breasted front, box back finished with side plaits and belt. Leg of mutton sleeves, made with puff and fancy turnover cuffs. Gunmetal buttons. Facing of same material in front. Broadcloth trimming around the neck and cuffs finished with silk braid and silk soutache. Very stylish. Colors, blue with red broadcloth, or brown with castor color broadcloth. State color when ordering.
Price........ .. ..**$3.75**

If by mail, postage extra, 25 cents.

No. 17C2919 CHILD'S THREE-QUARTER COAT. Made of fine all silk peau de soie, double breasted front, loose back with fancy belt. Large circular collar, fancy sleeves with puff, turnover cuffs. Pearl buttons. Trimmings of cream colored lace medallions around collar and white silk stitching. Lined throughout with light blue sateen. Very pretty garment. Color, black only.
Price.........................**$3.95**

If by mail, postage extra, 30 cents.

No. 17C2895 CHILD'S LONG REEFER COAT. Made of all wool ladies' cloth, double breasted front, box back, finished with a fancy belt. Imitation collar, shoulder capes and straps over shoulders. Puff sleeves, fancy turnover cuffs. Patch pockets. Fancy metal buttons. Trimmings of fancy silk braid around the capes and cuffs, and embroidered silk eagle on sleeve. Lined throughout with sateen. Colors, blue or brown.
Price........ **$1.75**

If by mail, postage extra, 20 cents.

No. 17C2904 CHILD'S LONG REEFER COAT. Made of all wool covert cloth, collarless effect, double breasted front, loose back made with box and side plaits, finished with fancy belt. Stylish puff sleeves, fancy turnover cuffs. Fancy metal buttons. Facing of same material. Trimmings of brown leather colored broadcloth around the neck. Color, castor only, with trimmings as described. Price...**$3.35**

If by mail, postage extra, 20 cents.

No. 17C2912 CHILD'S THREE-QUARTER TOP COAT. Made of all wool covert cloth, double breasted front, collarless effect, loose back finished with belt, fancy sleeves with stylish puff and turnover cuffs. Facing in front of same material. Fancy metal buttons. Self trimming around the neck and silk braid forming small circles and green velvet trimming inside of circles. Color, castor only.
Price..........**$3.75**

If by mail, postage extra, 25 cents.

No. 17C2923 CHILD'S THREE-QUARTER COAT. Made of very fine changeable silk, one of the newest ideas and very pretty, made with double breasted front, loose back with fancy belt. Fancy puff sleeves and turnover cuffs. Facing in front of same material. Shoulder capes trimmed with cream color lace embroidery. Lined throughout with light blue sateen. Colors, red green changeable or blue green changeable. State color when ordering. Price.....................**$4.95**

If by mail, postage extra, 30 cents.

No. 17C2898 CHILD'S LONG REEFER COAT. Made of all wool covert cloth, collarless effect, double breasted front, box back finished with belt. Stylish sleeves finished with puff, turnover cuffs. Nice gilt button trimmings. Facing in front of same material. Very neat. Color, castor only. Price.....................**$2.75**

If by mail, postage extra, 20 cents.

No. 17C2907 CHILD'S THREE-QUARTER COAT. Made of all wool, medium weight thibet cloth, very good, serviceable material, collarless effect, double breasted front, loose back finished with fancy belt. Stylish sleeves finished with puff and fancy turnover cuffs. Fancy gunmetal buttons. Facing of the same material. Velvet trimming around the neck and cuffs. Colors, bright red with green velvet or royal blue with red velvet. Price.... **$3.50**

If by mail, postage extra, 25 cents.

No. 17C2916 CHILD'S THREE-QUARTER TOP COAT. Made of fine all silk peau de soie, double breasted front, loose back finished with fancy belt. Shoulder capes. Pearl buttons. Trimmings of fancy white braid around collar, capes, belt and cuffs. Full puff sleeves. Lined throughout with light blue sateen. Color, black only with white trimming.

Price..........**$3.50**

If by mail, postage extra, 30 cents.

No. 17C2925 CHILD'S THREE-QUARTER COAT. Made of all silk peau de soie, double breasted front, loose finished with belt. Fancy puff sleeves, turnover cuffs. Pearl buttons. Lined throughout with blue sateen. Large collar made of peau de soie silk and stitched with white silk. Lace collar as shown in illustration. Very showy garment. Color, black only, with cream colored lace. Price...**$4.95**

If by mail, postage extra, 30 cents.

The New Spring Shirtwaist Suit

Designs by

Mrs. Ralston

Drawings by

Thomas Mitchell Peirce

The gown shown below would be pretty made in silk or linen, either in a plain or checked material, and is a useful model for general every-day wear.

NO. 1598.—Patterns for this shirtwaist can be supplied in six sizes: 32-42 bust measure. Price, including Chart Model, 15 cents, post-free. Material required: medium size (36-inch bust): 36 inches wide, 3 yards. In ordering ask for No. 1598. Send all orders, with money inclosed, to The Journal's Pattern Bureau.

NO. 1599.—Patterns for this ten-gored skirt can be supplied in six sizes: 22-32 waist measure. Price, including Chart Model, 15 cents, post-free. Material required: medium size (24-inch waist): 36 inches wide, 7 yards. In ordering ask for No. 1599. Send all orders, with money inclosed to The Journal's Pattern Bureau.

The suit illustrated below would be pretty made in voile or foulard silk. The skirt is a plain circular one with a wide box-plaited back.

NO. 1604.—Patterns for this bodice with vest front and shirred side front can be supplied in six sizes: 32-42 bust measure. Price, including Chart Model, 15 cents, post-free. Material required: medium size (36-inch bust): 36 inches wide, 3½ yards. In ordering ask for No. 1604. Send all orders, with money inclosed, to The Journal's Pattern Bureau.

NO. 1589.—Patterns for this circular skirt with double box-plait at the centre back, in round or walking length, can be supplied in five sizes: 22-30 waist measure. Price, including Chart Model, 15 cents, post-free. Material required: medium size (24-inch waist): 36 inches wide, 6¾ yards. In ordering ask for No. 1589. Send all orders, with money inclosed, to The Journal's Pattern Bureau.

1572-1614

A pretty design for a street shirtwaist suit. The skirt is cut in two sections and is a "gored circular" one. The bodice is trimmed with bias folds edged with braid.

NO. 1572.—Patterns for this bodice with three shaped bias folds and vest of tucked chiffon can be supplied in six sizes: 32-42 bust measure. Price, including Chart Model, 15 cents, post-free. In ordering ask for No. 1572. Send all orders, with money inclosed, to The Journal's Pattern Bureau.

NO. 1614.—Patterns for this tunic skirt with circular flounce and seven-gored foundation can be supplied in five sizes: 22-30 waist measure. Price, including Chart Model, 15 cents, post-free. In ordering ask for No. 1614. Send all orders, with money inclosed, to The Journal's Pattern Bureau.

1598-1599

1604-1589

Little Men and Women in Their Spring Clothes

By Mrs. Ralston

Drawings by Grace H. H. Cochrane

FASHIONS for children haven't budged. It is still cleanliness, comfort and economy, and a little of each of these ingredients mixed together will produce style. A few novelties have crept in and may be said to have taken a place with the standard fashions of children's clothes—such, for instance, as the circular-cut coat. This model is used for the tiny little tots in their first short coats of white Bedford cloth all the way up to the long three-quarter-length coats worn by girls from twelve to seventeen years.

IN LETTING down or letting out last year's outgrown clothes you will find that the common cotton and linen braids are very useful things; for instance, in lengthening a washed-out or outgrown skirt you can add a straight band of plain white goods covered with narrow rows of cotton braid fagot-stitched together with the prevailing color of the gown. In choosing a thread for the fagot-stitching you can always match the faded, washed-out appearance of last summer's gown. This same idea of fagot-stitched braid can also be used for letting down sleeves, making deep cuffs of the bands. If, however, this is too much work, and the dress isn't worth so much trouble, it would be better just to cut the sleeves off at the elbows and to make a guimpe to wear with the dress. Another way is to cut the sleeves

THE small-check plaids and ginghams are used for both best and every-day dresses, but are treated differently in their make-up. For instance, in the better dresses the mercerized finished goods are used, trimmed with bertha ruffles and guimpes of all-over embroidered muslins, with sashes or belts also of the embroidery. For plain, knockabout dresses the plaid and check ginghams, as well as the linens, madrases and cheviots, are used, these dresses being made up absolutely without trimming except stitching, and, possibly, turnover collars and cuffs of plain white.

NOW about coats for children. For boys from two to ten years you cannot have anything nicer than the plain box-coats of serge or covert cloth, in navy blues, tans and scarlets; the scarlets, of course, are only suitable for the wee little ones. For girls the coats to wear for all occasions with any gown, either cotton or woolen, are the navy blue serges, and the dark, small-checked goods, and the rough hopsacking and tweeds. These coats may be made in a straight, double-breasted box shape or the three-quarter-length circular-shaped coats. For summer wear they are mostly unlined except the sleeves, and are finished with stitching and buttons to match.

1905

Children's Summer Playday Clothes

Designs by Mrs. Ralston

Drawings by Grace H. H. Cochrane

Of Dimity or Percale

A Plaid Gingham Dress

Attractive in Wool or Linen

Make in Gingham, Linen or Madras

Suitable in White or Colored Linens

For Knockabout in a Tiny Checked Gingham

For Every Day in Colored Chambray, and for Best in White Nainsook

Suitable to Develop in White or Colored Wash Materials

Pretty Girl Papers

By Emma E. Walker, M.D.

Drawings by Katharine N. Richardson

What the Advertised Cosmetics and "Beautifiers" Really Are

IT WILL doubtless interest many of my JOURNAL girls to know the "true inwardness" of some of the well-known "secret preparations" for sale on the market to-day. One of these is a "balm." It is put up in a cheap glass flask, tied with a bit of ribbon. The ingredients of this "magic beautifier" besides water are the oxide of zinc and corrosive sublimate—a deadly poison. The price of the flask with its contents is $1.50, which is gladly paid by many a poor girl. The real cost is not more than ten cents.

Another preparation is a moth and freckle lotion. It is made up of "corrosive sublimate in almond paste or emulsion with water." It is also sold at the modest cost of $1.50, its worth being at most ten cents.

THERE is a soap which, when stamped with the magic name and scented, sells for fifty cents. In reality it is only an ordinary toilet soap which usually sells for ten cents a cake. The "cream" is a mixture of glycerine, zinc oxide and mercuric chloride (corrosive sublimate), scented with rose. These "famous" preparations have been the means of coining thousands of dollars for their ingenious promulgator, while in reality they are ordinary, cheap preparations condemned by physicians especially on account of the corrosive sublimate found in most of them.

Many powders contain lead. Indeed, some have been found by analyses to consist almost entirely of carbonate of lead—commonly known as white lead.

HAVE you not often noticed the effect of bad health on the skin? Perhaps no part of the body is so quick to show it. Physicians are realizing more and more the connection between the condition of the health and the appearance of the skin, and do not treat lightly the case of a girl who presents herself with a blotchy complexion. The trouble is not merely superficial, but demands skillful insight and treatment. The cause of this condition must be removed before the complexion will clear. Overeating, constipation, a sedentary life, breathing impure air, lack of sleep, nervous overstrain, violent emotions,

"A Sedentary Life is Bound to Show its Effect"

such as anger—all these are bound to show their unpleasant effects sooner or later in the skin, which is the index of what is going on throughout the whole economy.

A CELEBRATED dermatologist told me the other day of an experience he once had at a mineral-bath resort. He was called in haste to attend a well-known actress. On entering the room he found his patient literally "black in the face"—and neck. She was in the habit of using some cosmetic which contained lead. Consequently, the effect of her first sulphur bath was most appalling. The discoloration affected not only the surface of the skin but also showed itself down deep in the pores. She was a sorry-looking sight. When sulphur comes in contact with

"Rouge for Theatrical Purposes is Indispensable"

lead the effect is disastrous to beauty. Soap and water have no effect on such discoloration, which looks like indelible ink. The sebaceous matter in the pores gets mixed with the lead, and the ordinary blackhead looks fair in comparison with the result. The only way to get rid of these little black plugs is to squeeze them out.

BUT discoloration from the use of lead powders is one of their least harmful effects. I know of a girl who came to her physician one day with all of the symptoms of chronic lead poisoning. Her hands and arms were weak and unsteady. She found it difficult to write, and walking had become a task. She suffered from colic, and her digestion was deranged. She had a coppery taste in her mouth every morning on waking. There was an ugly dark blue line at the margin of her gums. She grew worse until she could neither pick up nor hold anything with her hands. She first noticed the weakness in her hands at a "taffy-pulling," where she dropped a skillet of hot syrup. At last she could not extend her fingers, and what is known as "wrist-drop" developed. Her hands dropped at the wrist and she had no power to raise them. Her back was so weak that she could not hold herself up, but leaned her body over to the old-fashioned "Grecian bend." The first physician whom she consulted thought that she had spinal disease. He fitted her with a brace, but her condition grew worse, and a second physician was called in. After a careful examination he pronounced it a case of chronic lead poisoning. This is only one of many similar cases. Delirium and convulsions have been caused by the long-continued use of lead powders.

A CERTAIN preparation that is advertised to produce rosy cheeks without the help of rouge consists of a powdered silicious sponge. When examined under the microscope it is seen to be made up of multitudes of tiny silicious needles. These stick into the skin, irritating it, thus causing it to redden.

Good Health for Girls

J. D. A. Electrolysis consists in the application of an electric needle to the root of the hair in order to kill it. The method is not practicable when the growth is luxuriant. The X-ray is sometimes used for this purpose. The expense of this treatment will depend upon the amount of work to be done and upon the physician consulted.

Birthmarks may sometimes be removed by electrolysis and by high frequency currents. The success of the treatment will depend upon the depth of the blemish.

INTERESTED READER. The causes of "moth-patches" are obscure. They appear to be due to certain internal disorders, fading away when these troubles are relieved.

Flat-foot is seldom caused by walking, as the foot is strengthened by this exercise. Weakness and long standing, and especially the habit of turning the foot outward, are the general causes of this deformity.

MARGARET R. A thin neck is sometimes due to the stiff, high collars that a girl wears. Try soft stocks for a while.

If you indulge in cold baths drink something hot just before taking the plunge.

SUBSCRIBER. A lotion for blackheads is carbonate of magnesia and zinc oxide, each 1 drachm; rose-water, 4 ounces. This is to be shaken and mopped on the spots, and later the bulk of the "worm" may be gently pressed out, after the face is softened with hot water. A reliable cream is then applied. A lotion for pimples is: Precipitate of sulphur, 1 drachm; tincture of camphor, 1 drachm; rose-water, 4 ounces. This may be applied several times a day.

A red nose is due primarily to a disturbance of the circulation. The blood-vessels of the nose become congested and finally permanently enlarged so that the nose is constantly red. Electrolysis is the best remedy for this condition. By this method the little blood-vessels are destroyed and the nose is restored to its normal color.

VIOLET R. Do not try to change the color of your hair. Anything artificial is sure to be detected and is always unlovely. You cannot make straight hair curly.

For the girl who is too plump no amount of treatment will be so helpful in decreasing her weight as a persistent course of vigorous daily exercise which brings the perspiration. She should, of course, be moderate in her diet.

AMANDA. If your skin is firm and tough enough to endure a specially vigorous rub after your morning bath you may use Turkish towels that have been slightly starched.

Nancy's First Housekeeping

By Anna Browning Doughten

EVER since I left school at the age of sixteen I had been earning my own living. The death of my father and mother soon after condemned me to a boarding-house existence.

I cannot remember the time when Jim Hancock and I first decided that we would be married some day. Jim was a clerk in the National Bank of a Jersey town of five thousand inhabitants, about fifteen miles from Philadelphia. We announced our engagement when he was made teller of the bank on a salary of fifteen dollars a week, and when it was raised to eighteen dollars we were married. The Hancocks for several generations had been quite important people in the town. Mrs. Hancock had been nice to me, but was afraid I would not be content to settle down to housekeeping after my contact with the business world. She did not realize that I had learned to value a home, having been without one, and that my business training would be no drawback to housekeeping. Jim declared that he was not marrying for a housekeeper, but for a wife and comrade; however, I was determined to be a good housekeeper as well as a comrade.

WE DECIDED to be married on the first of September, my twenty-third birthday — Jim was twenty-six — and such planning as we did in the two months before the ceremony! Eighteen dollars a week seems like riches, but when you plan out the expenses it is gone before you know it. We had made up our minds not to economize in quality since it was not necessary to furnish a house completely in the beginning. I had attended lectures on cooking and domestic science, so I had lots of theories. Jim was in sympathy with my ideals, if only I would promise to have one article of food at each meal which he could surely eat.

The house was the first thing to be chosen. I had read somewhere that the amount of rent a month should not be higher than one week's income, and as we wanted to lay by for a rainy day we could not pay a cent over fourteen dollars. I intended to do my own work, and, in a general way, knew what I wanted. It is singular from what a different standpoint you consider a house when you mean to do all the work. We went house-hunting three consecutive Saturday afternoons, and we did grow so discouraged. The whole world seemed to be against our obtaining a house, but I knew too much about boarding to consent to spend our first year in a boarding-house. There were a couple of attractive, good-sized houses, with quite large grounds, for eighteen dollars a month, and Jim wanted to decide on one of these; but we had been carefully figuring out our income, and I knew it would then be impossible to save a cent. When I thought of the work and worry and expense of taking care of one of those houses I stood firm.

JIM had three hundred dollars saved for furnishing the house, and I had enough for my trousseau and household linen, and we did not mean to run into debt. Jim also had seventy-five dollars put aside for our wedding trip, and was tremendously surprised when I suggested that we spend our honeymoon in our own home, getting it ready, and use that money for painting, for picture mouldings and the many incidentals. He grew to like the idea and called me a sensible girl, and I do not believe any one ever had a nicer, more lasting or more substantial honeymoon.

There were many things to do before we were married, and we were more than busy. We had the living-room, dining-room and hall painted in green and cream, the dividing line being a picture moulding in the living-room and hall, and a plate-rail in the dining-room. The bedrooms were a clear, golden brown up to the picture moulding, and above that a soft, warm yellow. The bathroom and kitchen we had painted white, the final coat being an enamel paint. We had the wood taken away from in front of the plumbing in both kitchen and bathroom. I shall never forget the massacre of roaches which followed. We had all the pipes and the bathtub and sink painted with the white enamel paint. It did look so pure and clean and sanitary, and the enamel paint is most easily washed; but we discovered that where there was much hot water used it had an exasperating fashion of peeling. We afterward found that we would be obliged to repaint the bathtub every three months to keep it in good condition. That was one of our mistakes, but the paint was attractive at first.

Our rooms were none of them large, and we had decided to have a buffet-table instead of a sideboard, as it cost less, took up less room, and, to my mind, was prettier. We found a most attractive one for thirty-nine dollars and fifty cents, which had drawers enough to take the place of a sideboard. The round table, with a six-foot extension, cost twenty dollars, and was beautiful. We bought four chairs at three dollars and fifty cents each, and two armchairs at five dollars each, and then we wanted a china-closet. There was an enticing one offered for thirty-eight dollars and fifty cents, but we turned our backs on temptation, choosing a plainer, smaller one for fifteen dollars, which made the total cost ninety-eight dollars and fifty cents.

WE WANTED to furnish the kitchen for fifty dollars, and I had to go over the list many times, cutting out the utensils which were not absolutely necessary, and even then we ran over the price. My chief extravagance was aluminum for my teakettle and saucepans, but in the long run that has proved an economy, for aluminum is light and easily cleaned, and while it will lose its brilliant polish unless very carefully washed, it will wear for years. The refrigerator seemed like an extravagance when an ice-box was three or four dollars cheaper, but the salesman explained the theory of cold air falling so convincingly, and the ice-box looked so impossible to keep clean, that we wondered how we even considered it, and I have never been sorry for my decision, although Mrs. Hancock still maintains that an ice-box is more economical. The refrigerator was zinc-lined, with a coating of white enamel paint. We bought part of an outfit for washing, for, although we expected to put most of our wash outside to be done, I meant to wash our unstarched underclothes, handkerchiefs, and my own collars and cuffs.

THE following is the list of kitchen articles, and what we paid for each:

One gas-stove	$12.00
One zinc-topped table	4.50
One refrigerator	18.00
Two chairs	3.00
One washtub	.75
One washboard	.40
One set of irons	.70
Five dozen clothespins	.10
Two clothesprops	.20
One ironing-board	.60
Twenty-five yards of clothesline	.25
One aluminum teakettle	2.50
One three-quart aluminum saucepan (without lid)	.50
One two-quart aluminum saucepan (without lid)	.35
One six-quart soup-kettle	1.50
Tin flour-canister	.75
Six glass jars for dry groceries	.75
One galvanized iron bucket	.30
One galvanized iron garbage-can	.60
One roasting-pan	.35
One omelet-pan	.30
One tin draining-basket	.75
One white granite dishpan	1.00
One sieve	.10
Salt-box	.15
Soap-cup	.15
Grater	.15
Nutmeg-grater	.05
Colander	.20
Muffin-tins	.35
Measuring-cup	.10
Apple-corer	.05
Egg-whip	.05
Iron meat-fork	.10
Iron basting-spoon	.10
Dustpan	.12
Dustbrush	.25
Scrubbing-brush	.10
Broom	.25
Icepick	.15
French paring-knife	.35
Large bread-knife	.60
Meat-grinder	.90
Can-opener	.10
Corkscrew	.20
Six assorted white granite bowls	1.80
Four white granite plates	.60
Three kitchen knives and forks	.75
Three solid nickel teaspoons	.25
Three solid nickel tablespoons	.50
Chain pot-cleaner	.10
Skimmer	.05
Rolling-pin	.10
Bread-board	.40
Potato-masher	.10
Three bread-pans	.60
One jelly-mould	.30
Six custard-cups	.50
Dipper	.10
Spatula	.30
Total expenditure	$61.17

Counting my brother's wedding gift we had three hundred and fifty dollars for furnishing our house. The following were our expenses:

Bedroom furniture	$52.00
Dining-room furniture	98.50
Kitchen furnishings	61.17
Dinner-set	12.00
Cartage and expressage	11.00
Total expenditure	$234.67

This left us one hundred and fifteen dollars and thirty-three cents for rugs and furnishing the rest of the house, and we meant to do this gradually after we were married. The wedding-trip money just covered the improvements of the inside of the house.

WE WERE married very quietly in Philadelphia, spent the night at a hotel there, and came right to our own home the next morning. We had arranged to take our meals at a boarding-house near by while getting our home in a livable condition. It seemed as if a bit of Heaven had come down into our lives when Jim unlocked the door, and crossing the threshold hand in hand, like two children, we began our new existence together.

1905

Nancy's First Housekeeping

By Anna Browning Doughten

DRAWN BY ANNA S. HICKS

OUR first home meal was to be Sunday's breakfast, so on Friday afternoon, while Jim was busy in the garden, I sat down with pad and pencil to make out the week's bills-of-fare and my marketing lists. I was to have several dollars extra for the first stock of groceries, for lots of things had to be purchased in large enough quantities to last several weeks. At first visions passed through my head of buying in large quantities; but when I calculated the prices it was utterly out of the question. However, I was convinced that it was the cheapest way, and finally by saving whatever I could each week I bought many groceries in wholesale quantities.

First, I made out the bills-of-fare without thinking much about cost, then put down the probable prices, and the amount was several dollars more than I could spend; so I went over the list, crossing out unnecessaries and substituting cheaper articles wherever possible, until the amount was about right; then I went over it all again, and made out a list for groceries, one for meat and one for green vegetables and fruit. Everything that would keep I bought on Saturday for the whole week. I wanted to do my marketing only twice a week, for I think housekeepers lose time, temper and money by running to market at the last minute in a great hurry. Every morning I meant to visit my refrigerator and use the left-overs for luncheon, so in making out the bills-of-fare each week I could only put down the probable dishes for that meal.

List of Groceries

One gallon of olive oil	$2.00
Twenty-five pounds of flour	.75
Salt	.05
Pepper	.10
One quart of vinegar	.10
Half a pound of tea	.30
One bottle of vanilla extract	.15
Box of cocoa	.25
One pound of crackers	.15
Two pounds of sal soda	.05
Two packages of baking soda	.05
Box of baking powder	.25
Two gallons of kerosene oil	.24
Two cakes of hand soap	.16
Two cakes of washing soap	$ .14
One pint of molasses	.08
Half a dozen lemons	.10
One pound of rolled oats	.03
One package of tapioca	.10
One package of gelatine	.10
One package of junket tablets	.10
One pound of rice	.10
Box of cereal	.13
Five pounds of sugar	.25
Cloves	.10
Cinnamon	.10
Nutmeg	.10
Allspice	.10
Mace	.10
Quarter of a pound of ginger	.15
One bottle of Worcestershire sauce	.25
One bottle of ketchup	.25
One quart of ammonia	.60
One pint of alcohol	.40
One pound of cheese	.17
One dozen and a half eggs	.38
One pound and a half of butter	.45
Half a pound of coffee	.17
Eighteen rolls	.18
Three loaves of bread	.15
One pound of prunes	.12
One pint of dried soup beans	.04
Total	$9.54

List for the Butcher

SATURDAY

Four pounds of pinbone roast	$ .56
One pound of mutton chops from the loin	.14

WEDNESDAY

One pound and a half of rump steak	.27
Total	$ .97

List of Vegetables and Fruit

SATURDAY

Half basket of apples	$ .30
One dozen oranges	.30
Parsley	.05
One basket of white potatoes	.40
One head of cabbage	.05
One head of lettuce	.10
Quarter of a peck of sweet potatoes	.10
One quart of onions	.08
One bunch of beets	.04

WEDNESDAY

One bunch of celery	.13
Total	$1.55

Ice	$ .50
Six quarts of milk	.48
Cream	.18
Two pounds of flounder	.20
Total	$1.36

Expenses

Groceries	$9.54
Meat	.97
Vegetables and fruit	1.55
Ice, etc.	1.36
Grand total	$13.42

My first week cost more than I had thought it would, but the second left me with the dollar for incidentals untouched, and after a while I learned the prices of foods, and how to manage the money to better advantage.

❧

SUNDAY morning about eight o'clock I suddenly realized that all the breakfast we were to have that day was to be cooked by me. The next thing I knew I had on my long kimono and slippers, and was hurrying quietly downstairs. I filled the kettle and lighted a burner under it, then went back again for my cold bath, and to dress. In my trousseau were a couple of gray gingham gowns with short skirts, elbow sleeves, and sailor collars of white embroidery, and without any standing collars, into which I could slip hurriedly, and yet look neat and attractive, and over these dresses I put a checked bib-apron.

The water was just boiling when I reached the kitchen. I put the coffee in the upper glass part of my French coffee-pot, and the boiling water in the lower part, and lighted the alcohol lamp. While I was setting the table I started the oven of the gas-stove, put our three rolls in the oven to warm, and three pieces of bread on the broiler to toast. Presently there was a decided burnt odor, and three pieces of charcoal were on the broiler, and the rolls were dark brown. The table was set by this time, and the coffee was made, so I watched the second lot of toast carefully. The eggs poached beautifully, but alas, in lifting them on to the toast one broke and ran all over the plate. I could have sat down and cried, but I carefully took out the broken egg, wiped off the dish, and poached another egg. I turned off the oven burners, put the eggs and the rolls inside, leaving the door open, and called Jim.

He smiled at my flushed face, but forbore to make remarks. Suddenly I realized how silly it was to let such little things make me unhappy, and I did not mind any more. The table was bare, with linen doilies, and there was a bunch of nasturtiums in the centre, and it was with great satisfaction that we sat down to our first meal in our own home.

First Week's Bills-of-Fare

Sunday

BREAKFAST
Apples
Poached Eggs on Toast
Coffee   Rolls

DINNER
Pinbone Roast
Browned Potatoes
Creamed Cabbage
Rice Pudding

SUPPER
Cold Roast Beef
Cabbage Salad
Crackers and Cheese
Sliced Oranges

❧

Monday

BREAKFAST
Oranges
Cereal with Cream
Coffee   Rolls

LUNCHEON
Minced Beef on Toast
Sweet Potatoes
Apple Sauce

SUPPER
Mutton Chops
Boiled Rice
Creamed Onions
Junket

❧

Tuesday

BREAKFAST
Baked Apples
Scrambled Eggs
Coffee   Rolls

LUNCHEON
Bean Soup
Lettuce Salad
Crackers and Cheese
Stewed Pears

SUPPER
Meat Croquettes
Browned Sweet Potatoes
Beets
Apple Tapioca

❧

Wednesday

BREAKFAST
Stewed Prunes
Oatmeal with Cream
Coffee   Rolls

LUNCHEON
Brown Stew
Cole-Slaw
Sliced Oranges

SUPPER
Beefsteak
Stewed Dried Beans
Creamed Cabbage
Cup Custard

❧

Thursday

BREAKFAST
Oranges
Oatmeal with Cream
Coffee   Toast

LUNCHEON
Vegetable Soup
Cabbage Salad
Cocoa   Gingerbread

SUPPER
Beefsteak
Baked Potatoes
Creamed Celery
Prune Soufflé

❧

Friday

BREAKFAST
Apples
Cereal with Cream
Coffee   Rolls

LUNCHEON
Welsh Rarebit
Lettuce Salad
Coffee

SUPPER
Boiled Flounder with
Drawn-butter Sauce
Mashed Potatoes
Celery with French
Dressing
Lemon Jelly

❧

Saturday

BREAKFAST
Stewed Prunes
Oatmeal with Cream
Coffee   Rolls

LUNCHEON
Cream of Celery Soup
Omelet
Lettuce and Cabbage
Salad
Fruit

SUPPER
Creamed Fish
Potato Salad
Lemon Jelly

IT SEEMED to me that I learned more in my first week of housekeeping than in all my previous life, and by the end of the second week I could cook ordinary things quite well, but it was more than a month before we had any guests, and then they were invited almost with terror. I wanted Jim to be as pleased with his housekeeper as he was with his wife, and he did seem to be; and even when I was most tired and most discouraged and things went most wrong—and housekeeping, with or without a maid, is not easy—the fact that we had our own home just for us two, and that we were growing closer and closer together in our daily life, was more than enough compensation, and I never, for one moment, felt that I would exchange places with any woman in this whole round world.

Dainty Bags for Easter

Illustrations from Photographs Sent to Dolly's Sewing-Basket in Prize Competition

FOR SMALL PIECES OF LAUNDRY

A PET cat, yawning, inspired the making of this bag. Two pieces of cardboard were cut in the shape of a cat's head. One piece was covered with white Canton flannel and the black part with velvet—the features being colored with ink. The bag was made of pink cotton material sewed around the gaping mouth of the under piece of cardboard which had been covered with pink. Ribbon strings were attached and the two parts glued together. Whiskers were made of waxed thread.

CHILD'S SCHOOL-BAG

THE wear and tear on a school-bag necessitates the use of durable material in the making of one, and this design shows a good model in tan-colored burlap. The small figures were done in long-stitch with brown raffia, the initials in cross-stitch with orange raffia. Handle of brown raffia braided.

CONCERTINA PATCH-BAG

THIS very odd but roomy bag was made of inch-wide strips of flowered material with a cord stitched in the edges alternately on the right and wrong sides. The strips were mitred about six inches apart to shape the bag in a square. A six-inch strip of the material was allowed for the top, with a hem one inch and a half wide through which to run a cord. A loop of the cord was also taken across the top to serve as a handle. When empty the bag collapses as shown in the small illustration below.

DOUBLE LAUNDRY-BAG

DESIGNED for a housekeeper's use. The two ends of a three-yard piece of calico were turned back to the centre, thus forming two bags three-fourths of a yard deep. A facing of calico across the centre was made into two casings for the draw-strings of the two bags. Each bag has an outside pocket for a laundry list and a pencil.

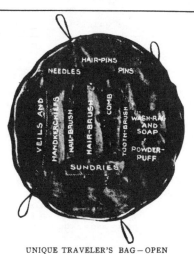

UNIQUE TRAVELER'S BAG—OPEN

BAG CLOSED AND READY FOR A TRIP

AS A CHANGE from the ofttimes burdensome suit-case, this traveler's bag will be welcome to many a girl for its handy size and convenient pockets. A dressing-sacque or nightgown may be slipped in with one's toilet articles. The outside is made of brown leather twenty-four inches in diameter, and the lining is of brown linen. The draw-strings at the sides are made of four strands of buckskin, while the portions between the strings are folded in and held together by snap fasteners sewed on the inside of the leather.

Awarded the First Prize

LEATHER SHOPPING-BAG

MADE of brown leather with a pyrographic design of clover leaves. The pocket with the clasp was designed for small change and car tickets, while a similar one on the back makes a safe place for more valuable articles. Any number of inside pockets could be arranged if desired.

EVENING BAG IN SILK AND LEATHER

REQUIRING one-quarter of a yard of silk, one yard of cord and two pieces of leather four inches by seven. Either burn or tool a design on the leather. The scrolled edges of the leather were stitched on the silk straight across; then the two pieces were placed together and stitched at the bottom and sides, the seam in the silk at the sides being made on the inside. The casing and hem are made as usual.

A NEW-STYLE BAG FOR FANCY WORK

Little Easter Presents

Designed by Antonie Ehrlich

Baby's tambourine crocheted in white and yellow Germantown wool. Directions 10 cents.

Crocheted socks in blue and white Saxony. Directions 15 cents.

Thumbless mittens knitted in white Saxony yarn. Directions 10 cents.

Knitted cap in pink split zephyr. Directions 25 cents.

Coin bag crocheted in silk with gold beads. Directions 15 cents.

Knitted sacque in white Saxony with taffeta ribbon strings. Directions 25 cents.

Knitted socks in pink and white Saxony. Directions 15 cents.

Knitted cap in pink Saxony with pink and white striped edge, and pink satin ribbon strings. Directions 25 cents.

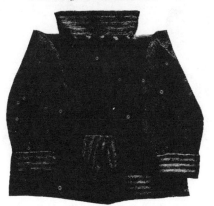

Knitted sacque in pink Saxony with pink and white striped edge, collar and cuffs. Directions 25 cents.

Back view of knitted sacque in pink Saxony with striped trimming.

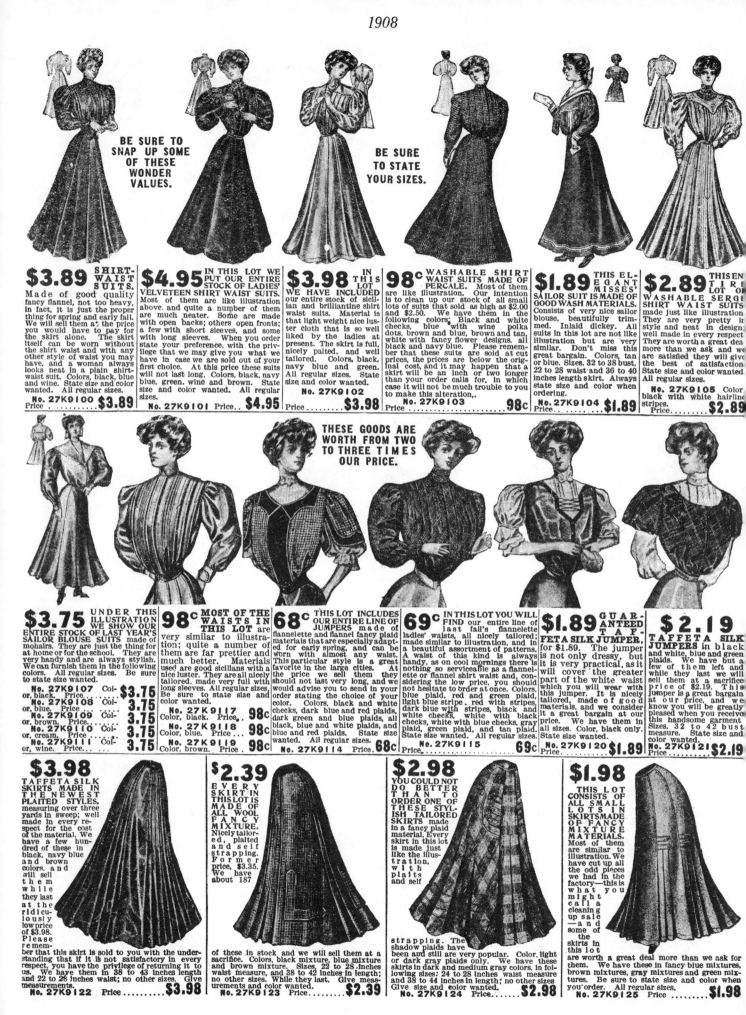

$3.89 SHIRT-WAIST SUITS. Made of good quality fancy flannel, not too heavy, in fact, it is just the proper thing for spring and early fall. We will sell them at the price you would have to pay for the skirt alone. The skirt itself can be worn without the shirt waist and with any other style of waist you may have, and a woman always looks neat in a plain shirt-waist suit. Colors, black, blue and wine. State size and color wanted. All regular sizes. No. 27K9100 Price.......**$3.89**

$4.95 IN THIS LOT WE PUT OUR ENTIRE STOCK OF LADIES VELVETEEN SHIRT WAIST SUITS. Most of them are like illustration above, and quite a number of them are much neater. Some are made with open backs; others open fronts; a few with short sleeves, and some with long sleeves. When you order state your preference, with the privilege that we may give you what we have in case we are out of your first choice. At this price these suits will not last long. Colors, black, navy blue, green, wine and brown. State size and color wanted. All regular sizes. No. 27K9101 Price..**$4.95**

$3.98 IN THIS LOT WE HAVE INCLUDED our entire stock of sicilian and brilliantine shirt waist suits. Material is that light weight nice luster cloth that is so well liked by the ladies at present. The skirt is full, nicely paited, and well tailored. Colors, black, navy blue and green. All regular sizes. State size and color wanted. No. 27K9102 Price.......**$3.98**

98c WASHABLE SHIRT WAIST SUITS MADE OF PERCALE. Most of them are like illustration. Our intention is to clean up our stock of all small lots of suits that sold as high as $2.00 and $2.50. We have them in the following colors, Black and white checks, blue with wine polka dots, brown and blue, brown and tan, white with fancy flower designs, all black and navy blue. Please remember that these suits are sold at cut prices, the prices are below the original cost, and it may happen that a skirt will be an inch or two longer than your order calls for, in which case it will not be much trouble to you to make this alteration,. No. 27K9103 Price.......**98c**

$1.89 THIS ELEGANT MISSES' SAILOR SUIT IS MADE OF GOOD WASH MATERIALS. Consists of very nice sailor blouse, beautifully trimmed. Inlaid dickey. All suits in this lot are not like illustration but are very similar. Don't miss this great bargain. Colors, tan or blue. Sizes, 32 to 38 bust, 22 to 28 waist and 36 to 40 inches length skirt. Always state size and color when ordering. No. 27K9104 Price...**$1.89**

$2.89 THIS ENTIRE LOT OF WASHABLE SERGE SHIRT WAIST SUITS made just like illustration. They are very pretty in style and neat in design; well made in every respect. They are worth a great deal more than we ask and we are satisfied they will give the best of satisfaction. State size and color wanted. All regular sizes. No. 27K9105 Color, black with white hairline stripes. Price.......**$2.89**

THESE GOODS ARE WORTH FROM TWO TO THREE TIMES OUR PRICE.

$3.75 UNDER THIS ILLUSTRATION WE SHOW OUR ENTIRE STOCK OF LAST YEAR'S SAILOR SUITS made of mohairs. They are just the thing for at home or for the school. They are very handy and are always stylish. We can furnish them in the following colors. All regular sizes. Be sure to state size wanted.
No. 27K9107 Color, black. Price....**$3.75**
No. 27K9108 Color, blue. Price....**3.75**
No. 27K9109 Color, brown. Price....**3.75**
No. 27K9110 Color, cream. Price....**3.75**
No. 27K9111 Color, wine. Price....**3.75**

98c MOST OF THE WAISTS IN THIS LOT are very similar to illustration; quite a number of them are far prettier and much better. Materials used are good sicilians with a nice luster. They are all nicely tailored, made very full with long sleeves. All regular sizes. Be sure to state size and color wanted.
No. 27K9117 Color, black. Price....**98c**
No. 27K9118 Color, blue. Price....**98c**
No. 27K9119 Color, brown. Price....**98c**

68c THIS LOT INCLUDES OUR ENTIRE LINE OF JUMPERS made of flannelette and flannel fancy plaid materials that are especially adapted for early spring, and can be worn with almost any waist. This particular style is a great favorite in the large cities. At the price we sell them they should not last very long, and we would advise you to send in your order stating the choice of your color. Colors, black and white checks, dark blue and red plaids, dark green and blue plaids, all black, blue and white plaids, and blue and red plaids. State size wanted. All regular sizes. No. 27K9114 Price..**68c**

69c IN THIS LOT YOU WILL FIND our entire line of last fall's flannelette ladies' waists, all nicely tailored; made similar to illustration, and in a beautiful assortment of patterns. A waist of this kind is always handy, as on cool mornings there is nothing so serviceable as a flannelette or flannel shirt waist and, considering the low price, you should not hesitate to order at once. Colors, blue plaid, red and green plaid, light blue stripe, red with stripes, dark blue with stripes, black and white checks, white with black checks, white with blue checks, gray plaid, green plaid, and tan plaid. State size wanted. All regular sizes. No. 27K9115 Price.......**69c**

$1.89 GUARANTEED TAFFETA SILK JUMPER, for $1.89. The jumper is not only dressy, but it is very practical, as it will cover the greater part of the white waist which you will wear with this jumper. It is nicely tailored, made of good materials, and we consider it a great bargain at our price. We have them in all sizes. Color, black only. State size wanted. No. 27K9120 Price.......**$1.89**

$2.19 TAFFETA SILK JUMPERS in black and white, blue and green plaids. We have but a few of them left and while they last we will sell them at a sacrifice price of $2.19. This jumper is a great bargain at our price, and we know you will be greatly pleased when you receive this handsome garment. Sizes, 32 to 42 bust measure. State size and color wanted. No. 27K9121 Price....**$2.19**

$3.98 TAFFETA SILK SKIRTS MADE IN THE NEWEST PLAITED STYLES, measuring over three yards in sweep; well made in every respect for the cost of the material. We have a few hundred of these in black, navy blue and brown colors, and will sell them while they last at the ridiculously low price of $3.98. Please remember that this skirt is sold to you with the understanding that if it is not satisfactory in every respect, you have the privilege of returning it to us. We have them in 38 to 43 inches length and 22 to 28 inches waist; no other sizes. Give measurements. No. 27K9122 Price.......**$3.98**

$2.39 EVERY SKIRT IN THIS LOT IS MADE OF ALL WOOL FANCY MIXTURE. Nicely tailored, plaited and self strapping. Former price, $3.35. We have about 187 of these in stock and we will sell them at a sacrifice. Colors, black mixture, blue mixture and brown mixture. Sizes, 22 to 28 inches waist measure, and 38 to 42 inches in length; no other sizes. While they last. Give measurements and color wanted. No. 27K9123 Price.......**$2.39**

$2.98 YOU COULD NOT DO BETTER THAN TO ORDER ONE OF THESE STYLISH TAILORED SKIRTS made in a fancy plaid material. Every skirt in this lot is made just like the illustration, with plaits and self strapping. The shadow plaids have been and still are very popular. Color, light or dark gray plaids only. We have these skirts in dark and medium gray colors, in following sizes: 24 to 28 inches waist measure and 38 to 44 inches in length; no other sizes Give size and color wanted. No. 27K9124 Price.......**$2.98**

$1.98 THIS LOT CONSISTS OF ALL SMALL LOTS IN SKIRTS MADE OF FANCY MIXTURE MATERIALS. Most of them are similar to illustration. We have cut up all the odd pieces we had in the factory—this is what you might call a cleaning up sale—and some of the skirts in this lot are worth a great deal more than we ask for them. We have these in fancy blue mixtures, brown mixtures, gray mixtures and green mixtures. Be sure to state size and color when you order. All regular sizes. No. 27K9125 Price.......**$1.98**

BE SURE TO SNAP UP SOME OF THESE WONDER VALUES.

BE SURE TO STATE YOUR SIZES.

This Bonnet Certainly Reflects Good Style. Milliners Ask $3.00.

Our Price, $1.69.

No. 18K15470 Very dainty bonnet at an exceedingly low price. Strictly hand made on a wire frame. The high rolling brim is covered with a row of imported German braid in combination with plaited and shirred milliners' mull. The entire ball crown and upper brim are finished with this same fine braid sewed row and row. A very stylish trimming effect of feather aigrettes tipped with very tiny spangled petals arise from the center of a ribbon rosette made of the best quality narrow black taffeta ribbon. On the right of the brim appears a cut jet barette.

Ties of No. 12 black taffeta ribbon are applied at the back and complete the trimming of this exceptional model. Can be ordered in all black as described, or black with a touch of lavender or a touch of white. Please mention color. Price......$1.69

All Hand Made Poke Bonnet Style, Beautifully Trimmed, $2.38.

No. 18K15475 Our very finest poke bonnet style for girls up to twelve years of age. This child's hat is strictly hand made on a wire frame with the entire upper and under brim very closely covered with shirred pink milliners' mull with numerous rows of tucking. This gives a soft, fluffy effect and is exceptionally pretty. The large bell crown is entirely covered with silk pyroxylin braid

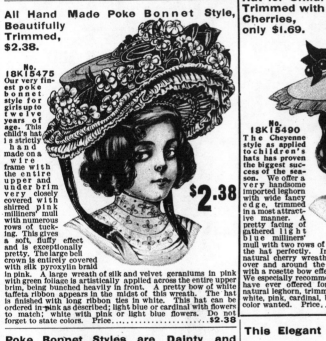

in pink. A large wreath of silk and velvet geraniums in pink with green foliage is artistically applied across the entire upper brim, being bunched heavily in front. A pretty bow of white taffeta ribbon appears in the midst of this wreath. The hat is finished with long ribbon ties in white. This hat can be ordered in pink as described; light blue or cardinal with flowers to match; white with pink or light blue flowers. Do not forget to state colors. Price.....................$2.38

Poke Bonnet Styles are Dainty and Stylish. This $2.50 Value Only $1.48.

No. 18K15480 For little children and girls up to twelve years of age there is nothing prettier than a poke bonnet style. We illustrate an imported leghorn shaped into this popular effect, having a facing of light blue milliners' mull very closely gathered with eight rows of close tucks. The edge of the hat is bound with light blue silk velvetta. The crown trimming consists of a pretty wreath of

tiny white daisies twisted through a very large rosette trimming of light blue mull and light blue taffeta ribbon. Ties of light blue taffeta ribbon extend from the back of the hat, giving a dainty finish to this handsome little style. Can be ordered as described in natural leghorn with light blue trimming; or with white, pink or red trimming. Please state color.
Price.................................$1.48

Only the Best Materials are Used in this Elegant and Refined Bonnet, $2.68.

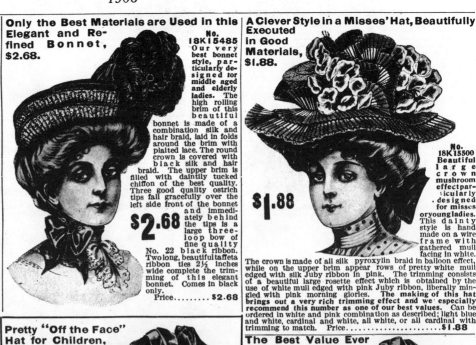

No. 18K15485 Our very best bonnet style, particularly designed for middle aged and elderly ladies. The high rolling brim of this beautiful bonnet is made of a combination silk and hair braid, laid in folds around the brim with plaited lace. The round crown is covered with black silk and hair braid. The upper brim is filled with daintily tucked chiffon of the best quality. Three good quality ostrich tips fall gracefully over the left side front of the bonnet and immediately behind the tips is a large three-loop bow of fine quality No. 22 black ribbon. Two long, beautiful taffeta ribbon ties 2½ inches wide complete the trimming of this stylish bonnet. Comes in black only.
Price........$2.68

Pretty "Off the Face" Hat for Children, Trimmed with Cherries, only $1.69.

No. 18K15490 The Cheyenne style as applied to children's hats has proven the biggest success of the season. We offer a very handsome imported leghorn with wide fancy edge, trimmed in a most attractive manner. A pretty facing of gathered light blue milliners' mull with two rows of tucks finishes the entire under brim of the hat perfectly. In front and at the edge of the brim a natural cherry wreath with foliage is applied which extends over and around the entire crown. This is daintily set off with a rosette bow effect of narrow taffeta ribbon in light blue. We especially recommend this hat as one of the best values we have ever offered for children's wear. Can be ordered in natural leghorn, trimmed with light blue as described; or with white, pink, cardinal, brown or navy trimming. Always give color wanted. Price............................$1.69

This Elegant Trimmed Leghorn is an Extra Special Offer at $1.95.

No. 18K15495 One of our very best styles in fancy edged fine imported leghorns for misses and children. The imported leghorn used in this hat is of extra fine quality and will prove highly satisfactory to you. The most effective trimming is obtained by the use of a wreath of imported velvet forget me nots in light blue sprayed with tiny full blown June roses. Fine quality white taffeta ribbon is gathered in rosette effect in the front and entirely around the brim of the hat close to the crown. This dainty little child's hat is exceedingly pretty as described in natural leghorn with light blue trimming; may also be ordered with white, pink or red trimming. Please give color.
Price..................................$1.95

A Clever Style in a Misses' Hat, Beautifully Executed in Good Materials, $1.88.

No. 18K15500 Beautiful large crown mushroom effect particularly designed for misses or young ladies. This dainty style is hand made on a wire frame with gathered mull facing in white.

The crown is made of all silk pyroxylin braid in balloon effect, while on the upper brim appear rows of pretty white mull edged with silk Juby ribbon in pink. The trimming consists of a beautiful large rosette effect which is obtained by the use of white mull edged with pink Juby ribbon, liberally mingled with pink morning glories. The making of this hat brings out a very rich trimming effect and we especially recommend this number as one of our best values. Can be ordered in white and pink combination as described; light blue and white, cardinal and white, all white, or all cardinal with trimming to match. Price......................$1.88

The Best Value Ever Offered in Children's Trimmed Leghorns at $1.25.

No. 18K15505 A tremendous value in good quality leghorn hat, attractively trimmed for children. Never before have we offered such an exceptional value as this hat, which we illustrate. We use a very good quality imported leghorn with a fancy edge, the entire under brim being faced with white milliners' mull shirred in two rows of tiny tucks. Loops of narrow white taffeta ribbon complete a pretty bandeau trimming. A wreath of white daisies with yellow centers extends from the front entirely around the brim to the drooping back of the hat. On the side front of the crown appears a rosette bow of narrow white taffeta ribbon braced with wire. This ribbon is drawn entirely around the crown and gives a decidedly pretty finish to the hat. Comes in natural leghorn with pink, white, light blue or red trimming.
Price....................................$1.25

Pretty Imported Body Hat, $1.95.

No. 18K15510 This stylish child's hat is made of an imported body hat in cream color natural straw, and is woven in fancy design.

Body hats allow of most original ideas in shapes and our style as illustrated shows one of the best. The trimmings consist of a large wreath effect of silk centered apple blossoms in pink. Intermingled with the flowers appears a novelty effect of plaited ribbon, edged on mull which is laid around the entire upper brim of the hat. The bandeau trimming of twisted light blue taffeta ribbon, ending in loops, completes the trimming of this very stylish hat. Can be ordered in natural and light blue as described, or with pink, white or red trimming. Remember to state color. Price.................$1.95

LADIES' SUMMER UNION SUITS

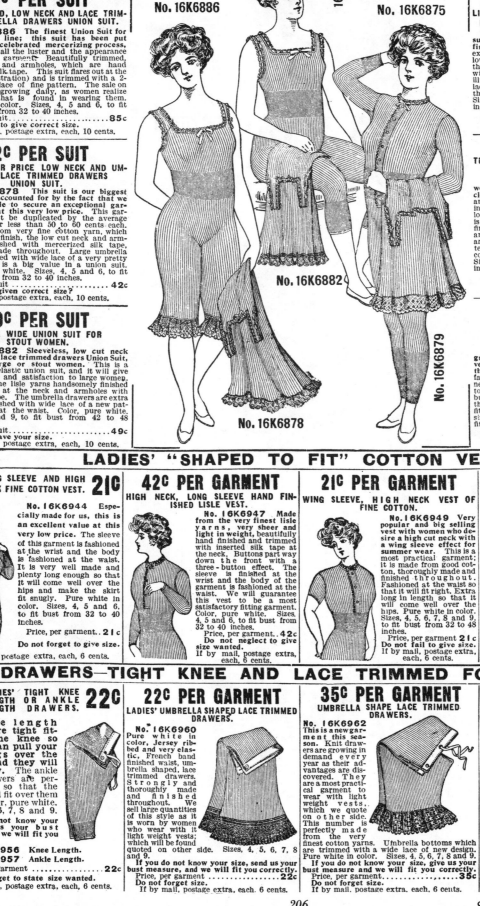

No. 16K6886   No. 16K6872   No. 16K6875

No. 16K6882

No. 16K6878

No. 16K6879

REDUCTIONS IN PRICE

85c PER SUIT

SILK FINISHED, LOW NECK AND LACE TRIMMED UMBRELLA DRAWERS UNION SUIT.

No. 16K6886 The finest Union Suit for ladies in our line; this suit has been put through the celebrated mercerizing process, which gives it all the luster and the appearance of an all silk garment. Beautifully trimmed, low cut neck and armholes, which are hand finished with silk tape. This suit flares out at the knees (see illustration) and is trimmed with a 2-inch torchon lace of fine pattern. The sale on union suits is growing daily, as women realize the comfort that is found in wearing them. Pure white in color. Sizes, 4, 5 and 6, to fit bust measure from 32 to 40 inches.

Price, per suit....................**85c**

Do not fail to give correct size.

If by mail, postage extra, each, 10 cents.

42c PER SUIT

OUR POPULAR PRICE LOW NECK AND UMBRELLA LACE TRIMMED DRAWERS UNION SUIT.

No. 16K6878 This suit is our biggest seller and is accounted for by the fact that we have been able to secure an exceptional garment to sell at this very low price. This garment could not be duplicated by the average retail store for less than 50 to 60 cents each. It is made from very fine cotton yarn, which is given a lisle finish, the low cut neck and armholes are finished with mercerized silk tape, beautifully made throughout. Large umbrella bottoms finished with wide lace of a very pretty design. This is a big value in a union suit. Color a pure white. Sizes, 4, 5 and 6, to fit bust measure from 32 to 40 inches.

Price, per suit **42c**

Have you given correct size?

If by mail, postage extra, each, 10 cents.

49c PER SUIT

EXTRA WIDE UNION SUIT FOR STOUT WOMEN.

No. 16K6882 Sleeveless, low cut neck and umbrella lace trimmed drawers Union Suit, made for large or stout women. This is a good big full elastic union suit, and it will give great comfort and satisfaction to large women. Made from fine lisle yarns handsomely finished and trimmed at the neck and armholes with mercerized tape. The umbrella drawers are extra large and finished with wide lace of a new pattern, shaped at the waist. Color, pure white. Sizes, 7, 8 and 9, to fit bust from 42 to 48 inches.

Price, per suit....................**49c**

We must have your size.

If by mail, postage extra, each, 10 cents.

BIGGER VALUES

58c PER SUIT

LISLE FINISH, LOW CUT NECK, LACE TRIMMED UMBRELLA DRAWERS UNION SUIT.

No. 16K6879 This is a very practical suit for summer wear as it is very sheer and fine. Made from the finest lisle yarns and exquisitely hand finished throughout; the low cut neck is trimmed with a silk ribbon; the umbrella bottom drawers are finished with an imported lace of a new design. (See illustration.) This is positively a big value for ladies who desire a high grade union suit at this remarkably low price. Color, a pure white. Sizes, 4, 5 and 6, to fit bust measure from 32 to 40 inches.

Price, per suit **58c**

Do not forget size wanted.

If by mail, postage extra, each, 10 cents.

42c PER SUIT

TIGHT KNEE, KNEE LENGTH, LOW NECK UNION SUIT.

No. 16K6872 A most practical suit for women desiring a Union Suit that fits the limbs closely. This suit comes a trifle below the knee and is finished so that you can pull the stockings up over the suit. It is sleeveless, with a low cut neck finished with mercerized tape, and is made from the finest yarn which is lisle finished. Well trimmed and perfectly made and finished throughout. All of our union suits are fashioned at the waist, and we will guarantee them to fit perfectly if you give us the correct size. This suit is pure white in color. Sizes, 4, 5 and 6, to fit bust from 32 to 40 inches.

Price, per suit.....................**42c**

Do not forget size wanted.

If by mail, postage extra, each, 9 cents.

42c PER SUIT

ANKLE LENGTH, HIGH NECK AND LONG SLEEVE UNION SUIT.

No. 16K6875 Union Suit, worn by a great many women all the year around. It is very sheer and fine, and is a splendid value at this price. Long sleeves and ankle length, fashioned at the wrist and ankle to fit; high neck, trimmed with a mercerized tape. Buttons down the front to the waist line with seven buttons, fashioned at the waist. We know that this suit will give satisfaction and that it will fit correctly providing you give us the proper size. Color, pure white. Sizes, 4, 5 and 6, to fit bust from 32 to 40 inches.

Price, per suit.....................**42c**

Have you given us the right size?

If by mail, postage extra, each, 12 cents.

LADIES' "SHAPED TO FIT" COTTON VESTS.

21c LONG SLEEVE AND HIGH NECK FINE COTTON VEST. 21c

No. 16K6944 Especially made for us, this is an excellent value at this very low price. The sleeve of this garment is fashioned at the wrist and the body is fashioned at the waist. It is very well made and plenty long enough so that it will come well over the hips and make the skirt fit snugly. Pure white in color. Sizes, 4, 5 and 6, to fit bust from 32 to 40 inches.

Price, per garment..**21c**

Do not forget to give size.

If by mail, postage extra, each, 6 cents.

42c PER GARMENT

HIGH NECK, LONG SLEEVE HAND FINISHED LISLE VEST.

No. 16K6947 Made from the very finest lisle yarns, very sheer and light in weight, beautifully hand finished and trimmed with inserted silk tape at the neck. Buttons part way down the front with a three-button effect. The sleeve is finished at the wrist and the body of the garment is fashioned at the waist. We will guarantee this vest to be a most satisfactory fitting garment. Color, pure white. Sizes, 4, 5 and 6, to fit bust from 32 to 40 inches.

Price, per garment....**42c**

Do not neglect to give size wanted.

If by mail, postage extra, each, 6 cents.

21c PER GARMENT

WING SLEEVE, HIGH NECK VEST OF FINE COTTON.

No. 16K6949 Very popular and big selling vest with women who desire a high cut neck with a wing sleeve effect for summer wear. This is a most practical garment; it is made from good cotton, thoroughly made and finished throughout. Fashioned at the waist so that it will fit right. Extra long in length so that it will come well over the hips. Pure white in color. Sizes, 4, 5, 6, 7, 8 and 9, to fit bust from 32 to 48 inches.

Price, per garment **21c**

Do not fail to give size.

If by mail, postage extra, each, 6 cents.

23c EXTRA LARGE SIZE FOR STOUT WOMEN, LONG SLEEVE, HIGH NECK VEST 23c

No. 16K6952 This vest is made from good cotton, fine and light in weight. It is worn by a great many women in all seasons of the year. Very elastic and fashioned at the waist so that it will fit snugly, long sleeves which are shaped at the wrist to fit properly. Buttons part way down the front with a three-button effect, finished at the neck with mercerized tape. Color, pure white. Sizes, 7, 8 and 9, to fit bust from 42 to 48 inches.

Price, per garment. **23c**

Have you given us size?

If by mail, postage extra, each, 6 cents.

DRAWERS—TIGHT KNEE AND LACE TRIMMED FOR SUMMER.

22c LADIES' TIGHT KNEE LENGTH OR ANKLE LENGTH DRAWERS. 22c

The knee length drawers are tight fitting at the knee so that you can pull your stockings over the drawers and they will fit properly. The ankle length drawers are perfect fitting so that the stocking will fit over them neatly. Color, pure white. Sizes, 4, 5, 6, 7, 8 and 9.

If you do not know your size, give us your bust measure and we will fit you correctly.

No. 16K6956 Knee Length.

No. 16K6957 Ankle Length.

Price, per garment....................**22c**

Do not forget to state size wanted.

If by mail, postage extra, each, 6 cents.

22c PER GARMENT

LADIES' UMBRELLA SHAPED LACE TRIMMED DRAWERS.

No. 16K6960 Pure white in color, Jersey ribbed and very elastic, French band finished waist, umbrella shaped, lace trimmed drawers. Strongly and thoroughly made and finished throughout. We sell large quantities of this style as it is worn by women who wear with it light weight vests; which will be found quoted on other side. Sizes, 4, 5, 6, 7, 8 and 9.

If you do not know your size, send us your bust measure, and we will fit you correctly.

Price, per garment....................**22c**

Do not forget size.

If by mail, postage extra, each, 6 cents.

35c PER GARMENT

UMBRELLA SHAPE LACE TRIMMED DRAWERS.

No. 16K6962 This is a new garment this season. Knit drawers are growing in demand every year as their advantages are discovered. They are a most practical garment to wear with light weight vests, which we quote on other side. This number is perfectly made from the very finest cotton yarns. Umbrella bottoms which are trimmed with a wide lace of new design. Pure white in color. Sizes, 4, 5, 6, 7, 8 and 9.

If you do not know your size, give us your bust measure, and we will fit you correctly.

Price, per garment.......................**35c**

Do not forget size.

If by mail, postage extra, each, 6 cents.

42c OUR BEST VALUE, UMBRELLA SHAPED, LACE TRIMMED DRAWERS. 42c

No. 16K6990 Hand finished drawers, they are beautifully made and finished throughout, puckering strings at the waist which will make the garment fit snugly. The umbrella bottoms are finished with an extra wide imported torchon lace slightly flaring. These drawers are made from the finest lisle yarns, pure white in color. Sizes, 4, 5, 6, 7, 8 and 9. If you do not know your size, give us your bust measure, and we will fit you correctly.

Price, per garment....................**42c**

Do not forget size.

If by mail, postage extra, each, 6 cents.

Sears, Roebuck & Co.

Part IV

Narrow Skirts and the New Century

1909–1920

The atmosphere of the twentieth century was one of enlightenment toward women. Wyoming had led the way in granting women the right to vote, and by 1912 eight more states — all of them in the west — had followed suit. Under the progressive leadership of President Theodore Roosevelt the government had become active in the social and welfare fields, and many states enacted laws regulating working conditions for women and children and granting public aid to mothers with dependent children.

Women's fashions were also reflecting the new more liberal attitudes. The heavy, bulky, awkward skirt fashions that had been in vogue for more than half a century were making way for lighter, slimmer, more form-fitting styles, better suited for the more active lives of twentieth century women.

By 1909 or 1910 the last vestages of the bustle had finally disappeared, and thus it was that the stylish lass dancing to music from one of Tom Edison's phonographs was most likely clad in a close fitting skirt, little different but for length from those being worn today.

Why Don't YOU Get This Phonograph

On FREE TRIAL?

For almost three years I have been making the most liberal phonograph offer ever known! I have given hosts of people the opportunity of hearing the genuine Edison Phonograph right in their own homes without charging them a single penny. So far you have missed all this. Why? Possibly you don't quite understand my offer yet. Listen—

MY OFFER:

I will send you this Genuine Edison Standard Outfit (the newest model), complete with one dozen Edison Gold Moulded Records, for an absolutely free trial. I don't ask any money down or in advance. There are no C. O. D. shipments; no leases or mortgages on the outfit; no papers of any sort to sign. Absolutely nothing but a plain out-and-out offer to ship you this Phonograph together with a dozen records of your own selection on a free trial so that you can hear it and play it in your own home. I can't make this offer any plainer, any clearer, any better than it is. There is no catch about it anywhere. If you will stop and think just a moment, you will realize that the high standing of this concern would absolutely prohibit anything except a straightforward offer.

WHY I WANT to Lend You this Phonograph:

I know that there are thousands and thousands of people who have never heard the Genuine Edison Phonograph. I can't tell you one twentieth of the wonders of the Edison, nothing I can say or write will make you actually hear the grand full beauty of its tones. No words can begin to describe the tender, delicate sweetness with which the genuine new style Edison reproduces the soft, pleading notes of the flute, or the thunderous, crashing harmony of a full brass band selection. And you can get the records in any language you wish. *The only way to make you actually realize these things for yourself is to loan you a Genuine Edison Phonograph free and let you try it.*

Our Easy Payment Plan.

I have decided on an easy payment plan that gives you absolute use of the phonograph while paying for it. $2.00 a month pays for an outfit. There is absolutely no lease or mortgage of any kind, guarantee from a third party, no going before a notary public, and the payments are so very small and our terms so liberal that you never notice the payments.

If You Want to Keep It

that is, if you wish to make the Phonograph your own, you may do so, but it is not compulsory. I am asking you merely to send for a free demonstration.

You Don't Have to Buy It:

All I ask you to do is to invite as many as possible of your friends to hear this wonderful new style Edison. You will want to do that anyway because you will be giving them genuine pleasure. I feel absolutely certain that there will be at least one and probably more who will want an Edison of their own. If they don't, if not a single one of them orders a Phonograph (and this sometimes happens) I won't blame you in the slightest. I shall feel that you have done your part when you have given these free concerts You won't be asked to act as our agent or even assist in the sale of a single instrument.

Get the Latest Edison Catalogs.

Just sign your name and address on the attached coupon now and mail it to us. I will send you our superbly illustrated Edison Phonograph Catalog, the very latest list of Edison Gold Moulded Records (over 1,500 of them in all languages) and our Free Trial Certificate entitling you to this grand offer. Sign the coupon now, get these catalogs and select your records at once. Remember the free concerts. Sign the coupon right now.

LOOK FOR THIS
TRADE MARK
ON EVERY INSTRUMENT

Thomas A. Edison.

F. K. BABSON, Edison Phon. Distrib'rs, Edison Block, Dept. 2031, CHICAGO

F. K. BABSON, Edison Phonograph Distributors, Edison Block, Suite 2031, Chicago, Ill.

Please send me without any obligations, your 1908 Edison Phonograph Catalog, list of Edison Gold Moulded Records and Free Trial Certificate entitling me to your grand offer, all free.

Name ....

Address ....

Sign and Mail this Coupon Today.

The Latest Paris and New York Fashions

These patterns are all the latest Paris and New York modes, and are unequaled for style, accuracy of fit, simplicity and economy. Full descriptions and directions—as to the number of yards of material required, the number and names of the different pieces in the pattern, how to cut and fit and put the garment together, are sent with each pattern, with a picture of the garment to go by. An allowance has been made in these patterns for seams. For waist-pattern, give bust measure in inches. For skirt-pattern, give waist measure in inches. For misses, boys, girls or children, give years. Order patterns by number. Each number counts as a pattern.

SPECIAL—If you will send us ONE NEW yearly subscription to this paper at our regular subscription-price of 20 cents a year, we will send Happy Hours one year to the address of the subscriber, and we will send you one of the patterns named below to reward you for your time and trouble. Address HAPPY HOURS, Augusta, Maine.

2621

2429

2344

2435

1938
2388

2432

2341

2391

2396

2397 Shirt Waist
2379 Knicker-bockers

2428 Dress
1405 Guimpe

2655

2656

2624

2661

2628

2622

2636

2630

2625

2626

2644

The Latest Paris and New York Fashions

These patterns are all the latest Paris and New York modes, and are unequaled for style, accuracy of fit, simplicity and **economy.** Full descriptions and directions—as to the number of yards of material required, the number and names of the different pieces in the pattern, how to cut and fit and put the garment together, are sent with each pattern, with a picture of the garment to go by. An allowance has been made in these patterns for seams. For waist-pattern, **give bust measure in inches.** For skirt-pattern, **give waist measure in inches.** For misses, boys, girls or children, give years. Order patterns by number. **Each number counts as a pattern.**

SPECIAL—If you will send us **ONE NEW** yearly subscription to this paper at our regular subscription-price of **20 cents** a year, we will send Happy Hours one year to the address of the subscriber, and we will send you one of the patterns named below to reward you for your time and trouble. Address **HAPPY HOURS,** Augusta, Maine.

THE LATEST PARIS AND NEW YORK FASHIONS

These patterns are all the latest Paris and New York modes, and are unequaled for style, accuracy of fit, simplicity and **economy.** Full descriptions and directions—as to the number of yards of material required, the number and names of the different pieces in the pattern, how to cut and fit and put the garment together, are sent with each pattern, with a picture of the garment to go by. An allowance has been made in these patterns for seams. For waist-pattern, **give bust measure in inches.** For skirt-pattern, **give waist measure in inches.** For misses, boys, girls or children, give years. Order patterns by number. **Each number counts as a pattern.**

SPECIAL—If you will send us **ONE NEW** yearly subscription to this paper at our regular subscription-price of **20 cents** a year, we will send you **one** of the patterns named below to reward you for your time and trouble. Address **HAPPY HOURS, Augusta, Maine.**

ANY PATTERN WILL BE SENT ON RECEIPT OF 10 CENTS

Happy Hours

Separate Waist or Tunic, No 4812

Separate Waist or Tunic, No. 4812.—Charming indeed is the model pictured, and its grace and beauty are only exceeded by its extreme usefulness. Developed in any of the soft weaves of cloth, silk or sheer materials that shops are showing, it may be worn over another gown. This pattern is cut in 5 sizes, from 32 to 40 inches bust measure. To copy it in the medium sizes, it requires, 2⅜ yards 44 inches wide. Price of pattern 10 cents.

Vanity Boxes.—Vanity boxes are an important part of a motoring outfit, and as often as not hang from the neck chain. Some are assuming the aspect of flat lockets; these open to display a powder puff, while inside is quite a sufficient stock of powder. Some are fashioned like small watches of hammered or dull gold or enamel, sometimes bearing a monogram, sometimes jeweled.

Metal Girdles.—The flexible metal girdles, so much in vogue, take the form of serpents with metal eyes, a jeweled pendant in their mouths. These girdles are generally lined with black velvet; some are copies of Egyptian possessions, others reproduce some quaint Japanese creations; to meet the demands of to-day they must be barbaric and intricate of design.

Simple and Effective, No. 4791.—The best Parisian and American designers still hold to the long diagonal lines of the distinctly Moyenne type. This frock should be developed in some soft weave of cloth, such as cashmere or Henrietta. The plaited skirt that is used for both house and street wear is cleverly

THE LATEST PARIS AND NEW YORK FASHIONS

DIRECTIONS FOR ORDERING.—Full descriptions and directions—as to the number of yards of material required, the number and names of the different pieces in the pattern, how to cut and fit and put the garment together, are sent with each pattern. An allowance has been made in these patterns for seams. For waist-pattern, **give bust measure in inches.** For skirt-pattern, **give waist measure in inches.** For misses, boys, girls or children, give years. Order patterns by number. **Each number counts as a pattern.**

SPECIAL OFFER.—If you will send us ONE NEW yearly subscription to this paper at our regular subscription-price of 20 CENTS a year, we will send you ONE of the patterns named below to reward you for your time and trouble. Address

HAPPY HOURS, Augusta, Maine

Simple and Effective, No. 4791   *Novel Coat, No. 4803*

introduced. This pattern is cut in 6 sizes from 32 to 42 inches bust measure. To copy it in the medium sizes it requires 6⅝ yards 36 inches wide. Price of pattern 10 cents.

For the Small Boy, No. 3117.—Mothers will find it economy to make blouses for the school-boy at home. Not only are they cheaper than when bought ready-made, but a much better quality of material can be had, which means that they will wear longer. This pattern is cut in 7 sizes, 4 to 16 years. To copy it in the 10-year size, it requires 1⅞ yards of material 36 inches wide. Price of pattern 10 cents.

For the Small Boy, No. 3117

Novel Coat, No. 4803.—A variation from the straight Moyenne lines to which we have been accustomed is the blouse coat pictured. The material employed for its construction should be of the softest and finest weaves one can afford; unlike the strictly tailored models, silk, velvet and similar materials may be used for its development. This pattern is cut in 5 sizes, from 32 to 40 inches bust measure. To copy it in the medium sizes, it requires 3½ yards 36 inches wide for the short length, and 5 yards 36 inches wide for the long length. Price of pattern 10 cents.

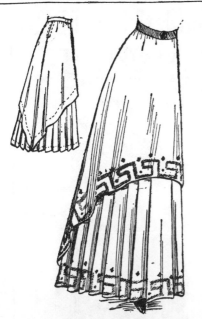

Ladies' Tunic=Skirt. No. 4932

THE LATEST PARIS AND NEW YORK FASHIONS

DIRECTIONS FOR ORDERING.—Full descriptions and directions—as to the number of yards of material required, the number and names of the different pieces in the pattern, how to cut and fit and put the garment together, are sent with each pattern.   An allowance has been made in these patterns for seams.   For waist-pattern, **give bust measure in inches.**   For skirt-pattern, **give waist measure in inches.**   For misses, boys, girls or children, give years. Order patterns by number.   **Each number counts as a pattern.**

SPECIAL OFFER.—If you will send us ONE NEW yearly subscription to this paper at our regular subscription-price of 25 CENTS a year, we will send you ONE of the patterns named below to reward you for your time and trouble.

See our offer on page 19.

Address HAPPY HOURS, Augusta, Maine

Ladies' Yoke Kitchen-Apron, No. 4560.— Pattern No. 4560 is cut in sizes from 32 to 44 inches bust measure. To make the apron in the medium size will require 5¼ yards of ma-

Ladies' Tunic Skirt. No. 4932.—This skirt has a five-gore foundation to which the kilt plaiting is attached. Over this is the tunic. The skirt will be in good style in any summer material: lawn, pongee, gingham, linen, etc. In place of the border a band of embroidery may be used with good effect. Pattern No. 4932 is cut in sizes from 22 to 32 inches waist measure. To make the skirt in the medium size will require 9 yards of bordered material 32 inches wide, or 7¾ yards of material 36 inches wide without border.   Price of pattern, 10 cents.

Ladies' Shirtwaist, No. 4841.—This waist shows one of the most desirable of the plain styles of the present season. It is suitable for wear with tailormade suits and also with separate skirts; it can be made of taffeta, foulard, linen, madras, percale or plain calico. If desired it can be embroidered on the panels of the front when made of linen or pongee. Pattern No. 4841 is cut in sizes from 32 to 42 inches bust measure. To make the shirtwaist in the medium size will require 2½ yards of material 36 inches wide.   Price of pattern, 10 cents.

Ladies' Dressing-Sacque, No. 3593.—The dressing-sacque is one of the most comfortable articles in a woman's wardrobe and can be

Ladies' Nine-Gore Skirt, No. 4450.—This style of skirt is suited to all narrow materials, such as taffeta, and also to pongee, linen, brilliantine and the like. If made of some mannish tailor-cloth it may have bands of braid and be very nice. Pattern No. 4450 is cut in sizes from 22 to 32 inches waist measure.   To make the skirt in the medium size will require 5¼ yards of material 36 inches wide or 5 yards the same width if made without folds. Price of pattern, 10 cents.

Ladies' Combination. Forming Tight-Fitting Corset-Cover and Open Circular Drawers, No. 4363.—Pattern No. 4363 is cut in sizes from 32 to 44 inches bust measure. To make the combination in the medium size will require 2¼ yards of material 36 inches wide and 4½ yards of 5-inch edging for ruffles, and 3 yards of narrow edging. Price of pattern, 10 cents.

Girls' Sailor-Blouse Dress, No. 3748.—Pattern No. 3748 is cut in sizes for from 6 to 12 years. To make the dress in the 8-year size will require 4 yards of material 36 inches wide. Price of pattern, 10 cents.

Girls' One-Piece Jumper Apron, No. 4036.— Pattern No. 4036 is cut in sizes for from 6 to 12

Ladies' Yoke Kitchen=Apron. No. 4560

terial 36 inches wide, with sleeves, or 4⅝ yards of goods 36 inches wide, without sleeves. Price of pattern, 10 cents.

Ladies' Shirtwaist. No. 4841

made of almost anything. It looks best, perhaps, in challis or in some of the pretty figured lawns which are to be bought for a trifle. Pattern No. 3593 is cut in sizes from 32 to 44 inches bust measure. To make the dressing-sacque in the medium size will require 3½ yards of material 36 inches wide. Price of pattern, 10 cents.

Ladies' Dressing=Sacque. No. 3593

years. To make the apron in the 8-year size will require 1½ yards of material 36 inches wide. Price of pattern, 10 cents.

GREEN SATIN COATS

Among the smart afternoon and evening wraps are long, voluminous coats of bright-green satin.

OUR BEAUTIFUL NEW FALL FASHION CATALOGUE IS NOW READY

Would You Like a Copy? We Will Gladly Send It to You FREE

Don't try to do your Fall shopping until you have seen this handsome Book. It will save you considerable money on your Fall and Winter Clothing

No. 2P97
WAIST
$1.00

YOUR COPY OF THIS BEAUTIFUL FASHION BOOK IS FREE!

Be sure to write for it today

You will surely be delighted when you look through the pages of our new Fall and Winter Catalogue, for you will find in it all the very newest styles. It has 210 pages beautifully illustrated and giving accurate descriptions of just what will be worn in New York City during the Fall and Winter. You will find splendid bargains in this book in

Ladies' Suits	Hosiery	Gloves
Ladies' Dresses	Colored Petticoats	Millinery
Ladies' Skirts	Corsets	Misses' and Children's
Ladies' Waists	Sweaters	Wear
Ladies' Coats	Neckwear	Baby's Clothes
Ladies' Furs	Underwear	Men's and Boys'Cloth-
Ladies' Lingerie	Shoes	ing and Furnishings

Our Catalogue is a guide to good taste in dress. A postal card brings it to you FREE by return mail.

The stylish garments illustrated on this page are splendid examples of the wonderful values you receive when you do your shopping at Bellas Hess & Co.'s. The fact that we send you every article you buy from us with all mail or express charges prepaid is another point that every economical woman will appreciate. You need only send us the prices quoted on this page or in our Catalogue and you are put to no further expense.

OUR GUARANTEE: Remember that we positively guarantee to please you. If you are not satisfied with any article you purchase from us, same can be returned at our expense and we will refund your money immediately.

No. 1P99
SUIT
$15.00

DESCRIPTIONS OF THE STYLISH GARMENTS ILLUSTRATED ON THIS PAGE

No. 3P98
SKIRT
$4.98

1P99 A Beautifully Tailored Ultra Fashionable New Style Suit of fine all-wool Fancy Cheviot of extra fine quality. The single-breasted coat is semi-fitted and 32 inches long. Collar, lapels and all edges are handsomely finished with silk braid. Braid trims the cuffs in combination with small buttons and simulated buttonholes and the two slit pockets are edged with braid to match, center seam in back of coat below waist line is braid trimmed to simulate an inverted vent. Back is also finished with five buttons. Coat fastens with silk braid covered buttons with velvet centers. The notched collar is of the finest quality velvet. Coat is richly lined with Belding's guaranteed satin. The skirt has a wide plait effect in front extending from waist line to bottom. This plait is edged with braid and trimmed with buttons and braid-buttonholes. Has fashionable bodice top and a deep plait on each side falling from below the knee; panel box-plaited back, stitched down as far as the knee. Suit comes in black, navy blue, Edison blue or brown, all with black braid trimming. Sizes 32 to 44 bust measure, 23 to 30 waist, 37 to 44 skirt length, also proportioned to fit misses and small women, sizes 32 to 38 bust, 23 to 26 waist and 37 to 43 skirt length. Special price, Express Prepaid **$15.00**

2P97 Very Dressy Well-Made Waist of Sheer Striped Japonika Silk, a beautiful fabric which is a mixture of silk and cotton, but looks like pure silk. Waist has yoke and chemisette of tucked net and two revers of plain messaline silk, trimmed with crochet buttons and fancy cord and tassel effect. Short sleeves finished with tucked net cuffs piped with self material. Fastens invisibly in back. A wonderful value. Comes in navy blue or black, with white stripe. 32 to 44 bust measure, Mail or Express Prepaid **$1.00**

3P98 Beautiful Paris Model Plaited Skirt. A charming design which is going to be all the rage. Made of fine quality all-worsted Panama Cloth in either black or navy blue. Upper part of skirt designed with a deep yoke fitting with perfect smoothness over hips and fastening through scallops at left side with braid covered buttons. Skirt has the graceful bodice top, lower part of model hanging in straight lines with the fulness laid in fine knife plaits all around. Very comfortable for walking and absolutely the newest thing. Sizes 23 to 30 waist, 37 to 44 inches front length. Express Prepaid **$4.98**

3P98A Same style Skirt as 3P98 made of finest imported all-worsted black voile. Express Prepaid. **$5.98**.
3P98B. We can supply this Voile Skirt with a handsome black taffeta silk drop skirt attached. Express Prepaid, **$8.98**.

BELLAS HESS & CO
WASHINGTON, MORTON & BARROW STS.
NEW YORK CITY, N.Y.

We pay the postage or expressage on everything you order from our Catalogue or from this page. Think how much this saves you!

The New Season's Dresses Suggesting the Tailored Touch

4679—A simplicity, that lends an air of distinction, is the characteristic quality of this little gown of light gray worsted, being relieved without depreciation by a single revers and cuffs of olive green velvet, and edge trimming of fancy, black braid. Small silver ball buttons ornament the strip of braid that defines the front closing. Venise allover is used for the high collar and undersleeves but these may be omitted if the wearer should prefer a round neck and short sleeves. The tucks at the shoulders are made after the shoulder seams are closed, and give an appearance of breadth to the figure. The skirt, which measures about $2\frac{3}{8}$ yards around the bottom, is made up of 5 gores.

Costume No. 4679 is in sizes 32, 34, 36, 38, 40, 42, 44 and 46 inches bust measure. Size 36 requires $4\frac{1}{4}$ yards of 44-inch material. Price, 15 cents.

4658—Navy blue satin was used in the development of this most attractive, semi-tailored dress with yoke of écru filet lace and bertha collar of champagne colored taffeta embroidered in a self-tone. Individuality marks the waist with its drop-shoulder sleeve and broad tucks which continue down the skirt producing long, graceful lines from shoulder to hem. A lining is supplied for the waist, the neck of which is cut out under the lace yoke. Where a too transparent yoke and collar are not liked, the lace may be lined with white, or covered with dark blue chiffon. The dress closes at the left front and measures about 3 yards around the lower edge.

Costume 4658 is in sizes 32, 34, 36, 38, 40, 42, 44 and 46 inches bust measure. Size 36 requires $6\frac{1}{2}$ yards of 36-inch material, 1 yard lining and $\frac{3}{8}$ yard of 18-inch allover lace. Price, 15 cents. Embroidery design No. 11742, price, 15 cents for either perforated or transfer pattern.

4245—Black and white shepherd checks, while perennial as far as ordinary usage is concerned, have been receiving more than the usual attention from fashionable dressers during the past Spring and Summer. The design of the tailored frock illustrated is admirably suited to this fabric and is made even more effective by the well-cut collar and revers of light gray broadcloth. The little vest-like shield is made of the same material. A touch of color is introduced in the bright red ball buttons that are used in two sizes. While the pattern does not include a standing collar, a separate collar of lace may be worn if desired. The dress measures $2\frac{1}{8}$ yards at the bottom.

Costume No. 4245 is in sizes 32, 34, 36, 38 and 40 inches bust measure. Size 36 requires $4\frac{1}{4}$ yards of 44-inch material with $\frac{3}{4}$ yard of contrasting broadcloth Price, 15 cents.

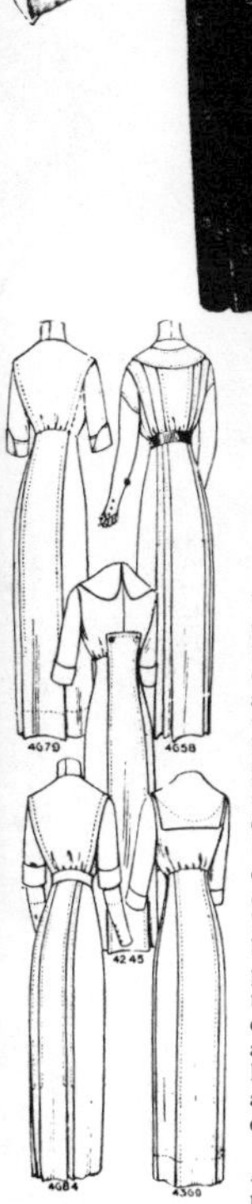

4684—While it has heretofore proved impossible to dislodge the two-piece suit from popular favor, the one-piece dress occupies a position which even the much beloved suit cannot replace. Dressiness is one of the chief characteristics of the costume, and no matter how simply it is made, there is a certain air of becoming formality about it that makes a woman feel well dressed. Then, too, it is so easy to slip on, and there is no laborious adjustment at the waistline, which is always more or less necessary to insure a sightly joining between waist and skirt. The frock illustrated embodies all of the becoming and convenient attributes of a well-designed, one-piece costume. It is here represented in tobacco brown cheviot with vest of chamois colored satin and topaz crystal buttons, small ones on the vest and larger ones for the skirt closing. The soutache braiding is most effective on the waist and can be easily done by the amateur with the aid of a transfer pattern. A three-piece body lining is supplied, upon which the lace yoke is mounted, the lining being cut away underneath. If desired, chiffon may be used under this and under the collar, if too great a transparency is objectionable. The sleeve may be in full length or short, with cuffs and lace under-sleeves. The skirt, a six-gored model with front gore in single, and back gore in double box-plait effect, measures $2\frac{3}{8}$ yards around the lower edge.

Costume No. 4684 is in sizes 32, 34, 36, 38, 40, 42, 44, 46 and 48 inches bust measure. Size 36 requires $4\frac{1}{4}$ yards of 44-inch material, $\frac{3}{4}$ yard 18-inch allover lace, and $\frac{7}{8}$ yard 36-inch lining. Price, 15 cents. Braiding design No. 11809, price, 20 cents.

4369—Strikingly simple is this one-piece dress of dark blue-grey broadcloth with trimmings of deep blue satin. A yoke or chemisette of allover Irish lace is worn with the dress, unless a low neck is preferred. Small ball buttons of dark blue and the buckle of smoked pearl are in harmony with the color scheme of the fabrics. No lining is required and a choice of two shapes is permitted in the collar, the back of which may be cut in square or rounded outline. Among other fabrics suited to the design are serge, broadcloth, cheviot or one of the new corded silk materials. The skirt is cut in five gores and measures $2\frac{1}{4}$ yards around the lower edge.

Costume No. 4369 is in sizes 32, 34, 36, 38, 40, 42, 44 and 46 inches bust measure. Size 36 requires $3\frac{1}{4}$ yards of 54-inch material with $\frac{3}{4}$ yard of 27-inch satin. Price, 15 cents.

One-piece dresses are one of the strongest of recent fashion notes. We predict for them as large a vogue in materials suitable for Fall and Winter as they have achieved in linens and other wash fabrics. Their popularity goes hand in hand with the demand for long coats. The newest form of coat for general and sporting wear is the Mackinaw coat made on mannish lines and reaches to a little below the knee only.

Long, Decided Lines Prevail in Simple Frocks

THE trig, one-piece dresses illustrated here are conspicuous for their simplicity. Their excellent style is due to the chic lines and the small amount of trimming employed. Indeed, much embellishment along this line is impractical and in poor taste for frocks that will have to stand much wear. Women are beginning to understand and appreciate the value of good lines and are depending more upon them than anything else. They are beginning to realize that an inexpensive material, made up in a smart, becoming and appropriate style, is far more effective than an expensive fabric, developed in an unsuitable fashion and laden with trimmings that really ought to have no place in frocks of this character.

Every one of the dresses pictured is suitable for general utility wear, and the fact that they are in one piece makes them doubly desirable, for they can be quickly and easily slipped on of a morning, especially those that button in front. And then the fear and consciousness of waist and skirt forever separating is entirely obviated.

4624—Serge heads the list for Fall materials because of its serviceability and adaptability. It can be had in different weights and qualities. The dark blue French serge used for the model illustrated has a soft, fine finish and is just about the right weight for an early Fall costume. White broadcloth made an effective collar and cuff set in this instance, but satin, ribbed silks, taffeta, tucked lawn or lace suggest attractive substitutes. The front and back sections of this frock are in panel style, which is generally so becoming by reason of its tendency to emphasize the length from shoulder to hem. The pattern provides for either a high or open neck and the one-piece sleeves can be made in full or shorter length. The six-gored skirt comes in regulation or shorter length and closes to the left of center front under plait. The width around lower edge of skirt is about 2⅜ yards.

Costume No. **4624** is in sizes 32, 34, 36, 38, 40, 42, 44, 46 and 48 inches bust measure. A medium size requires 4½ yards of 44-inch material, with ½ yard contrasting material 36 inches wide. Price, 15 cents.

4676—There is a broad expression of the present style tendencies in this handsome, pearl gray challis frock with delft blue, diamond-shaped figures. The sleeve comprises several fashionable points such as the cap suggestion, the comfortable fulness at the elbow and the unique shape of the cuff with its pointed upper edge. It is a type of sleeve that will without doubt be in demand, since the long sleeves have returned to popular favor. The smart bands of gray silk not only add a pretty trimming note, but also accentuate the best lines in the model. The plaited section at the right side of the skirt is a new idea heralding the return of plaits. The five-gored skirt has a box-plait in the back and a plait at each side of it, making the back view as interesting as the front. The width around the lower edge of the skirt is about 2⅜ yards.

No. **4676** is in sizes 32, 34, 36, 38, 40, 42, 44 and 46 inches bust measure. A medium size requires 8½ yards of material 27 inches wide, with 1 yard contrasting material for bands and ½ yard of lace 18 inches wide for yoke and collar. Price, 15 cents.

4254—Brown and white checked taffeta was a decidedly appropriate selection for this extremely simple, girlish dress. The style is so unassuming that the material can afford to be striking in contrast. White satin formed the pointed collar and wide cuffs. The back view of the model shows the point of the collar extending almost to the waistline. This style of collar is receiving much consideration from fashionable dressers, inasmuch as it is a charming deviation from the usual shapes. The sleeves are set into the armhole and stitched flat. This is a pleasant change from the kimono sleeve. The smart skirt has the approved high, slightly curved waistline and is in three pieces, with a broad, stitched box-plait at the back. The closing is effected at the left side front. The skirt, which is in regulation or shorter length, measures 2¼ yards around the lower edge.

Costume No. **4254** is in sizes 32, 34, 36, 38, 40 and 42 inches bust measure. A medium size requires 7½ yards of 27-inch taffeta, with ½ yard satin 36 inches wide. Price, 15 cents.

4590—The original of this dress was shown in tan worsted showing a green stripe, with collar and cuffs of tan broadcloth. The green buttons, imitating jade, were an important trimming factor, for they introduced the new craze for colored buttons. Loops of green rat-tail cord set them off to excellent advantage. The continuous front closing supplies the length of line needed by the short or stout woman. Here, too, the sleeve set into a stitched armhole is noted. This effect aims to bring out the charming contour of the shoulders. Two styles of collars are given. The six-gored skirt in regulation or shorter length has an inverted plait in the lower part of each side seam, made conspicuous by three buttons as pictured in the sketch. The width around the lower edge of skirt is about 2¼ yards.

Costume No. **4590** is in sizes 32, 34, 36, 38, 40, 42, 44, 46 and 48 inches bust measure. A medium size requires 4 yards of 44-inch material, with ⅝ yard contrasting material 27 inches wide. Price, 15 cents.

4673—A suitable fabric for a dress of this kind is cashmere or light weight serge. They lend themselves excellently to the application of embroidery, as demonstrated in the illustration. Dark blue cashmere with Copenhagen blue embroidery is an attractive combination. Two kinds of buttons are used. Small, blue crystal buttons adorned the collar, the upper portion of the side closing and the cuffs, while larger, blue, bone buttons are employed for the closing. This is quite an odd disposition that proved very effective. The tucks over the shoulders are exploited on many of the smartest dresses and produce a mere suggestion of blousiness in the waist. This model has two-seam sleeves which may be cut in full length or shorter, while the adjustable shield is to be used if the high neck is preferred. The width of the six-gored skirt around the lower edge is 2⅝ yards, indicating a slight increase over last season's.

Costume No. **4673** is cut in sizes 32, 34, 36, 38, 40, 42, 44, 46 and 48 inches bust measure. A medium size needs 4¾ yards of 44-inch material. Price, 15 cents. Scallop design No. 11662, price, 15 cents for either perforated or transfer pattern.

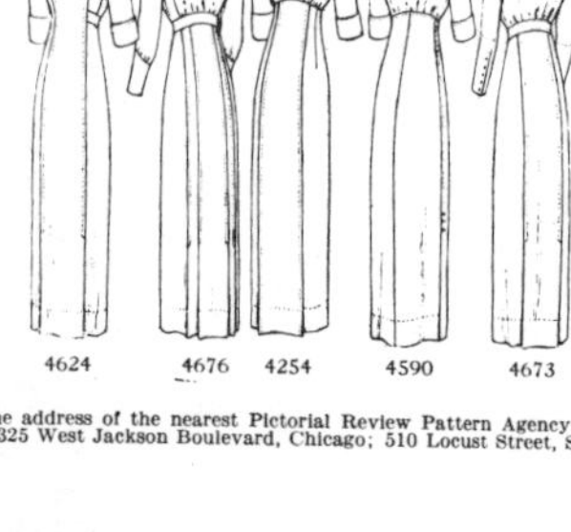

4624 4676 4254 4590 4673

Front Closings a Prominent Dress Feature

WHEN considering the general effect of the present development of fashions one is struck by the absence of the ornate. Day dresses show graceful, straight lines which are delightfully satisfying to the artistic eye. The small necessity for trimmings on gowns that must see much wear is an indication of good taste and a proof that women's dress is more and more adapting itself to real needs. This means also that greater attention must be given to the actual design and lines of a model.

4508—The color combination of materials used in the make-up of this stylish looking model was remarkably effective. Brown and white checked taffeta supplied the fabric for the body of the dress, plain butter colored Brussels net the yoke, and light, sage green velvet was used for the pipings. This design is a striking example of the simplicity that is the most prominent characteristic of fashionable gowning to-day. The model is adapted to various figures. The slender woman, of course, will look well in it, and the long lines tend to lengthen the short figure. Cutting up the width of the gown, as it were, does much to diminish the breadth of the stout figure. The waist is made without a lining and a choice is given of high or round neck. The sleeves are in one piece and in short length only. Front and back panels, in box plait effect form two of the six gores of which the skirt is composed. While the skirt illustrated is in regulation length, the pattern is perforated for a shorter length, the width around the lower edge being about 2 yards. The closing is arranged at the center back, the panel concealing that in the skirt. Serge, cashmere, challis and light-weight novelty mixtures are equally well adapted to a dress of this kind. Costume No. **4508** is in sizes 32, 34, 36, 38, 40, 42 and 44 inches bust measure. Size 36 requires 5 yards of 36-inch material, with $\frac{1}{2}$ yard of net 18 inches wide for yoke. Price, 15 cents.

4571—A model that will be of special interest is shown under this number. The amateur dressmaker will get an idea of what may be accomplished with simple materials and smart outlines. Particular attention is called to the delightfully attractive cut of the collar. Many women find it unusually becoming. It gives width to the shoulders and is one of the very newest ideas of the best Parisian dressmakers who are using it in many variations. A collar of this kind stamps a garment as up-to-date. Navy blue serge was used in this instance, with chemisette and collar of cream white satin. Some of the new colored crystal buttons are used to add a note of contrast. If desired satin, silk serge, whipcord or a light-weight, gray mixture might be substituted, with chemisette, collar and cuffs of contrasting colored broadcloth, faille or lace trimmed lawn. No lining is required, and if desired the large shoulder collar may be omitted and a high collar used instead. The skirt, a six-gored model measuring $2\frac{1}{4}$ yards around the lower edge, closes in the front in a slightly diagonal line, while the backs are lapped under the deep hem-tuck.

Costume **4571** is in sizes 32, 34, 36, 38, 40, 42, 44 and 46 inches bust measure. Size 36 requires $4\frac{1}{2}$ yards of 44-inch material, with $\frac{5}{8}$ yard of contrasting goods 27 inches wide. Price, 15 cents. Braiding design No. 11818 ($1\frac{1}{4}$ inch wide), 20 cents for perforated pattern.

4612—Delightfully unique is the design here illustrated in a new silk, known as tourist cloth, which is a reproduction of the light-weight, gray woolen, mannish materials. While exceedingly pliant it will give excellent wear and has been designed to serve for a material for Fall dresses just as foulard is used for Spring. Silk serge, messaline and light-weight woolen fabrics are suggested as substitutes. The plaited drapery on the waist is original in conception and appears to be a continuation of the uniquely cut front gore of the skirt. This gore, while the full length in front, cuts diagonally across the right side, tapering until it disappears under the back panel. Another fashionable feature of the waist is the large armhole and set-in sleeve that brings out the pretty contour of the shoulder so effectively. The gores of the skirt are cut irregularly. The front and right side are in upper and lower sections, while there are two regular gores on the left side and a panel at the back. The width around the lower edge is about 2 yards.

Costume No. **4612** is in sizes 32, 34, 36, 38, 40, 42 and 44 inches bust measure. Size 36 requires $5\frac{3}{4}$ yards of 36-inch material. Price, 15 cents.

4204-4645—Light gray cheviot with light blue broadcloth and dark gray rat-tail cord were used in developing this charming dress design, which shows many unusually pretty features. A round yoke, like that represented in the model, accentuates the rounded contour of neck and face, and should be readily chosen by the woman whose features and neck need the softening effect. The outline of the waist closing is particularly pleasing, and no doubt the woman with a taste for the unusual will welcome this pretty deviation from the regulation form of closing. A three-piece body lining is supplied, and if desired a high collar may be added. The lapping of the side seam and the use of the loops and buttons, apparently to hold the edges in place, is a clever detail that helps bring the skirt in harmony with the waist. The former is made up of six gores and has a plait at the lower part of each seam, making the width fully $2\frac{3}{4}$ yards around the lower edge.

Waist No. **4204** is in sizes 32, 34, 36, 38, 40 and 42 inches bust measure. Size 36 requires $1\frac{1}{2}$ yard of 44-inch material with $\frac{1}{2}$ yard of 27-inch contrasting material and $1\frac{7}{8}$ yard of lining. Price, 15 cents. Skirt No. **4645** is in sizes 21, 22, 24, 26, 28, 30, 32, 34, and 36 inches waist measure. Size 26 requires $3\frac{1}{4}$ yards of 44-inch material. Price, 15 cents. Braiding design No. 11818 ($1\frac{1}{4}$ inch wide), price, 20 cents for perforated pattern.

4664-4683—The Robespierre collar alone would proclaim the smartness of this design, as this form of neck finish is one of the most prominent features in the dress of the Directoire period, which are strongly influencing present fashions. One reproduction in dark green velveteen resulted in a rich looking costume. In this instance white satin was used for the collar and tie. High luster, black braid outlines the front closing and is stitched to the waist to simulate the wide armhole effect. Other suitable fabrics are serge, satin, corduroy, etc. The skirt, a five-gored model, has three side plaits at the back and one at center front and measures 2 yards around the lower edge.

4508 4571 4612 4204-4645 4664-4683

Waist No. **4664** is in sizes 32, 34, 36, 38, 40, 42 and 44 inches bust measure. Size 36 requires $1\frac{3}{4}$ yard of 44-inch material. Price, 15 cents. Skirt No. **4683** is in sizes 21, 22, 24, 26, 28, 30, 32, 34 and 36 inches waist measure. Size 26 requires $2\frac{7}{8}$ yards of 44-inch material. Price, 15 cents.

For a complete assortment of Costume Designs . . THE FASHION BOOK, FALL NUMBER; for sale at all agencies at 20 cents a copy including one pattern—by mail 30 cents from The Pictorial Review Company, New York.

Tunics and Panniers Prominent in Evening Gowns

4710-4562—The attractively shaped tunic and the gracefully cut skirt give this gown the stamp of originality. Venise allover was never used to better advantage, and as this form of lace usually demands an edge finish of some kind, one of the new Venise edgings in the flat, ball effect is suggested. Combinations of several kinds of lace on the one gown are in high favor, so shadow lace was selected for the crosspiece at the front of the waist and for the sleeve ruffles. For the dress proper old blue satin was used, the girdle being trimmed with sapphire blue, velvet ribbon and rhinestone buckles. A body lining is supplied, and the use of full length or short sleeves is optional. The skirt is in three pieces—front gore and two overlapping back gores—and may have an eight or fourteen-inch train. Greater freedom in walking is imparted by the alluring little slash in the bottom of the skirt, but if this is considered too daring, the opening may be filled in with a plaited fan of chiffon or lace. Width around the lower edge is 2¾ yards.

Waist No. 4710 is in sizes 32, 34, 36, 38, 40, 42 and 44 inches bust measure. Size 36 requires 4 yards of 27-inch allover lace, 1½ yard of 36-inch satin for foundation waist, with an extra ¾ yard for girdle. Price, 15 cents. Skirt No. 4562, in sizes 21, 22, 24, 26, 28, 30 and 32 inches waist measure, requires 4 yards of 36-inch satin for size 26. Price, 15 cents.

Pliability is the keynote of all the fashionable, Fall dress fabrics. The satin faced silks, in particular, will be favored for gowns for evening and dressy day wear. Charmeuse, crêpe de chine and crêpe meteor will prove fashionable selections.

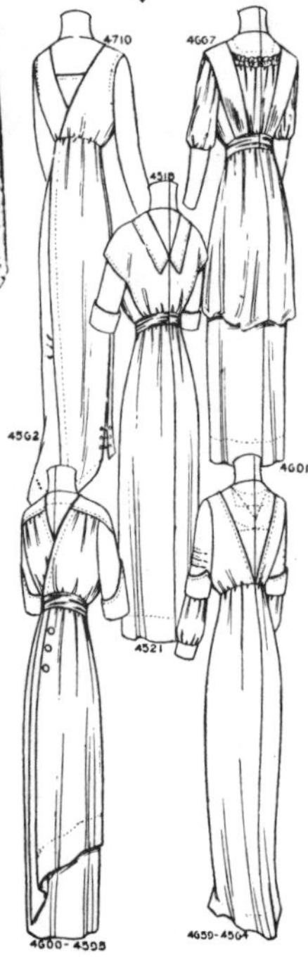

4667-4601—The pannier is the distinguishing style feature of this exquisite evening gown, for which were used light green chiffon, allover Bohemian lace (which is one of the newest Fall types) and black velvet ribbon. Princess lace was used for the bretelle ruffles. A lining or foundation is supplied for the waist and is here made of white satin over which the full front and back of chiffon are draped. If the waist is selected for day wear, it may be made with high neck and long sleeves. The skirt, in high waistline, has a circular foundation which may be in sweep or walking length, and measures 2⅛ yards around the lower edge in the sweep length.

Waist No. 4667 is in sizes 32, 34, 36, 38, 40, 42 and 44 inches bust measure. Size 36 requires 2 yards of 36-inch chiffon and 2 yards of 36-inch satin for waist, with 3½ yards of lace for bretelle ruffles. Price, 15 cents. Skirt No. 4601 is in sizes 21, 22, 24, 26, 28, 30 and 32 inches waist measure. Size 26 requires 5 yards of 18-inch allover lace and 2 yards of chiffon 36 inches wide. Price, 15 cents.

4518-4521—The widely contrasting silks used in the making of this gown produced a strikingly unique ensemble. For the skirt, a black and white figured satin was employed, while plain black, brocaded crêpe furnished the material for the waist. The latter is unusually attractive in cut. There is a regular underbody, which may be finished with high neck. Over this is posed the pointed drape, which is held in with a black velvet girdle. An Irish lace collar finishes the neck. The skirt is one of the graceful three-gored models that is slightly gathered at the back and sides. A high waistline is featured and the regulation or sweep length, the width around the latter being about 2⅜ yards. Waist No. 4518 is in sizes 32, 34, 36, 38, 40, 42 and 44 inches bust measure. Size 36 requires 3½ yards of 27-inch material. Price, 15 cents. Skirt No. 4521 is in sizes 21, 22, 24, 26, 28, 30, 32 and 34 inches waist measure. Size 26 requires 4⅜ yards of 27-inch material. Price, 15 cents.

4600-4595—Remarkably graceful is this model, which might serve as a theater or dinner gown, or for dressy day wear. Its most valuable style detail is the attractive shoulder yoke, that brings out the pretty contours of the shoulders and otherwise adds to the good lines of the figure. This yoke also provides an opportunity for the use of lace or contrasting material. The gown as illustrated attests to the great vogue for black and white; black satin is used for the foundation skirt and waist and for the waist trimming, the surplice waist and tunic being of white chiffon edged with pearl and jet galloon. A lining or foundation is supplied for the waist, and is usually made of the same material as the skirt. The entire gown might be made of charmeuse, voile, etc., if desired, with shoulder yokes of lace. The circular skirt may be in regulation or sweep length. The width around lower edge of sweep is about 2 yards.

Waist No. 4600 is in sizes 32, 34, 36, 38, 40, 42, 44 and 46 inches bust measure. Size 36 requires 1¾ yard of 36-inch satin for foundation and trimming, with 1½ yard of 40-inch chiffon. Price, 15 cents. Skirt No. 4595 is in sizes 21, 22, 24, 26, 28, 30 and 32 inches waist measure. Size 26 requires 2¼ yards of 36-inch material for foundation, and 1½ yard of 40-inch chiffon for tunic. Price, 15 cents.

4659-4564—Fancy striped voile proved a dainty selection for this pretty model, which is suitable for evening wear. With the yoke, and with or without the addition of the high collar, the model is adapted to day wear. In the latter case such materials as charmeuse, serge, broadcloth, etc. are suggested. A body-lining is supplied, and the under-sleeve shown in the back view is also provided. The skirt, a circular model, in sweep or regulation length, with high waistline, measures 2⅜ yards around the bottom.

Waist No. 4659 is in sizes 32, 34, 36, 38, 40, 42 and 44 inches bust measure. Size 36 requires 2⅛ yards of 36-inch material, 1¼ yard 36-inch lining and ⅜ yard 18-inch allover lace. Price, 15 cents. Skirt No. 4564 is in sizes 21, 22, 24, 26, 28, 30 and 32 inches waist measure. Size 26 requires 2¼ yards of 36-inch material, with 9 yards of lace edging for skirt and sleeve ruffles. Price, 15 cents.

Directoire Collars and Vest Effects Leading Features

4671-4674—The original, looped drapery of the skirt renders this gown individual in appearance. As is readily seen, it is a modification of the fashionable pannier and is best developed in soft, sheer fabrics. If desired the entire gown might be made of navy blue satin charmeuse or the waist and skirt drapery might be of chiffon, marquisette or net, and the plaited flounce of satin or charmeuse. A pretty braiding design, in a self-color, is used to outline the edge of overskirt and cuff and forms the motif that adorns the waist front. Dark blue crystal buttons and cream white, allover net or lace complete the trimming scheme. A three-piece lining is used for the waist, and the pattern also provides for full length sleeves. Where these are preferred, the lining is faced with the material, from the lower edge up to the perforations under the sleeve-cap, and the full undersleeve is omitted. A two-gored skirt serves as a foundation to which the plaited flounce is attached.

Waist No. 4671 is in sizes 32, 34, 36, 38, 40, 42, 44 and 46 inches bust measure. Size 36 requires 2¼ yards of 36-inch material and 2 yards of lining 36 inches wide. Price, 15 cents. Skirt No. 4674 is in sizes 21, 22, 24, 26, 28, 30, 32 and 34 inches waist measure. Size 26 requires 4½ yards of 36-inch material with 1¾ yard of lining. Price, 15 cents. Braiding design 11506, perforated pattern, 20 cents; transfer pattern, 10 cents.

4372—One of the newest features of this attractive costume is the simulated vest of satin. Judging by the frequency with which the vest is met in imported models and by the warm reception already given it by American women, this form of trimming, together with the Directoire collar, bids fair to attain a sweeping popularity. Another smart detail is the petticoat effect of the skirt; in a very dressy gown this is often of the same fabric as the vest. For the gown illustrated, sage green silk serge striped with darker green was used. The large collar, that might be cut with a deep or shallow rounded back, was made of sage green faille silk, being in this instance embroidered with darker green. While the turn-over collar of Venise lace, on top of the large collar, is very effective it is not absolutely necessary. The attached skirt is in three pieces—a large front and side portion, lengthened by an underskirt or petticoat section, and a back gore in panel effect. The width around the bottom is 1⅞ yard.

Costume No. 4372 is in sizes 32, 34, 36, 38, 40, 42 and 44 inches bust measure. Size 36 requires 6 yards of 36-inch material with ⅝ yard of lining for vest foundation and ⅝ yard of 27-inch contrasting material for large collar and cuffs. Price, 15 cents. Embroidery design No. 11742, price, 15 cents for either perforated or transfer pattern.

4691-4708—The prominent note of this gown is its marked Directoire tendency, as manifested in the Robespierre collar and vest. French and American designers are following the dress of that period in many details and with most satisfactory results. The costume illustrated is also an example of the strong vogue for black and white. Black charmeuse was used with collar foundation, vest and narrow panel on the skirt of white satin. Black jet buttons are an additional style note, as jet in the form of buttons and trimmings is again fashionable in certain combinations. If the open neck at the front is not admired, a separate collar of lace may be worn underneath. The skirt, one of the very latest models, has a tunic overdrapery suggestive of the modish pannier, its draped fulness being attached under the panel back. A side-plaited flounce attached to a six-gored upper portion forms the foundation skirt. The width around the lower edge of flounce is about 4½ yards.

Waist No. 4691 is in sizes 32, 34, 36, 38, 40, 42, 44 and 46 inches bust measure. Size 36 requires 1⅞ yards of 36-inch material. Price, 15 cents. Skirt No. 4708 is in sizes 21, 22, 24, 26, 28, 30, 32 and 34 inches waist measure. Size 26 requires 7¼ yards of 36-inch material, with ¾ yard of 27-inch satin for entire inserted section. Price, 15 cents. Braiding design No. 11818 (1¼ inch wide), price, 20 cents for perforated pattern.

4364—Light gray broadcloth was selected for this charming design, which could be suitably worn for afternoon dress occasions, or the less formal evening functions. With the gray broadcloth were combined darker chiffon velvet for the large collar and white satin for the inserted front section, which in the waist suggests a vest. A body lining is supplied in the pattern. The attached skirt is in 5 gores and may be in regulation or shorter length. It measures about 1⅞ yard around the lower edge.

Costume No. 4364 is in sizes 32, 34, 36, 38, 40, 42, 44 and 46 inches bust measure. Size 36 requires 3¼ yards of 54-inch material with a nap, 1¼ yard of 27-inch lining and ¾ yard of 18-inch allover lace, with 1 yard contrasting material for inserted section. Price, 15 cents. Braiding design No. 11602, perforated pattern, 20 cents.

4675-4670—The Directoire or Robespierre collar is shown in still another variation in this model; combined with the large revers it is in its characteristic setting. Navy blue cheviot with black satin are shown here. The waist is made without a lining, but patterns of the shield and standing collar are supplied. The skirt, a six-gored model, measures 2⅞ yards around the lower edge.

Waist No. 4675, in sizes 32, 34, 36, 38, 40, 42 and 44 inches bust measure. Size 36 requires 2 yards of 44-inch material, ⅞ yard of 27-inch satin and ¾ yard 18-inch allover lace. Price, 15 cents. Skirt No. 4670, in sizes 21, 22, 24, 26, 28, 30, 32, 34 and 36 inches waist measure. Size 26 requires 3½ yards of 44-inch material. Price, 15 cents.

Various Types of Smart Coats and Suits for Fall

4692-4689—Distinguished and quite military in aspect is this suit of taupe colored, wide wale cheviot with dark, imitation amber buttons which, by the way, are the latest cry in imported fashions. The coat, with its large revers and Robespierre collar, is strongly suggestive of the Directoire period, which is again supplying the style motif for Fall. A collar such as this lends a certain dignity to the wearer and is, in this instance, underfaced with light taupe satin. The same satin underfaces the revers and lines the garment. Being only semitailored and slightly bloused, this coat is easy to fit, and is ideal for the home dressmaker. The cutaway portion, which may be cut shorter if desired, is also remarkably simple, being fitted at the back with two darts, and joins to the waist portion by means of a belt. The skirt illustrates the return to favor of plaits, which, in various arrangements, are a feature of some of the very latest models. While the slender, straight lines are retained, many women will welcome the greater width imparted by the introduction of the plaits. This skirt is cut in eight gores, and measures about $2\frac{5}{8}$ yards around the lower edge.

Coat No. **4692** is in sizes 32, 34, 36, 38, 40, 42 and 44 inches bust measure; size 36 requires $2\frac{5}{8}$ yards of 54-inch material. Price, 15 cents. Skirt No. **4689** is in sizes 21, 22, 24, 26, 28, 30, 32, 34 and 36 inches waist measure; size 26 requires $3\frac{1}{8}$ yards of 54-inch material. Price, 15 cents.

4699-4670—The popular, navy blue or black serge would make a natty suit of this model, the smartness of which is demonstrated by the short coat in cutaway outline, and by the dainty little vest of scarlet broadcloth. The coat may be in 32 or 34-inch length. One of the latest of trimming ideas, namely the plain braid binding, gives exceptional style value to the garment and is practical as well, as it protects the edges, which are always subjected to much wear. Whipcord, tweed and cheviot could also be used, while a strong vogue is springing up for tailored suits of heavy silk serge, silk whipcord and the corded silks. Any of these might be substituted with good results. The skirt is a smart, 6-gored model showing the introduction of plaits and measures about $2\frac{7}{8}$ yards around the lower edge.

Coat No. **4699** is in sizes 32, 34, 36, 38, 40, 42, 44 and 46 inches bust measure; size 36 requires $3\frac{1}{4}$ yards of 44-inch material. Price, 15 cents. Skirt No. **4670** is in sizes 21, 22, 24, 26, 28, 30, 32, 34 and 36 inches waist measure; size 26 requires $3\frac{1}{2}$ yards of 44-inch material. Price, 15 cents.

4681-4683—The garment illustrated, known as the Mackinaw coat, is one of the newest adaptations of a man's garment to the feminine wardrobe. It is shorter than the regular auto or polo coats that have become such a necessity, and for that reason the newer model will be preferred by many. This curtailment of length lessens the weight of the garment considerably. This fact will make for popularity for general use, as the weight of the heavy coats frequently becomes a burden in any but extremely cold weather. The home dressmaker will have no difficulty in making this loose-fitting garment, and it will, without doubt, prove an excellent investment to the economical dresser. A coat of this character made of one of the new coatings in large checks or rough mixtures will be invaluable for business, outing or knock-about wear.

The skirt is a 5-gored design with an unusual distribution of plaits; one at the center front, under which the opening is arranged, and three side plaits at the back. The width around the lower edge is about two yards.

Coat No. **4681** is in sizes 32, 34, 36, 38, 40, 42 and 44 inches bust measure. Size 36 requires 3 yards of 54-inch material. Price, 15 cents. Skirt No. **4683** is in sizes 21, 22, 24, 26, 28, 30, 32, 34 and 36 inches waist measure. Size 26 requires $2\frac{7}{8}$ yards of 44-inch material without nap. Price, 15 cents.

4701-4606—Many new style features are represented in this suit. The cutaway outline of the coat is one and the chic vest another; but most prominent by far is the new collar in modified Robespierre effect. The last is growing in favor and is shown on almost every kind of feminine garment. A handsome suit could be made like the model by using one of the new heavy silk suitings in côtelé or ribbed effect. Serge, cheviot, vigoureaux, English tweed and other light-weight suitings are also adapted, with collar of velvet and vest of contrasting satin or broadcloth. The skirt, a six-gored model on fashionable lines, has a plait in the lower part of each seam, producing a comfortable width of $2\frac{5}{8}$ yards around the lower edge.

Coat No. **4701** is in sizes 32, 34, 36, 38, 40, 42, 44 and 46 inches bust measure. Size 36 requires $3\frac{1}{4}$ yards of 44-inch material, with $\frac{7}{8}$ yard of 18-inch contrasting material for vest. Price, 15 cents. Skirt No. **4606** is in sizes 21, 22, 24, 26, 28, 30, 32 and 34 inches waist measure. Size 26 requires $2\frac{3}{4}$ yards of 44-inch material without a nap. Price, 15 cents.

4175-4093—Navy blue serge appears to experience no falling off in its enormous popularity, and this trig little suit shows it in one of its best applications. The edge-binding of fine black braid adds a novel touch to a suit, that depends otherwise for its style on the excellent lines of both coat and skirt. The former, 28 inches in length, is one of the much admired short coats, which continue to hold popular fancy because of the youthful appearance they give the average figure. The skirt is cut in six gores, those in front and back suggesting double box-plaits, and measures $2\frac{3}{4}$ yards around the lower edge.

Coat No. **4175** is in sizes 32, 34, 36, 38, 40, 42 and 44 inches bust measure. Size 36 requires 3 yards of 44-inch material. Price, 15 cents. Skirt No. **4093** is in sizes 22, 24, 26, 28 and 30 inches waist measure. Size 26 requires 3 yards of 44-inch material. Price, 15 cents.

Types of Dressy Waists and Skirts

4667—Bretelles are much used on the newest dressy blouses. They are recommended for the stout woman, as they cut up the breadth across the front and back and give a length of line that is very becoming. This waist may be made without them if desired. Long sleeves may be used in place of those shown. Waist No. 4667 is in sizes 32, 34, 36, 38, 40, 42 and 44 inches bust measure. Size 36 requires 2 yards of 36-inch material, 2 yards lining 36 inches wide, 1 yard allover lace 18 inches wide and 2 yards lace banding for bretelles. Price, 15 cents.

4671—Cream white messaline and baby Irish allover made this a dressy looking waist. The undersleeves, though very pretty, are a matter of choice. The box plaits simulate bretelles, and are accentuated by the tuck at each side. A lining is supplied and the undersleeves may be made in full length. Waist No. 4671 is in sizes 32, 34, 36, 38, 40, 42, 44 and 46 inches bust measure. Size 36 requires 2¼ yards of 36-inch material, with 2 yards of 36-inch lining and 1¼ yard allover lace, 18 inches wide. Price, 15 cents. Embroidery design No. 11741, price, 15 cents for either perforated or transfer pattern.

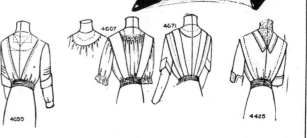

4659—The revers really furnish the distinguishing note of this model. Very wide lace frilling as a sleeve finish is growing in popularity because of its effectiveness. The pattern provides for undersleeves which may be used to complete the length of the sleeves. No. 4659 is in sizes 32, 34, 36, 38, 40, 42 and 44 inches bust measure. Size 36 requires 1¾ yard of 44-inch material with 1¼ yard lining 36 inches wide, ⅝ yard allover lace 18 inches wide, 1¼ yard lace 18 inches wide for revers and cuffs and 1 yard lace frilling. Price, 15 cents.

4425-4695—A conservative costume, especially adapted to the matronly figure is depicted in this illustration. It embodies the ultra fashionable in skirt styles namely, the plaited flounce and the tunic which is in four pieces. The flounce is attached to a seven-gored foundation. The width around lower edge of flounce is about 3¾ yards. Dark blue striped silk developed the original model, the cross arrangement of the stripes on revers and cuffs affording an effective self-trimming. Dark blue serge in this style, with revers and cuffs of black satin would make a serviceable frock. Waist No. 4425 is in sizes 32, 34, 36, 38, 40, 42 and 44 inches bust measure. Size 36 requires 2⅛ yards of 36-inch material with ⅜ yard of 27-inch lining for peplum and ⅞ yard of 18-inch allover lace. Price, 15 cents. Skirt No. 4695 is in sizes 21, 22, 24, 26, 28, 30, 32 and 34 inches waist measure. Size 26 requires 5¾ yards of 36-inch material with 2⅝ yards lining 36 inches wide for foundation. Price, 15 cents.

While the return to the normal waistline has been much discussed by those interested in fashion and its changes, a large number of the latest productions in gowns and skirts continue to show the graceful, high waisted effects.

New Blouse and Skirt Designs

4669–4683—The groups of tucks prettily arranged below the deep yoke at back and front give a pleasing fulness to this white habutai silk waist. The five-gored skirt of blue serge closes to the left of center front, the width around lower edge being about 2 yards.

Waist No. 4669 is in sizes 32, 34, 36, 38, 40, 42, 44, 46 and 48 inches bust measure. Size 36 requires $2\frac{5}{8}$ yards of 36-inch material. Price, 15 cents. Skirt No. 4683 is in sizes 21, 22, 24, 26, 28, 30, 32, 34 and 36 inches waist measure. Size 26 requires $2\frac{7}{8}$ yards of 44-inch material. Price, 15 cents.

4691—Inexpressibly chic is this blouse style adapted from the Directoire period. It is excellent for combinations of contrasting materials. Black and white satin are suggested with sapphire crystal buttons as a contrasting note. Lace frills in the long modish sleeves and the tiny lace chemisette below the Robespierre collar are smart touches that indicate the latest fashion tendency.

Waist No. 4691 is in sizes 32, 34, 36, 38, 40, 42, 44, and 46 inches bust measure. Size 36 requires $1\frac{7}{8}$ yard of satin 36 inches wide with $\frac{3}{4}$ yard of contrasting material 18 inches wide for vest and collar and $\frac{1}{4}$ yard lining 36 inches wide. Price, 15 cents.

4664—The sloping front closing, the wide, stitched, simulated armholes, the collar and side frill are style features of the moment. Checked taffeta is here illustrated.

Waist No. 4664 is in sizes 32, 34, 36, 38, 40, 42 and 44 inches bust measure. Size 36 requires 3 yards of 27-inch material with $\frac{3}{4}$ yard contrasting material 27 inches wide for collar and cuffs, and 1 yard lace for frill. Price, 15 cents.

4675—Here is another type of Directoire blouse which promises to be very popular this coming season. The high collar and revers are as a rule generally becoming. The shield is detachable. This blouse would reproduce delightfully in charmeuse and is an excellent style for serge or broadcloth with a skirt of the same material. Waist No. 4675 is in sizes 32, 34, 36, 38, 40, 42 and 44 inches bust measure. Size 36 requires $2\frac{1}{2}$ yards of 36-inch material with $\frac{3}{8}$ yard lining 27 inches wide, $\frac{3}{4}$ yard contrasting material 27 inches wide and $\frac{3}{4}$ yard net, 18 inches wide. Price, 15 cents.

4670—The separate skirt has increased in popularity since the long coat has become so prominent a garment. One of wide wale diagonal suiting made on this order and ornamented with crystal buttons would serve admirably with a waist of silk or lingerie fabric. It closes to the left of center front and under plait, and comes in regulation or shorter length. The width around the lower edge is about $2\frac{7}{8}$ yards. Skirt No. 4670 is in sizes 21, 22, 24, 26, 28, 30, 32, 34 and 36 inches waist measure. Size 26 requires $3\frac{1}{2}$ yards of 44-inch material. Price, 15 cents.

Pretty Models for the Younger Set

4686

4678

4492

4403

4265

4686
4405
4711
4680
4678
4492
4265

4678—Brown and white shepherd check is well suited to the development of this youthful costume. The vest effect, peplum and fashionable sleeves are interesting features. The skirt is a six-gored model and measures 2½ yards around the lower edge. Costume No. 4678 is in sizes 14, 16, 18 and 20 years. Size 16 requires 5¾ yards of 36-inch material, with ½ yard all-over lace 18 inches wide. Price, 15 cents.

4492—The back closing makes this an attractive variation of the Norfolk waist. The skirt closes to the left of center back under plait, and measures 1⅞ yard around the lower edge. Costume No. 4492 is in sizes 14, 16, 18 and 20 years. Size 16 requires 5¼ yards of 36-inch material. Price, 15 cents. Braiding design No. 11153, price, 35 cents for perforated pattern.

Fetching Garments for Schoolgirls

4693–4489—This delightfully girlish Norfolk suit was made of brown corduroy. A shawl collar may be substituted and a deep yoke used if desired. The skirt, with inverted plait at center back, measures $2\frac{1}{8}$ yards around lower edge. Coat No. 4693 is in sizes 14, 16, 18 and 20 years. Size 16 requires $3\frac{1}{4}$ yards of 44-inch material. Price, 15 cents. Skirt No. 4489 is in sizes 14, 16, 18 and 20 years. Size 16 requires $2\frac{3}{8}$ yards of 44-inch material. Price, 10 cents.

4487—An ideal dress for early Fall wear without a coat, and later on under a long one, is shown in this sketch. The box plait at the back broadens at the waistline to meet the skirt panel, giving the effect of a continuous plait. The width around lower edge of attached five-gored skirt is about $2\frac{3}{8}$ yards. Costume No. 4487 is in sizes 14, 16, 18 and 20 years. A 16-year size requires $3\frac{3}{4}$ yards of 44-inch material, with $\frac{3}{4}$ yard 27-inch contrasting silk.

Embroidery a Favorite Detail in Lingerie

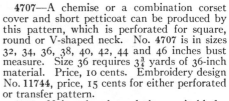

3762 — The front of this fetching nightgown is gathered in Empire style, but it may hang free if preferred. The sleeves may be in elbow length. No. 3762 is in sizes 32, 36, 40 and 44 inches bust measure. Size 36 requires 4¼ yards of 45-inch material with 1½ yard insertion, 3¼ yards edging, 2½ yards beading and 3 yards ribbon. Price, 15 cents.

3908 — The fact that the yoke and sleeve caps are in one piece renders the making of this gown a very simple undertaking indeed. It slips on over the head. No. 3908 is in sizes 32, 36 and 40 inches bust measure. Size 36 requires 3¾ yards of 45-inch material and 4 yards insertion. Price, 15 cents. Embroidery design No. 11615, perforated pattern, 20 cents; transfer pattern, 15 cents.

4707 — A chemise or a combination corset cover and short petticoat can be produced by this pattern, which is perforated for square, round or V-shaped neck. No. 4707 is in sizes 32, 34, 36, 38, 40, 42, 44 and 46 inches bust measure. Size 36 requires 3¾ yards of 36-inch material. Price, 10 cents. Embroidery design No. 11744, price, 15 cents for either perforated or transfer pattern.

4570 — Nainsook or long-cloth are suitable for the nightgown with sailor collar, pocket and cuffs, outlined with hemstitching or veining. Machine embroidered, colored edge banding is also suggested. No. 4570 is in sizes 32, 36, 40, 44 and 48 inches bust measure. Size 36 requires 4⅛ yards of 45-inch material. Price, 15 cents.

4550 — Combination undergarments consisting of a corset cover and open drawers, like the one illustrated, are conducive to that snugness of fit so essential to the fashionable, slender silhouette. The lower edge of drawers may be drawn in or may hang free. No. 4550 is in sizes 32, 34, 36, 38, 40, 42, 44, 46 and 48 inches bust measure. Size 36 requires 2½ yards of 40-inch material, 3 yards insertion and 7½ yards edging. Price, 15 cents. Embroidery design No. 11103, price, 10 cents for perforated pattern.

Dainty and Serviceable Wear for Little Ones

4668   4698   4431   4702   4240

4666

4668—This charmingly quaint design for a little girl's dress is shown in tan colored cheviot with brown velvet trimmings and belt. No. 4668 is in sizes 6, 8, 10 and 12 years. The 8-year size requires 4 yards of 27-inch material, with $\frac{1}{2}$ yard of 18-inch contrasting material. Price, 15 cents.

4698—Here is a dainty frock of white lawn trimmed with insertion. It can also be made with bretelles, full length sleeves and a high neck. No. 4698 is in sizes 2, 4, 6 and 8 years. The 4-year size requires $2\frac{1}{4}$ yards of 36-inch material. Price, 10 cents.

4431—Natural colored pongee was used for this dear little dress, that can be either smocked or shirred. No. 4431 is in sizes 4, 6, 8; 10 and 12 years. The 8-year size takes $3\frac{1}{8}$ yards of 36-inch material. Price, 15 cents. Smocking design No. 11752, perforated pattern 15 cents; transfer pattern, 10 cents.

4702—Point d'esprit net, Valenciennes edging and allover lace with pale blue satin made this an attractive little frock. No. 4702 is in sizes 4, 6, 8, 10 and 12 years. The 8-year size requires 4 yards of 27-inch material, $\frac{1}{2}$ yard of 36-inch satin and $11\frac{3}{4}$ yards of edging. Price, 15 cents.

4240—Nothing could be more attractive than a frock like the model made up in white batiste with Valenciennes edging. No. 4240 is in sizes 6, 8, 10 and 12 years. The 8-year size requires 4 yards of 27-inch material and 5 yards of insertion. Price, 15 cents. Embroidery design No. 11751, 15 cents for perforated pattern.

4666—A serviceable and pretty coat is here shown in black and white checked coating. No. 4666 is in sizes 4, 6, 8, 10 and 12 years. The 8-year size requires $2\frac{1}{2}$ yards of 54-inch material. Price, 15 cents.

4534—A simple gown like the model, in navy blue velveteen, would be appropriate for "Sunday best." Serge and mixtures give good service. No. 4534 is in sizes 6, 8, 10, 12 and 14 years. The 10-year size takes $4\frac{1}{4}$ yards of 27-inch material. Price, 15 cents.

4687—Among suitable materials for rompers are gingham, chambray, linen, and galatea. No. 4687 is in sizes 2, 4, 6 and 8 years. The 4-year size takes 3 yards of 27-inch material. Price, 10 cents.

4478-4690—Boys' shirt blouse, in sizes 6, 8, 10, 12, 14 and 16 years. The 12-year size requires $2\frac{1}{4}$ yards of 36-inch material. Price, 10 cents. Trousers No. 4690, in sizes 3, 4, 6, 8, 10, 12, 14 and 16 years. The 12-year size requires $\frac{7}{8}$ yard of 54-inch material. Price, 10 cents.

Striking Designs in Children's Frocks

4704

4295

4697

4663

4310

4660

4166

4704—Blue and green checked worsted with green silk collar would.be smart for this one-piece dress. No. 4704 is in sizes 4, 6, 8, 10 and 12 years. An 8-year size requires $3\frac{1}{2}$ yards of 36-inch material, with $\frac{3}{8}$ yard of 27-inch silk for collar. Price, 15 cents.

4295—This style is suited to serge, challis and albatross. No. 4295 is in sizes 2, 4, 6 and 8 years. A 4-year size requires $2\frac{1}{2}$ yards of 36-inch material. Price, 15 cents. Scallop design No. 11661, price, 15 cents for either perforated or transfer pattern.

4697—Dress with side closing, in sizes 4, 6, 8, 10 and 12 years. An 8-year size takes $3\frac{1}{4}$ yards of 36-inch material, with $\frac{1}{2}$ yard contrasting material 27 inches wide for collar. Price, 15 cents. Emblem design No. 11745, perforated pattern, 15 cents; transfer pattern, 10 cents.

4663—In this dress choice is given between a large collar in pointed or round outline. No. 4663 is in sizes 6, 8, 10 and 12 years. An 8-year size requires $2\frac{1}{2}$ yards of 44-inch material, with 1 yard contrasting material 18 inches wide. Price, 15 cents.

4310—Child's dress, sizes 2, 4, 6 and 8 years. A 4-year size requires $2\frac{1}{8}$ yards of 36-inch material. If made of embroidery flouncing, $1\frac{1}{4}$ yard 25 inches deep, with $\frac{1}{2}$ yard material 36 inches wide for the sleeves and $2\frac{3}{4}$ yards of beading will be necessary. Price, 10 cents.

4660—In sizes 6, 8, 10 and 12 years. An 8-year size requires $2\frac{1}{2}$ yards of 44-inch material and 1 yard lining 27 inches wide for underbody. Price, 15 cents.

4700—This dress is in sizes 4, 6, 8, 10 and 12 years. An 8-year size requires $2\frac{3}{4}$ yards of 44-inch material and $\frac{1}{2}$ yard of 44-inch broadcloth for collar and shield. Price, 15 cents. Emblem design 11745, price, 15 cents for perforated pattern; 10 cents for transfer pattern.

4166—Dress with yoke-panel, in sizes 2, 4, 6 and 8 years. A 4-year size requires $1\frac{1}{4}$ yard of 44-inch material. Price, 10 cents.

4336—Child's tucked dress, in sizes $\frac{1}{2}$, 1, 2 and 4 years. A 2-year size requires $1\frac{3}{4}$ yard of 44-inch material with 4 yards insertion. Price, 10 cents.

4661—In sizes 4, 6 and 8 years. A 6-year size requires $2\frac{3}{4}$ yards of 44-inch material, with $\frac{1}{2}$ yard contrasting material 18 inches wide. Price, 15 cents.

Practical Ideas in Infants' Attire

4060—This practical, little, one-piece apron buttons at the side. It may be adorned with the nursery rhyme, in outline stitch, to please the little ones. No. 4060 is in sizes 2, 4, 6 and 8 years. The 4-year size requires $1\frac{3}{8}$ yard of 27-inch material. Price, 10 cents. Embroidery design No. 11760, perforated pattern, 25 cents.

4263—The sleeves of these rompers are cut in one with the body, but there is a seam on the shoulder. Gingham, chambray, kindergarten cloth and madras are suitable fabrics. No. 4263 is in sizes 1, 2, 4 and 6 years. The 4-year size requires $3\frac{1}{2}$ yards of 27-inch material. Price, 10 cents.

4653—Embroidery flouncing was used for this little dress. The hand embroidery on yoke and sleeve bands is made by embroidery design No. 11569, the perforated pattern of which costs 25 cents. No. 4653 is in sizes $\frac{1}{2}$, 1, 2 and 4 years. The 2-year size requires $2\frac{5}{8}$ yards of 27-inch material. Price, 10 cents.

4628—The pattern for this infant's kimono is perforated for dressing sack length. No. 4628 is in one size only, and takes 2 yards of 36-inch material for kimono, and $1\frac{1}{8}$ yard of contrasting material for bands, or $\frac{7}{8}$ yard of 36-inch material for sack, and $\frac{5}{8}$ yard for bands. Price, 10 cents.

4685—Here is a dainty little cap, which may be trimmed with hand embroidery or plaited frilling. No. 4685 is in sizes 1, 2, 3 and 4 years. The 3-year size requires $\frac{3}{4}$ yard of 20-inch material. Price, 10 cents. Embroidery design, No. 11739, perforated pattern, 15 cents; transfer pattern, 15 cents.

4662—The use of the hood or collar with this infants' single or double cape is optional. In one size only and takes $3\frac{5}{8}$ yards of 36-inch fabric. Price, 15 cents. Embroidery design No. 11751, perforated pattern, 15 cents.

4649—This underwear set consists of an underwaist, knickerbocker and plain drawers and a petticoat, with attached underbody. No. 4649 is in sizes 2, 3, 4, 6 and 8 years. The 4-year size requires $1\frac{1}{2}$ yard of 36-inch material for either drawers and waist, and $1\frac{1}{4}$ yard for petticoat with underbody. Price, 15 cents.

4709—The pattern of this child's night-dress, which may be opened at front or back, is in sizes $\frac{1}{2}$, 1, 2, 3, 4 and 5 years. The 2-year size requires $2\frac{3}{8}$ yards of 27-inch material. Price, 10 cents.

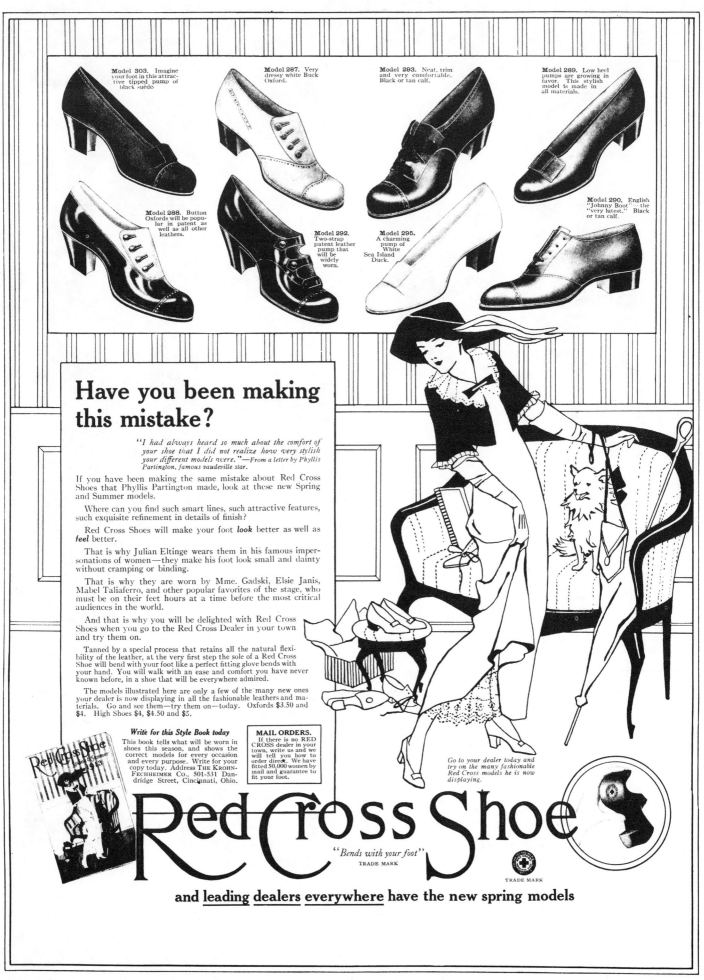

Model 303. Imagine your foot in this attractive tipped pump of black suède.

Model 287. Very dressy white Buck Oxford.

Model 293. Neat, trim and very comfortable. Black or tan calf.

Model 289. Low heel pumps are growing in favor. This stylish model is made in all materials.

Model 288. Button Oxfords will be popular in patent as well as all other leathers.

Model 292. Two-strap patent leather pump that will be widely worn.

Model 295. A charming pump of White Sea Island Duck.

Model 290. English "Johnny Boot"—the "very latest." Black or tan calf.

Have you been making this mistake?

"I had always heard so much about the comfort of your shoe that I did not realize how very stylish your different models were."—From a letter by Phyllis Partington, famous vaudeville star.

If you have been making the same mistake about Red Cross Shoes that Phyllis Partington made, look at these new Spring and Summer models.

Where can you find such smart lines, such attractive features, such exquisite refinement in details of finish?

Red Cross Shoes will make your foot *look* better as well as *feel* better.

That is why Julian Eltinge wears them in his famous impersonations of women—they make his foot look small and dainty without cramping or binding.

That is why they are worn by Mme. Gadski, Elsie Janis, Mabel Taliaferro, and other popular favorites of the stage, who must be on their feet hours at a time before the most critical audiences in the world.

And that is why you will be delighted with Red Cross Shoes when you go to the Red Cross Dealer in your town and try them on.

Tanned by a special process that retains all the natural flexibility of the leather, at the very first step the sole of a Red Cross Shoe will bend with your foot like a perfect fitting glove bends with your hand. You will walk with an ease and comfort you have never known before, in a shoe that will be everywhere admired.

The models illustrated here are only a few of the many new ones your dealer is now displaying in all the fashionable leathers and materials. Go and see them—try them on—today. Oxfords $3.50 and $4. High Shoes $4, $4.50 and $5.

Write for this Style Book today
This book tells what will be worn in shoes this season, and shows the correct models for every occasion and every purpose. Write for your copy today. Address THE KROHN-FECHHEIMER CO., 501-531 Dandridge Street, Cincinnati, Ohio.

MAIL ORDERS.
If there is no RED CROSS dealer in your town, write us and we will tell you how to order direct. We have fitted 50,000 women by mail and guarantee to fit your foot.

Go to your dealer today and try on the many fashionable Red Cross models he is now displaying.

Red Cross Shoe
"Bends with your foot"
TRADE MARK

TRADE MARK

and leading dealers everywhere have the new spring models

The
Cookery Department

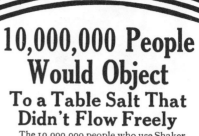

Fireless Cooker Preserving

By Margaret Soundstrom

IN bygone days, preserving time was fraught with many trials. It meant an upset kitchen, tired nerves and continual bending over a hot fire with your head in a cloud of steam for fear anything should burn, or cook too long or too fast. The result was that no matter how much domestic pride there was in the heart of the housewife, she honestly dreaded this time more than she cared to admit.

But in these days, this preserving siege can be managed very differently; for, with the use of the fireless cooker, the confusion and heat of the old-fashioned methods are done away with. The fruit to be "put up" is not only perfectly cooked, but it retains much more of its original flavor, runs no risk of being scorched, does not cook rapidly, and if reasonable attention is given to the amount of time required for the cooking, it retains its original shape.

If a number of different kinds of fruit are to be "put up" the same day, there is ample opportunity to prepare one kind, while another batch of fruit is in the cooker. Thus time is saved, the kitchen is cool and comfortable to work in, and preserving can be looked forward to as a perfectly comfortable occupation, even for a rather warm day.

In using a fireless cooker for this purpose there are a few rules that must be kept in mind in order to insure success. Never attempt to use either unripe or overripe fruit; it must be solid and just ripe. Have the fruit jars, caps, the bands that fasten them, as well as the glasses for jellies, sterilized.

Sweet Watermelon Rind

DIVIDE a watermelon into quarters and trim away the green outside rind. Scoop out all of the soft, red inside, leaving only the solid, white part. Cut this into strips, and cover with cold water, with one tablespoonful of salt to every quart. Let stand overnight. Drain and rinse thoroughly; then put in the cooker pail. Fill it about one-third full with water, bring to boiling point, and put in the cooker for ten hours. Drain carefully, weigh, and for each pound use one-half cupful of water and three quarters of a pound of white sugar. Heat until boiling, skim, and add one teaspoonful of ground ginger root and a lemon with rind, cut in thin, lengthwise pieces. Add the melon rind, boil fifteen minutes, and pack into pint jars. Boil syrup ten minutes, pour over the melon, and seal immediately.

Blackberry Jam

CAREFULLY wash blackberries which are just ripe. Weigh them, put them into the cooker pail, and set over the fire. As they gradually heat, mash the berries, add to them their weight in granulated sugar, and when boiling, put into the cooker for two hours. Strain off the juice, and boil until it jellies; then add the berries, heat until boiling, and pour into sterilized jars. Seal the jars immediately with paraffin.

Preserved Pears With Ginger

PEARS with ginger and lemon make a very palatable preserve, especially if made in a fireless cooker where the slow process of steaming causes the flavor of the ginger and lemon to thoroughly permeate the fruit.

Select firm, ripe Bartlett pears; peel and weigh. To every pound of fruit add one of sugar; one lemon with the rind, cut into long strips; one ounce of green ginger root cut into shreds, and a half cupful of water. Put these in a cooker pail, making first a layer of pears, then sugar, ginger root and lemon, and repeat until the pail is nearly filled. Pour on the water, and set on the fire to heat slowly until boiling. Put in the cooker for two or three hours, according to the hardness of the pears. When sufficiently cooked, drain and put into jars. Reheat the syrup with lemon and ginger and boil until thick and clear. Skim, arrange ginger and lemon with the pears, add the boiling syrup and seal immediately.

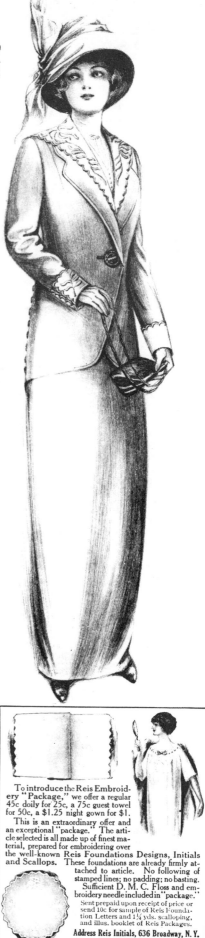

Victrola X, $75
Shown in illustration. With Victor record albums, $85

Victrola XI, $100
Shown in illustration

On the porch with your friends and a Victor-Victrola

An impromptu dance with a Victor-Victrola

Take a Victrola with you when you go away this summer

Whether you go to the country, mountains, or seashore for the summer, or just camp out for a week or so, you'll be glad of the companionship of the Victrola.

This wonderful instrument enables you to take with you wherever you go the most celebrated bands, the greatest opera artists, the most famous instrumentalists, and the cleverest comedians—to play and sing for you at your leisure, to provide music for your dances, to make your vacation thoroughly enjoyable.

And even if you don't go away, a Victrola will entertain you and give you a delightful "vacation" right at home.

You can buy a Victrola for $15, $25, $40, $50, $75, $100, $150, $200.

Any Victor dealer in any city in the world will gladly play your favorite music and demonstrate the Victrola to you.

Victor Talking Machine Co., Camden, N. J., U. S. A.
Berliner Gramophone Co., Montreal, Canadian Distributors

Always use Victor Machines with Victor Records and Victor Needles—*the combination.* There is no other way to get the unequaled Victor tone.

Victor Steel Needles, 5 cents per 100
Victor Fibre Needles, 50 cents per 100 (can be repointed and used eight times)

Victor
"HIS MASTER'S VOICE"
REG. U.S. PAT. OFF.

The music of the Victor-Victrola is particularly enjoyable on the water

The Victor-Victrola is an important part of the camping outfit

Victrola IX, $50
Shown in illustration

Victrola IV, $15
Shown in illustration

Ladies' Waist, No. 6717.—Linen, crepe de Chine or madras can be used to make this waist. The body and sleeves are cut in one piece. The seam can be used at the back or not, as preferred. The pattern, No. 6717, is cut in sizes from 34 to 44 inches bust measure. Price of pattern, 10 cents.

Children's Rompers, No. 6737.—This simplest of garments may be worn over the underwear or with only the flannels beneath it. The closing of the waist is in the back, and the trousers button across the back at the waistline. The pattern, 6737 is cut in sizes for 2, 4 and 6 years. Price of pattern, 10 cents.

Girls' Dress, No. 7331.—A practical frock for the schoolgirl is shown in this model. It has a guimpe which may be in one piece or in two, according to the width of the material, and over this a sacque garment which closes at the side of the front, and is belted in a trifle at the waistline. The guimpe or underwaist can be made of batiste or other wash-material, while silk or woolen fabrics are more suitable for the outer dress. The dress-pattern, No. 7331, is cut in sizes for 4, 6, 8, 10 and 12 years. Price of pattern, 10 cents.

Girls' Dress, No. 6728.—Linen, gingham or serge can be used to make this dress, with the trimming of contrasting material. The blouse is made with the body and sleeve-sections in one. The skirt is cut in two pieces, and closes at the left side. The pattern, No. 6728, is cut in sizes, for 8, 10, 12 and 14 years. Price of pattern, 10 cents.

Boys' Suit, No. 6783.—This suit shows the Russian type in an attractive form. The blouse is plain, with front closing, and a collar at the neck. With the suit trousers are provided, and these may be left straight and open at the knee or drawn in and gathered. The pattern, No. 6783, is cut in sizes for 2, 4 and 6 years. Price of pattern, 10 cents.

Ladies' Shirtwaist, No. 7318.—The collar and vest of this blouse are cut in one piece. Front and back are plain, and the roomy sleeve may end in a straight cuff at the wrist or be shortened to the elbow with a turn-back cuff, provided in the pattern. Such materials as silk, voile, challis, cashmere, and waist flannels are nice for these waists, with a contrasting color to trim.

Girls' Dress, No. 7326. — This dainty frock has a plain blouse with surplice closing in front, and with a small chemisette and a large collar trimming the neck. These may be omitted. The sleeves may be made short or long. The skirt is straight at both edges, and is nearly covered by the little tunic, which is of circular cut and which may have plain or scalloped edges. In using two materials for this frock one of them may well be silk of contrasting color. The dress-pattern, No. 7326, is cut in sizes for 6, 8, 10, 12 and 14 years. Price of pattern, 10 cents.

Ladies' Shirtwaist, No. 6851.—This waist offers a novelty in the arrangement of the neck. This is open, with a large collar, but the same collar may be pushed close to the throat and held up by a strap, loosened when the wearer wishes. The rest of the waist is on regulation lines. The pattern, No. 6851, is cut in sizes from 34 to 44 inches bust measure. Price of pattern, 10 cents.

Ladies' Kimono, No. 7311.—This graceful gown is made with a short Empire bodice cut in one with the short sleeves. The skirts have but little fulness and flare at the lower edge. All free edges are trimmed with a contrasting fabric. Cotton crepe, challis, cashmere, wash-silk, and similar materials are used for these gowns. The kimono-pattern, No. 7311, is cut in sizes for 36, 40 and 44 inches bust measure. Price of pattern, 10 cents.

Ladies' House - Dress, No. 7337.—The closing of this dress is placed at the left side of the front, and the edges of this and of the neck are trimmed with a bias band of contrasting material. The loose sleeves may be long or short. The skirt fits neatly at the top, and is also closed at the left side of the front. Wash-materials, cashmere, challis, and the like are used for these dresses, with braid or bias bands of material as trimming. The dress-pattern, No. 7337, is cut in sizes from 34 to 46 inches bust measure. Price of pattern, 10 cents.

Girls' Dress, No. 6867.—This is a good design for wearing over the school frock. Front and back are each in one piece, the closing in the back. The sleeves extend to the neck-edge, forming a yoke on each shoulder. The neck is open, the sleeves short, and all free edges are trimmed with banding. The pattern, No. 6867, is cut in sizes for 4, 6, 8, 10 and 12 years. Price of pattern, 10 cents.

Ladies' Apron, No. 6865.—This is one of the favorite bungalow aprons made with a small waist with sleeves and body cut in one, closing in the back, and joined to a skirt which completely covers that of the dress. The pattern, No. 6865, is cut in sizes from 34 to 44 inches bust measure. Price of pattern, 10 cents.

Ladies' Waist, No. 6960.—A plain model, with high neck, the material gathered at the base of the collar. The sleeve is inset with an enlarged armhole. Suitable for crepe fabrics, taffeta, satin, etc. The pattern, No. 6960, is cut in sizes from 34 to 44 inches bust measure. To make the waist in the medium size will require 2⅝ yards of 36-inch material. Price of pattern, 10 cents.

Boys' Russian Suit, No. 6981.—For very little boys. The blouse closes far over at the side and along the shoulder. The neck has a plain band collar, and the long sleeves have a group of tucks at the wrist. The pattern, No. 6981, is cut in sizes for 1 and 2 years. To make the suit in the 2-year size will require 1½ yards of 44-inch material. Price of pattern, 10 cents.

Girl Doll's Set of clothes, No. 6943.—The set consists of blouse, hat and bloomers or skirt. The skirt is set on the outside of the waist which is in Dutch style with front closing.

Ladies' Overblouse, No. 6989.—Two patterns are here given, one with jacket front and back, open neck, flare collar and small revers. The other closes in the back, has a deep rounded neck in front and a tuck at each shoulder.

Ladies' Skirt, No. 6975.—A two-gore model made with raised or regulation waistline. It is gathered across the back and has a small, plaited inset at the lower half of the side seams. The pattern, No. 6975, is cut in sizes from 22 to 32 inches waist measure. To make the skirt in the medium size will require 2⅝ yards of 54-inch material.

Children's Dress, No. 6971.—Long-waisted blouse, with diagonal front closing, drop-shoulder and bishop sleeve, long or short. Fancy collar and small shield. The skirt is straight and plaited. The pattern, No. 6971, is cut in sizes for 4, 6 and 8 years.

Girls' Coat, No. 6973.—A plain box coat with double-breasted closing, sleeves extending to neck-edge and either a small collar and revers, or a small turnover collar for side-front closing. Patch-pockets, which may be omitted. The pattern, No. 6973, is cut in sizes for 4, 6, 8, 10, 12 and 14 years. To make the coat in the medium size will require 1¾ yards of 54-inch material.

Ladies' Waist, No. 6968.—Made with raglan sleeve forming small shoulder-yoke. The back is plain, the fronts gathered at the top. A small collar trims the open neck and a gathered girdle extends below the waist. The pattern, No. 6968, is cut in sizes from 34 to 44 inches bust measure. To make the waist in the medium size will require 2¼ yards of 36-inch material and 1 yard of 36-inch contrasting fabric to trim as shown. Price of pattern, 10 cents.

Misses' Dress, No. 6988.—The plain blouse closes in front, the open neck has a small, fancy collar. Sleeves are full-length and plain with cuff. The skirt has a deep yoke and side-front closing; the lower portion has three gores. The pattern, No. 6988, is cut in sizes for 14, 16, 18 and 20 years. To make the dress in the medium size will require 3⅜ yards of 44-inch material, with ½ yard of 27-inch contrasting goods. Price of pattern, 10 cents.

Ladies' House-Dress, No. 6984.—The plain waist has bishop sleeves, full-length or shorter, front closing, high neck. The skirt has seven gores, and is gathered across the back, closing at the side of the front. The pattern, No. 6984, is cut in sizes from 34 to 44 inches bust measure. To make the dress in the medium size will require 3⅞ yards of 44-inch material. Price of pattern, 10 cents.

Ladies' Dress, No. 6972.—Showing the popular chemise tunic, full-length from shoulder to hem. Sleeves are attached to a separate guimpe which shows as a small yoke in front. Standing turnover collar and a three-gore foundation-skirt with straight lower sections. The pattern, No. 6972, is cut in sizes from 34 to 42 inches bust measure. To make the dress in the medium size will require 2 yards of 54-inch material, with 1½ yards of 36-inch satin. Price of pattern, 10 cents.

Ladies' Apron, No. 6977.—The front panel is plain and slightly shaped to the figure. The sides have their forward half extended as straps across the shoulders and the balance gathered into a waistband. There is also a patch-pocket of reasonable size. The pattern, No. 6977, is cut in sizes for 36, 40 and 44 inches bust measure. To make the apron in the medium size will require 4⅛ yards of 36-inch material. Price of pattern, 10 cents.

Ladies' Dressing - Sacque, No. 7842.—This model, inviting you to take comfort, suggests something you will want many times during the summer. The collar, in contrasting goods, continues its line down the front either side, in scalloped outline. Cuffs on short sleeves are similarly favored, but cuffs and collar may be plain if desired. The sacque-pattern, No. 7842, is cut in sizes for 36, 40 and 44 inches bust measure. Price of pattern, 10 cents.

Girls' Dress, No. 7814. — A very fetching little frock with front closing and a removable shield. Novelty striped material for the collar, cuffs and belt at a lowered waistline where the waist-body is gathered front and back. The skirt is plaited. The dress-pattern, No. 7814, is cut in sizes for from 6 to 14 years. Price of pattern, 10 cents.

Children's Dress, No. 7831.—Can you think of anything more fascinatingly odd than this dress design? Any girl will want such a treat, and the mother will find the making a pleasurable task. The model is made to slip on over the head, has a separate guimpe with closing at the front, and long or short sleeves. The dress-pattern, No. 7831, is cut in sizes for 4, 6, 8 and 10 years. Price of pattern, 10 cents.

Ladies' Apron, No. 7846. — In every way worthy of your approval, this apron has a very full body- and skirt-section — the closing is at the front with loops and buttons. Contrasting goods contributes the collar, cuffs and belt, as well as a pocket of generous size in each side of the front. A square yoke gives the garment balance, and long or short sleeves may be used. The apron-pattern, No. 7846, is cut in sizes for 36, 40 and 44 inches bust measure. Price of pattern, 10 cents.

Ladies' Shirtwaist, No. 7832.—An irresistible model in plain and striped silk, or your choice of fabrics and colors, or in solid white. The shoulder-fronts are gathered, and in the back at the waistline, the fulness is gathered under a stay belt. A very pretty collar notched at each shoulder has a frill which continues down the front of the waist where the closing is made. The shirtwaist-pattern, No. 7832, is cut in sizes from 36 to 44 inches bust measure. Price of pattern, 10 cents.

Ladies' Bathing-Suit, No. 7854.—As attractive as it should be, but in no way conspicuous by its style, is this bathing-suit in combination effect. The blouse is gathered at the waist, under a belt of the contrasting goods cut bias; the bias stripe is used on the collar, sleeve-ends, and to outline the closing at the left side of the front. The skirt has three gores. The bathing-suit-pattern, No. 7854, is cut in sizes for 36, 40 and 42 inches bust measure.

Girls' Dress, No. 7823. — This design recalls the suspender style, buttoning on the shoulder over a separate guimpe that has charming sleeves finished with frills. Scalloping finishes the scooped - out front of the dress, and shoulder-straps. The plaited skirt is in two gores and has panel front. The dress-pattern, No. 7823, is cut in sizes for 6, 8, 10, 12 and 14 years. Price of pattern, 10 cents.

Ladies' Shirtwaist, No. 7860.—For the esteem of the discriminating woman this waist was planned. Figured and plain material are advantageously used, but all one material will be just as desirable. A deep cape collar, cut in points, covers the entire front, and has a frill all around its edge; the full sleeves are gathered to deep cuffs. The shirtwaist-pattern, No. 7860, is cut in sizes from 34 to 42 inches bust measure. Price of pattern, 10 cents.

Ladies' Skirt, No. 7833. — A tasteful model in four gores, with its closing at the left side of the front. Introducing a plaited section at each side of the hips, gives a panel front, and a yoke is suggested by the button trimming as pictured.

Children's Dress, No. 7847. — A very good design for contrasting material. The frock is in one piece; the shoulder-straps, finish of the sleeves and a belt, run through lengthwise slashes at a lowered waistline, are of plaid material cut bias. The closing is at the back, and long or short sleeves may be used. The dress-pattern, No. 7847, is cut in sizes for 2, 4 and 6 years.

Ladies' Waist, No. 7851. — Another fetching style in a shirtwaist combining two materials in two shades of color. The pretty surplice vest — button-trimmed — has picot edge to make it "perfect."

Girls' Dress, No. 7830. — This answers the question how to make a trim, smart little dress on simple lines but with the "something catchy" in its style. Notice the closing-outline, and the shaping of the bodice, and a tuck in each front, turned toward the armhole. The long waist - body is gathered to a skirt which is plaited. The dress-pattern, No. 7830, is cut in sizes for 6, 8, 10 and 12 years.

Women's Dresses of Fashion

31T6575—Navy blue.
31T6576—Dark brown.
31T6577—Black.
EACH
$24.95

A DRESS WHICH WILL APPEAL to the woman desiring something not too fussy and yet possessing style. The material is ALL WOOL FRENCH SERGE, and the waist with round neck has cluster of pin tucks above girdle. Close fitting sleeves attached to fine mull underwaist are tucked and composition button trimmed. Skirt, pin tucked at hips, has button trimmed open plait from tucks to bottom of skirt on each side and short double button trimmed side drapes. Girdle has sash at left side. Fastens at left side and has skirt SWEEP of about 52 inches. Women's sizes only. **Give measurements.** Average shipping weight, 2 pounds.

31T6570
Silk Taffeta
$24⁷⁵

31T6570—Navy blue.
31T6571—Gray.
31T6572—Black.
EACH
$24.75

ONE OF THE SEASON'S FASHIONABLE FABRICS—lustrous ALL SILK TAFFETA—is used in this attractive dress. Round neck is edged with taffeta and waist front is embroidered with self and contrasting color and button trimmed on left side. Row of buttons trim back of waist. Georgette crepe sleeves are finished off with triple taffeta cuffs and the crushed girdle has sash with tassels. The softly gathered graduated tunic skirt has SWEEP of about 68 inches and dress fastens at left side. Women's sizes only. **Give measurements.** Average shipping weight, 1¾ pounds.

31T6575
French Serge
$24⁹⁵

31T6580
Sicilian
$12⁸⁵

31T6580—Navy blue.
31T6581—Brown.
EACH
$12.85

A SERVICEABLE AND FASHIONABLE women's dress of SICILIAN CLOTH, about two-thirds mohair and one-third cotton. Waist with loose panel front, buttoning through with smoke pearl buttons on each side, continues into girdle with sash in back, set off with celluloid buckle. Collar and turnback cuffs of self material, also panel of waist, are edged with contrasting color mercerized cotton poplin, and waist is lined with voile. Skirt has full straight tunic trimmed with pin tucks and SWEEP of about 74 inches. Women's sizes only. **Give measurements.** Average shipping weight, 2 pounds.

31T6585
Wool Mixed Shadow Check
$10²⁵

31T6585—Navy blue.
31T6586—Wine.
31T6587—Black.
EACH
$10.25

WOMEN'S DRESS OF MIXED SHADOW CHECK, about 50 per cent each of wool and cotton, following the long straight lines dictated by latest fashion. Tucked panel in front and back of waist are set off on each side with self material button trimmed straps. Collar and turnback cuffs are of contrasting color taffeta and girdle is of self material. The pretty straight line skirt has cluster of pin tucks near bottom and SWEEP of about 60 inches. Women's sizes only. **Give measurements.** Average shipping weight, 2 pounds.

For sizes see page 63.

62⁵
123T
Sears, Roebuck and Co.
Chicago

239

Sears, Roebuck & Co.

New Styles for Stout Women

31T6740
Wool
Poplin
$27.50

31T6745
Satin
Messaline
$24.75

31T6750
Wool Mixed
Serge
$12.98

31T6755
French Serge
and Georgette Crepe
$29.85

SIZES Dresses offered on this page are especially adapted for **stout figures** and can be furnished in the following sizes only: 39, 41, 43, 45, 47, 49, 51 and 53 inches bust measure, 29 up to and including 44 inches waist measure and front skirt length of 39 inches, with basted hem. **Be sure to give bust, chest and waist measures.** For simple measuring instructions, see order blanks in back of catalog.

31T6740—Navy blue.
31T6741—Black. EACH **$27.50**
THE STRAIGHT LINES OF THIS DRESS, made of excellent quality medium weight ALL WOOL POPLIN, have a tendency to give height and slenderness and make it particularly appropriate for stout women. The collar and vestee are of silk and cotton poplin and vestee is trimmed with small satin covered buttons. Sleeves are trimmed with row of good quality buttons. Waist is lined with mull. The skirt is most attractive, being made with long side drapery and short peplum effect, peplum and drapery being trimmed with embroidery and braid. The wide girdle is finished off with sash in back. Fastens in front and has skirt SWEEP of about 70 inches. Stout women's sizes only. **Give measurements.** Average shpg. wt., 2½ lbs.

31T6745—Navy blue. EACH
31T6746—Taupe.
31T6747—Black. **$24.75**
DESIGNED ESPECIALLY FOR WOMEN OF FULL FIGURE and made of good quality lustrous ALL SILK SATIN MESSALINE. The prettily embroidered vestee of Georgette crepe is attached to Jap silk underwaist and neck, at each side, set off with fold of white Georgette crepe. Georgette crepe collar at back is handsomely embroidered to match vestee. The stylish sleeves are of Georgette crepe, hemstitched and picot edged at cuffs. The extra wide, crushed girdle sets off the pretty tunic skirt which is softly draped at right side. Fastens in front and has skirt SWEEP of about 70 inches. Stout women's sizes only. **Give measurements.** Average shipping weight, 2 pounds.

31T6750—Navy blue. EACH
31T6751—Dark green.
31T6752—Black. **$12.98**
AN INEXPENSIVE AND PRACTICAL DRESS, made of good quality SERGE, about 50 per cent each of wool and cotton. This cloth possesses excellent wearing quality and the straight plaited style is particularly becoming to stout women. Dress is made the same both front and back, and waist front, belt and box plaits are trimmed with military braid and good quality buttons. The large collar is of silk and cotton poplin. Fastens under plait at left side and has skirt SWEEP of about 80 inches. Stout women's sizes only. **Give measurements.** Average shpg. wt., 2¼ pounds.

31T6755—Navy blue. EACH
31T6756—Black. **$29.85**
A STUNNING DRESS for stout women made of excellent quality ALL WOOL FRENCH SERGE with sleeves and upper part of overskirt of Georgette crepe. The pretty vestee is of white Georgette crepe softly plaited, and is attached to underwaist of Jap silk. The waist front, sleeves and tunic of skirt are handsomely embroidered with jet beads and tunic on each side in front is picot edged. Note the pretty flared serge cuffs. Fastens in front and has skirt SWEEP of about 68 inches. You will be delighted with the quality of this dress. Stout women's sizes only. **Give measurements.** Average shipping weight, 2¼ pounds.

Junior Misses' Fall and Winter Coats

These Coats Are Made to Fit Junior Misses and Small Women Only. Average shipping weight of muffs, 2 lbs.

Ages, years	15	17	19
Bust measure, inches	34	36	38
Average length		45	inches

Velour Cloth Coat. Made of a heavy weight wool mixed velour cloth, about 80 per cent wool, balance cotton, which will give splendid wear. Coat is unlined and cut 45 inches long in this season's most popular style, in loose back effect. Large convertible high grade moleskin fur cloth collar, closely resembles real mole fur. Patch pockets. **State age and bust measure.** Average shipping weight, 5 pounds.
17 T 2500—Navy blue.
17 T 2501—Brown.
17 T 2502—Dark green.
17 T 2503—Burgundy.
Price,
each............ $16.50

17 T 2505
Velour Coating
$12.48

17 T 2515
Velour Plush
$14.98

17 T 2510
Astrakhan Cloth
$12.98

17 T 2500
Velour Cloth
$16.50

17 T 2525
Fancy Mixture
$9.98

17 T 2520
Velour Cloth
$15.98

Fall and Winter Coat of Velour Coating. Made of a heavy weight wool mixed velour coating, about 80 per cent wool, balance cotton. Coat is 45 inches long with belted back. Full cuffs, button trimmed. Unlined and has large collar and pockets of gray chinchilla fur cloth which closely resembles real chinchilla fur. **Mention age and bust measure.** Average shipping weight, 5 pounds.
17 T 2505—Dark navy blue.
17 T 2506—Dark brown.
17 T 2507—Dark green.
17 T 2508—Dark burgundy.
Price,
each.... $12.48

Astrakhan Cloth Coat. Made of good quality astrakhan cloth, woven of mohair in small close curls. Coat is cut in loose fitting belted style with slash pockets. Large collar and full cuffs are of lustrous velour plush in color to harmonize. Lined throughout with serviceable wearing mercerized sateen. **Give age and bust measure.** Average shipping weight, 5 lbs.
17 T 2510—Navy blue.
17 T 2511—Brown.
17 T 2512—Black.
Price
each... $12.98
17 T 3294—Velour Plush Muff in colors to match trimming on coat.
Price,
each...... $2.19

Velour Plush Coat. Made of lustrous velour plush, woven of fine cotton yarn, very rich and silklike in appearance. Cut in the latest style, showing loose yoke back. Large convertible collar, full cuffs and patch pockets are of same material. Lined with good wearing flowered sateen. **State age and bust measure.**
17 T 2515—Navy blue.
17 T 2516—Brown.
17 T 2517—Green.
17 T 2518—Burgundy.
17 T 2519—Black.
Price,
each...... $14.98
17 T 3294—Velour Plush Muff. (Not illustrated.) Colors to match coat. **State color.**
Price,
each....... $2.19

Velour Cloth Coat. Made of a heavy weight velour cloth, about 80 per cent wool, balance fine quality cotton yarn. Coat is unlined, has inverted plait in back. Convertible collar, full cuffs and fancy pockets. **Mention age and bust measure.** Average shipping weight, 5 pounds.
17 T 2520—Navy blue.
17 T 2521—Brown.
17 T 2522—Dark green.
17 T 2523—Burgundy.
Price,
each.................. $15.98

Fancy Mixture Cloth Coat. Made of a heavy Winter weight cloth that is woven in dark harmonizing colors in a fancy mixed design, about 50 per cent wool, balance cotton, which will give good wear. Coat is unlined, cut 45 inches long and has large collar of lustrous velour plush to match trimming on pockets and back of belt. **Be sure to state age and bust measure.** Average shipping weight, 4½ pounds.
17 T 2525—Fancy mixture.
Price,
each.................... $9.98

26₃ **Sears, Roebuck and Co.**
106T **Chicago**

Women's Fur Coatees

These attractive coatees are very stylish with suits and dresses.

41T7017

41T7019

	Price
41T7017—Taupe Coney Coatee...	**$57.00**
41T7018—Black Coney Coatee....	**57.00**

Coney Fur Coatee in either taupe gray or black. Made of the soft silky haired coney fur, with large shawl collar which can be worn as in illustration or close up around the neck. All around belt, two pockets. Satin lined. Average shipping weight, 4½ pounds.

	Price
41T7019—Taupe Marmot Coatee..	**$51.00**
41T7020—Kolinsky Marmot Coatee..................	**51.00**

High Grade Marmot Fur Coatee in the new taupe shade or kolinsky (dark brown shade). A short haired glossy durable fur in a popular style. Two pockets. Silk lining. Average shipping weight, 3¼ pounds.

41T7021—Black Nearseal Coatee...........**$150.00**

41T7022—Black Hudson Seal Coatee...........**$330.00**

Women's Fashionable Large Coatee from fine grade nearseal (imported sheared coney), or Hudson seal (plucked, clipped and tip dyed muskrat). Brocaded silk lined. Average shipping weight, 3½ pounds.

41T7023—Japanese Mink Coatee (mink shade).**$175.00**

Women's Fancy Coatee from the short haired soft Japanese mink in imitation of American mink. These coatees are very popular and also very serviceable. All around belt. Silk lined. Average shipping weight, 3½ pounds.

41T7021

41T7023

Sears, Roebuck and Co.
Chicago   40T

2127

Attractive Choker Scarfs

41T7087

41T7067

41T7078

41T7091

41T7083

41T7067—Stone Marten Opossum Choker Scarf. (Natural Opossum Brown Tipped)..................$13.25

41T7068—Taupe Gray Opossum Choker Scarf..................13.25

41T7069—Brown Coney Choker Scarf. 9.55
41T7070—Black Coney Choker Scarf.. 9.55
41T7071—Taupe Coney Choker Scarf. 9.55

One-Skin Double Furred Choker Scarf from long glossy haired opossum or imported sheared coney. See illustration above Av. shpg. wt., 1 lb.

41T7087—Lucille Brown Fox Scarf..................$25.75

41T7088—Taupe Gray Fox Scarf. 25.75
41T7089—Red Fox Scarf....... 25.75
41T7090—Black Fox Scarf...... 30.00

Women's Double Furred Choker Scarfs from imported fox skins, a soft fluffy fur. Can be worn as in illustration or opened up and thrown loose across shoulders. Av. shpg. wt., 1¼ lbs.

41T7091—Hudson Seal Scarf..................$36.00

41T7092—Taupe Nutria Scarf. (South American Beaver)... 30.00

41T7093—Marten Scarf. (Natural Skunk)... 54.00

41T7094—Black Nearseal Scarf. (Imported Sheared Coney) 16.75

41T7095—Taupe Gray Squirrel...... 36.00

Attractive Choker Style Tie Scarf. Can also be worn loose across shoulders. See above for various furs and colors. Av. shpg. wt., 1 lb.

41T7078—American Red Fox Scarf......$54.00

41T7079—American Taupe Gray Fox Scarf 69.00

41T7080—American Lucille Brown Fox Scarf.............. 69.00

41T7081—Natural Skunk Scarf.... 63.00

41T7082—Taupe Wolf Scarf........ 33.00

New Style Animal Double Furred Choker Scarfs can be worn as in illustration above or opened up and thrown loose across shoulders. See above for prices and colors and kind of fur. Av. shpg. wt., 1¼ lbs.

41T7083—Natural Kit Fox Scarf. (Natural Brown and Gray Tipped).......$33.00

41T7084—Poiret Brown Fox Scarf. (Medium Brown)... 39.00

41T7085—Kolinsky (Dark) Brown Marmot Scarf... 15.00

41T7086—Natural Skunk Scarf...... 69.00

Attractive Style Two-Skin Effect Double Furred Choker Scarf. Can be worn as in illustration or opened across shoulders. Average shipping weight, 1¼ pounds.

Sears, Roebuck and Co.
Chicago   129

78T9156

78T9161

78T9166

78T9171

High Grade Dress Hats Choice Each $5⁷⁵

78T9176

Average shipping weight of hats, 2¾ pounds.

78T9156—A very popular large mesh veil with wide grosgrain ribbon band is trimmed on this very smart sailor made entirely of good quality silk faced velvet. A small bud and green leaves form the trimming. Colors: Black, navy blue, taupe gray or purple. State color.

78T9161—A beautiful handmade ribbon rose and clusters of small silk covered berries trimmed on the front of this pretty straight brim sailor. Made of good quality silk faced velvet, the edge prettily shirred. Band and bow of good grosgrain ribbon. Colors: Black with pink flower; black with gold color flower; navy blue with Copenhagen blue flower; purple with pink flower; taupe gray with pink flower. State color.

78T9166—Popular "Mitzi" sailor. Made of good quality silk faced velvet, with facing of satin. Trimmed at back with three genuine ostrich tips and wide bow of moire ribbon, the ribbon also trimmed across the front of hat. Colors: Solid black; black with Copenhagen blue facing and black plumes; taupe gray with Copenhagen blue facing and Copenhagen blue plumes; navy blue with sand color facing and navy blue plumes. State color.

78T9171—Becoming dress hat made entirely of good quality silk faced velvet, the crown prettily draped. Genuine ostrich plume trimming, about 13½ inches long. Colors: Peacock blue top with black facing and blue plume; black top with rose color facing and black plume; sand color top with black facing and sand color plume; taupe gray top with Copenhagen blue facing and gray plume, or solid black hat. State color.

78T9176—An unusually smart turban style. Made of very fine quality mirrored silk faced velvet. Rounded brim is made in deep folds and closely shirred. Trimming wing effect made of velvet to match hat. Colors: Black, navy blue, taupe gray, dark brown, cherry red. State color.

78T9181—Very smart close fitting turban. Made entirely of good quality silk faced velvet. Has a double outer brim, the corners being turned back to give a touch of color. Four small ostrich rosettes and tiny bows of grosgrain ribbon. Colors: Black and Copenhagen blue combination; black and sand color combination; solid black; taupe gray and peacock blue combination; dark brown and sand combination. State color.

78T9186—An unusually smart rolling brim hat. Made of good quality silk faced velvet prettily draped. Grosgrain ribbon inserted in edge of brim; large ostrich pompon trimming. Colors: Taupe gray hat with rose color ostrich; navy blue hat with Copenhagen blue ostrich; Copenhagen blue hat with sand color ostrich; black hat with sand color ostrich; black hat with black ostrich. All ribbon to match ostrich. State color.

78T9196—One of the season's most popular hats. Made of good quality silk faced velvet, with folded drape of fine quality satin around crown. Perfectly beautiful jet black ornament appliqued across front of brim. Colors: Peacock blue, dark brown, taupe gray, or black. State color.

78T9181

78T9186

78T9191

78T9201

78T9191—Large sailor made of silk faced velvet, underbrim of good quality satin. Prettily trimmed with popular pompon made of glossy ostrich fiber. Band and small bow of grosgrain ribbon. This shape is becoming to both young and mature women and the light facings give a most pleasing contrast of color. Colors: Black with Copenhagen blue facing; navy blue with pearl gray facing; taupe gray with Copenhagen blue facing; Copenhagen blue with sand color facing; solid black. All with black pompons. State color wanted.

78T9196

78T9201—A band of prettily curled genuine ostrich is trimmed around entire brim of this small poke shape hat. Made of good quality silk faced velvet, the upper brim in color to match ostrich. Colors: Black with rose color ostrich; black with sand color ostrich; taupe gray with Copenhagen blue ostrich; navy blue with pearl gray ostrich; solid black. State color.

Sears, Roebuck and Co.
Chicago

₃**147**

Smart Middies and Smocks

Be sure to state size when ordering.

27T431
Serge
$3.59

27T4315
$2.98

27T4290
$2.25

27T4305
$1.79

27T4285
$1.59

27T4320
$1.35

27T4295
$2.98

Latest Style Embroidered Smock. Made of a good quality firmly woven cotton material which resembles pure linen. Collar trimmed with hand embroidery as shown. Black poplin tie. Skirt of middy trimmed with three rows of braid. A splendid value. Sizes, 32 to 44 inches bust measure. **State size.** Shipping weight, 10 ounces.

27T4290—Blue.
27T4291—Rose.
27T4292—Green.
27T4293—White.
Price,
each............ **$2.25**

Shepherd Check Middy Coat. Made of good quality black and white woven check cotton material. Collar, cuffs and pockets trimmed with good quality blue cotton material, as shown. Trimmed with large pearl buttons. A very practical and serviceable garment. Carefully made. Sizes, 32 to 44 inches bust measure. **State size.** Shipping weight, 10 ounces.

27T4305 — Black and white check.
Price,
each............ **$1.79**

A New and Popular Style Smock made of firmly woven cotton material, closely resembling a linen crash. Front and pockets daintily embroidered. Piping around yoke and cuffs as shown. Garment closes down center front plait. A very stylish garment. Sizes, 32 to 44 inches bust measure. **State size.** Shipping weight, 10 ounces.

27T4315—Light tan.
27T4316—Blue.
27T4317—Rose.
27T4318—All white.
Price,
each............ **$2.98**

Regulation Middy for Girls in the popular co-ed style. Made of splendid quality firmly woven Hill's jean. Wide band at bottom trimmed with buttons as shown. Neck trimmed with silk lace. A splendid garment. Sizes, 6, 8, 10, 12 and 14. **State size.** Shipping weight, 10 oz.

27T4320
All white.
27T4321
White with blue.
27T4322
White with red.
Price,
each...... **$1.35**

On color pages 53 and 54 we show most stylish garments which will be in vogue during the Fall season, 1919, and Spring, 1920. All excellent values.

Good Quality Blue Serge Middy Blouse. Material is firmly woven wool mixed serge, about one-third wool, balance cotton. Deep yoke and slash pocket on front as shown. Braiding around collar and open cuffs. Wide band at bottom finished with silk laces. Embroidered emblem on sleeve. Sizes, 32 to 44 inches bust measure. **State size.** Shipping weight, 10 ounces.

27T4310 — Navy blue.
Price,
each **$3.59**

Regulation Middy Blouse in the most popular style. This middy is made of fine quality firmly woven Hill's jean, which is a splendid wearing material. Collar and cuffs trimmed with braiding as shown. Deep yoke with a slash pocket and tie as illustrated. Sizes, 32 to 44 inches bust measure. **State size.** Shipping weight, 10 oz.

27T4285—White with blue.
27T4286—White with red.
27T4287—All white.
Price,
each............ **$1.59**

Beautiful Round Neck Embroidered Smock. Made of firmly woven cotton material, resembling pure linen. Attractively embroidered on front as shown. Front trimmed with inverted box plaits as shown. A very stylish garment. Splendid value. Sizes, 32 to 44 inches bust measure. **State size.** Shipping weight, 10 ounces.

27T4295—Blue and white.
27T4296—Rose and white.
27T4297—All white.
Price,
each............ **$2.98**

Sears, Roebuck and Co.
Chicago
123T

Smart Styles for This Season

27T4030
Voile
$2.25

27T4040
Silk
Crepe
De Chine
$7.50

27T4050
Silk Georgette
Crepe
$10.95

27T4035
Silk Georgette Crepe
$7.95

27T4025
Silk
Georgette Crepe
$5.50

All Silk Georgette Crepe Waist. This is a very popular and stylish collarless model. Fancy yoke around front and back of neck daintily embroidered and trimmed as shown. Front panel trimmed with narrow tucks and side plaits. All seams hemstitched. Splendid value. Sizes, 34 to 46 inches bust measure. **State size.** Shipping weight, 14 ounces.

27T4035—White.
27T4036—Flesh.
27T4037 Bisque tan.
27T4038 Navy blue.
Price, each,
$7.95

White Cotton Voile Waist. Front panel daintily pin tucked and trimmed with side plaits and pearl buttons as shown. Collar plaited and trimmed all around with Valenciennes lace edging. Turnback cuffs to match. All seams hemstitched. Sizes, 34 to 46 inches bust measure.

State size.
Shipping weight, 14 ounces.
27T4030 White.
Price, each,
$2.25

All Silk Georgette Crepe and Silk Lace Waist. Over-panel, both front and back, trimmed with hemstitching and narrow plaits as shown. Long sash ties around waist at side. A very dressy and practical garment. Sizes, 34 to 46 inches bust measure. **State size.** Shipping weight, 14 ounces.

27T4050 White.
27T4051 Flesh.
27T4052 Black.
Price, each,
$10.95

A Very Stylish Tailored Model of good quality all silk crepe de chine. This waist may be worn buttoned high around the neck or open as shown. Fronts trimmed with narrow pin tucks and plaits. All seams hemstitched. Sizes, 34 to 46 inches bust measure. **State size.** Shpg. wt., 14 oz.

27T4040—Flesh.
27T4041—White.
27T4042 Bisque tan.
27T4043 Navy blue.
27T4044 Black.
Price, each,
$7.50

All Silk Georgette Crepe Waist. Attractive collarless model with front embroidered and beaded as shown. Piping around neck and cuffs to match color of embroidery. All seams hemstitched. Good value. Sizes, 34 to 46 inches bust measure. **State size.** Average shipping weight, 14 ounces.

27T4025 White.
27T4026 Flesh.
27T4027 Navy blue.
27T4028 Bisque tan.
Price, each,
$5.50

Price, 98c Each
38T6161
Women's Good Quality Cambric Underskirt. Flounce finished with a solid scalloped embroidery edge. A tailored underskirt throughout. Lengths, 34 to 42 inches. State length. Shipping weight, 10 ounces.

STOUT SIZES.
Price, $1.18 Each
38T8433
Same as above, for stout women. 60 inches hip measure. Lengths, 38 to 42 inches. State length. Shipping wt., 12 ounces.

Price, 98c Each
38T6128
Women's Good Quality Cambric Underskirt. Has flounce of pretty pattern embroidery. A neat appearing and serviceable skirt. Lengths, 34 to 42 inches. State length. Shipping weight, 10 ounces.

STOUT SIZES.
Price, $1.18 Each
38T8403
Same as above, for stout women. 60 inches hip measure. Lengths, 38 to 42 inches. State length. Shipping wt., 12 ounces.

MUSLINS

Price, $2.38 Each
38T6399
Women's Nainsook Princess Slip. Flounce and cover of this garment are made of good quality embroidery, in a neat design. Ribbon run embroidered beading at waist. Ribbon draw at neck. Arm openings and back of neck edged with embroidery. Sizes, 34 to 44 inches bust measure. State size. Shipping wt., 10 oz.

Price, 98c Each
38T6114
Women's Envelope Chemise. Made of good quality crossbar nainsook. Neck and arm openings and bottom lace edged. Ribbon draw at neck. Sizes, 34 to 44 inches bust measure. State size. Shipping weight, 7 ounces.

Price, $1.28 Each
38T6102
Women's Nainsook Envelope Chemise. Trimmed. Embroidery arm openings and bottom lace edged. Ribbon draw. Sizes, 34 to 44 inches bust measure. State size. Shipping weight, 8 ounces.

Price, $1.48 Each
38T8425—STOUT SIZES.
Same as above, for stout women. Sizes, 46 to 50 inches bust measure. State size. Shipping wt., 10 ounces.

Price, $1.58 Each
38T6103
Women's Nainsook Combination Envelope Chemise and Bloomer. The latest style in women's undergarments. Front embroidered in dainty colors, shirred and hemstitched. Bottoms shirred and neatly trimmed with lace. Neck and arm openings lace edged. Buttons at crotch. Sizes, 34 to 44 inches bust measure. State size. Shipping weight, 8 ounces.

Price, $1.39 Each
38T6163
Women's Good Quality Cambric Underskirt. Flounce of attractive design embroidery with scalloped edge. Lengths, 34 to 42 inches. State length. Shipping weight, 10 ounces.

Price, $1.98 Each
38T6160
Women's Good Quality Cambric Underskirt. Deep flounce of beautiful embroidery, with wide band of insertion. Has underlay. Lengths, 34 to 42 in. State length. Shpg. wt., 12 oz.

STOUT SIZES.
Price, $2.28 Each
38T8424
Same as above, for stout women. 60 in. hip measure. Lengths, 38 to 42 inches. State length. Shipping weight, 14 ounces.

STANDARD QUALITY.
All our standard quality cambric and nainsook average sixty-eight threads one way (warp) and fifty-six threads the other way (filling) to the inch. We do not carry any lower grades.

Price, $1.38 Each
38T6101
Women's Good Quality Nainsook Envelope Chemise. Camisole style. Wide band at top hemstitched and embroidered in floral design of dainty colors. Bottom neatly hemstitched. Silk ribbon shoulder straps. Sizes, 34 to 44 inches bust measure. State size. Shipping weight, 7 ounces.

Price, 79c Each
38T6159
Women's Bloomers. Made of cambric. Have elastic at waist and knees. Well made throughout and cut over full size patterns. Sizes, small, medium and large. Lengths, 26, 28 and 30 inches. State size. Shipping weight, 8 ounces.

Price, 98c Each
38T8434—STOUT SIZES.
Same as above, for stout women. Hip, 58 inches. Length, 32 inches. Shipping weight, 11 ounces.

Sears, Roebuck and Co.
Chicago
3265

BRASSIERES CORSET COVERS DRAWERS

Price, $2.38 Each
38T9716—Flesh color. Women's Good Quality Crepe de Chine Silk Camisole. Embroidered in floral design in contrasting colors. Trimmed with lavender satin ribbon in scalloped effect. Shoulder straps to match. Buttons under arm. Ribbon draw. Elastic waistband. Packed in box. Sizes, 34 to 44 inches bust measure. **State size.** ← Shipping weight, 9 ounces.

Price, 48c Each
38T6388 Women's Good Quality Nainsook Corset Cover. Made in camisole style. Top and shoulder straps neatly hemstitched. Ribbon draw. Elastic at waist. Closes in front. Sizes, 34 to 44 inches bust measure. **State size.** Shipping weight, 4 ounces. →

Price, 49c Each
38T4503 Women's Cambric Brassiere. Front yoke of neat pattern lace. Arm openings and neck lace edged. Rustproof boning. Closes in front with hooks and eyes. Reinforced under arms. Sizes, 34 to 48 inches bust measure. **State size.** Shipping weight, 4 ounces. →

Price, 98c Each
38T6379—Women's Nainsook Corset Cover. Yoke, front, back and short sleeves of allover and filet lace. Sizes, 34 to 44 in. bust. **State size.** Shpg. wt., 4 oz.

Price, $1.28 Each
38T8411—STOUT SIZES. Same as above. Sizes, 46 to 50 in. bust measure. **State size.** Shpg. wt., 5 oz.

Price, 89c Each
38T6387 Women's Corset Cover. Front embroidery and back nainsook. Sizes, 34 to 44 in. bust measure. **State size.** Shpg. wt., 3 oz.

Price, 98c Each
38T8430—STOUT SIZES. Same as above. Sizes, 46 to 50 inches bust measure. **State size.** Shipping weight, 5 ounces.

Price, 48c Each
38T6376 Women's Good Quality Nainsook Corset Cover. Ribbon draw at neck. Sizes, 34 to 44 inches bust measure. **State size.** Shipping weight, 4 ounces.

Price, $1.38 Each
38T6381 Women's Corset Cover. Front and back, short sleeves, made of good quality embroidery in beautiful design. Ribbon draw at neck. Sizes, 34 to 44 inches bust measure. **State size.** Shpg. wt., 4 oz.

Price, 85c Each
38T6152—Open.
38T6153—Closed.
Women's Embroidery Trimmed Cambric Drawers. Lengths, 23 to 29 inches **State length.** Shipping weight, 8 ounces.

STOUT SIZES

Price, 98c Each
38T8409—Open.
38T8410—Closed.
Same as above. Lengths, 23 to 29 inches. **State length.** Shipping wt., 9 oz.

Price, 79c Each
38T4527 Women's Brassiere in Camisole Style. Made of batiste. Yoke, front and back trimmed with good quality embroidery. Tape shoulder straps. Closes in front with hooks and eyes. Sizes, 34 to 48 inches bust measure. **State size.** Shipping weight, 4 ounces.

Price, 49c Each
38T4502 Women's Cambric Brassiere. Front yoke trimmed with embroidery. Neck and arm openings edged with lace. Reinforced under arms. Rustproof boning. Closes in front with hooks and eyes. Sizes, 34 to 48 inches bust measure. **State size.** Shipping weight, 4 ounces.

Price, 79c Each
38T6150—Open.
38T6151—Closed.
Women's Nainsook Drawers, Lace Trimmed. Lengths, 23 to 29 in. **State length.** Shpg. wt., 8 oz.

STOUT SIZES

Price, 89c Each
38T8407—Open.
38T8408—Closed.
Same as above. Lengths, 23 to 29 inches. **State length.** Shipping wt., 9 oz.

Price, $1.38 Each
← 38T4524—Pink.
Women's Silk Bust Confiner. Made of good quality washable satin. Has elastic insert in back. Satin ribbon shoulder straps. Rustproof boning. Ribbon draw. Closes in back with hooks and eyes. Sizes, 34 to 48 inches bust measure. **State size.** Shpg. wt., 7 oz.

Price, 59c Each
38T4525—Pink.
38T4526—White.
Women's Bust Confiner. Made of good quality madras, elastic back. Rustproof boning. Front closing. Sizes, 34 to 48 inches bust measure. **State size.** Shipping wt., 5 oz.

Price, 68c Each ←
38T4528 Women's Bust Confiner. Front made of embroidery. Back of batiste. Elastic in back. Rustproof boning. Closes in front. Sizes, 34 to 48 inches bust measure. **State size.** Shpg. wt., 4 oz.

Price, 98c Each
38T6156—Black.
38T6157—White.
Women's Sateen Bloomers. Elastic at waist and knees. Lengths, 26, 28 and 30 inches. **State length.** Shpg. wt., 9 oz.

STOUT SIZES

Price, $1.12 Each
38T8438—Black.
Same as above. 58-in. hip. Length, 32 inches. Shipping weight, 10 ounces.

Price, $3.98 Each
38T9721—Pink.
38T9722—White.
38T9723—Black.
Women's Silk Bloomers. Made of good quality washable satin. Bottoms double shirred with elastic. Elastic waistband. Comes in small, medium and large, or lengths 26, 28 and 30 in. **State size.** Shpg. wt., 14 oz.

← Price, 58c Each
38T4507 Women's Ventilated Bust Confiner. Made of good quality batiste. Has elastic insert in back. Rustproof boning. Closes in front. Sizes, 34 to 48 inches bust measure. **State size.** Shpg. wt., 4 oz.

Sears, Roebuck and Co.
Chicago

263

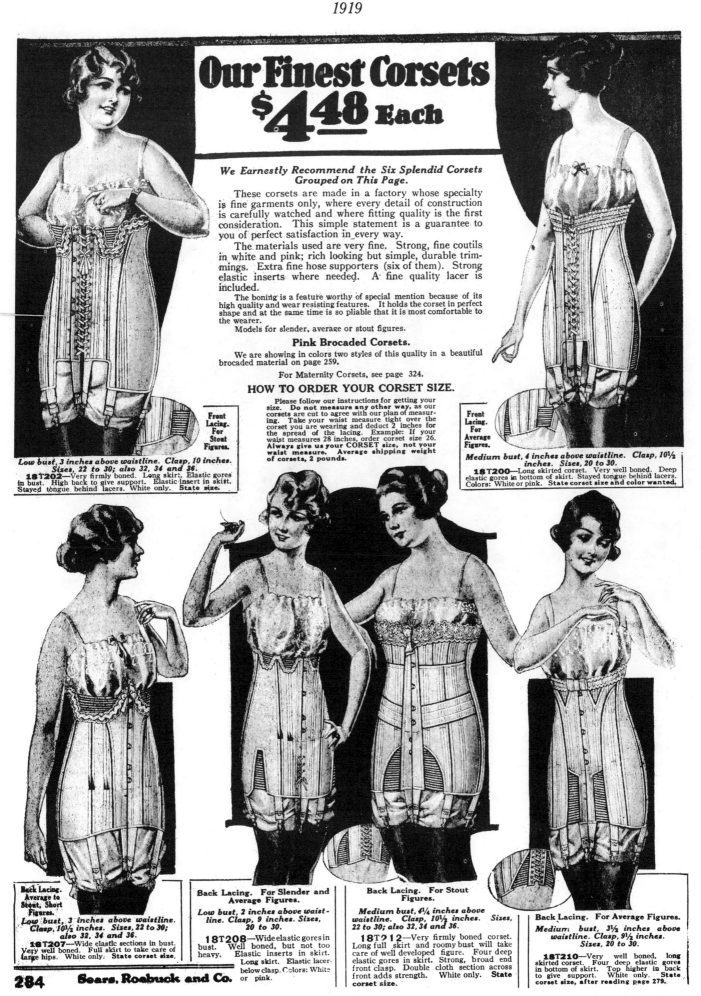

Our Finest Corsets
$4.48 Each

We Earnestly Recommend the Six Splendid Corsets Grouped on This Page.

These corsets are made in a factory whose specialty is fine garments only, where every detail of construction is carefully watched and where fitting quality is the first consideration. This simple statement is a guarantee to you of perfect satisfaction in every way.

The materials used are very fine. Strong, fine coutils in white and pink; rich looking but simple, durable trimmings. Extra fine hose supporters (six of them). Strong elastic inserts where needed. A fine quality lacer is included.

The boning is a feature worthy of special mention because of its high quality and wear resisting features. It holds the corset in perfect shape and at the same time is so pliable that it is most comfortable to the wearer.

Models for slender, average or stout figures.

Pink Brocaded Corsets.

We are showing in colors two styles of this quality in a beautiful brocaded material on page 259.

For Maternity Corsets, see page 324.

HOW TO ORDER YOUR CORSET SIZE.

Please follow our instructions for getting your size. Do not measure any other way, as our corsets are cut to agree with our plan of measuring. Take your waist measure tight over the corset you are wearing and deduct 2 inches for the spread of the lacing. Example: If your waist measures 28 inches, order corset size 26. Always give us your CORSET size, not your waist measure. Average shipping weight of corsets, 2 pounds.

Front Lacing. For Stout Figures.

Low bust, 3 inches above waistline. Clasp, 10 inches. Sizes, 22 to 30; also 32, 34 and 36.

18T202—Very firmly boned. Long skirt. Elastic gores in bust. High back to give support. Elastic insert in skirt. Stayed tongue behind lacers. White only. State size.

Front Lacing. For Average Figures.

Medium bust, 4 inches above waistline. Clasp, 10½ inches. Sizes, 20 to 30.

18T200—Long skirted corset. Very well boned. Deep elastic gores in bottom of skirt. Stayed tongue behind lacers. Colors: White or pink. State corset size and color wanted.

Back Lacing. Average to Stout, Short Figures.

Low bust, 3 inches above waistline. Clasp, 10½ inches. Sizes, 22 to 30; also 32, 34 and 36.

18T207—Wide elastic sections in bust. Very well boned. Full skirt to take care of large hips. White only. State corset size.

Back Lacing. For Slender and Average Figures.

Low bust, 2 inches above waistline. Clasp, 9 inches. Sizes, 20 to 30.

18T208—Wide elastic gores in bust. Well boned, but not too heavy. Elastic inserts in skirt. Long skirt. Elastic lacer below clasp. Colors: White or pink.

Back Lacing. For Stout Figures.

Medium bust, 4¼ inches above waistline. Clasp, 10½ inches. Sizes, 22 to 30; also 32, 34 and 36.

18T212—Very firmly boned corset. Long full skirt and roomy bust will take care of well developed figure. Four deep elastic gores in skirt. Strong, broad end front clasp. Double cloth section across front adds strength. White only. State corset size.

Back Lacing. For Average Figures.

Medium bust, 3½ inches above waistline. Clasp, 9½ inches. Sizes, 20 to 30.

18T210—Very well boned, long skirted corset. Four deep elastic gores in bottom of skirt. Top higher in back to give support. White only. State corset size, after reading page 279.

284 Sears, Roebuck and Co.

FIVE SPECIAL BARGAINS FOR WOMEN AND CHILDREN

The sweaters shown on this page are made for wear and service. They are well finished throughout and we believe them to be excellent values at the prices we ask. They are sure to give complete satisfaction.

Be sure to order 2 inches larger than your actual bust measure.

Price, 98c Each

38T9310—Gray.

Women's Heavy Weight Cotton Sweater Coat. Has roll collar, two pockets. An unusual value at this price. Will give long service. Sizes, 34 to 44 inches bust measure. **State size.** Shipping weight, 1¾ pounds.

Price, $4.98 Each
XX Large.
38T9455—Gray.
38T9456—Navy blue.
38T9457—Maroon.

Women's Extra Size Sweater Coat. Heavy weight. Knit from nearly one-half wool, balance cotton. Has roll collar and two pockets. Well made and will give long service. Sizes, 50, 52 and 54 inches bust measure. **State size.** Shipping weight, 3¾ pounds.

Price, $2.38 Each

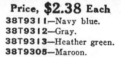

38T9311—Navy blue.
38T9312—Gray.
38T9313—Heather green.
38T9305—Maroon.

Women's Heavy Weight Sweater Coat. Very practical for everyday wear. Has shawl collar and two pockets. Knit from 90 per cent cotton and 10 per cent wool. Sizes, 34 to 44 inches bust measure. **State size.** Shipping weight, 2½ pounds.

BUILT FOR SERVICE.

Price, 89c Each

38T9543—Gray.

Schoolgirls' Heavy Weight Cotton Sweater Coat. Has roll collar and two pockets. Will give protection and wear exceptionally well. Ages, 7 to 12 years. **State age.** Shipping weight, 1⅜ lbs.

Price, $1.98 Each

38T9547—Navy blue.
38T9548—Gray.
38T9549—Heather green.
38T9550—Maroon.

Schoolgirls' Heavy Weight Sweater Coat. Knit from 90 per cent cotton and 10 per cent wool. Has roll collar and two pockets. Well made, warm and serviceable. Ages, 7 to 12 years. **State age.** Shipping wt., 1¾ pounds.

Sears, Roebuck and Co.
Chicago

267

Sears, Roebuck & Co.

Women's Dress Shoes

15T1377
The Pair, $7.00
Patent Leather
Vamp Lace—
Dull Leather Top
—Military Heel—
Flexible McKay
Sewed Sole.
*Sizes, 2½ to 8.
Wide widths.
Shipping wt.,
1½ lbs.*

15T1394
The Pair, $7.00
All Black Vici Kid
Lace—Medium Heel With
Rubber Top Lift—Flexible
McKay Sewed Sole.
*Sizes, 2½ to 8.
Wide widths.
Shipping wt., 1½ lbs.*

15T1393 Pair, $7.00
Patent Leather Vamp
Button—Dull Leather
Top—French Heel—
Flexible McKay Sewed
Sole.
*Sizes, 2½ to 8. Wide widths.
Shipping wt., 1¼ lbs.*

The shoes on this
page come in wide
widths only.

Be sure to
state size.

15T1363
Pair, $6.95
All Black
Vici Kid Lace
—French Heel
—Flexible McKay
Sewed Sole.
*Sizes, 2½ to 8. Wide widths.
Shipping wt., 1¾ lbs.*

See order blanks
in back of catalog
for shoe size meas-
uring chart.

15T1395
Pair, $6.50
Black Glazed
Horsehide Lace —
Military Heel With
Rubber Top Lift—McKay
Sewed Sole.
*Sizes, 2½ to 8. Wide widths.
Shipping wt., 1½ lbs.*

15T1335
The Pair, $6.00
Gunmetal Finish
Side Leather Lace — Dull
Leather Top—Military Heel
—McKay Sewed Sole.
*Sizes, 2½ to 8. Wide widths.
Shipping wt., 1¾ lbs.*

15T1396
The Pair, $6.50
Black Glazed Horse-
hide Vamp Lace — Dull
Leather Top—French Heel
—McKay Sewed Sole.
*Sizes, 2½ to 8. Wide widths.
Shipping wt., 1½ lbs.*

Unless otherwise stated, heels are made with two
or three lifts of leather on the wearing surface, the
rest of the heel consisting of fiber board.

Sears, Roebuck and Co.
Chicago   33T
2 **179**

Children's and Little Girls' Fur Sets

For ages from 2 to 7 years.

41T7650

41T7670

41T7610

41T7600

NEW YORK

41T7665

41T7605

41T7640

41T7660

41T7625

41T7650—Tan and Black.
Price.....................**$8.75**
Child's Natural Holland Genet Cat Set. Animal style scarf, melon muff, satin lined. Ages, 3 to 7 years. Average shipping weight, 1¾ pounds.

41T7600—Children's White Angora Fur Set. Price.......$3.00
Neck piece and front of the muff are made from white Angora fur. The back of the muff is made from short curly lambs' wool. Ages, 2 to 5 years. Average shipping weight of set, 1½ pounds.

41T7640—Blue Gray Goat Set. Price.................$5.95
41T7645—Brown Goat Set.
Price......................5.95
Children's Imported China Goat Set in blue gray or brown. The blue gray imitates blue wolf, the brown imitates brown bear. Serviceable long haired fur. Animal style scarf and pillow style muff. Satin lined set. Ages, 3 to 7 years. Average shipping weight, 1¾ lbs.

41T7660—White Set. Price.......$10.75
Little Girls' White Iceland Fox Fur Set. Long haired soft fluffy combed Thibet fur animal scarf, ball muff. Satin lined set. Ages, 3 to 7 years. Average shipping weight, 1½ pounds.

41T7625—Tiger Coney Set. Price...$7.85
41T7630—Natural Tan and Gray Coney Set. Price................. 7.85
41T7635 — White Coney Ermine Set. Price................. 9.00
Little Girls' Imported Coney Fur Set in tan and black to imitate tiger or natural tan and gray or in white coney fur in imitation of ermine. Animal style scarf and melon muff. Set satin lined. Ages, 3 to 7 years. Average shipping weight, 2 pounds.

41T7670—Natural Nutria Set. Price...............$18.75
41T7675—Silver Tipped Coney Set. Price...........10.75
Little Girls' Fur Set from natural nutria (South American beaver) or silver tipped coney to resemble silver fox. Coatee effect scarf and melon muff with ruching. Set silk lined. Ages, 3 to 7 years. Average shipping wt., 1¾ lbs.

41T7665—Brown and Gray Tipped Set. Price.........$24.00
Our Finest Grade Set for little girls. Made from natural brown and gray tipped kit fox skins. Animal style scarf with silk ruching and lining. Canteen style muff with silk lining and ruching. Ages, 3 to 7 years. Av. shpg. wt., 2 lbs.

41T7605—White Set.
Price.....................**$4.75**
Little Girls' Angora Trimmed Fur Set. The neck piece and muff are made from short curly lambs' wool, trimmed with white Angora fur. Muff is trimmed with a purse and silk bow. Ages, 2 to 5 years. Average shipping weight, 1½ pounds.

41T7610—Brown and White Coney Set. Price...$7.85
41T7615—Natural and White Coney Set. Price.. 7.85
41T7620 — Black, Tan and White Coney Set. Price....... 7.85
Imported Coney Fur Set in brown and white, natural tan and gray and white, tan and black in imitation of tiger fur with white trimming. Animal style scarf and canteen style muff. Set satin lined. Ages, 3 to 7 years. Average shipping weight, 1½ pounds.

141

Girls' Winter Coats, Bonnets and Muffs

Ages, years	2	3	4	5	6
Length, inches	22	24	26	27	28

Bonnets and muffs are sold separately. Average shipping weight, 10 ounces. State age and color when ordering. All bonnets have silk ribbon ties.

Following Descriptions Are for Coats Shown on Opposite Page.

Astrakhan Cloth Coat. Made of good quality astrakhan cloth, woven of glossy mohair in small close curls. Has collar and belt of lustrous velour plush. Lined throughout with good quality mercerized sateen. **State age.** Average shipping weight, 2¼ pounds.
17T3060—Brown.
17T3061—Navy blue.
17T3062—Dark Copenhagen blue.
17T3064—Black. Price, each.. **$5.79**
17T3205—Velour Plush Muff in colors to match trimming on coat. Price.. **89c**
17T3305—Velour Plush Bonnet in colors to match trimming on coat. Price.. **$1.19**

Velour Plush Coat. Made of lustrous silklike velour plush, woven of fine quality cotton yarn. Coat has sash belt, slash pockets and shirred back. Deep collar trimmed with edging of chinchilla fur cloth. Lined with good quality mercerized sateen. **Mention age.** Av. shpg. wt., 2½ lbs.
17T3070—Burgundy.
17T3071—Navy blue.
17T3072—Liberty (medium) blue.
17T3073—Brown.
17T3074—Dark green.
17T3075—Black. Price, each.. **$6.79**
17T3310—Velour Plush Bonnet in colors to match coat. State color. Price.. **$1.29**

Velour Plush Coat. Woven of fine quality cotton yarn, very silklike. Coat is trimmed with beaver fur cloth edging, woven of mohair to resemble real beaver fur. Lined with mercerized sateen. **State age.** Average shipping weight, 2½ lbs.
17T3080—Liberty blue.
17T3081—Navy blue.
17T3082—Brown.
17T3083—Dark green.
17T3084—Burgundy.
17T3085—Black. Price, each.. **$6.98**
17T3205—Velour Plush Muff in colors to match coat. Price.. **89c**
17T3345—Velour Plush Semi-Hat. Silk lined. To match coat. State color. Price.. **$1.48**

All Wool Soft Finish Broadcloth Coat. An unusually fine fabric. Cut in latest style with yoke back. Collar and cuffs of black silk seal plush. Garment has interlining for additional warmth. Lined with mercerized sateen. **State age.** Average shipping wt., 2½ lbs.
17T3090—Victory red.
17T3091—Navy blue.
17T3092—Pekin (greenish) blue.
17T3093—Tan. Price, each.. **$10.50**
17T3200—Black Silk Seal Plush Muff to match trimming on coat. Price.. **$1.29**
17T3300—Black Silk Seal Plush Bonnet. Silk lined. Price.. **$1.69**

Velour Plush Coat. Woven of fine quality cotton yarn, very silky. Deep inverted side plaits trimmed with smoke pearl buttons. Coat has trimming of beaver fur cloth closely resembling real beaver fur. Lined with mercerized sateen. **State age.** Average shipping weight, 2½ lbs.
17T3100—Green.
17T3101—Navy blue.
17T3102—Liberty blue.
17T3103—Brown.
17T3104—Burgundy.
17T3105—Black. Price, each.. **$6.98**
17T3215—Beaver Fur Cloth Muff to match trimming on coat. Price.. **98c**
17T3345—Velour Plush Semi-Hat to match coat. Silk lined. Price.. **$1.48**

Lustrous Velour Corduroy Coat. Collar and cuffs of gray chinchilla fur cloth, woven of mohair to resemble real beaver fur. Lined with good quality mercerized sateen. **State age.** Average shipping wt., 2½ lbs.
17T3110—Navy blue.
17T3111—Liberty (medium) blue.
17T3112—Brown.
17T3113—Dark green.
17T3114—Burgundy.
17T3115—Black. Price.. **$5.35**
17T3220—Gray Chinchilla Fur Cloth Muff to match trimming on coat. Price.. **98c**
17T3325—Velour Corduroy Bonnet. State color. Price.. **98c**

Velour Corduroy Coat. Made with yoke back. Collar and cuffs of lustrous velour plush. Lined with mercerized sateen. **State age.** Average shipping wt., 2½ lbs.
17T3120—Brown.
17T3121—Navy blue.
17T3122—Dark Copenhagen blue.
17T3123—Dark green.
17T3124—Burgundy.
17T3125—Black. Price.. **$5.98**
17T3210—Corduroy Muff. State color. Price.. **85c**
17T3320—Velour Plush Bonnet to match trimming on coat. Price.. **98c**

Black Silk Seal Plush Coat. This smart double breasted style is made of our best quality silk seal plush. Has all round buckle trimmed belt. Wide collar and cuffs of beaver fur cloth, woven of lustrous mohair to resemble the real beaver fur. Lined with excellent quality mercerized sateen that will give good wear. **State age.** Average shipping weight, 2½ pounds.
17T3130—Black. Price, each.. **$9.95**
17T3200—Black Silk Seal Plush Muff to match coat. (Not illustrated.) Price.. **$1.29**
17T3300—Black Silk Seal Plush Bonnet to match coat. Silk lined. Price.. **$1.69**

Curly Bearskin Cloth Coat. Woven of mohair in large lustrous curls. Made in loose box style with double breasted front fastened with white pearl buttons. Coat has full turnback cuffs and is lined throughout with good quality mercerized sateen in harmonizing colors. **State color.** Average shpg. wt., 2½ lbs.
17T3140—Red.
17T3141—White.
17T3142—Gray. Price.. **$3.98**
17T3240—Curly Bearskin Cloth Muff in colors to match coat. State color. Price.. **79c**
17T3340—Curly Bearskin Cloth Bonnet in colors to match coat. State color. Price.. **98c**

Fancy Velour Plush Coat. Cut from novelty velour plush with a pleasing pin stripe effect. Coat has plaited yoke back, double belt, pearl buttons and buckles. Novelty collar of black silk seal plush. Lined with mercerized sateen. **State age.** Average shipping weight, 2½ lbs.
17T3150—Green.
17T3151—Brown.
17T3152—Burgundy.
17T3153—Liberty (medium) blue. Price, each.. **$7.98**
17T3200—Black Silk Seal Plush Muff to match trimming on coat. Price.. **$1.29**
17T3300—Black Silk Seal Plush Bonnet to match trimming on coat. Silk lined. Price.. **$1.69**

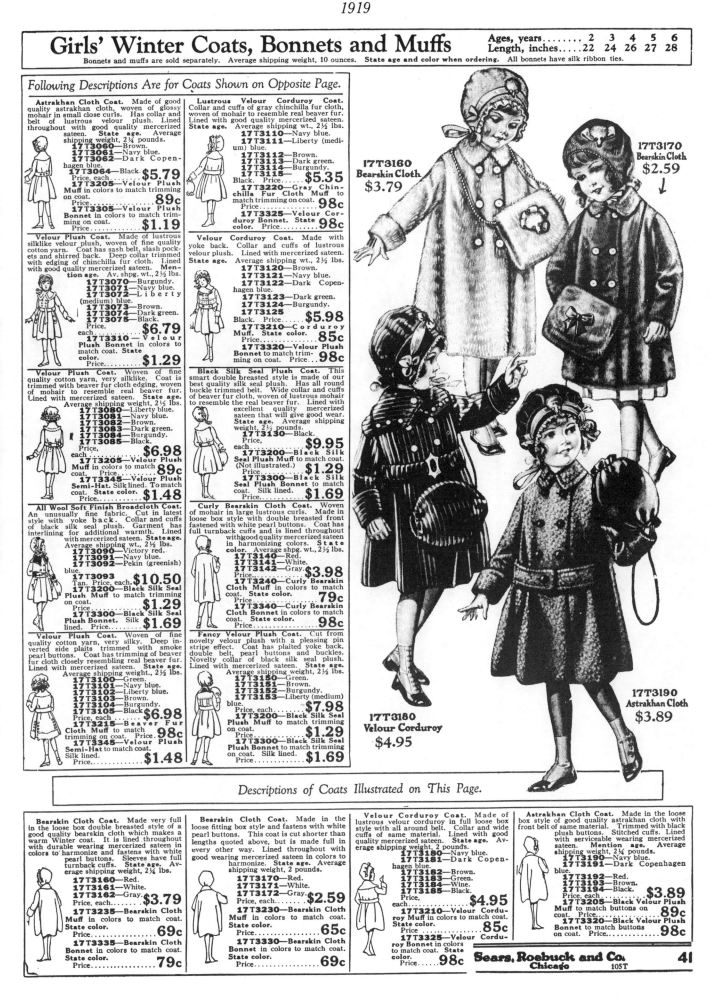

17T3160
Bearskin Cloth
$3.79

17T3170
Bearskin Cloth
$2.59

17T3180
Velour Corduroy
$4.95

17T3190
Astrakhan Cloth
$3.89

Descriptions of Coats Illustrated on This Page.

Bearskin Cloth Coat. Made very full in the loose box double breasted style of a good quality bearskin cloth which makes a warm Winter coat. It is lined throughout with durable wearing mercerized sateen in colors to harmonize and fastens with white pearl buttons. Sleeves have full turnback cuffs. **State age.** Average shipping weight, 2¼ lbs.
17T3160—Red.
17T3161—White.
17T3162—Gray. Price, each.. **$3.79**
17T3235—Bearskin Cloth Muff in colors to match coat. State color. Price.. **69c**
17T3335—Bearskin Cloth Bonnet in colors to match coat. State color. Price.. **79c**

Bearskin Cloth Coat. Made in the loose fitting box style and fastens with white pearl buttons. This coat is cut shorter than lengths quoted above, but is made full in every other way. Lined throughout with good wearing mercerized sateen in colors to harmonize. **State age.** Average shipping weight, 2 pounds.
17T3170—Red.
17T3171—White.
17T3172—Gray. Price, each.. **$2.59**
17T3230—Bearskin Cloth Muff in colors to match coat. State color. Price.. **65c**
17T3330—Bearskin Cloth Bonnet in colors to match coat. Price.. **69c**

Velour Corduroy Coat. Made of lustrous velour corduroy in full loose box style with all around belt. Collar and wide cuffs of same material. Lined with good quality mercerized sateen. **State age.** Average shipping weight, 2 pounds.
17T3180—Navy blue.
17T3181—Dark Copenhagen blue.
17T3182—Brown.
17T3183—Green.
17T3184—Wine.
17T3185—Black. Price, each.. **$4.95**
17T3210—Velour Corduroy Muff in colors to match coat. State color. Price.. **85c**
17T3325—Velour Corduroy Bonnet in colors to match coat. State color. Price.. **98c**

Astrakhan Cloth Coat. Made in the loose box style of good quality astrakhan cloth with front belt of same material. Trimmed with black plush buttons. Stitched cuffs. Lined with serviceable wearing mercerized sateen. **Mention age.** Average shipping weight, 2¼ pounds.
17T3190—Navy blue.
17T3191—Dark Copenhagen blue.
17T3192—Red.
17T3193—Brown.
17T3194—Black. Price, each.. **$3.89**
17T3205—Black Velour Plush Muff to match buttons on coat. Price.. **89c**
17T3320—Black Velour Plush Bonnet to match buttons on coat. Price.. **98c**

Sears, Roebuck and Co.
Chicago
105T
41

Pretty Styles

Sizes, 7 to 14

State size when ordering.

Sizes	7	8	10	12	14
Average bust measure, inches	28	29	30	31½	33
Average length, inches	27	28	32	38	42

Descriptions of dresses illustrated on opposite page.

31T4020—Navy blue. EACH **$14.95**
THERE IS UNUSUAL CHARM about this little girls' dress, appropriate for either very best or more common wear. Made of ALL WOOL FRENCH SERGE, an always fashionable and splendid wearing material, it features the much desired plaited skirt. All around belt with softly tied sash of self material at side of front. The neat plaiting on cuffs and down front of waist daintily trims this smart little frock. Buttons down side of waist and tucks on part of vestee add further touches of dressiness. Closes invisibly at side of front. Sizes, 7 to 14. State size. Average shipping weight, 1¼ pounds.

31T4025—Wine.
31T4026—Navy blue. EACH **$3.48**
THIS DRESS OF PRACTICAL STYLE is made of COTTON SERGE, a popular and service giving material. Dress has tucked waist buttoning visibly down front and gathered skirt with box plait in front. Piping of harmonizing color neatly finishes the pointed flap on convenient pockets, cuffs and all around belt. The becoming cotton linene collar is daintily embroidered. Sizes, 7 to 14. State size. Average shipping weight, 1¼ pounds.

31T4030—Navy blue.
31T4031—Wine. EACH **$5.48**
HERE IS A VERY TRIM LOOKING POPULAR STYLE for school or general wear. Made of COTTON WARP SERGE, nearly one-half wool, a well known, durable fabric. Dress has all around plaited skirt with wide box plait in front and back, and novel cut belt buttoning in back. Silk tie and rows of braid on cuffs, shawl collar and shield add neat finishing touches to this practical little dress. Closes at side of front. Sizes, 7 to 14. State size. Average shipping weight, 1¼ pounds.

31T4035—Rose.
31T4036—Green.
31T4037—Copenhagen blue. EACH **$6.79**
THIS DRESS MADE OF BATISTE, a medium weight material, half wool, half cotton, embodies some of the smartest style features. Button trimmed tucked waist and all around belt with graceful sash of self material in back. The collar and cuffs are trimmed with fringe. Skirt has rows of shirring below belt and patch pockets are trimmed with pin tucks. Closes invisibly in back. Sizes, 7 to 14. State size. Average shipping weight, 1 pound.

31T4040—Brown.
31T4041—Navy blue. EACH **$6.98**
YOUR DAUGHTER WILL BE PLEASED with this neat looking dress for her school days. Made of HALF WOOL, HALF COTTON CASHMERE, a soft closely woven material. Gathered skirt has plaits in front and the all around detachable belt is embroidered in front in harmonizing colors. Becoming collar of white pique and plaid silk bow tie. Closes invisibly at side of front. Sizes, 7 to 14. State size. Average shipping weight, 1½ pounds.

31T4045—Blue and tan plaid. EACH **$3.79**
THIS SPLENDID DRESS of attractive COTTON PLAID SUITING, a material of durable wearing qualities, has the much desired plaited skirt with shapely pockets. Trim touches are added by the becoming white pique collar, with tie, cuffs and flap on pockets neatly hemstitched. White pearl buttons trim the waist and the all around belt. Closes visibly down side of front. Sizes, 7 to 14. State size. Average shipping weight, 1¼ pounds.

31T4050—Navy blue.
31T4051—Wine. EACH **$7.48**
BECOMINGNESS OF DESIGN AND MATERIAL, and warmth and serviceability are features which make this pretty VELVETEEN CORDUROY dress very desirable. Dress is gracefully gathered all around, with pretty detachable belt buttoning in front. Collar, vestee effect, cuffs and flap of patch pockets are of contrasting color poplin. Collar and front of waist trimmed with featherstitching. Closes invisibly at side of front. Sizes 7 to 14. State size. Average shipping weight, 2 pounds.

31T4055—Green.
31T4056—Navy blue.
31T4057—Rose. EACH **$14.35**
THIS DRESSY MODEL is made of good quality SILK TAFFETA, a fabric appreciated for its rich, lustrous beauty. Dress is softly gathered all around at waist, with full length panel front and panel from waist in back. Trimmed with pin tucks and pearl buttons. Becoming round neck with white silk plaited frill. Sash with bow in back. Closes invisibly down side of front. Sizes, 7 to 14. State size. Average shipping weight, 1 pound.

31T4060—Navy blue.
31T4061—Wine. EACH **$5.98**
DELIGHTFULLY GIRLISH STYLE distinguishes this serviceable dress of durable COTTON WARP SERGE, nearly half wool. Dress has inverted plaits in back and front of skirt, closing invisibly at side of front. Plaid silk taffeta collar and cuffs attractively trim this little dress. The buttons on waist and detachable belt with piped slash in front add further neat touches. Cord tie with soft tassels. Sizes, 7 to 14. State size. Average shipping weight, 1½ pounds.

31T4065—White.
31T4066—Pink. EACH **$12.95**
THIS EXQUISITE LITTLE FROCK, made of all silk CHIFFON, a very soft dainty material, displays all the grace and becomingness so much desired for special occasions. The fine lace at neck, on sleeves and folds of softly gathered skirt, and the pretty embroidery on front of waist add to its daintiness. Sash of satin ribbon softly tied in back. Elbow length sleeves. Closes invisibly in back. Sizes, 7 to 14. State size. Average shipping weight, 1 pound.

3IT4070

31T4070 Navy blue.
31T4071 Wine. EACH **$4.98**
THIS DRESS of good wearing quality SERGE, nearly 50 per cent wool balance cotton, is becoming and always popular, giving graceful lines to the girl between the ages of 7 to 14. The long collar forming tabs below waist, detachable belt and cuffs are neatly trimmed with stitching of harmonizing color. A row of dainty buttons on vestee effect adds further neat finishing touches. Closes invisibly at side of front. State size. See scale of proportionate sizes on this page. Average shipping weight, 1¼ pounds.

31T4075 Blue.
31T4076 Rose. EACH **$3.24**
VERY SMART AND BECOMING is this little frock made in combination of solid color washable cotton POPLIN and PLAID GINGHAM. New style collar and cuffs of plaid are very attractive with the dainty stitching and fold of solid material. Dress is further trimmed with pearl buttons and imitation buttonholes. Imitation patent leather belt. Closes invisibly at side. Sizes, 7 to 14. State size. Av. shpg. wt., 1¼ pounds.

31T4080 Navy blue. EACH **$11.75**
YOUTHFULNESS AND FASHIONABLE STRAIGHT LINES make this splendid wearing ALL WOOL SERGE sailor dress a becoming and comfortable style for young girls. Dress has full length box plaits in front and back with belt fastening in front. The white braid on cuffs, sailor collar ornamented with embroidered stars, and emblem on left sleeve and white pique shield, effectively trim this pretty dress. Sailor tie. Invisible front closing. Sizes, 7 to 14. State size. See size scale on this page.

3IT4075

3IT4080

31T4085 Black and white check. EACH **$3.69**
THIS TRIM LOOKING DRESS is made of universally popular COTTON SHEPHERD CHECK of pleasing weight and serviceability. Dress is gathered with plaits in front and has an all around belt. Front of waist in panel effect is trimmed with bands of part wool serge in harmonizing color, as are the convenient patch pockets. Neat finishing touches are added by the cuffs, button trimmed part wool serge collar and ornamental cord. Closes invisibly in back. Sizes, 7 to 14. State size. Average shipping weight, 1¼ pounds.

3IT4085

31T4090 Blue.
31T4091 Wine. EACH **$3.29**
FOR THE MILD WINTER DAYS this dress, made of good wearing quality COTTON SERGE, will serve very nicely. Skirt has box plait in front and large convenient pockets. Collar and piping on cuff effect sleeves and front of belt is of contrasting color cotton linene. The metal buttons on waist and belt are an attractive trimming. Closes in front. Sizes, 7 to 14. State size. See scale of sizes on this page.

3IT4095

3IT4090

31T4095—Tan khaki twill with blouse. EACH **$2.48**
31T4096—Tan khaki twill with bib. **1.65**
31T4097—Blue chambray with blouse. **2.39**
31T4098—Blue chambray with bib. **1.48**
GIRLS' OVERALLS OF DURABLE MATERIALS. Made in one-piece style, with drop seat. The pearl buttons and patch pockets add to the appearance of this neat style. Elastic band at knees. Sizes, 7 to 14. State size. Average shipping weight, 1¼ pounds.

Sears, Roebuck and Co. 5**123**

The End

Sources

The American Woman, Vickery and Hill Publishing Co., Augusta, Me., 1905, 1906 (various issues)

Der Bazar—Illustrirte Damen-Zeitung, L. Schaefer, Berlin, 1860-1865 (various issues)

Godey's Lady's Book and Magazine, Godey's Lady's Book Publishing Company (Limited), Philadelphia, 1878 (various issues)

Happy Hours Magazine, Hill & Company, Augusta, Me., 1883, 1884, 1909, 1910 (various issues)

Harper's Bazar, Harper and Brothers, New York, 1870 (various issues)

Harper's New Monthly Magazine, Harper and Brothers, 1854 (various issues)

Harper's Weekly, Harper and Brothers, New York, 1857 (various issues)

Hearth and Home, Vickery and Hill Publishing Co., Augusta, Me., 1915, 1916 (various issues)

The Ladies Home Journal, Curtis Publishing Company, Philadelphia, 1886, 1887, 1888, 1889, 1894, 1905 (various issues)

Ladies' Indispensable Assistant, New York, 1852., Reprint Edition by Cookbook Collector's Library, Louisville, 1971.

Coming Styles, Marshall Field and Company, Chicago, 1896.

Montgomery Ward and Company General Catalogue, Montgomery Ward and Company, Chicago, 1894

Peterson's Magazine, Philadelphia, 1883 (various issues)

Pictorial Review, The Pictorial Review Company, New York, 1912 (various issues)

Sears, Roebuck and Company General Catalogues, Sears Roebuck and Company, Chicago, 1908, 1919, ibid., Sears, Roebuck and Company Fashion Catalogues, 1903, 1905

Young, Agnes Brooks, *Recurring Cycles of Fashion,* Harper & Brothers, New York, 1937